BECOMING IMPERIAL CITIZENS

NEXT WAVE: New Directions in Women's Studies
*A series edited by Inderpal Grewal, Caren Kaplan,
and Robyn Wiegman*

Becoming Imperial Citizens

Indians in the Late-Victorian Empire

Sukanya Banerjee

DUKE UNIVERSITY PRESS   DURHAM AND LONDON   2010

© 2010 Duke University Press
All rights reserved
Designed by C. H. Westmoreland
Typeset in Adobe Caslon by Achorn International Inc.
Library of Congress Cataloging-in-Publication Data appear on the
last printed page of this book.

Contents

ACKNOWLEDGMENTS vii

INTRODUCTION: Imperial Citizenship: Nation, Empire, Narrative 1

1. Of the Indian Economy and the English Polls 36

2. South Africa, Indentured Labor, and the Question of Credit 75

3. The Professional Citizen in/and the Zenana 116

4. Bureaucratic Modernity, the Indian Civil Service, and Grammars of Nationalism 150

AFTERWORD 191

NOTES 197

BIBLIOGRAPHY 235

INDEX 265

Acknowledgments

One of the singular pleasures of completing a project of this nature is the opportunity it provides to thank the numerous individuals and institutions who have helped in its making.

It is a pleasure to express my indebtedness to Parama Roy, who read this work from its earliest stages. Over the years, her exacting standards have been equaled only by her unmatched intellectual generosity and critical wisdom. I cannot thank her enough for asking the questions she did. I am indeed fortunate to have had her as my advisor, and I remain thankful for her continued friendship and mentoring.

My thanks to Joseph Childers for his critical input and support of my work. Had it not been for his innovative approach to the nineteenth century, I would have arrived at it very differently. I am grateful to Lisa Lowe for her feedback on very early stages of this project and for her support long after. George Haggerty has been a wonderful teacher and mentor, for which many thanks. For all her encouragement of my work and the joy of her company, my thanks to Piya Chatterjee.

My deepest thanks to all those who have read this work in various sections or forms. My thanks to Jennifer Brody for receiving the manuscript so warmly and for her help at critical moments. Geraldine Forbes's comments on a version of chapter 3 and her help with some details has meant a lot to me. Bishnupriya Ghosh remains a wonderful ally, and I am grateful for her insightful comments and unwavering support. Inderpal Grewal has read and supported this work at various stages, for which I remain grateful. Many thanks to Kumkum Sangari for reading a version of the manuscript in its entirety and for her thoughtful suggestions and friendship. Mrinalini Sinha read sections of this work at a later stage; I truly appreciate her support. It was a wonderful surprise to receive Richard Sorabji's very generous response to a version of chapter 3. I remain thankful to James Vernon for supporting this project at an early stage and for some very helpful suggestions.

Rosemary George, Rajeswari Sunder Rajan, and another reader for Duke University Press have been incomparably generous with their feedback and support. My deepest thanks to them: their astute engagement with the manuscript helped me think through it in new ways.

I would also like to thank the following people, whose advice or interest in this work—be it in the form of questions, informal conversations, correspondence, or more formal conference feedback—has meant much to me: Srimati Basu, Elleke Boehmer, Marcus Bullock, Dipesh Chakrabarty, Aparna Devare, Jane Gallop, Engseng Ho, Andrew Kincaid, Caroline Levine, Teresa Mangum, Kathy Psomiades, Barbara Ramusack, Mitra Sharafi, Daniel Sherman, Sandhya Shetty, Amardeep Singh, Ashwini Tambe, Sylvia Vatuk, and Kamal Verma. I would also like to thank the audiences and organizers at the following conferences and seminars where I have repeatedly presented various sections of the work: Inter-Disciplinary Nineteenth Century Studies Conference; North American Victorian Studies Association Conference; Fin de Siècle Seminar Series, Oxford University; South Asian Literary Association Conference; and the South Asia conference at the University of Wisconsin, Madison.

A project of this nature cannot be undertaken without considerable institutional support, and for this I remain grateful to the Graduate School of the University of Wisconsin, Milwaukee for its consistent support over the years, in the form of Arts and Humanities Travel Awards and a very timely Graduate School Research Committee Award. Thanks to Steve Atkinson for all his help. Separate fellowships at the university's Center for 21st Century Studies and its Center for Women's Studies provided an important forum for interdisciplinary discussions and also helped speed this project along. I am grateful to the College of Letters and Sciences and the Center for International Education for travel funding.

A fellowship at the Institute for Humanities Research at the University of Wisconsin, Madison helped bring the project to completion. A summer research fellowship from the National Endowment for the Humanities was critical in the final stages, and I deeply appreciate the support.

For all their help, I would like to thank the librarians and staff at the following institutions: the Oriental and India Office Collections of the British Library; the Newspaper Library, in London; the National Archives of India, in New Delhi; and the National Library, in Kolkata. My thanks, too, to the staff at the Inter Library Loan Office of the

University of Wisconsin, Milwaukee for keeping up with my endless requests for loans (and renewals).

I am grateful for the support of my colleagues in the English department at Milwaukee and the department chairs, Mickey Noonan, Jim Sappenfield, Alice Gillam, and Andy Martin. Gwynne Kennedy and Kristie Hamilton have been exemplary in their collegiality; I am immeasurably grateful for their friendship and scholarly support over the years. Mary Louise Buley-Meissner is unfailing in her support and good cheer.

Ken Wissoker has been an exemplary editor. My deepest thanks for his interest in this project and his imaginative support throughout; it has truly been a pleasure to work with him. My thanks to Courtney Berger and Leigh Barnwell for shepherding the manuscript through the production process. Pam Morrison has been unfailingly helpful. My thanks for her meticulous attention to detail. I am grateful to Fred Kameny for his help in this final stages.

I cannot even begin to thank my family for everything they have done and continue to do for me: gratitude of that order belies acknowledgement. My parents, Susmita and Probal Banerjee, continue to sustain me with unconditional love and support. Without them this process, and much else, would have been unimaginable, if not impossible. Mark Netzloff, who has lived with this manuscript with boundless humor and patience, has also helped me live beyond it. Apart from everything else, I have benefited greatly from his academic companionship, critical insight (and proofreading). To each of them my deepest thanks. My thanks, too, to Jhumpa and Speranza (sadly departed), whose feline company vastly enlivened the process of writing.

Finally, this is in loving memory of Kalyani Devi, who remains extraordinary.

INTRODUCTION

Imperial Citizenship: Nation, Empire, Narrative

Does imperialism mean Canada for the Empire, Australia for the Empire, India for the Empire, or can there be two definitions for subjects of one and the same Empire? If there is but one recognized definition under the flag over which the sun is supposed never to set, then it is for us to see that *no injustice shall minimise the rights or privileges of that citizenship, whether that holder is black or white* (emphasis in the original).—Memorandum from Hindu Friend Society, Victoria, British Columbia, 1911[1]

[Moolchand] is and has been a quiet inoffensive law-abiding citizen, and can in no sense be deemed to be a danger to the State of Western Australia . . . His rights as a British subject were secured to him by the Mutiny Proclamation of 1859 [*sic*], and by the Proclamation of His Majesty at the Delhi Durbar in 1901, and it is not within the competency of the Australian legislature or executive to override those proclamations . . . the Magna Charta [*sic*] of the rights and privileges of the people of India.—Petition on behalf of Moolchand Shivcharan Dass, Australia, October 30, 1905[2]

We are not Englishmen or men of English race or extraction, but we are British subjects, the citizens of a great and free empire; we live under the protecting shadows of one of the noblest constitutions the world has ever seen. The rights of Englishmen are ours, their privileges are ours, their constitution is ours. But we are excluded from them.—Surendranath Banerjea, Calcutta, January 14, 1893[3]

Uttered at different moments across the British Empire by Indian subjects of the Crown, the lines quoted above posit a relation with the imperial polity that strains against the Indians' status as subject. If political subjecthood denotes, among other things, an entitlement or protection based on fealty,[4] then the first two quotes emanate very clearly from a recognition by the Indians of their status as subjects of the British Crown. However, in forwarding claims that Indians were evidently entitled to as subjects, these statements also accomplish something else: they belie the inscriptions denoting the subjecthood that formed the basis for such claims.[5] By arguing that there cannot be "two definitions for subjects of one and the same Empire," the members of the Indian delegation in Canada seek to overcome the discrimination against them as "Indians." Interestingly, while the petition was from the Hindu Friend Society, its list of grievances included the plight of Sikhs and Muslims of Indian origin resident in Canada as well. The expanded reference hints at the inadequacy of the petitioners' self-identification as "Hindu," gesturing instead to the viability of a more commodious and unmarked nomenclature. In a different but related vein, the petition forwarded on behalf of Moolchand, an Indian of modest means from Bombay—he was stated to be "poor" in the petition—absorbs the class-stratified restrictions imposed on Indians in Australia (Moolchand was being deported because he could not prove he was a "merchant, student, or tourist traveler").[6] The logic of the petition, in fact, fuses Moolchand with an abstract body politic that overrides such class markings by gathering him within the folds of "the rights and privileges of the people of India" guaranteed by the Crown. What drives each of these statements is a belief in the transformative potential of their claims, a transformation implicitly effected by and through the rhetorical positing of a formal equality. Moolchand and the Indians in Canada attempt, in the full enjoyment of their status as British subjects, to simultaneously transcend the inscription—"poor," "black," even "Indian"—marking their position *as* subjects: in articulating a formal equivalence, a position of abstract equality that reframes the basis for entitlement, they attempt to take on the mantle of citizens.

Constituting Citizenship

While the memorandum from Canada and Moolchand's petition formulate citizenship where it is evinced most starkly—the question of entry or exit[7]—the statement by Surendranath Banerjea, one of the progenitors of the Indian nationalist movement that gained momentum from the 1880s onward, situates citizenship in the context where it is seen to matter most: political representation. While I will presently discuss Banerjea's prefatory statement from 1893, it is worth mentioning here an observation made by him in 1897 that anticipates the rhetorical framework of the petitions forwarded by Moolchand and the Indians in Canada. Appealing for representative government in India, Banerjea had argued that Indians, despite their vastly different history, should be "admitted into the rights of British citizens."[8] Indians, according to him, should be incorporated as citizens not necessarily in recognition of their status as Indians (even though that identity had, according to Banerjea, an illustrious lineage), but because such incorporation would be in keeping with the notions of justice and liberty enshrined in the liberal ideals of citizenship. Banerjea was confident that such ideals were valued deeply by the British, "to whatever party, to whatever creed, to whatever sect they might belong."[9] Significantly, Banerjea's understanding of citizenship, in both its liberal cast and its liberal framing of the British, was sustained by a familiar metaphor of familiality. He brought to attention how "England ... has justly been called the august mother of free nations," and the people of India "are children of that mother, and they claim their birthright."[10] The invocation of this strikingly feminized metaphor in a setting that must have been very nearly all male (Banerjea initially made these remarks at the University of Oxford Union) should come as no surprise, for it again illustrates how claims and configurations of political authority are articulated most effectively through an assumption of desires and impulses that are often heavily gendered.[11] What is of interest here, though, are the ways in which Banerjea's narrative of familiality, like Moolchand's framing of a quiescent respectability—Moolchand's inscription as "poor," after all, could be counterbalanced only by the knowledge that he was "quiet and law-abiding"—sustains liberal renditions of a formal equality, holding in delicate abeyance the marked status of subjecthood, whose differentiating logic otherwise ensured that the colonial state recognized Indians "only as subjects, not citizens."[12]

The state of suspended subjecthood approximated by Moolchand, Banerjea, and the Hindu Friend Society in Canada is worthy of note, for it marks a crucial transitory moment: in claiming their perceived rights as subjects of the Crown, British Indians simultaneously underwrite themselves as citizens of empire, imperial citizens. It is this transition and the narrativity that sustains it that this book examines, foregrounding the various rhetorical, affective, and thematic registers across which Indians formulated and laid claim to universalist ideals of citizenship over the late nineteenth century and the early twentieth. The emphasis on "imperial" citizens brings to light formulations of citizenship before the inception of the nation-state; it also indicates the ways in which the British Empire itself provided the ground for claiming citizenship even as the thrust of these claims implicitly critiqued British colonial practices. In following through with these formulations, however, the book does not presume to provide a comprehensive survey of Indian claims to imperial citizenship. Rather, in singling out some of the narrative trajectories through which notions of citizenship were formulated, it seeks to include British Indians in the broader debates on the evolving discourse of citizenship over the nineteenth century; it also attempts to uncover the contingent and overlapping genealogies of postcolonial citizenship.

By analyzing the formulations of citizenship well before decolonization, *Becoming Imperial Citizens* goes against the grain of reading British Indians only as subjects, and not as citizens. While the colonial state notoriously persisted in such a reading, the effects of that denial remain somewhat tangible in that even in the immensely rich body of scholarship on India in the late nineteenth century and the early twentieth, there is relatively little engagement with the contours of anticolonial critique or the formation of colonial subjectivities along the category of citizenship.[13] It may be that the post-Enlightenment provenance of modern citizenship preempts its consideration in analyses of anticolonialism and colonial subject formation that seek also to undermine hegemonic metanarratives of "Western" liberal modernity. But the fact that the category of the modern nation, though of similar lineage, finds easier recurrence in this context suggests that the relative reticence on citizenship as a category of study before decolonization may have more to do with its concatenation with ideologies of nationhood and the apparatus of the nation-state.[14] True, citizenship in its guise as a universal rights-bearing category was not formally codified till the drafting of the constitution of an independent India, but the fact of codification alone should not detract from the longer processes—partial, incomplete, flawed, and often futile—through which the *languages* of citizenship were refracted from at least the late nineteenth century. Bypassing the various ways in which the idea of citizenship was formulated in late-colonial India—often with tangible effect—blunts the efficacy and urgency that the category lent to anticolonial critique; it also overlooks the fact that it was the liberal premise of citizenship that presented itself as a viable mode of self-presentation by racialized colonial subjects well before the envisaging of an autonomous nation-state.

It is important to emphasize the "languages" of citizenship here, for this book situates citizenship not so much in the realm of statutory enactment as in the cultural, imaginative, and affective fields that both engender it and are constituted by it. Citizenship, as Lauren Berlant notes, is "continually produced out of a political, rhetorical, and economic struggle over who will count as 'the people' and how social membership will be measured and valued."[15] Following the nuances of its narrative formulations becomes one way, then, of registering the competing desires, objectives, and imaginings that constellate the "citizen." From the perspective of this study, emphasizing the narratives that undergird this process—rather than focusing solely on the statutory endpoint of citizenship—not only marks what was a momentous turn for racialized colonial subjects but also makes it possible to locate citizenship in an imperial context that is otherwise seen to preclude its possibility. In examining how British Indians formulated notions of citizenship across the British Empire during the late nineteenth century and the early twentieth, it is worth noting that the word "citizen" itself did not feature in common law, which spoke only of "subjects, naturalized subjects, and denizens."[16] In fact, it was not until the advent of the idea of a British Commonwealth of Nations that the word "citizen" gained currency in British nationality law. Thus, when Indians were purportedly denied citizenship, it was not a legally defined code of citizenship that they were deprived of, or desired. Rather, it was the *potential* of their position as subjects that was at stake, and it was a testing of the strength of this potential that yielded articulations and understandings of what it is to be a citizen in ways that animated the discourse of citizenship not only for Indians, but for Britons as well—providing what is an often overlapping genealogy of citizenship for Britain and its colonies.

Tracing this genealogy requires a textualization of citizenship, a mode of inquiry that is sensitive to the narrative constituents of its claims as well as its statutory prescriptions, both of which speak to the imaginative framings through which the category of citizenship consolidates itself. Such an interpretive filter places emphasis on citizenship as "social practice,"[17] an aspect of citizenship which, Seyla Benhabib notes, remains underexamined in studies of citizenship that otherwise tend to ignore the "dialogical" and "narrative" constructions of political selfhood.[18] The implications of this more expansive approach to citizenship have become especially relevant over the past few decades, as a rapidly reterritorializing global economy has in many ways unhinged citizenship from the referent that has grown to monopolize it since the nineteenth century: the nation-state. Outlining the transformation of the "national in its condition as foundational for citizenship,"[19] however, Saskia Sassen elaborates not so much the superseding of the nation-state as a remorphing that has positioned citizens differently in relation to it. In fact, the imperative for this book to reformulate citizenship does not stem from the much-celebrated demise of the nation-state (which, indeed, is not dead) but from a need to lay claims to the concomitant rights and responsibilities of citizenship in a "post-national" guise[20]—to understand, in other words, the modes of "flexible citizenship"[21] marking our contemporary transnational moment. Such negotiation asks for an understanding of citizenship that exceeds its nation-bound inscriptions. It also asks for an attentiveness to citizenship not as "a unitary institution," but as more of a conglomerate of "discrete but related aspects of the relationship between the individual and the polity."[22] Disaggregating citizenship thus enables a reckoning of it amid what can be the beguiling opacity of the nation-state. Conversely, that such an approach consequently braids in the formal, legalistic aspects of citizenship with what extends beyond statutory inscription is evident in Sassen's leaving open-ended the question of where the impact of citizenship in a changing political structure is now most evident: it could be, she notes, "in the formal rights of citizenship" or "in citizens' practices, or in the psychological dimensions of the institution."[23]

Textualizing citizenship, then, addresses the expanded ambit within which conventional markers of citizenship have been located. More specifically, with reference to South Asia, such an approach speaks to the endeavor of tracing a genealogy of rights.[24] And, especially important for the purposes of this book, it opens up a reading of British Indians in a guise they rarely come to focus in, that of the citizen. This is not to imply that citizenship is only a matter of semantic arrogation—that British Indians were recognized as citizens simply because they claimed to be. That can hardly be the case, not least because there never was a definitive code of imperial citizenship that Indians could demand.[25]

However, emphasizing the various articulations of citizenship that ensued in the absence of such a code draws attention to the extralegal life of citizenship, the modes of self-representation it generates even before it is codified, the political claims it triggers because it is deferred. It widens the frame for accommodating the category of citizenship, whose valence and contours at any given point should also take into account what it takes to *become* a citizen.[26] If, in the late colonial period, Indians were relegated to what Dipesh Chakrabarty terms the "waiting room of history"[27] that promised citizenship to colonial subjects while continuing to deny it, *Becoming Imperial Citizens* emphasizes how the waiting room becomes an important site in the study of citizenship precisely because it was remarkably prolific in generating claims to a citizenship that was otherwise withheld.

The emphasis on becoming a citizen in this book plays on both connotations of "becoming": implying a sense of process, as well as a somewhat prescriptive ideal of what is fitting or appropriate. Significantly, both implications resonate with the ideals of nineteenth-century liberalism, which, in its emphasis on the individual as a political agent, validated notions of development and perfectability,[28] with the latter often underwriting the continual necessity of the former. Such a dynamic manifested itself most visibly in colonies such as India, where one outcome of liberal imperial ideology was ensuring that Britain's civilizing mission could never be complete: Indians could never be quite ready for representative government. While this paradox of liberalism, as we might call it, has received due attention in analyses of colonialism and indeed sets the stage for the claims to citizenship that are of interest here, I would also like to situate it alongside other contradictions besetting or engendering liberal ideology in Victorian Britain, which has begun to receive renewed critical attention.[29] In her illuminating study of the vexed relation between liberal aspirations of individualism and the emphasis liberalism placed on the role of the state in augmenting the capacities of the individual, Lauren Goodlad notes that "Victorians who demanded effective governance [were also] confounded by their own ingrained liberal predilections" for "self-governance."[30] In a similar vein, Jordanna Bailkin points out that although, in its emphasis on trajectories of development, liberal ideology seemingly privileged temporality rather than location, the liberal "disavowal of place" nonetheless "went hand in hand with a profound concern for the impact of the material environment on individual and collective character."[31] A consideration here of these contradictions is prompted by the fact that areas of liberal interest and reform, such as political economy, indentured labor, or the electoral process, are key sites of engagement in this book. Therefore, to make note of the contradictions underlining liberal ideology is also to highlight how such contradictions were woven into the emergence of quintessentially Victorian institutions such as professionalism, the bureaucracy, and even the introduction of competitive examinations—all of which feature prominently in this study.[32] It is through sites such as these that this book traces the formulations of imperial citizenship, examining how the range of ideals engendered by such sites—be they bourgeois familiality, a preoccupation with cleanliness and circulation, notions of credit and creditworthiness, an emphasis on ideas of merit, or a privileging of professional expertise—provided narrative frames sustaining the logic of what were unprecedented colonial articulations of formal equality.

This is decidedly not to suggest that ideals and institutions bearing the imprint of Victorian liberalism were the sole support for Indian claims of citizenship, or that such sites were always already there, lying in unproblematic readiness to be harnessed in the service of colonial subjects. Rather, my interest in focusing on these sites is in part a reflection of the ongoing and valuable emphasis in nineteenth-century studies on tracing the mutually constitutive relationship between colony and metropole, instead of viewing their relation in terms of a discrete binarism. Antoinette Burton makes the excellent point that simply enumerating the colonial presence in metropolitan spaces is not enough, for it leaves intact the sense of Britain "as the centripetal origin of empire, rather than insisting on [its] interdependence" with it.[33] Literary and historical scholarship on nineteenth-century Britain and the British Empire has, at least over the last decade, taken due note of the irrefragable charge of empire in the making of metropolitan identities, as well as of the considerably dispersed provenance of metropolitan institutions. The renewed discussion of Victorian liberalism, too, acknowledges how colonial concerns informed its particular modes of articulation. Set against the rich backdrop of this discussion, one of the objectives of this book is to highlight colonial negotiations with emergent liberal institutions and values. The book undertakes to do so with a specificity that concretizes references to colonial influence or provenance, rendering colonial figures integral to discussions of Victorian liberalism as interlocutors, in ways that will also, it is hoped, deflect from a reification of their subject positions as "colonial."[34] To focus on more than an undifferentiated colonial presence or influence, in other words, is not to make here a token gesture of inclusiveness, nor is it to vivify colonial subjects as only marking the limits of liberal discourse—a position they are often cast in. Rather, it is to recognize that their making as British subjects also ensured that Western-educated Indians remained as variously invested (for better or worse) as their metropolitan counterparts were in the claims and institutions of liberalism, in ways that punctuated its turns with an immediacy whose critical resonance renders colonial negotiations indispensable to a textured study of what was a variegated unfolding of liberal ideology.[35]

Conversely, from the perspective of studies of South Asia, taking note of the various Victorian sites critical to the delineation of citizenship claims articulated by British Indians accounts for the salience of nineteenth-century liberal beliefs in equality and self-representation which—among other ideologies and traditions, to be sure—appealed in very obvious ways to the projects and aspirations of politically conscious middle-class Indians. For the purposes of this book, to emphasize this over what could have been an account of indigenous practices and institutions is not to be derailed by the derivativeness of the "Western" concept of liberal citizenship, or the Victorian ideals and institutions abetting in its formulation. Instead, it is to squarely acknowledge their inescapable prevalence in the genealogy of Indian citizenship, if only to emphasize their contingencies, limits, and, more important, their cross-hatched provenance.[36] In fact, tracing the colonial articulations and claims of formal equality within and through structures and institutions that implicate both Indians and Britons becomes one way of highlighting the "messiness of historical practices," which, Mrinalini Sinha rightly notes, marks the consolidation of a liberal discourse of citizenship not so much in terms of an imputed "purity," but as a multiply inflected discourse, if with universal potential and aspirations.[37] Here, an emphasis on the various narratives that lend coherence to the category of citizenship enables the argument in this book to track the overlapping trajectories through which the ideal of the universal citizen-subject assumed singularity. In this, I am specifically interested in how the narrative template undergirding formulations of the abstract citizen subject also unsettles its self-evident certitude. In other words, this study examines how the narrativity of citizenship, in shoring up its otherwise composite nature, also reveals the uncertain making of citizenship as a rational, unitary discourse: this does not necessarily situate citizenship within a discourse of an alternative modernity but argues for a more vexed and uneven notion of modernity on its own terms.[38]

The chapters of this book are organized around the writings of four Indians who were prominent in both colony and metropole: Dadabhai Naoroji, an economist, academic, and politician, who lived in England for nearly fifty years and who, in 1892, was elected to the British Parliament from Central Finsbury; Mohandas K. Gandhi, who, before attaining the status of "mahatma," was a law student in London and then a lawyer in South Africa for twenty-one years; Cornelia Sorabji, the first woman to study law at Oxford and the first Indian woman lawyer, who made a living representing veiled Indian women who were denied access to male lawyers; and Surendranath Banerjea, one of the earliest Indians to be admitted into ranks of the Indian Civil Service (ICS).

By canvassing the various incarnations and connotations of imperial citizenship, the book tracks how the notion plays out in sites directly associated with citizenship, such as electoral polls or the debates about the eligibility to vote (chapters 1 and 2), as well as in sites constitutive of it, such as the highly charged domain of female professionalism or the bureaucratic framework of the ICS (chapters 3 and 4). The book examines the question of citizenship as it emerged as a matter of political right, a node for self-fashioning, and a way of gaining cultural and social access. The chapters bring together a range of texts: economic treatises, autobiographies, legal reports, official petitions, fiction, election speeches, accounts of the zenana (the inner dwelling quarters of Indian homes reserved for women), and government records. The study includes a wide cast of characters, from Irish Home Rulers to colonial officials in South Africa; from indentured laborers stationed across the British Empire to middle-class British women seeking to enter the realm of professionalism; from Indian nationalists adopting a revolutionary credo to veiled Indian women forbidden to step beyond the confines of their homes. Situated at varying degrees from the scope and reach of the category of citizenship, this swath of characters, the book proposes, becomes indispensable in tracing the various narrative registers for articulating citizenship at a time when representative institutions in India were only a possibility and the law beguilingly evasive on the issue.

INTRODUCTION 11

Universal Problems

If it can be said that nineteenth-century liberalism cast itself in a universalist mold, inasmuch as it postulated that all humans are born free and equal, then its compromised universality manifested itself in the premise that Indians were never quite ready for self-governance or political representation ("always subject, never citizen"). This qualification in fact marks the inherent limit of modern citizenship derived from a liberal universality. For Immanuel Wallerstein, the history of citizenship in the nineteenth century reveals how the purportedly inclusive category of citizenship itself engendered binary distinctions (bourgeois and proletarian; man and woman; white and black; European and non-European), if only to curtail the "degree to which the proclaimed equality of all citizens was in fact realized."[39] Even if one were not entirely to go along with the premeditated causality implicit in Wallerstein's account, the role of the discourse of citizenship in the unfolding vocabulary of various forms of racial, gendered, or class-based stratifications has been demonstrated in several contexts.[40] In outlining the claims and formulations of citizenship, the following chapters point to the necessary unevenness of citizenship and the negative taxonomies it generates. However, while an understanding of the exclusionary nature of citizenship forms the backbone of the argument of this book, I would like to guard against a somewhat (liberal) utopian impulse that often accompanies the reading of citizenship and its histories, a reading that effectively attributes, as Joan Wallach Scott cautions, "earlier exclusions [of citizenship only] to temporary glitches in a perfectible, ever-expansive pluralist system."[41] An attentiveness to the formulations of citizenship bears amplitude precisely because it makes room for a materialist critique that underscores—with more nuance than theoretical presupposition alone can afford—how the narrativization of formal equality, even when prompted by the demand for inclusion, variously renders the effects of citizenship to be always double and partial.[42] The specificities of such an understanding reorient reparative discussions of the limits of liberal citizenship around an axis more complicated than that of benevolent inclusiveness alone.

In its emphasis on universality, liberal citizenship based itself on an abstract equality in which each individual is equivalent to every other, irrespective of class, race, gender, sexuality, ethnicity, language, etc. As is evident in the epigraphs to this chapter, such an understanding was a key factor in the articulations of an imperial citizenship. Indeed, as Sinha has shown, the Indian women's movement in the period between the two world wars argued for the franchise on the very basis of a universalistic rhetoric that was otherwise used to temporalize Indian claims to citizenship.[43] While the principle of universalism is in many ways an enabling one with reference to the liberal theory of citizenship, the abstract equality that constitutes its basis also absorbs, as does the homogenization of capital, material realities and historical particularities,[44] effecting an erasure that has provoked critiques of the universalizing thrust of both citizenship and capital.[45] The range of that critique cannot be enumerated here, but this study is attentive to how various cultural forms—different modes of articulation, memories, forgotten histories: various kinds of narrative, in short—have been posited as alternative sites to recuperate and reconfigure those erasures.[46] The role of narrative as counterpoise to the abstracting function of citizenship directs this study in very significant ways, but my interest also lies in tracing how narratives of citizenship mediated or approximated this abstraction in the first place. In other words, taking narrative to broadly signify the guiding structure of and for representation—as that which renders "human experience into a form assimilable to structures of meaning"[47]—this book takes into account how narratives ontologically "rescue" or reconfigure subjects in relation to the abstractions of liberal citizenship. It also takes as its object of study the narrative means through which the abstract ideal of citizenship was mediated in ways that shored up ideals of citizenship as well as colonial claims to it. In emphasizing narrative means, the study is attentive to particular modes of writing, such as the autobiography. However, rather than linking formulations of citizenship with generic literary forms alone, the book is more interested in tracing the narrative tropology and logic lending tenability to the material sites, imaginative economies, and competing desires that underwrote claims to an "abstract equality" that, from the perspective of colonial subjects marked by and through difference, was unprecedented. Such an approach reflects the attemps to expand both the realm of citizenship and the scope of literary analysis.[48]

Considering the contradictions characterizing nineteenth-century British liberal practice in its colonial guise, Uday S. Mehta has noted that although British liberalism favorably linked political power with "the rights of citizens," the very existence of the British Empire proved "that British power was overwhelmingly exercised over subjects rather than citizens."[49] Mehta's study has been influential in underlining how this exclusion of nineteenth-century liberalism was intrinsic rather than contradictory to its own logic. The liberal espousal of "universal capacities" that potentially rendered everyone equally eligible for political rights hinged after all on an underlying assumption, as Mehta so aptly notes, of a "thicker set of social credentials that constitute[d] the real bases of political inclusion."[50] John Stuart Mill could therefore hold forth on the virtues of representative government based on a universalist rhetoric, but, in what has become familiarly evident, he did so with the clause that there are "conditions of society in which a vigorous despotism is in itself the best mode of government for training the people in what is specifically wanting to render them capable of a higher civilization."[51] Having depicted India as "wanting" in this regard, it was but a short step for Mill to argue that India was not yet at that stage of civilization or, indeed, of political representation.

A reckoning of these limits of liberalism, particularly in their colonial manifestations, is certainly not new. What this book does, instead, is take up the narrative strategies through which these civilizational credentials were established or discredited by Indians in their specific negotiations with the extant rhetoric of liberal citizenship. Evidently, while a liberal understanding of formal equality was premised on the abstract individual, the deferral of what was understood to be political rights for Indians depended quite heavily on strategies of colonial rule, which ensured that natives were always represented in specific ways—denied the "benefits" of abstraction, as it were.[52] In following Indian attempts to claim the benefits of liberal political rhetoric, therefore, the argument here traces in part how they re-presented themselves, exceeding typological ascriptions or disenabling embodiments. An emphasis on the abstraction that engenders a formal, disembodied equality seems counterintuitive, especially in light of the critiques of liberal citizenship that rightly fault it for effacing individual particularities, cultural ascriptions, and gendered specificities. However, if one were to also keep in mind that, as Nancy Stepan notes, "the historical counterpart to the disembodiment of the individual citizen of modernity—an individual imagined stripped of all substantiation—was the [simultaneous] ontologizing via embodiment of their sex and racial difference" in ways that also instantiated reasons for disenfranchisement;[53] then, following the move toward an abstract equality constitutes an equally important step in tracking Indian responses to the colonial deferral of representative selfhood.[54]

My objective in examining the narrativization of an abstract equality by late-colonial Indian subjects—rather than only pursuing the more visibly recuperative project of reclaiming colonial subjects in their embodied particularity, important as that task still remains[55]—is impelled also by the need to underscore what are always checkered and uncertain formulations of the liberal universalist ideal. Such an exercise posits citizenship not as a stable, self-evident artifact of Enlightenment rationality but, as mentioned earlier, as something that lays itself bare as a more composite category, revealing the traces of its own constitution as a rational discourse, a designation that was itself the product of overlapping colonial strategies. That the post-Enlightenment premise of universal equality, based on a formal abstraction, itself hinged on the white, middle-class male as place-holder is inescapable, and the flawed implications of such a premise have animated valuable scholarship from several quarters. However, attending to the considerably vexed formulations generated across a range of contexts by even such a premise affords not only historical insight—in terms of the kinds of formulations made possible—but also opens up a more thoroughgoing engagement with the universalist ideal, revealing what at once comprised and compromised the understanding, if not actualization, of an abstract equality.[56] The imperative to highlight this negotiation lies in the fact that while the universalist scope of an abstract equality no doubt remains problematic, it still provides the basis for political struggle across various registers: as Rajeswari Sunder Rajan insightfully notes, "universal rights ... has a double politics: it is informed by a (constitutive) betrayal of the promise of universality but also provides the goal and (the) historical grounds of struggle in its name."[57] Tracing the negotiated formulations of citizenship that such an ideal engenders, especially for those beyond its pale, renders "the universal" more supple inasmuch as it irreducibly concatenates its efficacy with its contingency. I would like to state here that my argument does not view the narrative trajectory of a universalist rhetoric as necessarily emancipatory. I am interested, rather, in the narrative possibilities that the notion of formal equality enables, the imaginings and subject positions it engenders, and, more important, the social and embodied stratifications that it inaugurates, in ways that locate the universal, perforce as a site of ongoing negotiation.[58]

Referencing the instrumentality of formulations of universalism within the context of racial disqualification in the United States, Nikhil Pal Singh notes that the admission of racialized subjects "into an order of abstract equality or citizenship" also ensures that "the negative particularities of racial ascription [are overlooked] on the condition of an absolute rejection of any positive particularities that may have accrued."[59] Singh's caveat does well to urge again a mindfulness of the erasure that the universalist logic of citizenship entails. The study of imperial citizenship assumes relevance in this context as it provides an instance for considering how mediating an abstract equality does not necessarily have to be a zero-sum game, not the least because Indians claimed citizenship, as evident in the chapter's epigraphs, always as subjects of the Crown.[60] That such an iteration sanctioned the only possibility for claiming citizenship in some ways renders the claim to imperial citizenship a negative one. However, it also insistently gestures to the necessary doubleness of universal citizenship: Indians, after all, were "imperial" citizens, citizens only because of their position as localized "Indian" subjects of the Crown. Such doubling is symptomatic not just of imperial (or any) citizenship but, more broadly, of the principle of universalism itself, whose "impossible totalization [is] symbolized," Ernesto Laclau notes, "by particulars which contingently assume such a function."[61] In demanding what was historically and theoretically impossible, the very claims to imperial citizenship in fact assume a positive charge—not only because they continually run up against the conditions of their impossibility, but because in doing so, they insistently reference this doubleness, serving as a constant reminder of how the universal ideal of citizenship is instantiated, if only as a moment of capture.[62]

An analysis of the narrativity of citizenship allows for a reading of these constitutive moments of capture in a finer grain. Aligning the narrative registers of citizenship alongside its political histories, in fact, reveals the extent to which the affective and imaginative undertow of citizenship often naturalizes its theoretical paradoxes—its vacillations between the universal and particular, its doubleness. That the tensions between universalism and particularity, embodiment and disembodiedness, incorporation and abstraction have at once constituted and bedeviled formulations of citizenship since the late eighteenth century is evident in the proliferation of anatomical and social sciences that parallel the ascendancy of liberal norms of the unmarked, abstract subject.

It must be more than coincidence that the gothic mode of narrative,[63] with its preoccupation with various forms of bodiliness (dismemberment, transmogrification, transfiguration) also comes into its own during the late eighteenth century and the early nineteenth, the era of the birth of the modern citizen.[64] Evidently, the concept of citizenship insinuates itself through various modes of narrative that mediate its formal lapses: this book's analysis of the narrativity of citizenship, then, not only gives pause to consider how British Indians articulated themselves as citizens—important enough as that reminder stands—but also sheds light on the complex mutations of the category of citizenship itself.

In its examination of the various narrative registers, *Becoming Imperial Citizens* is therefore attentive to how the various sites that enable an articulation of the universalist ideal of citizenship—sites recognized as bearing the imprint of a rational modernity: credit, political economy, the bureaucracy, professionalism—do so by yielding a more layered, uncertain, and composite script, one that gestures to what remains spectral, takes recourse to idioms of liminality, dwells on failure, cites the ineffable or exorbitant, or pointedly mourns what cannot be represented. Yet the fact that these emerge through registers most available for approximating a formal equality underlines the theoretical travails of citizenship in ways that render citizenship itself a fugitive, if not gothic, concept.[65] Thus, while Tanika Sarkar's work on colonial India has been key in situating the question of citizenship "elsewhere"—that is, examining how political values were, contrary to conventional wisdom, articulated in the "private" sphere of women's lives even before they were articulated in the political and public realms[66]—*Becoming Imperial Citizens* examines the articulation of citizenship "otherwise," looking at how citizenship in the public and political realm, a realm considered more its own, finds cogent formulation through languages that are usually not considered its own.

Between Nation and Empire

In highlighting Indian claims to citizenship within the context of empire, this book also engages with the attendant problems of such claims as they play out in the absence of what has most commonly brought the universalist premise of citizenship into focus: the nation-state. Banerjea's comment, included as an epigraph, is revealing in this respect:

by claiming a language (if not a status) of citizenship on the very virtue of its denial, he clearly foregrounds the imperial aegis as the basis for delineating universal ideals of citizenship. The imperial terrain in fact assumes a particular charge in tracing the languages of imperial citizenship for Indians because it was precisely the unevenness of a common British subjecthood—the disjunction between the "equal treatment" advocated by and in an apparently liberal metropolis and the more exclusionary measures adopted by the Dominions, which were fashioning a citizenship for themselves—that provided the ground and a sense of urgency for Indian demands for self-representation.[67] Banerjea's statement, written in response to the exclusionary policies of the Indian Civil Service that effectively eliminated qualified Indians from the service, underlines a sense of imperial belonging even as it critiques the inequities of that position. For Banerjea, Indian inclusion in the ICS signaled the beginnings of nationalist political development, and his statement indicates how in the case of India, it was the empire, rather than a preexisting prototype of nation, that generated a consciousness of the formal equality of citizenship. The statement also underlines how, for those like Banerjea who steadfastly pursued the ideal of Indian self-government, thinking the nation did not preclude empire, resistance did not have to be wholly oppositional, and citizenship did not suggest only nation.

Rather than placing the apparent ambivalence of this statement along a nationalist teleology that would view it as an "undeveloped" phase of Indian nationalism, a point I will come to later, it is worth considering here the implication of the fact that conceiving of an imperial affiliation alongside a nationalist identification was, for Banerjea and many others, not entirely aporetic. It yielded, instead, a different temporality, a different cognitive map, an emotional scale that was differently charged. Indeed, for us not to read it as such would be to overlook the discrepant imaginings and expansive economies of affect that constitute the nation but evidently fall by the wayside of its more parochial discourse. However, to read beyond the parameters of nationalist discourse, to read citizenship as imperial, is not to kindle an imperialist nostalgia. Rather, it is to point to how the narratives of imperial citizenship deflect the singularity of nationhood. If the history of Indian nationalism has been primarily nationalist,[68] in that it posits the creation of the nation-state as its defining narrative, then a reading of imperial citizenship is part of an endeavor to "rescue history itself," as Prasenjit Duara puts it, "from the ideology of the nation-state,"⁶⁹ inasmuch as it illuminates what are always the multiple births of the nation-state, its stillborn progenies, and its arrested narratives. If history is guided by the inevitability of hindsight, and historicism empathizes with the victor,⁷⁰ then many of the narratives of imperial citizenship, though not always bearing fruit, make it difficult nonetheless to discern clearly who loses and why. They seek soberly to remind us that the present we inhabit is never without a certain invisible debt.

Banerjea's quote, however, is noteworthy on other counts as well. The English constitution that he so confidently lays claim to—"the rights of Englishmen are ours, their privileges are ours, their constitution is ours"—does not of course exist in any written form. Yet a study of Victorian culture reveals the extent to which the constitution was entrenched in cultural and political discourse. In fact, as James Vernon observes, because the constitution, unwritten as it was, was "used strategically as a language of legitimation, it was [also] continually reproduced in different and contrasting ways."⁷¹ Statements like Banerjea's participate in a similar reproduction in ways that signal, as this book traces, the extent to which the discourse of citizenship itself depended on an interpretive reconstitution of legislative enactments, or the lack thereof. Moreover, as Banerjea's statement makes abundantly clear—as do the petitions of the Indians in Canada and Moolchand—it is the status of British subjecthood, of allegiance to the Crown, that legitimates the demand for citizenship. In other words, it is as a subject of the Queen that Banerjea can position himself as a rights-bearing citizen in ways that not only make it difficult to extricate the rational, post-Enlightenment language of citizenship from a prior rhetoric of protected fealty but that also reconfigure predictable readings of anticolonialism.⁷² It is these related considerations that the rest of this introduction will pursue, but first, a sense of the imperial location that Banerjea so expansively gestures to.

While highlighting the various articulations of imperial citizenship, it is important to recognize the different valences that the concept of imperial citizenship accrued during the late nineteenth century and the early twentieth. The claims to citizenship advanced by figures like Dadabhai Naoroji or Mohandas K. Gandhi in the 1890s draw significantly on universalist ideals of citizenship in ways that differ from Cornelia Sorabji's and Surendranath Banerjea's points of reference a few decades later, when they retrospectively adduce citizenship through an emphasis on service, education, and civic self-fashioning.⁷³ Banerjea's ideations of imperial citizenship, in turn, both intersect with and depart from an official policy of imperial citizenship that, as Daniel Gorman has described, were beginning to be etched by the start of the twentieth century in a bid to engender imperial unity among the white settler colonies—policies which were not only doomed but which viewed the dependencies (such as India) on a lesser footing than the self-governing Dominions (Australia, Canada, New Zealand, and South Africa).[74] The fact that the claim to imperial citizenship had such different resonances for the figures under study underscores the importance of acknowledging what Ruth Lister describes as "citizenship regimes,"[75] the various interpretations accrued by citizenship at different historical moments as it is adjudicated through specific ways and toward different means. In reading the claims of citizenship forwarded by colonial subjects, it is important, then, to keep track of the changing import of citizenship in Britain as well.

While what was meant by citizenship in Britain by the mid-1860s dealt largely with the right to vote, the discussion of who qualified for that right revolved at different moments around different questions of class, race, ethnicity, gender, or morality.[76] Even as the franchise was posited as the eventual goal, it yielded different indices of citizenship along the way, such that before the franchise indeed became universal in Britain, it was civil rights that accounted more for understandings of citizenship.[77] In the campaigns leading up to the Second Reform Act, which significantly extended the franchise to working men in 1867, arguments broke from a moral radicalism of an earlier period to foreground the rational "respectable working man" who, it was felt, could and should be entrusted with the franchise, in the interest of public well-being.[78] While such a formulation implicitly excluded the possibility of giving women the right to vote, it did filter through to mid-century liberal suffragist demands that largely claimed the franchise in the name of the responsible working woman but that were uncomfortable with positing the working-class woman as the "autonomous woman" who was to be the anticipated bearer of liberal citizenship.[79] As we shall see, the construction of ideas of respectability to render citizenship legitimate, and the ambivalence of those ideas, also marked Gandhi's petitions to secure voting rights for Indians in Natal later in the century. To point this out is to emphasize that Indian claims to citizenship were part of the same history that was unfolding in Britain from the mid-nineteenth century onward. In fact, in noting that Indians were always subjects and never citizens, it is important to remember that until 1918—or for most of the period under study in this book—approximately 60 percent of adult men in Britain had the right to vote. Before 1867, the figure was roughly 20 percent.[80] That the trajectories of these two constituencies, Indians and Britons claiming political selfhood, should be intertwined—they could never, of course, be coincident—can hardly be overemphasized, not the least because claims for citizenship from both appealed to a common body, the British Parliament. To study the various gestations of citizenship in India in the late nineteenth century, then, requires more than a cursory engagement with Victorian Britain as well, and not just with the realm of parliamentary politics, but with the larger social and cultural milieu that effected and was affected by it.

This book consequently considers moments and concerns of Victorian Britain as much as those of India. It looks not just at the ways in which the empire was invoked to further Indians' claims for citizenship, but also at the erratic and uneven ways in which the empire featured in debates on citizenship in Britain itself. It is interested in moments such as the one in 1865, when John Bright, MP from Birmingham and an advocate of parliamentary reform, impassionedly declared before a Birmingham audience: "Why an Englishman, if he goes to the Cape, he can vote; if he goes farther to Australia, to the nascent empires of the New World, he can there vote; if he goes to the Canadian federation, he can there vote . . . It is only in his own country, on his own soil, where he was born, the very soil which he has enriched with his labour and with the sweat of his brow, that he is denied this right which in every other community of Englishmen in the world would be freely accorded to him."[81]

In fact, the establishment of representative self-government in the settler colonies and the rapidity with which they democratized citizenship put Britain on a somewhat uneven keel. The unexpected nature of this relationship was evident in the visit by the Australian activist, Vida Goldstein, to England in 1911 to support the suffragist campaign. Goldstein's visit was not, Angela Woollacott notes, along the lines of a colonial seeking advancement in the imperial metropolis; rather, Goldstein was in London as an "experienced voter from a progressive country who could extend the benefits of her knowledge to her beleaguered English sisters."[82]

With regard to the expansion of citizenship, it was the settler colonies, particularly Australia and New Zealand, which led the way. This expanded transimperial framework yielded historicist trajectories such as the one literally enacted at the opening ceremony in 1912 of the fair organized by the Women's Freedom League in Chelsea, at which, as it has been noted: "Oriental countries were the women's past, countries where women were disenfranchised represented the present, and countries where they were enfranchised were the future."[83] Britain most certainly did not emblematize the future, but British women made amends for this rather ignominious position by highlighting the deplorable and pathetic position of those in countries representing an anterior phase: the "Oriental woman," the Indian female subject.[84] The implications of this negotiation will be taken up in more detail in chapter 3, but it is important to note here that British suffragists used the figure of the Indian woman to counter the antisuffragist claim that they did not deserve the vote because they were unfit to govern the British Empire.[85] In other words, Indian women needed the kind of political and social work that only British women, in their capacity as imperial citizens, could undertake on their behalf. As Rosemary George succinctly notes, "the modern politically authoritative British woman was made in the colonies."[86]

What is of particular interest in this dynamic between Indian and British women is the emphasis on work, which is also something that comes through very prominently in Bright's statement, quoted earlier: "It is only in his own country, on his own soil, where he was born, the very soil which he has enriched with his labour and with the sweat of his brow, that [the Englishman] is denied this right." The question of labor or work evidently cannot be extricated from that of citizenship, and it assumes, in fact, a key role in this study—whether it be the question of Indian indentured laborers in South Africa, middle-class Britons seeking a career in the ICS, educated Indians judging the fruits of citizenship on the basis of employment opportunities, or that of middle-class British women underscoring their desirability as workers for and of empire. The question of work in its various forms generated, as it continues to do now, overlapping migratory patterns, yielding a diasporic imperial terrain that is impossible to ignore in this study of imperial citizenship.[87] The question of work was also, as has not been sufficiently acknowledged, at the core of early Indian claims to nationhood. Not only did the problem of Indian labor recur prominently in debates in the settler colonies—which, threatened by the import of cheap labor, discriminated against Indians, thus forcing the question of imperial citizenship—but the earliest nationalist demands, such as the ones formulated by the Indian National Congress soon after its creation in 1885, focused on questions of professionalization as embodied by the Indian Civil Service. In approaching the question of work from two ends of the spectrum, this study links the nineteenth-century Indian labor diaspora with the bourgeois envisionings of nation through the lens of professionalism, two movements that tend not to occupy the same analytical framework.[88] This book outlines, then, how, while the granting of responsible self-government in terms of complete legislative autonomy became the rallying cry of citizenship after the first two decades of the twentieth century in India, it had a more lateral scope in the preceding century, which provides alternate modes for understanding the demand for citizenship, as well as the impulse to nationhood.

Of Subjects and Citizens

No study of imperial citizenship in the Indian context can overlook the primacy of the Queen's Proclamation of 1858. Upon the termination of the East India Company's administrative tenure in India in the wake of the revolt of 1857, the Queen's Proclamation announced the sovereignty of the Crown over British India declaring: "all shall alike enjoy the equal and impartial protection of the Law ... And it is our further Will that, so far as may be Our Subjects, of whatever Race or Creed; be freely and impartially admitted to Offices in Our Service, the Duties of which they may be qualified, by their education, ability, and integrity, duly to observe."[89] The proclamation became the rallying point for British Indians during the latter decades of the nineteenth century, being hailed—be it in London, Natal, or Calcutta—as the Magna Carta for Indians. It features quite strategically in the writings of the principal figures in this study, whether used to argue for the suitability of an Indian to stand for Parliament in a working-class London constituency on an Irish Home Rule ticket (Naoroji); claim social respectability for expatriate Indian merchants and laborers in South Africa (Gandhi); gain access to the privatized spaces of the Indian zenana, as well as to travel to far-flung British Dominions (Sorabji); or protest against the arbitrary age restrictions of the ICS (Banerjea).

The colonial state, however, remained evasive about the proclamation, which was actually followed more in the breach than the observance of the aspirations quoted above. Bearing a highly ambivalent relationship with the colonial bureaucracy, which did not quite know how to disavow it, the proclamation in fact lent itself to reinscription by colonial subjects, which became the only mode of its coming into focus in the late nineteenth century and the early twentieth. It is also important to note that the proclamation was not prompted by the universalist imperative that undergirded the Virginia Declaration of Rights in 1776 or the Declaration of the Rights of Man and Citizen in France in 1789 (in fact, for obvious historical reasons, neither was the Magna Carta so fondly cited by Indians).[90] Promulgated in the aftermath of the revolt of 1857 and the harsh excesses of the "counter-insurgency" measures undertaken by the British, the proclamation was more conciliatory in objective, hoping to effect an equable transition of power from the East India Company to the Crown. That it went on to provide the cornerstone for Indian claims to a citizenship based on universalist notions of equality is indeed catachrestic. If, as Judith Butler notes, "exclusionary norms of universality can, through perverse reiterations, produce unconventional formulations of universality that mobilize a new set of demands,"[91] then the iterations invoking the proclamation as the standard bearer of universal rights are noteworthy because they reappropriate the proclamation in universal terms, in the first place.

As mentioned earlier, the category of citizen was not formally codified in British nationality law until well into the twentieth century. However, the idea of a common and equal status across the empire gained some currency toward the end of the nineteenth century, mainly as an attempt to balance the growing demand for autonomy from the settler colonies with Britain's imperial desire to remain at the helm of affairs.[92] The Imperial Conferences, held from 1887 onward in an attempt to establish a show of unity across a far-flung empire, tried to codify this common status. However, the Dominions, despite progressive legislation for their own inhabitants, railed against the implications of this purported imperial equality as it translated into a claim for citizenship rights for nonwhite subjects entering their territories. The British government, on the other hand, as will be shown in chapter 2, remained ambivalent on the issue, thus leaving the question of equal status contestable. Addressing the premiers of the self-governing colonies in 1897, for instance, Joseph Chamberlain stated: "We quite sympathise with the determination of the white inhabitants of the Colonies which are in comparatively close proximity to millions and hundreds of millions of

Asiatics that there should not be an influx of people alien in civilisation, alien in religion, alien in custom, whose influx moreover would most seriously interfere with the legitimate rights of existing labour population." Yet Chamberlain also felt compelled to remind this audience: "But we ask you also to bear in mind the traditions of the Empire which make no distinction in favor of, or against race or colour."[93]

The discussions at the Imperial Conferences eventually led to the passing of the British Nationality and Status of Aliens Act (henceforth BNSA) in 1914, codifying the common status throughout the empire of all subjects of the Crown. Notably, the act stated that "any person born within His Majesty's dominions and allegiance" was considered a natural-born British subject.[94] Moreover, the act also allowed for imperial certificates of naturalization, with which a person naturalized as a subject of the Crown in Britain or in any British possession would be recognized as a British subject throughout the empire, "entitled to all political and other rights, powers, and privileges, and be subject to all obligations, duties, and liabilities, to which a natural-born British subject is entitled to or subject."[95]

The BNSA perhaps went the furthest in laying the groundwork for a common status, but its scope was limited in reality, for it had to contend with the legislative authority of the self-governing colonies. Consequently, the much vaunted single imperial code created by the 1914 act proved chimerical, and a conference in London of prime ministers and representatives from the Dominions and India had to pass a resolution in 1921 urging that the "rights of such Indians to citizenship be recognized," noting "that there is incongruity between the position of India as an equal member of the British Empire, and the existence of disabilities upon British Indians lawfully domiciled in some other parts of the Empire."[96] Commenting on the conference proceedings, the London *Daily News* carried an article focusing on the Indian delegate, Srinivas Sastri. Describing how Sastri had been deputed to "fight for . . . equal rights for Indians within the Empire," the article quoted Sastri's ruminations on the apparent inequality in the self-governing Dominions: "I can't help wondering whether the Dominions realise the true meaning and greatness of the British Empire. Is it for them simply a matter of convenience, and trade connections of sentiment or do they grasp a conception of it far greater and higher than any of those bonds implied? If they do they must admit our rights as equal citizens of the Empire."[97] That

Sastri's position occasioned some disquiet is evident in a letter from Richard Jebb, an imperial journalist, to the editor of the *Morning Post*.[98] Referring to the "rights of His Majesty's Indian subjects in relation to the Self-governing Dominions," Jebb contended that the issue had been falsely argued on the basis of an erroneous understanding: that "there exists such a thing as a common 'citizenship' of the British Empire." If citizenship denoted a relation between the individual and the state wherein the citizen could "influence the policy of the State," then, for Jebb there can be no citizenship of the empire, for the "British Empire is not a State." "What has existed, does exist, and can continue to exist," he conceded, is "a status common to all the peoples of the British Empire as 'subjects' of the Britannic Crown." But that should not be confused or conflated with citizenship, for, according to Jebb, "citizenship includes subjecthood, but subjecthood does not include citizenship."[99] While Jebb's dismissal of Sastri's claim to imperial citizenship was actually correct in pointing out the absence of an overriding imperial state, it is worth reading the apparent certitude of Jebb's statement alongside the relatively indeterminate status of a common British subjecthood and the absence, at that point, of a legal category of citizenship.

While the status of a natural-born British subject was implicit in common law, there was no comprehensive statutory denotation of the status of a British subject until as late as the BNSA of 1914[100]—an act that, ironically enough, was introduced in the House of Commons by the Secretary for the Colonies. The significance of the BNSA lay in imparting what legal historians have described as "an appearance of solidity and certainty" to what was otherwise a "confused and unsettled state of the law at any earlier time."[101] As Ann Dummett and Andrew Nicol observe: "The history of British nationality law is a story without a central character."[102] In fact, it is quite remarkable how often the word "piecemeal" occurs in legal historians' attempts to trace the evolution of British nationality and subjecthood. Yet, like the unwritten constitution, the notion of who is a subject and consequently not a citizen could, as Jebb's letter to the editor implies, be referenced with evident conviction. Given that the common state of subjecthood itself was never fully codified until well into the twentieth century, and that the position of subject did not guarantee "automatic" or "inalienable" rights but only provided the ground to claim them,[103] the basis of such a conviction evidently was on a plane other than the juridico-legal. This not only explains why the distinction between citizenship and subjecthood was the focus of such insistent reiteration; it also marks the imperative for reading imperial citizenship beyond the realm of statutory enactment.

An approach that extends beyond the positivistic would also be very much in keeping with studies of colonial South Asia that, broadly speaking, have been sensitive to the need to integrate the subjective with "official" or "factual" evidence.[104] With reference to citizenship in particular, feminist scholars working on South Asia have accorded a thickness to juridico-legal readings of citizenship by situating them in a broader social—and sometimes even literary—matrix.[105] There has for a while also been an understanding of the necessity for a shift from "events" to "discourse" in readings of nationalism.[106] In narrativizing nationalism, or reading the history of nationalism as a narrative in itself, there has also been a scrutiny of the selectivity of that narrative, especially when it posits the nation-state as the singular objective of all energies directed against the "colonial." What is of particular interest here is the fact that this narrativization has warranted a running together of "anticolonial" with "nationalism," even though, as Sudipta Kaviraj notes, removing the British was not within the conceptual "horizon" of anticolonialism—which, in the late nineteenth century and the early twentieth, was primarily a critique of colonial rule.[107] In separating the anticolonial from what became the nationalist, Kaviraj marks the moment of transition from one to the other as the point at which anticolonialism identifies a collective identity, a "we" to oppose British rule.[108] Here, though, what can be drawn out further is the tension between the various notions of this collective identity and the discrepant ways in which the relation with British rule was envisaged. The notion of imperial citizenship teases out this tension, highlighting particularly how imperial loyalty played a mediating role in articulating the claims to rights and an equality of a "we," not the least because any rhetoric of citizenship hinges quite dramatically on notions of loyalty. That this loyalty should be expressed toward the Crown but on behalf of the equal rights of the Indian people against the inequities of a colonial government demands a more valenced study of anticolonialism than is afforded by a nationalist telos, which assumes the ouster of British rule as the predetermined motive of any anticolonial agitation.

A reading of imperial citizenship adds further nuance to an understanding of anticolonial politics because although the distinction between citizen and subject theoretically rests on the fact that the citizen, unlike the subject, owes allegiance to a sovereign body rather than a sovereign,[109] that distinction between citizen and subject could not be so readily discerned with regard to Britain. Whereas the French and American revolutions shifted the terms of political membership, the "allegiance of the subject to the king remained in place in England" as the guarantor of legal status despite the inroads made by parliamentary democracy,[110] producing therefore a "hybrid citizenship."[111] And for racialized colonial subjects, such allegiance gained special purchase, for it was only on the basis of their status as subjects of the Crown that they could argue for the privileges of citizenship in a rapidly changing imperial environment that was witnessing the emerging autonomy of the Dominions. At the Imperial War Conference in 1917, for instance, where the Indian delegation protested the nonobservance of the BNSA and the discriminatory measures adopted against Indians in settler colonies, the Indian delegate, Satyendra Sinha, went so far as to state that "India has in a peculiar degree a sense of loyalty to the person and throne of the monarch in Britain, and it would, therefore, give the greatest satisfaction to my countrymen that this Conference should unequivocally express its declaration that the monarchical form of government is best suited to the requirements of the Empire."[112] Relegated to the "waiting room of history," Indians could evidently argue for political inclusion on the strength of their allegiance, in ways that produced rather incongruous formulations of political selfhood. A similar dynamic is apparent in an earlier instance when Gandhi argues for the Indian right to the franchise in the self-governing colony of Natal by repeatedly emphasizing the Indian allegiance to the queen. Enunciations such as these need not be placed only along a nationalist teleology that traces the progressive development of Gandhi's nationalist consciousness from an earlier position of loyalty. Gandhi's statement, rather, can also be read as illustrating the paradox of a discourse of citizenship that can argue for formal equality only on the basis of allegiance to the monarch, imbricating a post-Enlightenment discourse of liberal citizenship with a discrepant familial loyalty that renders rational framings of citizenship hardly self-evident.

A reading that recognizes such expressions of loyalty not only as a limitation—a reading that the notion of imperial citizenship makes room for—also presses for a broader reconsideration of the role of loyalty in constituting colonial subjectivities. In doing so, it assigns a complexity to the understanding of loyalty, given that its perceived singularity, otherwise, has sifted rather predictable patterns of anticolonial resistance and also yielded exclusivist notions of the postcolonial nation-state and its citizenry.[113] By opening up a more commodious reading of loyalty, the figure of the imperial citizen further tweaks the binarized equation between colonizer and colonized that has by now been qualified considerably by an understanding of the inevitable and strategic intimacies, complementarities, reciprocities, and contiguities running through them. It seems impoverishing indeed to forfeit the enormously rich and complex interplay of relations that a foregrounding of the place of loyalty in studies of anticolonialism can yield, given that the issue of loyalty is foundational, as mentioned above, to the claims of imperial citizenship, as well as the anticolonial critiques engendered by such claims.

Nation, Empire, and Narration

While the loyalist (and royalist) moments seem discomfiting, they are also important in compounding the doubleness of citizenship. As the exchanges at the Imperial Conferences quoted above make evident, the vocabulary of citizenship, developed in and through the context of empire, contributed in no small measure to the adumbration of the Indian nation-to-be (the "imperial citizens" in this study are, with the exception of Sorabji, among the frontrunners of those who are recognized today in India as "nationalists"). Innovative scholarship on late-colonial India has focused on the global imaginary that enabled agendas of anticolonial critique and nationalist resistance[114] and variously made possible the conception of India "as a bounded national space and economy."[115] By placing the concept of citizenship within the more expansive domain of empire, this study makes a similar move, emphasizing, however, that although imperial citizenship becomes crucial to the etching of a national "we," it is more ambivalent in its bounded territoriality and affective sway. In fact, while the nation has been read likewise,[116] the question of citizenship has not incited the argument for such considered ambivalence, an effect, perhaps, of its appearing to be always already claimed and marshaled by a statist discourse.

Locating citizenship at a moment prior to the birth of the nation-state is revealing in this regard, for it uncovers the ambiguities of citizenship that are imputedly reined in by the stabilizing discourse of statehood.

The imperative to read citizenship "otherwise," in fact, is prompted by the central figures in this study, who—while deeply committed to "nation-building"—bore an uneven relation to a nationalist narrative of statehood. While Gandhi in many ways exceeded the programmatic agenda of the nation-state and Sorabji was marked antinationalist on account of her unstinted support for British rule, both Naoroji and Banerjea were associated with what has been termed the "moderate" phase of nationalist agitation.[117] This phase, it is commonly assumed, embodied but the initial and "incomplete" stage of Indian nationalism inasmuch as it did not elicit a full-fledged demand for immediate political autonomy. Rather, its "ambiguity"—the fact that its indisputable investment in the idea of the nation was charged with an equal commitment to an imperial affiliation[118]—was marked, as Sanjay Seth perceptively notes, in terms of a "lack."[119] At one level, one could say that conflating ambiguity with lack indicates a paucity of imagination. At a deeper level, however, it also reveals an inability to think about the nation beyond a particular trajectory or form of statehood. How, then, can one read the scripts of citizenship laid out by these figures—if only to underscore the contingency of nation-states and their histories and to invoke, however briefly, the alterity of pasts,[120] a task that assumes urgency in the face of an upsurge of majoritarian nationalisms that brook no such possibilities?

Homi Bhabha laid out the theoretical possibilities for such a move some time ago in his oft-cited "DissemiNation," making it difficult to presume "the homogenous and horizontal view" that is central to the modernizing gesture of nationhood.[121] Bhabha's argument disrupts the historicism of the nation, foregrounding its "double time," wherein the people are simultaneously the "historical 'objects' of a nationalist pedagogy" as well as the performative subjects who demonstrate the "prodigious living principle" that erases "any prior or originary presence of the nation-people."[122] Despite Bhabha's interrogation of the constituency of the nation, an interrogation that indeed grants a constitutive role to its margins and marginalized, there is, in his analysis, a certain givenness about the nation-space and the trajectory of the nation. His analysis of the "otherness" of the "people-as-one" builds upon an assumption of an already existing citizenry of "we the people." In fact, in avowedly distancing himself from the "discourse of nationalism"[123] or the "history of nationalist movements,"[124] he grants to them a settling that overlooks their otherwise fraught bearings. What if we considered those very histories and discourses? What if, rather than highlighting the liminality of the nation through a temporal axis, as Bhabha does, we seek to locate its liminality in other registers—where the people are both citizens and subjects, of both a nation and a multiply constituted empire? If the formal realism of the novel tied it in with the destiny of the nation and vice versa—giving nationalism, following Benedict Anderson's influential argument, a prominent place in English studies[125]—then what modes of narrative lend themselves to a re-visioning of the "citizen," imperial or otherwise?

In addressing these questions, one must bear in mind that the narrative form that emerged from the late eighteenth century onward, thematizing Benedict Anderson's homogenous empty time of the nation most directly, was that of the realist novel, which in foregrounding the central narrating subject also ushered in the post-Enlightenment citizen-subject.[126] In a later period, this narrative congruence led to reductive mappings of the narrative output of "Third World" intellectuals who apparently could not but write of the nation.[127] While such pronouncements have been rightly and vigorously disputed, it is true, too, that the novel has dominated postcolonial scholarship[128] inasmuch as it has provided—more readily even than poetry, a genre that historically has stirred nationalist feelings—what Jahan Ramazani describes as a "textual synecdoche" for the nation.[129] Without necessarily entering into a debate about the relative merits of poetry or prose vis-à-vis their relevance to the nation or postcolonial studies,[130] it is not difficult to surmise the instrumentality of the chronotope[131] of the realist novel for mapping the nation. Of course in its engagement with various narrative forms reflective of displacement, exile, and hybridity, postcolonial literary scholarship has acknowledged the preeminence of postmodern narratives, which in overturning the mimeticism or attempts at verisimilitude of the realist novel register the critiques of the nation as engendered by its betrayals.[132] This betrayal, or a poignant yet acute awareness of the failure of the nation to deliver on its promises, provides the dynamic for a great many writers, scholars, and critics of the late twentieth century, as indeed it does for Bhabha's ruminations in "DissemiNation." Such musings or narrative transgressions, however, tend to be attributed to and from a post-colonial vantage and aesthetic alone, consigning a limited narrative and affective mode to those situated at the emergence of the nation, historically. What of their sense of betrayal and displacement by the nation that is in the making, or yet-to-be made? What of the fictiveness of their extrafictional musings, the profound loss they write into the germinal imagining of the nation on a register that is imminently "political"—of the way they articulate themselves as citizens?

The increasing tempo of these questions indicates much that remains to be explored. With respect to South Asia, the literal displacement and loss that is synonymous with the birth of the nation has been painfully visible and chronicled in Partition narratives of violence that are still being recovered. I am interested here not just in an earlier historical moment, when the idea of the nation is yet rudimentary, but also in the other kind of violence that is enacted when the contingencies of the nation, and its various possibilities, are subsumed by a narrative hegemony that renders many without a narrative, as it were. This becomes starkly the case with Banerjea or Sorabji, who—finding themselves out of step with the nation, and even with the empire—have no narrative mode readily available to articulate their profound investment and engagement with both. It is necessary to emphasize their engagement with the politics of the nation and the empire, variously estranged as they may have been from both, for theirs is not a stance of cosmopolitan disengagement; rather, it is cosmopolitan inasmuch as it maps a different affective field in and through its engagements with the question of nation, a "discrepant cosmopolitanism" perhaps.[133] In this it is worth noting that the labeling of Banerjea as a "moderate" nationalist or Sorabji as "imperialist," is inflected by the spatialized chronology of the nation, a function, in fact, of a realist narrative chronotope. Reading their narratives through the lens of imperial citizenship, one that strains against the narrative sequence through which the nation unfolds itself, is not so much an act of retrieving these figures as one of noting the enabling yet confounding richness of a historical and conceptual contrapuntality that is smoothed over through narrative abetment, if not anything else. Quite simply, it is to gesture to narrative modes that limn other ways of imagining the nation and that remind us that the burden of narrativizing the birthing of the nation and its citizenry was not carried by the (realist) novel alone,[134] and that the space-time coordinates of realism have not always been key to the imagining of the community.[135]

It is in this spirit that the following chapters are also attentive to the languages of the gothic, of the spectral, of mourning, and of liminality, which insinuate themselves into formulations of a citizenship that is and is not of the nation-to-be. While chapter 1 takes up the gothic in a very literal sense, underlining how the tropology of fin de siècle gothic sustains the narrative logic of Naoroji's claims to citizenship, the later chapters also point to how the narrative modes of citizenship traffic with time, space, and bodies in ways that render citizenship itself, as suggested earlier, a gothic concept. In other words, the chapters examine how the narrative registers of imperial citizenship, in straining against their own possibilities of representation, constitute and reflect the necessary doubling of citizenship. They recognize, on the one hand, the theoretical travails of citizenship that are effected by the contradictory logic of the universal that is always "haunted," as Butler notes, by what it has to eponymously evacuate yet also nominate as its only mode of representation.[136] On the other hand, the chapters also undertake a materialist reading attentive to the particularities of the competing discourses that allow for the iteration of the subject as the abstract "citizen." And, as mentioned earlier, if the "citizen" emerges from the gaps of these often disjunctive frameworks in but a fleeting moment of capture, then the narratives underwriting citizenship serve not only to remind us of the necessary yet suspended return of the universal to its constitutive particulars, but also to point to the constitutive assumptions normalizing this vacillation and its consequent exclusions.

In focusing on the vectors of representation that also constitute claims for citizenship, the last two chapters look specifically at autobiographical texts. In contravention of the expectations from autobiographies written by members of a politically conscious colonized elite, Banerjea's *Nation in Making* and Sorabji's *India Calling* turn out, quite surprisingly, to be neither about their authors nor about the nation that they purport to write about. Rather, in imagining a nation that is not being made, in detailing an affective register that exceeds the conceptions of the nation that is being made, the autobiographies performatively constitute a nation that is not, in ways that warrant the recent shift in autobiography scholarship to the view that autobiographies in the early stages of decolonization were in some ways "always already postmodern, always already globalized."[137] Such confabulations, of course, were arrested by the nation that crystallized itself by claiming its narratives more confidently. Philip Holden points to how a succeeding generation of autobiographers witnessing the dawn of the Indian nation, such as Jawaharlal Nehru, write the time and space of the nation more legibly in its Enlightenment script.[138] While I generally agree with Holden's argument, I would like to use the reading of Banerjea's and Sorabji's autobiographies as a way of underlining their meditations with—not at a distance from—the legacies of the Enlightenment and its progeny that most surely drove their imagination even before the nation was born: citizenship. And if their autobiographies leave their subjects as signifiers rife with contradictory ascriptions—or evacuated of them all, rendering the autobiographical/colonial subject as only an absent presence—that is perhaps how the claim to equality by an abstract yet sedimented articulation of imperial citizenship would have it.

Chapter 1, "Of the Indian Economy and the English Polls," begins by examining Dadabhai Naoroji's economic treatise *Poverty and Un-British Rule in India* (1901), which presents a case for imperial citizenship by appealing to the principles of classical political economy. As the chapter points out, by arguing that Britain was draining India's wealth, thereby bleeding it to death, Naoroji uses blood and capital interchangeably—as indeed did Marx—to implicate colony and metropole in an imperial body politic that forces the question of imperial citizenship through an argument of economic sustenance and circulation. In addition to his economic analyses that attempted to forge an imperial citizenry, Naoroji also drove the question of imperial citizenship to Britain through his spectacular political career as a parliamentarian. In following Naoroji's election campaigns in Holborn and Central Finsbury in 1886 and 1892, the chapter shows how the narrativity of the gothic (which permeates *Poverty*'s sanguine argument in very generic ways) also unevenly fashions Naoroji's rhetorical presentation of himself as an imperial citizen eligible to represent a London constituency on an Irish Home Rule ticket. Given that his foray into metropolitan politics was marked by a racialized controversy that labeled him the "black man," the chapter draws attention to the shaping of Naoroji's rhetorical idioms of citizenship by racialized tropes that fed into a late-Victorian political vocabulary, which could at once accommodate and disavow the political claims of colonial subjects.

The question of electoral representation provides the backdrop for chapter 2, "South Africa, Indentured Labor, and the Question of Credit," which picks up the trail of imperial citizenship in South Africa. The chapter engages with the ways in which the site of indentured labor forced a discussion of imperial citizenship that drew the settler colonies, the government in Britain, and petitioners from India into a debate about the fate of expatriate Indians, indentured and otherwise, who were stationed in considerable numbers across the British Empire. The chapter draws particular attention to the expatriate Indian merchant community in Natal, whose members—on the verge of being disenfranchised in 1895—protested the racial inequalities they were subject to by pointing to the often inhuman treatment meted out to Indian indentured laborers by European settlers in South Africa. However, by examining the petitions of Indians in Natal and India, writings of Gandhi, reports of the Protector of Immigrants and the testimony of the laborers, the chapter highlights how Indian traders invoked bourgeois virtues of character and cleanliness through the narrative logic of credit in ways that marked their own eligibility for citizenship but accorded an ambiguous—indeed spectral—position to the indentured laborer whose very presence, though, made their claims of citizenship possible.

In contrast to an engagement with questions of indentured labor, chapter 3, "The Professional Citizen in/and the Zenana," takes up the question of citizenship through the relatively privileged idiom of professionalism but in ways that also encompass those occupying a marginal social position. Proposing that in privileging expertise rather than the individual, professionalism approximates the abstract equality of citizenship, this chapter investigates the value of a professional self-fashioning for the highly marked figure of the late-colonial female subject. The chapter reads *India Calling* (1934), the autobiography of Cornelia Sorabji, alongside her other unpublished writing, including her legal reports of her clients, the veiled Indian women, or *purdahnashins*. Focusing on Sorabji's representation of herself through the highly charged terrain of professionalism in late-Victorian Britain, as well as in her dealings with the marginalized purdahnashins in India, the chapter foregrounds how it was the site of professional labor—a site that evidently could be conveyed only through the language of liminality—through which Sorabji forged an idiom of citizenship for the colonial female subject, who was otherwise claimed by the gendered prescriptions of both imperial and nationalist modernities.

Chapter 4, "Bureaucratic Modernity, the Indian Civil Service, and Grammars of Nationalism" also furthers the consideration of the trope of professionalism but situates it in the realm of a bureaucratic modernity. It focuses on the ICS, which formed the backbone of the colonial administration in India. Examining the records of the Civil Service Commission, the debates surrounding the procedures of the rigorous examination that candidates had to take, and representations of the ICS in fictional works such as H. S. Cunningham's *Chronicles of Dustypore*

(1875) and G. O. Trevelyan's *The Competition Wallah* (1866), the chapter highlights how the metropolitan engagement with the terms of a bureaucratic modernity was as much about how to constitute the modern citizen as about governing India. The second section of the chapter reads *A Nation in Making* (1925), the autobiography of Surendranath Banerjea, one of the first Indians to be admitted into the ICS, which had been exclusively British. While the issue of Indian entry into the ICS provided a forum in the late nineteenth century for Indians to model a rhetoric of political rights based on formal equality, the latter half of the chapter also demonstrates how the ethos of a bureaucratic modernity rather than the ICS itself informed the narrative dynamic of Banerjea's rendition of an Indian public sphere and citizen body. In doing so, the chapter also traces the antagonisms precipitated by very different notions of masculinity, citizenship, and nation-space forwarded by Indian nationalism in the early twentieth century, such that a rhetoric of mourning—one that constantly questioned the here and now—counterintuitively became one way of configuring the "imperial" citizen even as the nation was historically being construed otherwise.

In drawing attention to the specific formulations of imperial citizenship, then, this book punctuates national histories and tests the contours of imperial geographies; by underscoring the doubleness of languages of citizenship, it renders its rationalist script more "centaur-like."[139] The book seeks to provide a new frame for considering colonial subjects. But by foregrounding the citizenship claims of a colonized people, the intent, as should be evident by now, is not to view citizenship itself as necessarily emancipatory or egalitarian. Rather, guided by an understanding of both the exclusions of citizenship and the normalizations effected by it, the formulations of citizenship traced by the following chapters highlight the narrative inscriptions of imperial citizenship that lend a genealogy to those exclusions and normalizations, thus forcing the gap which the seemingly foundational language of (national) citizenship seeks always to close.

CHAPTER ONE

Of the Indian Economy and the English Polls

Published in 1901, Dadabhai Naoroji's monumental *Poverty and Un-British Rule in India* is widely regarded as one of the founding texts of Indian nationalist economics. It does not enjoy quite the same currency, however, in cultural analyses of Indian nationalism. That relative lack of esteem is curious in light of the fact that *Poverty* generates its argument primarily through a critique of imperial policies in India, constructing an Indian body politic that even remodels Englishness in the process.[1] It is almost as if in providing the first statistical estimate of India's national income,[2] *Poverty* precludes itself from exegeses of nationalism that have come to view the nation as narrative. Indeed, the critical emphasis on the "writing" of the nation seems to have reproduced classificatory typologies of "economic nationalism" and "cultural nationalism," which have long constituted a divide in Indian historiography.[3] To be sure, the instrumental role played by nationalist economic analyses in launching populist anticolonial campaigns in India—such as *swadeshi*, which entailed the boycott of foreign goods—is widely accepted. But the economic analyses of thinkers like M. G. Ranade, R. C. Dutt, and Naoroji himself are known more for the various cultural outpourings they generated—nationalist songs of self-reliance, ballads, drama, and fiction—than for the narrative strategies or cultural idioms they deploy. It is perhaps the very logic that accorded primacy to these texts of economic analysis that cordons them off from an analysis of their narrative implications. Economic critiques of imperialism provided, as Manu Goswami notes, "the first sustained articulations of nationalism" by forwarding the notion of a "territorially delimited economic collective."[4] In claiming the colonial space in the name of a conceptual nation, however, Indian bourgeois nationalists of the late nineteenth century expressly excluded the "individual," the "cultural," or the "particular" from the abstract nation-space they so constructed, even as they sought to move away from the seemingly ahistorical, abstract models of classical political economy.[5] Therefore, while *Poverty*'s emphasis on providing a statistical critique of colonial rule in the name of a unified nation-space privileged its claims, it also cast the text in an angular relation with the social and cultural "life" of that emerging nation.

Political Economy and Fin de Siècle Gothic

Yet it is precisely this self-conscious definition of "the economic" that prompts a counterintuitive reading of a text like *Poverty*. After all, the authority that classical political economy appropriated for itself during the late eighteenth and early nineteenth centuries depended on rhetorical and discursive strategies that sought to demarcate "economic concerns" from those of "morality, religion, and social stability."[6] *Poverty*'s occlusion from the imaginative resonances of the nation could very well speak to the desired epistemological distinctions between what Mary Poovey describes as "figures of arithmetic and figures of speech."[7] From the nineteenth century onward, as Poovey outlines, the notion that numbers were "dull" and "dry" seemed to privilege their access to empirical knowledge in contrast to the "undue embellishment associated with fiction, hyperbole, and rhetoric."[8] But the distinction between "figures of arithmetic and figures of speech" was in itself discursive, concealing the extent to which the self-evident facticity of empirical data was permeated by imaginative processes. For instance, the census, which was instrumental in institutionalizing the regime of numbers, hinged, as has been pointed out, on a certain "mode of imagining the colonial state."[9] Even as the colonial administration in India relied heavily on a regime of numbers to regularize the otherwise recalcitrant features of the sociophysical landscape,[10] the rationale of the British census in India lay, as Gauri Viswanathan suggests, in "its meticulous construction of narrative plots."[11] The narrative and imaginative implications of the census serve as a useful entry point into *Poverty*, whose economic data are interspersed with Naoroji's letters, essays, and speeches written over the last few decades of the nineteenth century, which have otherwise been lost sight of in—or because of—*Poverty*'s designation as a pioneering work of Indian economic nationalism.

Reading *Poverty* "literarily" is also in keeping with a strand of economic analysis that argues for the ways in which economic arguments operate through discursive and rhetorical devices.[12] Such an approach is particularly important for the purposes of this chapter because it is by appealing to economic, political, and cultural registers that *Poverty* not only delimits a territorially defined nation-space, but also provides an early figuration of the Indian as citizen. The first section of this chapter examines how the narrative framing Naoroji's economic treatise brings together statistical calculations and ideas of bodily health, constructing an Indian body politic that not only erupts in moments of gothic dismemberment, but, in doing so, points to a consanguinity between colony and metropole envisaged by the free-trade principles of political economy but rarely followed in practice. In fact, the unlikely conjoining of the principles of political economy with elements of gothic narrative helps Naoroji formulate a unified imperial citizenry that brings together Indians and Britons, the only formulation, according to him, that could remedy the economic problems postulated by *Poverty*.

By juxtaposing a reading of *Poverty* with that of Naoroji's election campaigns—in 1892, he was elected to the British House of Commons from Central Finsbury—the second section of this chapter underlines how his self-representation as an imperial citizen before a metropolitan electorate borrowed from the same narrative corpus that had enabled him to present the urgency of India's economic condition to a metropolitan readership. In reading Naoroji's election campaigns, what is of particular interest is not only how he sought to dispel popular representations of the Irish—as he ran in an English constituency on an Irish Home Rule ticket—but also how he countered racialized perceptions of his own status as an Indian subject, as a "black man," an epithet bestowed upon him by Lord Salisbury, the Tory leader of the day. Naoroji's need to counteract the general English misapprehensions of the Irish was fairly obvious, given that the Irish demand for Home Rule, which had been gathering force during the second half of the nineteenth century, had precipitated the 1886 elections and also made the Irish monstrous in the popular imagination. However, the unprecedented nature of Naoroji's candidacy as an Indian subject demanding political rights, not only for himself but on behalf of an English electorate—thus making him a true imperial citizen—presented an entirely new challenge. To read how Naoroji was racialized in this endeavor is to draw attention to the twinning of the unfolding registers of race and citizenship. In emphasizing the coimplication of the discourse of race with that of citizenship, the chapter is sensitive to the fact that a racial vocabulary is often engendered by the technologies of citizenship. In reading the newspaper coverage of Naoroji as the "black man," however, the argument also considers how it was precisely the uncertainties underlining generalized articulations of race that, when placed alongside the purported certitudes of an emerging, allegedly scientific racial discourse, allowed for a discourse of citizenship that could at once accommodate and disavow the political claims of racialized colonial subjects.[13]

While the preoccupation of citizenship with questions of incorporation and abstraction makes itself evident in ways that I have broadly described as gothic,[14] this chapter is attentive to the specificities of fin de siècle metropolitan gothic fiction, whose popularity helps explain the resonance of the narrative registers through which *Poverty* (and Naoroji) appeared before a metropolitan audience. An emphasis on fin de siècle gothic is inescapable here, for its conventions provided a prism through which the English came to represent the colonies and colonial subjects in the latter decades of the nineteenth century, a fact well captured by Patrick Brantlinger's immensely suggestive term, the "imperial gothic."[15] Fin de siècle gothic fiction, with its stock—and motley—crew of half-breeds and half-beasts threatening to populate the metropolis, illustrates the profound contradictions and fears besetting an imperial polity that had extended its sway across a substantial portion of the earth yet dreaded the inevitable intimacies engendered by that expansion. Critical analyses of fin de siècle gothic production, though, tend to associate its prominence mostly with metropolitan writers, who alone are allowed the privilege of fear as well as that of self-recrimination and moral anxiety about the empire—an anxiety that manifested itself through the horrors of degeneracy, dissolution, and decay seen in the work of writers like H. G. Wells, H. Rider Haggard, Robert Louis Stevenson, and Bram Stoker (here I am referring more to Stoker's metropolitan location).

However, the tropology of the gothic was not confined to the realm of literary pursuits alone; it also lent itself to the formulation of political debates, as in the demand for Irish Home Rule. Moreover, the self-reflexivity that undergirded gothic imaginings was not only a metropolitan prerogative. Shifting the scope of the gothic from metropolitan writers as well as from the specific realm of literary production, this chapter highlights how Naoroji's statistical figuration of "un-British rule" expresses his concern about a rapidly denuding English identity, a concern that was spectacularized in all its hideous ramifications in the metropolitan fiction of the day. The irony, of course, is that it is Naoroji who points out what is un-British and, consequently, what is British. This considerably expands the rubric of the gothic, for even as metropolitan gothic reveled in moments of transmogrification and signaled the dissolution and degeneration of the English and their empire, its impetus always lay in redrawing national and cultural boundaries, enacting, in Cannon Schmitt's words, "the formation of England conceived as a nation and of English national subjects."[16] In this, Naoroji's appeal to concerns provoked by the gothic not only rendered those boundaries porous but also became instrumental in constructing colonial subjects—who more often than not featured as the gothic focus of English "fear"—as, in fact, "equal" citizens of the British Empire.

An invocation of the gothic in a discussion of an economic treatise such as *Poverty* bears ample warrant, for the connection between gothic narrative and classical political economy has long been apparent, given that Adam Smith's thesis of the self-regulation of market forces depends heavily on the symbolic and supernatural figure of the "invisible hand" that makes up for the lack of any adequate existing economic formulation.[17] Ghouls and vampires, we know, widely permeated Marx's critique of political economy as well.[18] *Poverty* is gothic insofar as its economic argument relies on "gothic effects."[19] If toward the end of the nineteenth century, the staple ingredients of earlier gothic narratives (such as haunted castles and torture chambers) were "supplanted by the threat of the decay and dissolution of one's personality,"[20] then Naoroji's central premise that England's economic and political practices in India at the time were symptomatic of a degenerating Englishness could hardly not tap into prevalent metropolitan doubts of self-identity in relation to empire, the hallmark of the "imperial gothic."[21] Moreover, as the proliferation of various kinds of anatomical and psychological discourses at the end of the century questioned the certitude of bodily boundaries and teleology,[22] the body itself emerged as the locus of gothic horror.[23] The economic argument of *Poverty* repeatedly returns to the image of bloodied, dismembered bodies (and the body politic) in order to attest to its prognosis of England's financial misrule. In doing so, *Poverty* certainly speaks to the corpus of narrative conventions characterizing fin de siècle gothic, but, as mentioned earlier, it also co-opts it to provide for a forum of representation and appeal for those most likely to be demonized by its implications, England's colonial "others."

Born to a Parsee family in Bombay in 1825, Naoroji distinguished himself as an academic. He became one of the first Indians to hold a professorship, when he was named Professor of Mathematics and Natural

Philosophy at Elphinstone College, in Bombay. Deeply involved in imparting a distinct agenda to Indian public life in Bombay, he reminisced in later years: "the six or seven years before I eventually came to England in 1855, ... were full of all sorts of reforms, social, educational, political, religious, etc. Ah, those years."[24] That he chose to move to England in 1855 to become a trading partner in an Indian commercial firm surprised everyone who knew him, given his academic and political standing in Bombay. His decision to do so was motivated by a desire to alert an English audience to the urgent need for reform in India, to establish, as one of his biographers puts it, "an intimate connexion [sic]" between England and India.[25] Naoroji lived in England until 1907, and although he spent time in India intermittently during that period, he immersed himself in the intellectual and political life of the imperial metropolis.[26] Although he lost the 1886 election in which he ran for Parliament from Holborn, he was elected as the Liberal candidate from Central Finsbury in 1892. In pursuing his goal of acquainting the English with Indian affairs, Naoroji was relentless in his exposition of the state of the Indian economy, which, over the years, was the subject of his painstaking and prolific calculations and statistical estimates.

Published in England in 1901, *Poverty* is a compilation of essays, statistical tables, official correspondence from and to Naoroji, reports of parliamentary commissions, and the texts of Naoroji's speeches in the House of Commons and elsewhere in England. Although most of the individual items in *Poverty* were originally addressed to English officials and politicians, the volume as a whole is aimed at a broader audience that is largely English as well, convinced as Naoroji was, as his prefatory comments indicate, that "a truly British course can and will certainly be vastly beneficent both to Britain and India" (*Poverty* v). Interestingly, not only does *Poverty* include Naoroji's writings, but it also presents the views and rebuttals of colonial administrators. The polyvocality of the volume is significant in emphasizing a dialogic relationship between colony and metropole. More important, the multiauthored and multilayered nature of the volume interpellates its (English) audience in a juridical role—not unlike the one popularized by gothic fiction throughout the nineteenth century[27]—the first step, perhaps, in their journey to become imperial citizens as well. As Naoroji states later: "I have not the least doubt in my mind about the conscience of England and Englishmen, that if they once clearly see the evil, they will *not shrink* to apply the proper remedies" (140; emphasis in the original). As a beneficiary of

Western education in India, Naoroji was quite unequivocal about the fruits of English liberalism. In fact, his interest in poverty in India arose from the consequences of what he felt was the good work done by the English. "English education," he notes, "has taught the highest political ideal of British citizenship and raised in the hearts of the educated Indians the hope and aspiration to be able to raise their countrymen to the same ideal citizenship" (vi). As quickly becomes clear in the book, the issue of poverty becomes symptomatic of—and even a displaced referent for—the failure of the English to fulfill their pledges of granting citizenship to Indians.[28] Referring to various acts of Parliament and the Queen's Proclamation of 1858, Naoroji presents "self-government under British paramountcy" as an index of "true British citizenship" (xiv), and it is the deferral of this political ideal that generates and frames the economic critique of his analysis of poverty.

While poverty operates very much as a metaphor for failed English promises, the text also provides ample evidence that it is a product of English economic policies. Even as Naoroji is careful to enumerate the "invaluable blessings" of British rule in India (*Poverty* 1), the moral valence of colonial governance is evaluated along a register that weaves political and economic rights into a consideration of the "moral": "I have as much desire," he remarked elsewhere, "to see the British connection with all its moral benefits continue for a *very* long time, as that India should not be starving and in distress."[29] That the moral and politico-economic categories should be welded into a common analytic framework is not surprising. John Ruskin, writing in 1860, had like many others deplored the precepts of political economy for presuming that "directions can be given for the gaining of wealth, irrespectively of the consideration of its moral sources."[30] The case of India, however, tweaked this argument, for it witnessed the twinning of the principles of political economy with a definite agenda of moral improvement. Past mercantilist policies of the East India Company had dismissed India's potential for social and moral improvement in the interest of protecting the company's monopoly. But the momentum gathered by ideas of free trade encouraged its lobbyists in Parliament to argue for the feasibility of free trade through an emphasis on the redeemability of Indian civilization, thus forging what Eric Stokes describes as an "alliance of attitude between the missionary and merchant."[31] In 1833, Thomas Babington Macaulay observed in a speech:

It would be, on the most selfish view of the case, far better for us that the people of India were well-governed and independent of us, than ill-governed and subject to us; that they were ruled by their own kings, but wearing our broadcloth, and working with our cutlery, than that they were performing their salaams to English collectors and magistrates, but were too ignorant to value, or too poor to buy, English manufactures. To trade with civilised men is infinitely more profitable than to govern savages.[32]

Macaulay's speech, referred to on numerous occasions by Naoroji, reflects the conjoining of the discourse of political economy with that of social, if not moral, reform. The earnest zeal to "improve" India, which formed the cornerstone of colonial liberal ideology, was evidently not divorced from the equally keen desire to ensure English profit. However, given that both these discourses were framed by an implicit attentiveness to the interests of the English nation (and a corresponding consciousness of English superiority), neither the goals of economic liberalism nor that of a liberal education could ever be fully realized in India's favor. And it is in this gap between the purported liberalism of political economy and its parochially mercantilist manifestation, between the universalistic assumptions of moral improvement and the belatedness of its political promises, that one can situate Naoroji's critique of Anglo-Indian relations and his alternative conception of an imperial citizenship—which could enable England to fulfill its highest ideals only by exceeding what Naoroji felt was a narrow envisioning of political economy.[33]

The thrust of the economic argument advanced by *Poverty* rests upon providing an estimate of the Indian national income, which, Naoroji argues, leaves very little for India after paying the necessary taxes and tributes to England. Simple as this argument may sound, Naoroji's achievement lies in actually computing the per capita national income, a task that had not been attempted before. Bringing together agricultural data from various provinces and the value of the manufacturing industries and other sources of wealth, he arrives at the total income of British India, which, when divided by the population, yields the per capita income (*Poverty* 23–25). The emergence of the per capita income after a series of lengthy calculations marks a turning point, for while it refers to the individual Indian, it is a figure that can be derived only by taking the whole population into account, thus accentuating the individual's organic relation with the collective figure of the population. When V. K. R. V. Rao took up the task of calculating the Indian national income years later, he commented: "there is a magic about the *per capita* National Income which ... appeal[s] to [people's] imagination."[34] The "magic" evidently lay in the trace of the nation that inhered in the per capita income: as Naoroji noted, what was important about the per capita income was that it signified "the whole actual, material, annual income of India ... available for the use of the *whole people of India*" (187; emphasis in the original). As a figure that derived from and established a "functional equivalence" between the members of the body politic it thus constituted, the per capita figure went a long way toward rendering that body a nation.[35]

However, it is significant that although *Poverty*'s income calculations produce an abstract reckoning of the "Indian" inasmuch as she or he is denuded of "irrational" inscriptions, the pivotal energy of these calculations comes from their reliance on the irreducibly marked body of the Indian indentured laborer, or "coolie," who was exported to overseas British colonies to meet the demand for cheap and exploitable labor that arose upon the British Parliament's abolition of slavery. In order to prove that India's per capita income was indeed insufficient, Naoroji compares it with figures denoting the cost of "necessary consumption," required for the "bare wants of a human being, to keep him in ordinary good health and decency" (*Poverty* 25). The itinerant figure of the emigrant laborer makes its way into the calculations as Naoroji computes the cost of the subsistence-level rations budgeted for the coolie's journey out of India. That the abject figure of the departing coolie, who becomes useful precisely because she or he was provided with "not the slightest luxury—no sugar or tea, or any little enjoyment of life but simple animal subsistence of coolies living in a state of quietude" (26), should become instrumental is ironic, given that the laborers are invoked as members of the body politic precisely at their moment of departure, a dynamic that is taken up further in the next chapter. What is of interest here is how figures such as that of the coolie, who are included within the body politic on account of their exclusion from the physical spaces of the nation, enable Naoroji to pronounce: "Such appears to be the condition of the masses of India. They do not get enough to provide the bare necessities of life" (31). While Naoroji extends his framework of reference to include other "examples" of subsistence-level existence by referring to agricultural laborers, he does not discuss possible modes of income redistribution that could ameliorate the situation, noting that possibility as a vital question but bracketing it off as one occupying an entirely different sphere of legislative argument (188). Rather, the economic imbalance literally embodied in and by the body of the coolie, and other laborers, becomes important in itself in Naoroji's presentation of an emaciated body politic. Having embodied the economic imbalance, the coolie recedes from the discussion altogether, only to be overshadowed by the educated Indian, whose fate is the one that looms large over Naoroji's arguments for citizenship, as I shall discuss later.

While Naoroji's calculation of the per capita income constitutes an Indian body politic in ways it had not been conceived of before, it is interesting to note that the body politic is also always on the point of dissolution. *Poverty* is replete with images of an exhausted body politic, one that on account of British economic practices is "on the verge," Naoroji emphasizes, "of being ground to dust" (*Poverty* 250). The predominant metaphor of *Poverty*, a metaphor that Naoroji is now credited for having introduced into Indian economic analysis, is that of the "drain." Calculating that India annually sends between £200 million and £300 million to England in the form of revenues that are never returned; payments for an administrative structure that fails to fulfill its promises; interest on loans, the benefits of which never filter down to the Indians; and a vast quantity of exports never balanced by imports, Naoroji asserts that it is the "exhaustion caused by the drain" that prevents India's relation with England from being a "healthy business" (33).

The idea of a "healthy business" is significant here, for with the increasing professionalization of medicine during the nineteenth century, the healthy body had become a normative criterion in England, institutionalizing a regime of public-health administration that also influenced areas such as education, sexuality, and sanitation. As Pamela Gilbert notes, by the 1860s, the importance of a healthy body and physical environment had been fairly well established, even in political discussions of citizenship.[36] The leitmotif running through discussions of health across various registers was a preoccupation with circulation. The well-known physician Thomas Southwood Smith wrote of bodily functions: "All vital processes are either processes of supply or processes of waste . . . Every moment old particles are carried out of the system; every moment new particles are introduced into it. The matter of which the body is composed is thus in a state of perpetual flux."[37] The circulatory processes of the body became the template for larger issues of social health and morality, such that "feeble water supplies, clogged drains, crowded courts and tenements, smoking fireplaces and furnaces,"[38] all impediments to circulation, also became a site for obsessive concern and correction over the course of the nineteenth century. Consequently, the results of an ineffective circulation, or of one gone awry, became the stuff of metropolitan gothic imaginings: an overriding concern about urban stench, in fact, distinguished late-Victorian gothic fiction from its earlier counterparts.[39] In a text such as Richard Jefferies's 1885 novel *After London*, as Alexandra Warwick observes, apocalyptic images of London's ruination are presented through images of a river overflowing its banks and sewage channels.[40] Clearly, a regulated water supply—and, consequently, the question of circulation and drainage—had assumed considerable significance. As Thomas Osborne puts it, tying the "body, city, and economy together into one system,"[41] drains emerged as a key artifact of Victorian society: "instead of commemorating themselves with great cathedrals, the Victorians built magnificent drains."[42]

Images of circulation remained crucial to economic formulations as well, and the healthy body politic was perceived as both a precondition for and an effect of the successful implementation of laissez faire principles of classical political economy.[43] But as Catherine Gallagher also points out, the body and the economy were not always homologous, and in Malthusian economics, for instance, "ideas of bodily well-being and economic circulation were frequently articulated both on and against each other."[44] It is noteworthy, then, that Naoroji argued for economic circulation by using the template of bodily well-being. He was certainly not alone in bringing the two sites together, for critiques of political economy, which were legion in this period, hinged on bodily metaphors as well. After all, it was in an essay titled "Veins of Wealth" that Ruskin took political economy to task for its disregard of natural human impulses in advocating a science of wealth.[45] While Naoroji's opposition to the drain of wealth from India resembled in many respects the criticisms leveled against political economy, he was actually arguing from the other side. Subscribing to a naturalization of economic processes—a naturalization based on the premise of the circulatory functions of the healthy body—Naoroji declaimed the drain as one that "set all the ordinary laws of political economy and justice at naught" (*Poverty* 125). That the correct working of the laws depended upon a "natural" circulation of wealth is evident from the following passage: "If, as in England, the revenue raised from the people *returned to the people*—if the income of railways and other public works taken from the people, returned to the people, to fructify in their pockets, then there would be no need for anxiety for finance or famines, or for pinching in salt, or poisoning with opium, millions of the human race. India would then pay with ease £100,000,000 or £200,000,000 of revenue, and would not be the worse for it" (201; emphasis in the original). What Naoroji objects to is not the fact that India pays vast sums to England; rather, it is the noncirculatory, hence unnatural and unhealthy, nature of this transaction that he decries. To be sure, Naoroji was certainly not the first to comment on England's draining of India: he quotes previous English administrators who had done so.[46] Naoroji's framing of the drain in terms of a larger argument about the healthy body politic, however, imbued the drain with a moral and political valence that came to bear upon the current state of India: as a result of the drain—the failure to observe the laws of political economy—India, *Poverty* insisted, was rapidly being reduced to a state of ill health, which highlighted in particular the moral failure of British rule.

Naoroji's emphasis on the draining of India was of course astute, for it emphasized a circulatory trope that was preeminent in the Victorian imagination, only that in this case, he also highlighted the potentially damaging effects of a "faulty draining" that was not inserted within a larger circulatory network or a "principle of exchange."[47] As an aside, it should be noted that recommendations for improved sanitation presented by reformers such as Edwin Chadwick, in his 1842 *Report on the Sanitary Condition of the Labouring Population of Great Britain*, had gone a long way in imposing a "sanitary policing"[48] of the native populace in India in ways that "colonized" the native body.[49] Incidentally, Chadwick was largely influenced by the ideas of Southwood Smith, who in turn developed his notions on public health based on reports from India and Egypt.[50] If all of this illuminates a network of ideas that was itself circulatory in its discussion of circulation and public health, then it is perhaps meet that Naoroji should have presented these ideas to a metropolitan audience, if only to indict it for its failure to approximate the ideals of circulation and a healthy body politic: the wheel indeed had come full circle.

As mentioned earlier, it is not so much the extraction of wealth that

Naoroji criticizes, but the patterns of circulation into which that wealth is routed (or not). That circulation was deemed important as the general prerequisite for both capital and bodily health is evident in the ways in which blood and money were used interchangeably and from the fact that a figure such as Dracula—a vampire who both hoards money and sucks blood—came to embody the anxieties of the late-Victorian period.[51] While the metaphor of vampirism was ripe for Naoroji's argument—Marx had already used the vampire analogy in *Capital*—Naoroji superimposed an implicitly more bloody scene of violence over that image. In *Poverty*, Naoroji repeatedly invokes Lord Salisbury's comment, made twenty-five years earlier, that "*India must be bled*." Conceding that "the injury is exaggerated in the case of India, where so much of the revenue is exported without direct equivalent," Salisbury, then Secretary of State for India, was nonetheless of the opinion that India must be bled more efficiently. In fact, he had even stated that "'the lancet should be directed to the parts where the blood is congested or at least sufficient, not to those' (the agricultural people) 'which are *already feeble from the want of it*'" (*Poverty* ix; emphasis in the original). Not only does Naoroji repeatedly refer to this statement, but he also points out how former foreign rulers in India "were like butchers hacking here and there." The British presence, by contrast, is far more devastating, for "the English with their scientific scalpel cut to the very heart," with the result that the wounds "are kept perpetually open and widening, by draining away the life-blood in a continuous stream" (211).[52]

Naoroji's critique of the scientific precision with which England "applies the lancet to India's heart," a metaphor that he uses repeatedly but also decries, echoes in some ways the outrage against vivisectionary techniques that were gaining precedence as a way of bolstering the scientific claims of medicine and surgery. H. G. Wells's 1896 *The Island of Doctor Moreau*, for instance, demonized the vivisectionist Moreau, who is portrayed throughout with "hands smeared red," and the entire narrative in fact has been described by one critic as "blood-spattered."[53] *Poverty* is not far from being blood-spattered itself, replete as it is with Naoroji's constant reminders of India's sanguinary loss. "Continuous and increasing 'bleeding,'" Naoroji reminds his audience, can only "reduce strength and kill" (*Poverty* 390). However, while the protests against vivisection were viewed as polarizing the argument along a split between rationality and sentimentality, with the antivivisectionists being seen to occupy the lower (and feminized) ground of emotion,[54] Naoroji effectively replicates the antivivisectionist technique of repeatedly portraying the pained body, but does so to argue for a "rational" adherence to market principles of economy. References to Salisbury's speech about the effective use of the lancet appear in the preface to *Poverty* and in its concluding pages, emerging as bookends to his argument. In fact, in the compilation of Naoroji's speeches that forms the coda to *Poverty*, Salisbury's memorable phrase, "India must be bled," appears as the title of Naoroji's public address at Walthamstow. Warning his audience that "it is at India's cost and blood that the Empire has been formed and maintained up to the present day" (645), Naoroji pronounces that "if the British public do not rouse themselves the blood of every man that dies there will lie on their head" (647).

The idea of the "sins" of empire coming to rest upon the uneasy conscience of the English was of course not new to the fin de siècle. In tandem with scientific theories of degeneracy and atavism that both fueled it and were fueled by it, metropolitan literary and popular culture in the late nineteenth century had been bedeviled by grotesque bodies: the brutish denizens of Moreau's island or the hideously beautiful Ayesha in Rider Hagard's *She* (1887), for instance. Naoroji's gory and retributive images of an India bleeding to death are significant, however, in that they provide a counterpoint to another bloodied moment marking Anglo-Indian relations in the nineteenth century: the revolt of 1857. His speech titled "India Must Be Bled" collapses the metaphor of blood, using it not just to denote money but, with reference to the revolt, blood itself: "In the time of the Indian Mutiny," Naoroji points out to his English audience, "you had only forty thousands troops there. It was the two hundred thousand Indian troops that shed their blood and fought your battles and that gave you this magnificent Empire" (*Poverty* 645). While Naoroji refers to the blood shed by Indian troops for the British, the images that circulated in the aftermath of the revolt, and which continued to circulate over the next several decades, were of the British blood shed by the mutineers. Significantly, most of the British casualties were lives lost in battle, rather than in gory scenes of calculated bloodshed. However, the latter emerged as the predominant image of the revolt: as Jenny Sharpe comments, "the image of death by disease or bullet wound [was] far less noble than that of helpless women and children being cut to pieces by leering sepoys with swords in hand."[55]

A site of massacre by the Hindu satrap Nana Saheb, in fact, was preserved with its dried blood as an enduring reminder (was any needed) of the barbarity of the natives.[56]

The gothicized images of bloodied, mutilated British bodies continued to gain purchase long after the revolt, if only to help the British come to terms with the central predicament precipitated by it.[57] With the transfer of power necessitated by the events of 1857, and the Queen's Proclamation of 1858 following thereafter, Indians, as mentioned earlier, were assured a certain parity with the Britons in rights and privileges—the tenets, in Naoroji's eyes, of citizenship. Despite the granting of these privileges, the memory of the revolt in India, along with colonial insurgencies elsewhere, increasingly cast doubt on the extent to which colonial populations could be included within the imperial embrace. As an article in the *Times* bemoaned, in the wake of the Morant Bay uprising in 1865 in Jamaica: "Alas for grand triumphs of humanity, and the improvement of races, and the removal of primeval curses, and the expenditure of twenty millions sterling, Jamaica herself gainsays the fact and belies herself, as we see today. It is that which vexes us more than even the Sepoy revolt."[58]

Such dismay reinforced scientific views of racial difference, and in a speech to the London Anthropological Society in 1866, James Hunt, one of its founders, observed that "the merest novice in the study of race-characteristics ought to know that we English can only successfully rule either Jamaica, New Zealand, the Cape, China, or India, by such men as Governor Eyre [Governor of Jamaica]."[59] In India, the memory of 1857 inaugurated a racial grammar of difference that fed upon itself, constructing the native male as savage, duplicitous, and ultimately irredeemable.[60] The specter of the revolt even haunted the Ilbert Bill controversy of 1883–84, when a proposed amendment to allow certain Indian officials to try European offenders was effectively vetoed with arguments that invoked the Indian rapacities of 1857.[61] Interestingly, the abiding memories of the revolt centered on the raped and mutilated body of the English woman as a testimony to Indian excess. The disfigured male English body was curiously absent, as the fragmented body of the male colonizer would surely have "negate[d] colonial power at the precise moment that it needed reinforcing."[62] In fact, it can be argued that the figure of the savage and lecherous mutineer was constructed to appease an English masculinity otherwise imperiled by the emergence of the newly formed Indian subject demanding the long-promised fruits of British education—the subject wanting to be a citizen. *Poverty* plays into this crisis of masculinity by clearing space for an English manliness: "India needs the help," Naoroji writes, of "manly, conscientious, true-hearted English gentlemen to study and probe her forlorn condition, and India may then fairly hope for ample redress ere long at England's hands and conscience" (*Poverty* 230). Since an idiom of gentlemanliness had emerged as the register for tracing the ascendancy of English bourgeois masculinity from the mid-1800s on, it is no small irony that Naoroji appeals to it to fulfill the aspirations of that constituency which most threatened it in the colonial theater: the emerging Indian middle class—known in Bengal, in fact, as the class of the *bhadralok* ("class of gentlemen").

While Naoroji tracked the drain along a number of different registers, unlike other contemporary Indian economic commentators, he insisted that it was affected by two elements: namely, the remittances paid to English officials employed in India, remittances that made their way back to England along with the pensions that were paid there; and, similarly, the remittances made by non-European officials serving in India (*Poverty* 38).[63] In other words, the drain, according to Naoroji, was aggravated most by the non-employment of educated Indians, members of the burgeoning native middle class—who, as he notes, "may beg in the streets or break stones on the roads for ought the rulers seem to care for their natural rights, position and duties in their own country" (205). It is not just the nonemployment of natives that Naoroji protests, but also the underemployment of professional Indians, who were consistently appointed to lower positions with lower wages despite "all professions of equality of all British subjects, without reference to colour or creed" (122). Quoting John Stuart Mill's dictum that "industry is limited by capital" (56), Naoroji posits a remedy for the drain by pointing out that salaries paid to Indians would accumulate and circulate capital within India, "enabl[ing] the agricultural as well as other industries to get the necessary life-blood for their maintenance and progress" (135). That the capital accumulated by educated natives should translate into the lifeblood of the country establishes a metonymic relationship between the middle-class Indian and the national body politic, wherein the educated native metaphorizes its bleeding and its remedy. For Naoroji, the question of securing employment for the educated Indian male in fact became the most urgent site for pressing forth the equalizing rhetoric of citizenship: apportioning employment to qualified

Indians was one way the British government could make good on the pledge in the Queen's Proclamation that "Indians shall be British citizens, with all the rights and duties of British citizenship" (394). In this, it is the educated native who is extrapolated on the national body politic, and the figure of the indentured or agricultural laborer, which was otherwise so instrumental in its conceptualization, recedes into the background: Naoroji dismisses the question of the employment of the "lower class of bodily and menial laborers" as but "India's crumbs in the lower employments of her children" (228).[64]

Naoroji's conflation of a liberal rhetoric of equality with economic opportunity for educated natives therefore articulates a notion of citizenship that operates through an uneven logic of class. However, if it is the figure of the educated, male native that is taken as the figure of the citizen, it is a grammar of feminized suffering that provides the narrative subtext of the problem of the drain and its proposed solution. As discussed above, the appeal to England to live up to its pledges of citizenship and employ Indians without prejudice emerges not only as a solution to the economic deficit posed by the drain, but also as a means to consolidate the professional aspirations of an Indian middle class. It ensures, also, the moral legitimacy of the English gentleman, who emblematizes a putative Englishness itself. As Naoroji notes, "I am writing to English *gentlemen*, and I have no fear that they will receive my sincere utterances with the generosity and love of justice of English gentlemen (*Poverty* 230; emphasis in the original).[65] This faith in Englishness, however, is tempered by several instances in *Poverty*, as when Naoroji observes that "England is now rearing up a body of Englishmen in India, trained up and accustomed to despotism," with the consequence that "the English in India, instead of raising India, are hitherto themselves descending and degenerating to the lower level of Asiatic despotism" (230). Stemming the drain, fulfilling Indian promises of citizenship, or rescuing the bleeding body politic becomes, then, as much a test of Englishness as had been the English "challenge" of an earlier era to rescue the immolated body of the Hindu widow about to commit sati, another arguably gothic encounter marking Anglo-Indian relations. *Poverty*'s array of statistical calculations highlighting the inequity of England's relation with India, in fact, feminizes the body politic it creates inasmuch as it calls for the same "manly" resolve that provided the legitimizing trope of English colonialism in India: the act of rescue that Gayatri Spivak formulates as the "white man saving the brown woman from the brown man,"⁶⁶ but which Lata Mani has also analyzed as providing the grounds of negotiation (and collusion) between colonial and native patriarchies.⁶⁷ The gendered dimension of the drain is evident in the fact that M. G. Ranade—like Naoroji, one of the early leaders of the Indian nationalist movement—made use of the same gendered logic, in his case, though, to argue that "to blame [India's economic] situation on the drain is hardly a fair or manly position to take up."⁶⁸ Regardless of their differing positions on the drain, what is common to both arguments is a feminized body politic that yields a vocabulary most adequate for presenting the middle-class Indian male as the emergent citizen—as well as consolidating the position of the English gentleman—even as such a framework disaccommodates other classed and gendered bodies from its largesse.

While the exigent logic of political economy effectively masks this central paradox of citizenship, Naoroji's notion of an imperial citizenry mediates what also emerges as the imminient incompatibility between ideas of the Indian body politic, bodily health, and free-trade principles of political economy. Having constructed an Indian body politic that could sustain itself only though a circulatory relationship with England, Naoroji is befuddled by the question of England's relation to this body politic. His ambivalence is evident in statements like "India sorely needs the aid of English capital; but it is English *capital* that she needs, and not the English invasion to come also and eat up both capital and produce" (*Poverty* 229; emphasis in the original). It is not that Naoroji is resentful of English presence in India; in fact, he fervently believes in its salutary effect. The problem lies not so much in the fact of English presence in India, but in that the English behave as "strangers," "foreigners," or "invaders." As Naoroji notes, "if every European coming to India would make it his home, so that the item of the 'home remittance and charges' is nearly eliminated, it would not matter at all" (136). The reality is that "every European," while in India, "is isolated from the people around him ... The people know not him, and he knows not, nor cares for, the people," with the result that "all [that the Europeans] effectually do is to eat the substance of India material and moral, while living there, and when they go, they carry away all they have acquired, and their pensions and future usefulness besides" (204).

The image of India being bled becomes correlative, then, with that of India being devoured, both images of a diminishing body politic pointing to the central failure of the English to adhere to the tenets of political economy. By making themselves alien to India, the English fail to realize, Naoroji notes, how they hurt their own economic interests, as a healthy India would have served to augment England's coffers. Illuminating the prudent logic of political economy through a sense of the perverse, Naoroji writes: "It is the pitiless eating of India's substance in India, and the further pitiless drain to England; in short it is the pitiless *perversion* of economic laws by the sad bleeding to which India is subjected that is destroying India.... Let natural and economic laws have their full and fair play, and India will become another England, with manifold greater benefit to England herself than at present" (*Poverty* 216; emphasis in the original). The conjunction of political economy with the language of the gothic—the image of a mother eating her child was a particularly potent gothic image in the nineteenth century[69]—makes room for an imperial citizenry that enables the workings of political economy in ways that stabilize the fear of transgression invoked by the gothic. As Naoroji had stated elsewhere, hopes for India's future resided in Englishmen's realizing that they "owe as much filial duty to India as to England, to the mother who has provided for them as to the mother who gave them birth" (*Essays* 45). In emphasizing India's coterminousness with England in *Poverty*, he interpellates the English within an imperial citizenry by recuperating a metaphor of filiation that counteracts the horror of England's otherwise unfamilial and "unnatural" relation with India. Such images, in fact, had been circulating in the vernacular press in India, where images of England devouring or sucking the blood out of *Bharat Mata* (Mother India) were quite common.[70]

But even as the gothicized spectacle of England's relation with India repeatedly foregrounds India's pained condition, Naoroji does not ask the English to "feel" the Indians' pain. While the centrality of sympathy in enabling bonds of sociality is indisputable, sympathy itself, it has been noted, is aroused by an imaginative identification with the suffering body on the part of the one who does not suffer.[71] *Poverty* does not ask for this kind of sympathetic exchange, for it never implies that the English are not also adversely affected by the drain. Rather, the goal of Naoroji's argument is to compel the English to realize the simultaneity of effects, to recognize that India's misfortune only erodes England's financial position, jeopardizing the interests of its population as well as its moral claims of Englishness. As Naoroji asks rhetorically, "while British India is thus crushed by a heavy tribute ... do the British industrial people or the great mass, derive such benefit as they ought to derive, with far greater benefit to England itself, besides benefiting India?" (*Poverty* 338). Driving home the point in a speech to the House of Commons, Naoroji had commented that even as the English had to be "selfish, [they should] be intelligently selfish, for [their] good can only come through India's good" (304).

Naoroji's resignation to British selfishness of course recalls Adam Smith's notion of the primacy of self-interest in human (and economic) behavior; in fact, it is this self-interest—"intelligent selfishness," as Naoroji would have it—that undergirds Naoroji's argument, more than the notion of sympathy that Smith had outlined earlier. Smith begins *The Theory of Moral Sentiments* with the remark that "how selfish soever man may be supposed, there are evidently some principles in his nature, which interest him in the fortune of others, and render their happiness necessary to him, though he derives nothing from it except the pleasure of seeing it."[72] By contrast, if Naoroji invoked sympathy for a bleeding, dismembered India, that sympathy was channeled by the tenets of political economy. It was prompted by the understanding, forwarded by political economists, that "only as a repository of vigor and sensation" could capital serve as a "guarantee of the corporate entity's future life."[73] But by deploying sympathy to emphasize the importance of a shared political and economic process between India and England, and to institute in fact an imperial citizenry, Naoroji inverts the "boundary-drawing" potential of sympathy as an affective injunction.[74] However, this is only in keeping with *Poverty*'s broader inversion—not only of the prerogatives of fin de siècle gothic but also of the boundaries between numbers and rhetoric and between the economic and the political—that displaces the abiding distinction between subject and citizen, in ways that also exceed the Indian national imaginary that *Poverty* seeks to project.

Imperial Citizens at the English Polls: The "Black Man" and the Irish

Nothing exemplifies the immediacy with which Naoroji presented the question of a shared imperial citizenry to an English audience more tellingly than his campaigns for Parliament. Given the lack of representative institutions in India, the imperial metropolis seemed to offer a more salubrious political climate to colonial subjects in the latter decades of the nineteenth century.[75] At an 1885 meeting of the newly formed Bombay Presidency Association, Naoroji commented on the importance of the upcoming elections in England: "the present occasion of the new elections is one of those rare occasions in which we can appeal to the whole nation" (*Essays* 293). The Third Reform Act had considerably expanded the electorate in 1884, and Naoroji's comment indicates that the desire to involve metropolitan electors more intimately with India coincided with what was to be an initiation into political life for many of them. If after the Second Reform Act took effect in 1867, the relationship between the new "working-class citizen" and the political process became crucial to a reexamination of the English nation,[76] then it seems fair to infer that the Third Reform Act, legislated at the apogee of Britain's imperial destiny, marked a critical moment in speculations about what the newly minted citizen's relation to the colonies could be. As Naoroji had pointed out as early as 1866, it was the "mischief of distance between the Englishman and the natives" that had precipitated many of India's problems (20–21); the increased political participation promised by the Third Reform Act thus offered him an opportunity to infuse the question of empire into the realm of an English nation that was still very much in the making, welding matters of nation and empire into a common analytical framework. But what exactly were the social, cultural, and political valences of such a framework in late-Victorian England? Through what idioms did Naoroji coalesce questions of the empire "out there" with the immediacy of concerns "at home"? And, for the purposes of the argument in this chapter, through what vectors did Naoroji present himself as an imperial citizen before a metropolitan audience?

Historical scholarship over the past decade has done much to shed light on Naoroji's unprecedented political career in England.[77] In focusing on the specific content of Naoroji's speeches and electoral addresses—which remain unexamined—this section reads his spectacular foray into English politics by highlighting the idioms through which a racialized colonial subject could interact with, and indeed seek to represent, a metropolitan populace. Catherine Hall has noted that from the middle of the nineteenth century onward, the colonies provided a "benchmark" for the English to "determine what they did not want to be and who they thought they were."[78] In this, the implications of Naoroji's campaign and electoral victory in fact run deeper. Hinging on the purported unity of an imperial citizenship that could bring the English and Indians together (as outlined in *Poverty*), Naoroji's campaigns articulate an English identity but, as also becomes clear, they offer a forum of representation for those otherwise excluded from the spaces of "Englishness" as it was being defined by the newly expanded electorate.

Although he had not explicitly stated his opinions on the subject, Naoroji had been considering the possibility of running for Parliament at the time of his address to the Bombay Presidency Association quoted earlier; in fact, he had already met with representatives of various sections of the Liberal Party in England. While his proposed candidacy was met with enthusiasm there, it was also accompanied by considerable doubt that he could even secure a nomination to any of the English constituencies: it was suggested that he would fare better with an Irish or Scottish constituency. Such anxieties proved unfounded, for the Executive Association of the Liberal Association of Holborn nominated him as its candidate in June 1886, and the *Holborn Guardian* endorsed his candidacy with considerable equanimity: "Although in the estimation of his countrymen he is a great authority on all questions affecting the interests of India, he is also intimately acquainted with the politics of this country, having resided here at one period of his life for many years, and taken an active interest in public matters."[79] Though more conservative, the *Times* also looked favorably upon his nomination, pointing out that in "20 years' residence in England [Naoroji] had made himself fully acquainted with the English political questions, and by returning him to the House of Commons, Holborn would prove itself one of the grandest constituencies in Great Britain."[80]

While the press coverage seemed to compensate for his foreignness by emphasizing his familiarity with England and English issues, Naoroji himself did not particularly care to deemphasize his Indian identity. In the 1886 election manifesto issued by the National Liberal Club, he began by identifying himself as a "man of strange name and race," but also announced later: "It is with special pride and pleasure that I, an Indian, address a Metropolitan Constituency as a candidate for the suffrages of the electors" (*Essays* 302–3). The perceived alienness of his name and racial identity, however, was offset by his statement that "I am an Indian subject of the Queen" (303). Articulations of personal loyalty to the monarch, as indicated in the introduction, made political capital for colonial subjects, introducing a note of familial affect in the imperial dynamic. Naoroji's stress on this relation with the queen also helped him strike a delicate balance between being at once foreign and familiar, similar to the balancing act attempted by the Indian prince and cricketer K. S. Ranjitsinhji, a contemporary of Naoroji who was also making inroads into the popular English imaginary at the time. Coincidentally, Ranji, as he came to be popularly known, was the first nonwhite player admitted to that bastion of Englishness, the English university cricket team, in the same year that Naoroji was elected to Parliament. In tracing the unexpected yet extraordinary ways in which Ranji endeared himself to the English, Satadru Sen notes how Ranji flaunted wealth (he owned the first automobile in Cambridge), but in ways that stopped just short of being "too exotic," thereby ensuring that he was seen as an "Indian who was wealthy and unusual enough to be glamorous, but English enough to be welcomed into the hearts, minds, and playing fields of England."[81] Though operating in a very different context, Naoroji's interaction with the English follows much the same logic: he was the "man of strange name and race" but also a "subject of the Queen." It was this admixture of novelty and familiarity that marked what I will argue was Naoroji's usefulness for an English electorate. But because the politics of the stump is very different from that of the cricket field (which is not without its own politics and stumps), one needs to follow closely the turns of Naoroji's electoral addresses. In this, it is significant that Naoroji's balancing act was mediated by a constituency that bore in itself an ambivalent relation to the English: the Irish.

As a Liberal candidate, Naoroji aligned himself with the party leader, William Gladstone, in his support for Irish Home Rule, announcing in his very first election speech that the issue of Ireland was "the burning question of the day" (*Essays* 304). Indeed the question of Irish Home Rule—allowing the Irish to have a parliament in Dublin, thus negating the effect of the 1801 Act of Union—proved highly contentious in the political discourse of the 1880s, even precipitating the 1886 elections. While the aging Gladstone called elections primarily to decide the Irish question, the Tory leader, Lord Salisbury, went on record against Irish Home Rule, commenting: "you would not confide free representative institutions to the Hottentots, for instance."[82] Salisbury's infelicitous comment was typical of the Anglo-Irish relationship, in which the English for several centuries had portrayed the Irish as poor, savage, even subhuman. Such characterizations became more pronounced in the nineteenth century, when the consequences of misdirected and exploitative English economic and political measures with relation to Ireland were attributed not to the ravages of English colonialism but to the blighted Irish population instead.

This was particularly true after the devastation of the potato famine in the middle of the century. Instead of paying attention to the economic causes of the famine, presented in Daniel O'Connell's Repeal of the Union campaign, the English press blamed Ireland's misfortunes on the ignorance, laziness, and filth of the Irish peasants, who apparently constituted "the missing link between the gorilla and the Negro."[83] The increasing political activism in Ireland and the growing momentum of popular outrage against English repression there resulted in the English having an even darker view of the Irish from the mid-1800s onward. While *Blackwood Magazine* described O'Connell's leadership as unleashing a "reign of terror . . . exercised by persons unseen and for causes unknown,"[84] a particularly lurid imaginary associated the political demands of the Repeal Association with the sinister influence of a Catholic priesthood. A pamphleteer put it this way:

> They stand at the altar, these dark ministers of a dark faith, arrayed in the mysterious power which their imagined authority over the next world gives them, and with the substantial power which they derive from their influence in this.
>
> When they speak, every voice is still; where they point the finger, the eyes of all follow it; and from the altar, inflamed by bigotry and delighting in blood, rush out the savage populace, to seize upon the victim, and to consign to destruction his property, his family, his home, and his life. Blood is the order—Blood is the cry—Blood is the doom.[85]

Stereotypical images of "Paddy" that had represented the Irish throughout the nineteenth century underwent a marked change. Although earlier images of Paddy had emphasized his emotional instability, inclination to violence, and general stupidity, the increasing political awareness of the Irish and the demand for Home Rule from certain sections in the latter decades of the century were met by a demonizing of the hitherto innocuous Paddy. Images of the Irish as vampires or as the "Irish Frankenstein" flooded the English press from the 1880s onward, and after the Phoenix Park murders of 1882—in which members of the Irish Invincibles assassinated prominent members of the Gladstone government—Irish leaders, especially, were caricatured as ape-like aberrations, "monstrous brutes without a touch of humanity."[86] Interestingly, at the height of the Home Rule movement, in October 1885, *Punch* ran an arresting image of the "Irish Vampire" preying on an English maiden (perhaps Britannia?) in repose; the *Irish Pilot* retaliated the next month by presenting "The English Vampire" pursuing a defiant Hibernia on the run. The gothic was evidently the chosen language of Anglo-Irish political representation.[87]

It was in this context of Anglo-Irish representation that Naoroji entered the electoral fray on an Irish Home Rule ticket. The potential of the gothic for portraying economic maladministration was obviously not new to him. Nor was he a stranger to economic analyses that dispensed with the providentiality of famine. The economic analysis of famine, in fact, had preoccupied the Indian intelligentsia over the last decades of the century. In 1900, R. C. Dutt presented a series of letters to the Indian viceroy, showing how the steady succession of famines in India was "due to the resourceless condition and the chronic poverty of the cultivators, caused by the over-assessment of the soil."[88] In 1881, Naoroji himself had submitted an extensive memorandum rectifying what he felt were the erroneous income assessments submitted by the Indian Famine Commission (*Poverty*, 220–30). In 1895, testifying before the Welby Commission that was probing India's financial administration, mainly at Naoroji's behest, he recalled William Hunter's observation a decade earlier that "forty years hereafter we should have had an Indian Ireland multiplied fifty-fold on our hands" (*Poverty* 308). Indeed, the problem of absentee-landlordism in Ireland that had "milked" Ireland[89] was closely related to Naoroji's thesis of the drain. But while he enlivened his drain theory with images of the bleeding, ravaged Indian body politic, Naoroji's representations of Ireland and the Irish were curiously bereft of such embellishment. As his election speeches reveal, Naoroji could speak of the Irish only in terms that consolidated metropolitan imperial discourse. While this can be explained by the exigencies of his position as a Liberal candidate espousing Irish Home Rule, which was more about political devolution rather than land reform, it does not fully account for Naoroji's overall silence on Ireland otherwise, given the overlapping trajectories of Irish and Indian anticolonialism.[90] In fact, while the similarity between Ireland and India (as well as other colonial constituencies) offered various forms of intercolonial solidarity,[91] reading the specific dynamics of Naoroji's election also reveals the subtle "intimacies of difference"[92] underpinning these alliances. In this, what Naoroji does not say about Irish suffering assumes significance inasmuch as what he does say about Ireland is formulated through depictions of what remains the polar opposite of gothic imagery (though always lying beneath its surface): the bourgeois family.

The familial trope of domesticity emerges as a familiarizing measure in Naoroji's speeches that seek to counteract popular images of the Irish—who, as he points out, were seen as "a bad lot . . . poor, wretched, ungrateful" (*Essays* 306). Acknowledging the primacy of untrammeled domestic space, his speeches elucidate the relationship that Ireland would share with England if Home Rule were to be granted: "What will Ireland be after it has this Home Rule? It will simply have its own household, just as a son who has come of age wishes to have a home in which his wife may be supreme" (*Essays* 305). Simply assuming that "because Ireland has a separate household, therefore she will also be separated from the Imperial firm" was, Naoroji assured his audience, sheer folly, especially if one took into account the economic and political benefits that Ireland would stand to gain if it were to remain within the empire (305).

By linking ideals of domestic autonomy with economic pragmatism, Naoroji was no doubt domesticating the Irish, representing them in terms of familiar middle-class values constituting a putative Englishness.[93] In emphasizing Ireland's self-interest in retaining its membership in the imperial family, the metaphor of familiality also provided a counterpoint to anxieties generated by claims such as that of Lord Salisbury, who had cautioned that granting Home Rule would be an "avowal that we were unable to satisfy even the most sacred obligations, and that all claims to protect or govern beyond our narrow island were at an end."[94] Countering Salisbury's insinuation of a failure to rule, Naoroji referred to him and his followers as "sham Unionists" who were defending an empire based on corruption, rather than a true union of "hearts and affections" (*Essays* 313). Couching the issue of administrative competence in strikingly familial terms, Naoroji encouraged the electors to forge an even more lasting bond by fulfilling their responsibilities to their Irish brethren. Pointing out that "when once an Englishman sees his mistake he has the moral courage to rectify it" (304), Naoroji impressed upon his audience that "it would be for the people of England to choose the good and reject the evil," and "the good was to do justice to Ireland" (312).

In moralizing the imperial duties of English electors with regard to Ireland, Naoroji was certainly reiterating the moral tone pervading Liberal rhetoric, which had, since the mid-1800s, employed a moral vocabulary to instill a feeling of citizenship among workingmen.[95] In this, the question of political reform had assumed moral proportions, being framed as a passage from darkness to light or from evil to good.[96] The question of political and labor reform, which assumed an even more central role in Naoroji's second election campaign in Central Finsbury, bears traces of this moral tone. Denouncing the injustice meted out to workingmen, Naoroji argued trenchantly in 1892 for an eight-hour workday, promising to devote himself "entirely, honestly, and thoroughly" to the "noble purpose."[97] The moral element of his crusade against injustice toward the working class, however, was interwoven with appeals to what he described as an equally moral commitment on the part of the newly enfranchised voters. "The eternal laws of justice and righteousness," he pronounced in 1892, "could never be broken." And if the people failed to "exercise their [new] power in doing justice to themselves, to their fellow-subjects in Ireland," and in turn, "their oppressed fellow-citizens in India," then, he noted, "the fault would be their own."[98] The moral duty of the voters, in other words, was presented on an imperial scale that punctuated the prose of political process with an "imperial conscience."

Naoroji's moral emphasis on a kindred connection between the Irish, English, and Indian populace was timely in addressing the glaring paradoxes in an emergent imperial genealogy. In 1883, J. R. Seeley, the Cambridge historian, remarking that the "word Empire seems too military and despotic to suit the relation of a mother-country to colonies," had invoked the familial metaphor to emphasize the need for England to review its relationship with its colonies.[99] The metaphor of the familial acquired considerable nuance, so much so that by 1897, Joseph Chamberlain expressed a preference for the phrase "Sister Nations" over "Mother Country and her Colonies."[100] India and Ireland, however, were excluded from England's imperative to regroup the self-governing colonies into an incipient "family of nations," and Naoroji's efforts to alert English voters to their duties toward the Irish and the Indians evidently mapped an alternative imperial connection, endorsing a metaphor of familial responsibility to ensure political development in colonial sites otherwise excluded from the emerging "commonwealth of nations." In fact, while the word "commonwealth" was being suggested to avoid the authoritative connotations of imperial rule in many quarters, it had begun to acquire a distinct racial charge by alluding to a familial metaphor of blood ties. As James Froude commented in 1886, the year of Naoroji's first election campaign: "The English race do not like to be parts of an empire. But a 'commonwealth' of Oceana held together by common blood, common interest, and a common pride in the great position which unity can secure—such a commonwealth as this may grow of itself if politicians can be induced to leave it alone."[101] Ironically, Naoroji chose precisely not to leave such a notion of the commonwealth alone. While a metaphor of family and "common blood" was being deployed to forward a particular racial argument, he charted a kindred network of affiliation and imperial unity that attempted to overcome the racialized limits of the imperial brethren.

The expanded parameters of the imperial brethren alternately conceived evidently depended, however—at least with reference to Ireland—on metaphors of bourgeois familiality that had been used to naturalize the English colonial exercise in Ireland since the early modern period.[102] Naoroji's own references to a familial relationship also served only to reinforce the subordinate relation already accorded to Ireland in the imperial equation. Yet it was evidently only through this normative rhetoric of familiality that Naoroji could nullify the threat posed by the Irish and also appeal to the English electorate as an Indian. An abiding feature of his speeches is his use of the example of Irish Home Rule to urge Londoners to ponder India's political fate as well. During his election campaign in Holborn in 1886, he observed that if English voters supported Gladstone in his struggle for Irish Home Rule, they would earn the blessings not only of "five millions of Irishmen, but they would also earn the blessing of fifty times five millions of the inhabitants of India" (*Essays* 315). Tying India's fortunes to those of Ireland had considerable precedence, for even imperial administrators had long acknowledged the many similarities in England's relations with India and Ireland.[103] The striking parallels in the English handling of affairs in India and Ireland, in fact, had led to strategic parliamentary alliances,[104] and Irish support was to vivify the Indian nationalist movement well into the twentieth century. The richness of the "internationalism" that the Irish dimension added to Indian politics is indeed noteworthy.[105] Naoroji's conjoining of Irish and Indian aspirations is therefore not novel, but it highlights, as mentioned earlier, certain anxieties that do not so much detract from the evident affinity between the two constituencies as indicate the uncertain logics underlining colonial articulations of citizenship—and, by extension, the permissible framing of such alliances.

The obviously Irish provenance of the Bengal Tenancy Act of 1885, for instance, had irked Indian opponents of the bill, who feared that the "importation of 'Irish' agitation" would disrupt social order in Bengal.[106] When the proposal for Naoroji's nomination from an Irish constituency arose again in 1888, Naoroji was cautioned by his friends in India that "'Dadabhai and Davitt' might become 'synonymous,' the one for fomenting Indian and the other Irish rebellion" (Michael Davitt, the founder of the Irish Land League, was elected to Parliament several times).[107] That the specter of an Irish insurgence haunted Indians agitating for political reform is evident in Naoroji's presidential address to the Indian National Congress in the same year as his Holborn candidacy. "Is this Congress," Naoroji asked rhetorically, "a nursery for sedition and rebellion against the English Government, or, is it another stone in the foundation of the stability of that Government?"[108] Naoroji's transposition of a politics of constitutionalism onto the Irish-Indian political agenda is not just typical of the Moderate politics that characterized his generation of Indians. Even as the Easter Uprising of 1916 significantly ignited popular nationalist feelings in India, someone like Bal Gangadhar Tilak, who was to play a significant role in steering the nationalist agenda away from the Moderates, adhered more to the model of Irish Home Rule advocated by Irish parliamentarians than to the extra-constitutional tactics of the Sinn Féin.[109] This is not to discount the possibility that censorship may have heavily shaped public remarks by Indian leaders, nor is it to overlook what indeed were the close affinities between Irish and Indian nationalism.[110] It is to highlight, instead, the fact that despite Ireland's political proximity to India, Indian representation of the Irish remained circumspect in many ways,[111] revealing the limits of intercolonial alliances and the unspoken protocols of what could be said and what remained unsayable. In Naoroji's public speeches, at least, the Irish are recuperated only through a metropolitan rhetoric of bourgeois familiality, upon which hangs heavy the untold histories of English economic injustice during the nineteenth century, thereby compounding the "ghostly persistence" of Irish suffering.[112] However, it is precisely through this lacuna of things left unsaid that Naoroji, an Indian, could present himself before a metropolitan electorate on a Home Rule ticket, as an imperial citizen.

His observations to the voters that although Home Rule had been "synonymous with rebellion" in the past, its leaders had now proven that "if they knew how to fight, they also knew how to make peace" (*Essays*

314–15) became necessary not only in rendering the Irish acceptable but in shoring up his own credentials for a metropolitan audience before whom he was on slippery, if not unprecedented, ground. An Indian's seeking an English seat on an Irish Home Rule ticket appealed to many divergent registers, as is evident in a milkman's statement reported in the liberal *Pall Mall Gazette*. The milkman, referred to as "Dowty," stated that he supported Gladstone but did not support the proposal for Home Rule, voicing the opinion that "the Irish members must stop at Westminster." He was keen, however, to vote for Naoroji, who he said was "as good as you or me be his face what colour it may." Besides, as he reportedly told the correspondent, he preferred having an "eloquent Hindoo to represent [him] than a noodle of a rich butterman, who can't say 'bo.'"[113]

The milkman's final comment highlights what was emphasized most during Naoroji's campaign: his eloquence and oratory. Describing his campaign debut at the Holborn Town Hall, the *Pall Mall Gazette* reported: "But before Mr. Naoroji had been speaking five minutes he held his audience in his hands, and had completely won their heart by his fluent periods, by his straightforward appeals and manly eloquence. If the incarnation of John Bull had made its appearance under the organ he could not have asked for a heartier or more unanimously enthusiastic reception."[114] In fact, the vigor with which Naoroji undertook an extensive program of campaign speeches—his nomination was announced only a few weeks before the vote—earned him his "colors," so to speak. The popular enthusiasm hailing his first campaign in 1886 was so palpable that "Invisible," who had speculated in the *Holborn Guardian* that Colonel Duncan, Naoroji's Tory opponent, "would be unopposed, doubtless,"[115] qualified his statement a week after Naoroji's hectic campaigning to comment that the contest in Holborn "will be pretty keen."[116]

The oratory of political leaders occupied a prominent position in popular English politics in the nineteenth century, with Gladstone's 1880 Midlothian campaign assuming mythic status. The verbal suasion of the leaders in fact suspended class barriers, enabling upper-class men to appeal to working-class constituencies.[117] In Naoroji's case, it appears to have even suspended his foreignness. "If Mr. Naoroji had changed his name to Mr. Brown or Mr. Jones," the *Pall Mall Gazette* noted, "no one would know him to be a Parsee."[118] It was not only his oratory but also his appearance that played a key role in naturalizing his presence in the

English electoral scene: as the *Gazette* added, "he has the appearance and the manner of a cultivated English gentleman."[119] Naoroji certainly appealed to established tropes of the Gentleman Leader, a role his financial position amply supported.[120] But if his alien identity could at all be subsumed by markers of English gentlemanliness, then Naoroji's case also reveals how this could be effected only through a confusion about or suspension of the specifics of his identity. His guarded representation of the Irish; the fact that he was Indian but lived in England for twenty years; his belonging to a religious minority, the Parsees, that was not seen to be representative of Indians—all these marked the limits of his identifiability, which went a long way in rendering Naoroji acceptable, for not only could he be "claimed" for Englishness, but he could be Anyman, Everyman, Citizen. No wonder, then, that his speeches representing a disembodied voice received such attention in the contemporary coverage of his campaigns. But a political culture that was equally visual—that had long mobilized iconic representations of political leaders—could not for long deflect attention from Naoroji's corporeality. The debate about who he was occurred to a significant extent at the level of visuality—how he looked and appeared—and it is the necessary indeterminacy of these debates that is key to a reading of his election campaigns.[121]

The verdict against Gladstone and the Home Rule Bill in the 1886 elections ensured Naoroji's defeat in a predominantly Conservative constituency. However, having polled a sizable 1,950 votes after a campaign that lasted only a few weeks, he was sufficiently encouraged to persevere in his electoral pursuit and nurture a constituency until the next election was announced. Deciding upon Central Finsbury in 1887, he set about wooing its largely urban, working-class electorate.[122] Perhaps because in contrast to his previous whirlwind campaign Naoroji now had more time to announce himself, his protracted presence raised pointed questions. As the *Times* reported on December 1, 1888, Lord Salisbury, then Tory Prime Minister, speaking in Edinburgh the night before, had attempted to explain Naoroji's defeat in Holborn with the observation that "I doubt if we have got to that point of view where a English constituency would elect a black man." Salisbury clarified that he was of course "using language in its colloquial sense, because I imagine the colour is not exactly black, but at all events, [Naoroji is] a man of another race."[123] Salisbury's unfortunate comment bestowed national prominence upon Naoroji, initiating a public debate that popularized him almost overnight as "Salisbury's black man."

The ignominy of the comment ignited a storm of protest in Britain, and much of the defense mounted on Naoroji's behalf actually referred to the kindred imperial affiliation he had been advocating. Signifying the ways in which he had appealed to and constituted a national English imaginary along the lines of an "imperial conscience," the *Manchester Guardian* expressed concern at Salisbury's remark, commenting that "many men will suppose that it is the voice of England speaking, and the country will be held responsible for one man's bile."[124] A letter to the *Daily News*, signed "A Yorkshireman," added to that sentiment, expressing the opinion that "his lordship's vulgar ebullition must be put down to his rancorous tongue, and to that 'spirit of contempt, hatred, and suspicion' which is in contrary to the principle of imperial unity as darkness is to light."[125] Another letter to the *Pall Mall Gazette*, signed "Anglo-Indian," expressed anguish at the fact that news of Salisbury's ill-chosen comment had been cabled to India and that "it will be known from Peshawar to Cape Comorin that a gentleman who is almost worshipped by large numbers of his compatriots has been contemptuously described by the Ranee Saheb's Wazeer ([roughly translated as "the Queen's Prime Minister"] as a "black man."[126] As the *Edinburgh Evening Dispatch* urged its readers, "we should lose no chance of obtaining information respecting India, and of placing ourselves in sympathy with our fellow subjects there."[127]

Even as recriminations against Salisbury flew thick and fast, most of them argued on the basis of an imperial unity that sought to accommodate Naoroji—and Indians—through a racial imaginary that specifically excluded the "fact of blackness." The injustice seemed to lie, as Antoinette Burton astutely comments, not in the fact that blackness had been unfairly represented, but that Naoroji had been represented as the "black man."[128] As the Edinburgh newspaper quoted above went on to note, "in point of fact our educated Hindoo fellow subjects are probably more nearly allied to us in race, and also in colour and civilization, than King Solomon in all his glory."[129] Referring to contemporary theories of a common Aryan ascendancy that supposedly united Indians and Britons, the *Manchester Guardian* stated, albeit facetiously, that Naoroji "is as much as an Aryan as Lord Salisbury himself, and indeed Professor MAX MULLER would tell us that it was as probable as not that some thousands of years ago Lord SALISBURY and Mr. NAOROJI had a common progenitor in the Caucasus or Central Asia."[130] Moreover, while Salisbury's comment was attributed to his aristocratic snobbishness and ignorance, a consideration of middle-class English values was invoked to counteract the possibility of such a notion gaining credence: "the stigmatizing of honoured subjects of her Majesty as 'black men' and 'niggers,'" the *Pall Mall Gazette* piously noted, "should be left to underbred subalterns."[131]

The "black man" episode evidently offered up a test of liberal citizenship, and popular opinion rose to the occasion. In all of this, though, there was endless speculation about the precise shade of Naoroji's skin color; after all, "the colour," as Salisbury had pointed out, was "not exactly black." While it was pointed out that "it was a shade or two fairer" than the previous representative from Central Finsbury,[132] the *Leeds Mercury* was of the opinion that "Mr. Naoroji is no more a black man than is Lord Salisbury."[133] The attempt to ascertain Naoroji's skin color, however, did not result in the exactitude that was hoped for. The confusion generated on that score was aided no doubt by Naoroji's class identity, which worked to keep his racial identity somewhat at bay.[134] It was also compounded in no small measure by the fact that he was a Parsee.

A minority community of Persian descent who followed the Zoroastrian faith, Parsees had first settled in India in the eleventh century, occupying a racially and culturally liminal position there.[135] Writing in the 1860s, Henry Maine had described the Bombay Parsees, Joan Leopold notes, as "an intellectual and [even] a racial bridge between the English and Hindus."[136] Naoroji himself was an active member of the Parsee community in Bombay and continued his engagement with Parsee affairs in England, even writing an essay on the status of Parsees.[137] Although he identified himself as a Parsee, that was by no means his only or primary register of self-representation. While he had appeared in a Parsee headgear at one of his early election meetings, he followed that up subsequently with "English" appearances, and he made no mention of his Parsee identity while introducing himself to the electors. Moreover, his own views on Parsee identity itself were considerably nuanced. In his writings, he distinguished Zoroastrianism from other Indian religions, but he also represented Parsees in proximity to other Indian communities, not as alien to them.[138] It is significant, then, that he was invoked as a Parsee, or that his Parsee identity was invoked in its non-Indianness, in ways that made it easier to claim that Naoroji appeared like Compton or Salisbury. Invoking him as a Parsee, though, compounded the indeterminacy of the Parsee identity while also frustrating attempts to categorize Naoroji as Indian. However, the point may well have been to establish his uncertain status, for beyond a certain point, the exact nature of his identity, or what exactly his skin color signified, did not seem to matter.

Burton suggests that "as long as Naoroji was neither fully black nor fully white, determining his color with certainty [seemed] unimportant," and Sumita Mukherjee points out that the question of Naoroji's skin color in fact remained a topic of debate even a few decades later.[139] The evident desire to *maintain* uncertainty about Naoroji's skin color can perhaps be understood in its instrumentality in keeping in abeyance the precepts of a biologically deterministic scientific vocabulary, which otherwise gained charge of the racial debates in the final decades of the nineteenth century.[140] In fact, the response to the "black man" controversy reveals how a liberal notion of imperial unity had to be—and could be—mobilized to counter the divisiveness of an imperial rhetoric increasingly centered on race characteristics. This is not to say that the defense mounted on Naoroji's behalf was willfully pitted against the findings of scientific racism, or that the idea of imperial unity never overlapped with the precepts of a scientific racial rhetoric. Rather, it is to point to the wide and shifting range of late-Victorian discussions on racialized colonial subjects, the unevenness of which in fact accounted for the ubiquity of a racial discourse that extended well beyond the parameters of scientific findings.[141]

The fact that Naoroji's identity could not be established beyond dermal doubt, that how he looked could not easily be attributed to who he was, that his racial identity did not seem to matter in the way it would to a scientific examination, succeeded, if by default, in making race actually "matter" even more—more, in fact, than what met the eye. The uncertainty surrounding Naoroji's appearance and identity in fact effectively furthered the ideological effects of nineteenth-century biological racism, in which race, as Robyn Wiegman notes in a related context, "was situated as more potentially than skin deep."[142] Moreover, in Naoroji's being "not exactly black," the fact that the ineligibility of blackness remained self-evident underlines how the "black man" episode inaugurated its own racial grammars of citizenship precisely through its eagerness to claim Naoroji as citizen. The pithy question posed by the *Leeds Mercury*—"But supposing he were black, would that make him less a citizen?"[143]—sums up, precisely in its earnestness, why even in their most liberal moments Victorians were unable to confidently answer that question in the negative.

On the one hand, Naoroji's indeterminacy—he was simultaneously referred to as "Parsee legislator," "eloquent Hindu," "first Indian M.P.," and "an English member for the 'Boro of Central Finsbury"—illuminates the permeability of Victorian modalities of representation, which, as Jennifer Brody notes, were located but "at the juncture of (falsely) conflicting categories," whose "shifting positions . . . complicate and even violate categories that are supposed to be whole, pure, and inviolate."[144] On the other hand, this meant that not only was Naoroji himself considered eligible to stand for elections, but also that he could stand in for those not incorporated in the liberal contract of citizenship. As the nature of the support for his campaigns (especially the second) indicates, the colonial subject could emerge as imperial citizen primarily as a cipher, representing those who could not be otherwise embodied within the metropolitan logics of political representation: women and laborers. One can perhaps go so far as to say that the uncertainties of Naoroji's corporeality enabled it to absorb the disembodying effects of the operations of citizenship and capital: it played off the facts that the actualization of the ideal citizen effaces the female body; and that capitalistic value surmounts, as will be discussed further in the next chapter, the physicality of labor. In fact, as Naoroji pointed out to an election gathering organized by the Federation of Trade and Labour Unions in 1892, "labour had as much claim to a proper share in everything as capital, for after all, capital was simply crystallized labour, stored up and preserved."[145] By way of drawing out the "congealed labour," Naoroji exhorted the gathered workingmen to exercise their newly found "sovereign power," the power to vote. Moreover, as a known supporter of the suffragist movement, he signed on to the manifesto of the Women's Franchise League, agreeing to its objective that "there is imperative and immediate need of vigorous action on the part of women to enforce their just claims to citizenship, and to establish themselves securely as members of the body politic."[146]

Thus even while Naoroji took care to introduce himself as an "Indian subject of the Queen," his emergence as imperial citizen operated through a simultaneous embodiment and disembodiment, incorporating the claims of women, laborers, and the Irish in ways that also suspended his own corporeality. If one were to further the narrative impulse of gothic tropologies so evident in Naoroji's own economic analysis, it would appear that the logic of his emergence as imperial citizen was in itself monstrous—monstrous not in a horrific voracity, but monstrous in that his body becomes "remarkably mobile, permeable, and infinitely interpretable," absorbing (and thereby nullifying) "as many fear-producing traits as possible into one body."[147] Judith Halberstam foregrounds this "technology of monstrosity" as one that normalizes the human; in presenting what is not-human, the monster provides, Halberstam notes, for "the invention of human as white, male, middle class, and heterosexual."[148] Naoroji's "monstrous" emergence as imperial citizen is clearly made possible by the normalizing rhetoric of citizenship that otherwise disaccommodates him as well as women and laborers. But if it is Naoroji's suspended particularity that renders him eligible for citizenship, in ways that can even be taken to underline the necessary disembodiment underlying the liberal abstract norm, then it is significant that this suspension holds only because Naoroji, in his particularity, absorbs the detritus—working-class, female, Irish—of that citizenship.

It is important to underline this "monstrous" aspect of imperial citizenship and to insistently read the narratives of English labor, English female disenfranchisement, and Irish political aspiration into Naoroji's electoral success, for he could have hardly made it on the basis of his educated Indian bourgeois identity, which could go only so far in saving him from Salisbury's attack. Despite apologizing for Salisbury's comment, the Liberal party in England vacillated on its nomination of Naoroji till the very end. Official opinion in India hardly considered him eligible for election to Parliament either. A significant coincidence that has been entirely overlooked by critical and biographical commentary on Naoroji is that on the very day of Salisbury's remark, the Viceroy of India, Lord Dufferin, addressed a gathering at Calcutta and referred to the leaders of the Indian National Congress as a "microscopic minority" incapable of self-governance. Dufferin's comment was widely noted at the time and has even found its way into present-day history textbooks in India (even as Salisbury's has not). The December 1, 1888, edition of the *Times* that carried Salisbury's speech is the same one that reported Dufferin's comment. The full text of Dufferin's speech appeared in the newspaper two days later, including the sentence in question: "Let no man imagine that the English Government would be content to allow this microscopic minority to control the administration of that majestic and multiform Empire, for whose safety and welfare they are responsible in the eyes of God and before the face of civilization!"[149] It is surprising that Dufferin's remark was directed against the Indian National Congress, because he was reportedly amenable to its founding in 1885.[150] At the time of its institution, the Congress consisted mostly of English-educated, middle- and upper-class Indians loyal to the empire, who did not conceive of or even desire the termination of English rule but petitioned only for a degree of equality and self-representation. They were men much like Naoroji. In fact, Naoroji was elected president of the Congress three times and was hailed in India as the "grand old man."

Even as Dufferin took pride in the fact that the Congress leaders were the "product of the system of education which [the British had] carried on during the last 30 years," he added that "30 years is a very short time in which to educe a self-governing nation from its primordial elements."[151] While Dufferin's comment recapitulates the liberal faith in improvement through education, his caveat also reveals the anxieties imperiling this faith in the wake of an emerging Indian professional, middle-class, male political identity that sought to claim the fruits of that education. Dufferin's statement in fact reinforces Salisbury's interest in safeguarding a racially marked superiority within the imperial formation. Ironically, Dufferin was both a Liberal and Irish. But he was from the land-owning Ulster elite, forever wary of Irish agitation, something which heavily informed his dealings in India: O'Connell, in C. A. Bayly's reading, evidently "haunted Dufferin's dreams like great Caesar's ghost."[152] That an imagery of haunting should suggest itself so readily to a historical analysis of the Irish-English-Indian triangulation should not be lost sight of, especially as one reads Dufferin's letter to the Secretary of State for India written several months before the Congress was founded. The educated Indian, "the Bengali babu," Dufferin observed, "has a great deal of Celtic perverseness, vivacity, and cunning, and seems to now be employed in setting up the machinery for a repeal agitation, something on the lines of O'Connell's Patriotic Associations."[153] Though coming from opposite ends of the political spectrum, the invocation of the "black man" and the intimations of "Celtic perverseness" both mark the limits of liberal citizenship. While Salisbury's and Dufferin's comments reveal the gothic imagery that articulates these limits (or makes them appear not so), it is ironic that Naoroji's emergence as imperial citizen alludes equally to a gothic logic in countering them.

Naoroji won the Central Finsbury seat in Parliament in the 1892 election. But he did so by a margin of only five votes, with his opponent forcing a recount. While this alludes tellingly to the highly contingent nature of his campaign and victory, the slim margin of victory should not undermine the momentous nature of Naoroji's success. In the aftermath of his victory, Naoroji joyously announced that the English electors had "won the gratitude of the hundreds of Millions of India," for "Indians now for the first time realized the fact that they were not merely subjects, but Citizens of the vast English Empire."[154] In India, R. M. Sayani, prominent member of the Congress, seemed to voice the elated Indian opinion when he noted: "I am not at all surprised that an English constituency should elect an Indian gentleman, for experience teaches us that the good people of England are always willing that their fellow-subjects, in whatever part of the Empire living . . . should have the same rights and privileges as they themselves."[155]

Despite the perceived triumph of a liberal ideology, however, the nature of Naoroji's election campaign, both in terms of his self-representation as well as his metropolitan reception, reveals how imperial citizenship emerged as a technology that was contingent and contrapuntal. Yet it was precisely its contingencies and discrepancies that enabled it to retain a resistant charge and gather momentum at different points and along different registers across the empire, as the following chapters will demonstrate. In Naoroji's case, the notion of an imperial citizenship allowed for a faith in a liberalism that for colonial subjects was always a little frayed at the edges. At a celebratory meeting of Indians living in London, one of the speakers thanked the voters of Central Finsbury for "the Liberal, the truly Liberal spirit, that spirit which allowed of no distinction of caste, colour, or creed."[156] At various meetings held in India to celebrate the event, Naoroji's election was held to be "a visible symbol, a practical proof of the vitality of that policy of political righteousness."[157] Naoroji's election was indeed a symbol—although one that concealed more than it revealed—but it is precisely in its symbolic nature that it contributed to the unfolding of a national identity in India over the last decades of the nineteenth century, which had witnessed an attempt to fashion political activity on a national rather than a provincial scale. As an article in *The Hindu* was to point out:

> To the Englishmen who are a united nation . . . the solitary Parsee that sits under the aegis of Mr. Gladstone may not be more than a two day's

wonder. But to us who are aware of the disintegrating influences of Indian society, . . . every constitutional move which . . . brings on a common platform the prince and the peasant, the Mahomedan aristocrat and the Hindu or Parsee plebian, is a God-send and affects us for good. Viewed in this light, the return to Parliament of Mr. Dadabhai Naoroji is full of instruction and encouragement.[158]

That it was as a Parsee, a figure marked in its indeterminacy in India, through which Naoroji could become metonymic of an emergent, unified body politic actually anticipates the tensions that were to riven the fashioning of this body politic. Significant for the purposes of this chapter, however, is how the liberal rubric of citizenship, as evident in the quote from *The Hindu*, allowed Naoroji to emerge as a symbol of and for a national identification, a symbol that, as chapter 4 indicates, was displaced by more parochial promptings. But as the current chapter makes evident, the grammars through which that citizenship was articulated also ensured that Naoroji's election and his emergence as imperial citizen always amounted to something more than it revealed, that Naoroji represented something more than he could embody. The *Times* was not far off the mark in declaring Naoroji's election a "romantic" event. The idea of a romance perhaps relays most tellingly the necessarily exorbitant nature of Naoroji's election, as well as his broader claims to citizenship. It speaks not only to the narrative excesses of his gothic critique of colonial economy but also to his own embodiment of what did not otherwise constitute Englishness, exclusions that, in his view of imperial citizenship, were un-British.

CHAPTER TWO

South Africa, Indentured Labor, and the Question of Credit

While Naoroji's unprecedented election victory was hailed as a "romance," Indians also noted that the results of the election proved that the British Empire had exceeded the political benevolence of that other great empire, that of the Romans. A meeting of Indians living in London took note of the fact that in contrast to the Romans, who "did not confer the same rights and privileges . . . on the sons of the conquered lands," the Englishman "not only took into his bosom such sons of the conquered lands as [he] considered fit for the trust, but went further and," as Naoroji's electoral success clearly evinced, "selected them to represent them in the Imperial Parliament."[1] Noteworthy on several counts, this statement reveals the Indian belief that the British empire exceeded the Roman empire in political benevolence. However, the statement also invokes a principle of imperial citizenship that is historically traced back to the Romans: the idea that subjects at different points of an expansive empire could lay claim to the same rights and immunities.[2] In Naoroji's case, what made this portability of rights appear doubly unique is that it had allowed him, an Indian, to be elected to the "Imperial Parliament" in London, "irrespective of race, color, or creed."[3] Equally notable is that the statement emanated from a meeting of Indians in London, indicating the extent to which it was the imperial metropolis that underwrote understandings of imperial citizenship: after all, Naoroji could hardly lay claim to the same political privilege in India.

"What Status Shall British Indians Occupy Outside India?"

Because the question of imperial citizenship is inherently mobile in both theory and practice, it beckons to its manifestations across the diasporic terrain of empire, which in fact prompted and chiseled understandings of citizenship even before it was articulated with tangible effect in India itself. This chapter traces the formulation of ideas of citizenship among the expatriate Indians in South Africa, not least because Naoroji, as a member of Parliament, was repeatedly enjoined to ameliorate the eroding political rights of the populous Indian community that had settled there, starting in the mid-nineteenth century. Following the fortunes of diasporic Indians also makes evident how the imperial metropolis itself became a mobile metaphor, which—in seeking to guarantee the rights of imperial citizenship to a migrant population—engendered idioms of citizenship that marked both its possibilities and its limits. More specifically, the chapter draws attention to the nineteenth-century history of indentured labor, which, in its proximity to questions of imperial citizenship, allows for a closer reading of the vexed language of cultural identification and political entitlement that emerges at the intersection of labor, citizenship, and capital. The first section of this chapter reads a variety of archival documents by way of recounting the delicate position of Indians, indentured and otherwise, in the South African province of Natal in the closing decades of the nineteenth century. Highlighting the ensuing rhetoric of citizenship formulated by Mohandas Gandhi, a resident of Natal at that time, the chapter then analyzes his formulation of ideas of imperial citizenship in his capacity as spokesperson for the Natal Indians. As Gandhi's maneuvers make clear, Indian claims of citizenship in colonial Natal were modeled on particular idioms of character, credit, and cleanliness in ways that rendered indentured laborers both indispensable to—and unrepresentable within—the rhetoric of imperial citizenship.

The fact that, by the end of the nineteenth century, more than 100,000 Indians resided in South Africa, with over 50,000 in Natal alone, bears witness to the tremendous mobility marking the nineteenth-century British Empire. This mobility was occasioned primarily by the demand for labor: in the aftermath of the abolition of slavery, the need for cheap labor was felt across the empire, from plantations in the Caribbean to those in Fiji, which inaugurated the importation of indentured Indian immigrants in large numbers.[4] Even as the system of indentured labor arose in the aftermath of slavery, it was always haunted by its specter. Ever zealous in their attempts to avoid replicating the ills of slavery, the governments of Britain, India, and various other colonies instituted an extensive system of checks and balances, documenting every aspect of indentureship in order to ensure the probity of the system. The compulsive nature of this documentation, a compulsiveness evident in the sheer voluminousness of the archive on indentured labor, may have been occasioned by the fact that the system of indentured labor was often not very different from the one it was designed to supersede, both in its recruitment and treatment of the workers. As an article in the *Pioneer of India* pointed out in 1871: "Some late judicial proceedings have established the fact that the enrolment of coolies for service in the West Indies, as pursued in Allahabad, differs in no essential respect, except one, from the old African slave trade. This one exception is that in the present case the victims are British subjects."[5] Key to establishing the distinction between indentureship and slavery was the principle of contract: unlike slaves, laborers were supposed to enter into indentureship on their own accord, taking advantage of the opportunity presented to them of improving their fortunes in other parts of the empire.[6] But for Indian laborers to be recognized as free-market agents, their legal status had to be established on terms of equality; in other words, the network of indentured labor legitimated itself on the premise that Indians were rights-bearing subjects, "formally free and equal"—that "they too were citizens of empire."[7] In what seems a strange paradox, then, the discourses of imperial citizenship and indentured labor became mutually constitutive, with the result that the relation between labor and citizenship took on an added edge in imperial debates—which in any case were reconfiguring the significance of categories such as "labor," "free labor," or even "freedom."[8] However, to what extent was the laborers' status as "formally free and equal" tenable, and to what extent could that status sustain claims of and for imperial citizenship?

As much depended on the legal status of the laborers, nineteenth-century discussions on indentured labor revolved around working conditions and the scope indentured laborers (commonly referred to as "coolies") had to seek redress for their grievances. This was particularly true in Natal, which had begun to import Indian laborers in 1859, when it was announced that "the fate of the colony hangs on a thread and that thread is labor."[9] From 1859 onward, indentured Indian laborers were brought under contract into Natal by European planters who found it unprofitable to hire native labor on their sugar plantations.[10] In order to ensure the continued presence of cheap Indian labor, indentured immigrants were compelled to serve a minimum of five years, after which they could choose to remain in Natal or return to India. Obliged to ensure reasonable and fair terms of indenture for its subjects, the Government of India laid down stipulations regarding the treatment of indentured laborers, but the actual conditions of the laborers fell far short of the terms settled upon, and in 1866, the *Natal Mercury* reported that a laborer from Calcutta had submitted a letter to the newspaper outlining the various hardships endured by the indentured laborers.[11] Despite the laborers' status as "'free' individuals, with rights in courts of law as subjects of the Crown,"[12] much of the problems of indentured labor lay, as the following incident demonstrates, in the inability to fully acknowledge the laborers' status as such. This difficulty denotes the extent to which the notion of "free labor" was more a colonial edifice to mark a Whiggish movement away from slavery, a movement that depended on—in what is important for the argument in this chapter—"making labor power into an exchangeable commodity" in ways that pitted capitalism against slavery.[13]

In 1871, the Protector of Immigrants in Natal, reporting on a complaint filed against a plantation owner, forwarded the following statement from an indentured laborer, Balakistna [*sic*]: "I served three years on Mr. Leicester's estate; he gave proper food and wages, but was very severe. If a coolly did not go to work one day he stopped two days' pay, and he often tied up coolies who made mistakes and flogged them and then put salt-water on their backs. I saw five or six coolies flogged two or three times."[14] This statement was corroborated by that of another laborer, Mooneswamy, who also recounted how Mr. Leicester, "a very bad gentleman," would pour saltwater on his back after beating him, adding that "he would sometimes put a rope around my neck and send me to the police."[15] The office of the Resident Magistrate in Natal, however, discounted the testimonies by producing the affidavit of another laborer, Veraputheran, who admitted that he, too, had been flogged by Mr. Leicester, but concluded his statement with the observation that "Mr. Lister [*sic*] did not strike the coolies very often. All the coolies seemed to like Mr. Lister."[16] To this, A. Mesham, the Acting Resident Magistrate, added that the statements made by Mooneswamy and Balakistna did "not appear to be wholly true," and that "Balakistna's character when at Mr. Lister's was not so good as it might have been."[17] Presented with this contrasting evidence from the indentured laborers and the colonial officials in Natal respectively, the Government of India noted that the aspersions on the laborers' characters seemed to be merely defensive allegations on the part of the colonial authorities in Natal. It conceded, however, that "it is difficult to arrive at a satisfactory conclusion when the only evidence is the assertion of the complainant made a long time after the event, and without the opportunity of supporting or refuting it by independent evidence."[18]

The unwillingness to accept Balakistna's testimony as credible evidence; the ease with which the testimony could be refuted by competing evidence; and, more important, the consequent need for "independent evidence" bespeaks the difficulty the governments—both in Natal and India—faced in accommodating indentured laborers within a framework of rights, even as both struggled to legitimate indentured labor on the basis of it. Contract labor to Natal was in fact suspended in 1871, with the Secretary of State for India noting that the system could not be resumed "until we are certified that the colonial authorities are awake to their duty towards Indian emigrants, and that effectual measures have been taken to ensure that class of Her Majesty's subjects full protection in Natal."[19] It is doubtful, however, if either government could ever fully ascertain how best to secure indentured laborers' interests in Natal. While the system was resumed in 1874, there was no appreciable difference in the treatment of indentured laborers. Rather, the argument for indenture was premised, as it had been elsewhere, on the supposed benefits the system offered to indigent migrants. The Natal Immigration Report for 1879 pointed out that, despite the many hardships indentured laborers had to face, the indentured Indian was "better off than were he to remain in his Native land."[20] The report based this observation on the fact that over the last six months of 1879, 3,000 indentured laborers had obtained discharge certificates upon the expiration of their contracts, and "these people were well dressed, and much improved in physique, and their appearance was most creditable, not only to themselves, but also to their employers."[21] Evidently, the Victorian mantra of improvement, particularly self-improvement, was touted in defense of a system that was otherwise at pains to account for the laborers as legal subjects. That this became something of a favored refrain is evident from the Report of the Protector of Immigrants of 1892, which echoed the same language, pointing out how the laborers obtaining their certificates of discharge "were well and nicely dressed and much improved in physique and general appearance, the result of five years' residence in this Colony." "It affords me great pleasure," the protector added, "to be able *again* to state that the Indians generally, resident in Natal, continue as heretofore to form a prosperous and orderly section of the population of the colony" (emphasis added).[22] In other words, by placing the onus of improvement upon the laborers, colonial officials could appear to mediate the otherwise thorny problem presented by the confounded interrelation between indenture and citizenship, capital and freedom. Ironically, in emphasizing "improvement," something manifested through the comportment and conduct of the coolies, the reports prepared by and for the Government of India relied on what the Natal administration had often used to discredit the laborers, the question of "character."

Linked to more secular notions of virtue, the category of character had assumed an evaluative aspect in the nineteenth century, occupying a prominent role in Victorian political thought. While what constituted character was infinitely interpretable, it lent itself in the lexicon of Victorian liberalism to particular connotations of integrity, industriousness, and self-possession, paving the way for the manifestation of a self-reliant individualism.[23] In a move that was perhaps not entirely unrelated, a similar preoccupation with character also trumpeted ideals of service and self-restraint in India in the late nineteenth century, though it has been pointed out that this emphasis also referred to more long-standing notions of "dharma" or "*brahmacharya*."[24] While the ramifications of the shift in political thinking enjoined by the ascendancy of "character" in both India and England will be examined further in the study of reforms of the Indian Civil Service in chapter 4, what is of interest here is the rather slippery relation between indentured laborers and the question of their character. Even as the system of indenture could be absolved to some degree on account of its apparent character-building virtue, invocations of character on behalf of the indentured laborers became much more complicated when character itself came to constitute a central feature of citizenship claims forwarded by expatriate Indians navigating the triangulated politics of London, Natal, and India. Although Indians did, by virtue of their status as subjects of the Crown, broadly claim their rights as *equal* citizens of empire—indeed, that case was made on behalf of the coolies while defending indentured labor—such expansive claims of citizenship also had to compete with a more restricted notion, in which not only were political rights commonly ascribed to the notion of citizenship not automatic, inherent, or consequent on one's humanity (or subjecthood to the Crown), but they prescribed certain expectations of character from the mid-1800s onward.[25] In pursuing the tangled discussions and declarations of character that ensued in Indian claims for citizenship, it is also worth noting that although the much improved character of the laborers at the expiration of their indentures seemed to justify indenture itself, the situation of the laborers during their indentures remained relatively unexplored.

While reports about the discharge of indentured laborers helped justify inducting more laborers into indenture, thereby ensuring a steady supply of labor, the formerly indentured Indians posed a problem for Natal. Called "free Indians," they were given the option of staying on in the colony. Those who stayed usually farmed or bought small plots of land on which they grew vegetables and fruits, selling their produce directly to customers at a cheaper price. The commercial success of the free Indians incurred the displeasure of the European shopkeepers, but the resentment against them was not as pronounced as the animosity that was aroused by the flourishing ventures established by the "passenger Indians," who had more financial capital at their disposal.[26] Passenger Indians, who came to South Africa during the last three decades of the nineteenth century, represented an entirely different constituency. They were called passenger Indians because, unlike the contracted laborers who were shipped at the planter's expense, they paid for their own passage to South Africa. On account of their considerable financial resources and acumen, they had been able to establish successful business ventures, forming an urban and propertied Indian community in the colony. The passenger Indians had arrived in South Africa only after a sizable population of Indian laborers had agreed to contracts with Natal planters. Referred to as "Arab traders" because a large number of them were Muslim, most of the passenger Indians were from Gujarat and had arrived in Natal by way of Mauritius, but the community included many Hindus and Memon traders as well.

The swelling number of formerly indentured Indians as well as passenger Indians was soon perceived by the white settlers as a threat to their political and economic interests, and the idea of an "Asiatic menace" began to acquire considerable currency in the last two decades of the century—especially because many of the passenger Indians acquired property and were eligible for the franchise under Natal law. And although the settlers had been able to pass discriminatory measures against the native African population in Natal and other provinces, the Indians could not be treated in the same way because of their legal and political status as British subjects.[27] As a legal deputation forwarded on behalf of the Crown against the measures proposed by the South African Republic reiterated, the word "native" does not include

"Her Majesty's Asiatic subjects resident in the South African Republic, consequently these Asiatics were entitled to full privileges of Europeans hereunder."[28] A deputation of this nature was in response to the fact that governments in the South African provinces, while unable to disenfranchise Indians or curb their economic rights, had undertaken a series of measures to contain what was perceived to be the growing influence and prosperity of the Indians. Such measures included enforcing vagrancy laws and strict sanitation codes against Indians, and restricting them to certain places and opportunities for business. The question of public health, hygiene, and sanitation became one of the primary channels through which Indians were racialized and subjected to restrictive measures, as the Crown would not consent to any formal discriminatory legislation against them. In this, the distinction between laborers and passenger Indians was soon collapsed, moneyed traders and indigent laborers were uniformly referred to as "coolies"—a word that acquired a pejorative undertone—and the question of filth and squalor in the colony became a "coolie problem."[29] As a petition forwarded to the Volksraad (the parliament of the South African Republic) on behalf of European residents stated, it was necessary to segregate Indians in order to check the spread of epidemics like cholera, given that "all sanitary measures are neglected in the extreme in the dwelling houses of the Arabians and coolies, and that their mode of living is loathsome."[30] Evidently, as Nayan Shah points out in a different but contemporaneous context, a discourse of health and hygiene played "a formidable role in cultural definitions of racial difference and the racial character of living conditions."[31] It is important, though, to emphasize the entwining of the health and sanitation measures in South Africa with the economic insecurities of European settlers. It is worthwhile to underscore that this entwining racialized Indians, rather than seeing South African Indians as always already racialized, for to do so not only demystifies race—given that by the end of the nineteenth century, most scientists believed that racial differences were fixed and inherited[32]—but also shows that, as mentioned in the previous chapter, the idioms of racial exclusion evolved through a correlation with the unfolding vocabulary of citizenship itself. The popular feeling that coolies were "some of the vilest wretches in the place" lent credence to efforts by the Durban Municipal Council, for instance, to exclude eligible Indians from the electoral rolls in 1877, making citizenship not a question of property ownership—a criterion that has always been exclusionary to begin with—but one that hinged on a more opaque notion of "race and respectability."[33] In the agitation for the Second Reform Act in Britain, the debate surrounding the franchise there had also leaned more toward the moral character and respectability of potential electors. The resonances of this shift in South Africa meant that in its alignment with respectability, citizenship could, despite overt protests from the British government, very easily become racialized, given that respectability was often couched in terms of seemingly quotidian details of cleanliness, even in metropolitan political debates.[34]

Placing all Indians in the category of "coolie" did not sit well in the expatriate community in Natal. In response to what seemed to them an opprobrious epithet, the passenger Indians heartily objected to being labeled as "coolies" and went to great lengths to maintain their distinction. Even as the Crown supported their claim, arguing in a stand-off with the Government of the South African Republic that "coolie" could refer only to Indian or Chinese coolie immigrants, for "the word 'coolie' as used officially in England is invariably limited to Asiatic labourers and does not embrace persons of a superior class,"[35] the semantic reach of the word "coolie" was never settled upon. The South African Republic, for instance, stubbornly maintained that "the word 'coolie' means in South Africa any person belonging to or descended from the native races of Asia,"[36] a position it could continue to hold, given the limited influence of the Crown in the settler colonies during the 1890s. In Britain, the Liberal government of the time held that the "surest way to preserving the Empire intact was through the efficacy of the local freedom, to be guided by local opinion, and to allow the colonies to develop according to their inclinations and interests."[37] Thus, while the British government had initially refused Natal's request for self-government in 1892, it acceded to the demand in 1893, granting Natal "responsible government," which meant that while the Home Government in Britain could theoretically veto laws passed by Natal, it could not interfere in the internal matters of Natal or other self-governing colonies.

The imperial sanction for self-governing colonies, however, posed a particular problem for the British government, for its philosophy of a "non-racial empire" was increasingly challenged by the "determination of the British settlers in South Africa, Australia, New Zealand, and Canada that theirs must be a 'White Man's country.'"[38] But even as the belief in the racial superiority of Anglo-Saxons had gained scientific endorsement, it was still deplored on moral grounds, and the need to preserve the moral tenor as well as the administrative stability of empire compelled the British government to persevere in its nonracial policy, even though that often went against the grain of popular racial sentiments and very likely the government's own impulses. In the settler colonies, however, perceptions of Anglo-Saxon superiority increasingly eclipsed official imperial policies of racial nondiscrimination, and the racial conundrum faced by Britain is tellingly articulated in a Colonial Office minute: "The whole subject is perhaps the most difficult we have had to deal with. The Colonies wish to exclude the Indians from spreading all over the Empire. If we agree, we are liable to forfeit the loyalty of the Indians. If we do not agree we forfeit the loyalty of the Colonists."[39] While the Home Government continued to oppose the discrimination and ill-treatment of Indians as a matter of policy, it preferred not to counter the workings of the Natal legislature with regard to its internal affairs, with the result that the visible loss of direct imperial authority jeopardized the legal and political rights of Indians resident in the settler colonies, leaving them very little recourse for appeal.[40] The lack of an effective framework of appeal for both indentured and free Indians; the desire of the British government to appease the settler colonies while maintaining its imperial constituency; the attempts, in turn, of the Natal legislature to assuage the interests of its European constituency; and the Indian government's efforts to ward off the specter of slavery—these interlocking factors allow one to trace the emergence of a language of citizenship among Indians in Natal, the logic of which also marked the emergence of a unified political sensibility among Indians at home and abroad.

Despite the receding political authority of the imperial metropolis in the settler colonies, Indians in South Africa continued to invoke metropolitan authority; in fact, the loss of metropolitan political influence was compensated for by direct appeals to the social and cultural ethos of the metropolis. A petition addressed to the Secretary of State for the Colonies from Indian traders in the South African Republic, for instance, described the position of traders in the following manner: "a body of respectable hard-working men whose position is so misunderstood that their very nationality is overlooked and a name labeled to them, which tends to place them in an exceedingly low level in the estimation of their fellow creatures."[41] Recognizably bourgeois attributes of thrift, industry, and competitiveness are trumpeted as the characteristic traits of the diasporic Indian merchant community, with the reminder that "the very foundation of English commerce lies in the fact of *our* being able to compete more successfully with other nations" (emphasis added).⁴² Thus claiming an Englishness, the petitioners express indignation at the lack of support from "fellow" English settlers in South Africa:

> To them the hatred of injustice, and the love of fair-play is inherent, and when it affects themselves, they have a method of insisting upon their own rights and liberties, whether under a foreign government or under their own. Possibly it has never struck them that the Indian merchant is also a British subject, and claims the same liberties and rights with equal justice. To say the very least of it, if we may be permitted to employ a phrase of Palmerston's days, it is very un-English to claim rights one would not allow to others. The right of trade as an equal privilege has, since the abolition of the Elizabethan monopolies become almost a part of the English constitution, and were anyone to interfere with that right, the privilege of British citizenship would suddenly come to the front.⁴³

Presenting themselves as rights-bearing subjects, the traders claim the "privilege of British citizenship" by affiliating themselves with a liberal bourgeois identity which, since the beginning of the nineteenth century, had displaced English feudal privilege through an emphasis on industriousness and entrepreneurship.⁴⁴ However, the very basis of appealing to the imperial metropolis was the logic of liberal universalism, that subjects of the Crown were guaranteed rights, irrespective of racial or ethnic distinctions. The traders claimed "the *same* liberties and rights with *equal* justice" (emphasis added). Yet they could evidently do so only through a bourgeois self-identification. The most significant upshot of this familiar discrepancy between the universalist basis of citizenship and a cultural articulation of it in bourgeois terms was that it put the indentured laborers in a very nebulous position in South Africa: on the one hand, their presence was legitimated by the fact that they were supposedly free and equal; yet, on the other hand, an acknowledgment of their presence seemed to impede the traders' attempts to safeguard the imperiled status of Indian rights to citizenship.

The quandary precipitated by this situation was evident in an incident that took place a few years before Natal was granted self-government. The constitutional autonomy already enjoyed by the Transvaal and the Orange Free State had resulted in discriminatory legislations against Indians in those territories, and the Indians in Natal, fearing that the colony would enact similar measures once it was granted self-government, formed the Durban Indian Committee in 1890 and sent a petition to the British government urging the continuance of British rule in Natal.[45] The petition was drafted by Fajalbhai Visram, a prominent trader in Bombay, who based it on a covering letter and a list of grievances sent to him by the Durban Indian Committee. Significantly, while the list of grievances forwarded to Visram indicated the committee's concern at the mistreatment of indentured Indians, the petition ultimately drafted by Visram, though appending the committee's list of grievances, did not make any mention of the indentured laborers. By framing the petition explicitly as a merchants' petition, Visram may have hoped to forestall the possibility that the British government would lump the Indian merchants in with the indentured laborers, an identification the traders expressly wished to avoid. If the omission of the laborers in Visram's formal petition was by design, then his intuitive caution proved well-founded, for upon receiving the petition, the Colonial Office in England promptly referred the matter to the office of the Protector of Indian Immigrants in Natal, an office created to supervise the general well-being of indentured laborers. The merchants categorically rejected the option of appealing to the protector's office, and in a strongly worded letter, Hajee Mahomed Hajee Dada, chairman of the Durban Indian Committee, stated:

> The channel through which it has been treated, however, is one I and my friends and people certainly do not recognize, and we are inclined to consider the step taken as an indignity, that you should have been instructed to take the matter up, as we are not in any way connected with your department, neither do we see what your department has to do with us.[46]

Dada's letter produced the desired result, for the Colonial Secretary's office in Natal offered to open up a direct line of communication with the merchants, thus circumventing the protector.[47] Though the traders' petition led to investigations into their condition in Natal, those investigations failed to provide any substantive results; however, they succeeded, as Maureen Swan notes, in differentiating the traders from the laborers and "bring[ing] the commercial elite firmly to the attention of appropriate officials in England, Natal and India."[48] Taking as a cue the merchants' obvious interest in differentiating themselves from the laborers, Swan suggests that they presented the laborers' grievances only as a way to protect their own position: listing the workers' mistreatment at the hands of the Natal administration was a ploy to highlight the indispensability of imperial supervision and thus forestall the establishment of responsible government in Natal, which would otherwise enjoy considerable leeway in legislating anti-Indian measures.[49] While the merchants' desire to emphasize a class identity distinct from that of the laborers is undeniable, the relationship between the traders and laborers can perhaps be read in terms other than that of a class polarization bridged only by vested mercantile motives. Rather, as the following section of this chapter demonstrates, a closer reading of the petitions of the Natal merchants reveals a far more fluid, if uncertain, relationship between the merchants and laborers, one that was modeled as much by the relationship that the Indian merchants were trying to forge for themselves with the metropolitan imperial authority as by the collective identity they were trying to consolidate in a bid to protect the legal standing and rights of expatriate Indians as a whole. If at stake in this double movement was the abiding question of "what status shall the British Indians occupy outside India?" then the figure that becomes important is that of the indentured laborer, who both enables and frustrates the answers to the question, as evinced by the appearance and disappearance of the laborer's plight from the petition of the Durban Indian Committee. Focusing on the erasure of the laborers and its significance to narrative formulations of imperial citizenship allows the second section of this chapter to draw attention to another figure, one who had posed with great urgency the question quoted above regarding the status of British Indians; one who was to diligently concern himself throughout his life with questions of labor and laborers; one who, fresh from his sojourn in late-Victorian London, arrived in South Africa in 1893 to emerge as the principal spokesperson of the Natal Indians: Mohandas Gandhi.

Gandhi's Credit

Born in the Indian state of Kathiawad in 1869, Gandhi traveled to England to study law in 1888. Although his arrival in England was steeped in trepidation and anxiety on account of his shyness and inexperience with the English language, he went on to stay in London for three years, immersing himself—as Naoroji did—in a variety of academic, intellectual, and philosophical pursuits. As one of his biographers notes, Gandhi's time in London was a period of "social, moral, and intellectual ferment."[50] In fact, so exhilarating was his experience there that when he left England after qualifying as a barrister, Gandhi wistfully remarked: "it was not without deep regret that I left dear London."[51] His return to India proved disappointing, for not only did his English legal training prevent him from practicing in the Indian courts, but he was also discouraged by what he saw as a marked change in the English attitude toward Indians. In England, as Judith Brown remarks, Gandhi had been able "to imbibe a sense of total equality with white subjects of the British empire,"[52] but his return to India alerted him to a pervasive English arrogance, wherein, as Gandhi notes in his autobiography, the arbitrariness of the "*sahib*'s will was law."[53] When an Indian firm in South Africa offered him a position, he readily accepted, glad as he was "somehow to leave India" (*Autobiography*, 101).

His eagerness to leave India proved premature because although South Africa offered him the opportunity to consolidate his professional status, it also emerged as a site that exacerbated the arbitrary colonial relations he had been troubled by in India. Though he initially planned to stay in South Africa for only one year, he remained voluntarily for twenty-one years, the length of his stay necessitated by his active involvement with the political fate of South African Indians. More often than not, Gandhi's years in South Africa come into critical focus primarily as the period when he developed his philosophy of *satyagraha*, which he describes as "the Force which is born of Truth and Love or non-violence."[54] Consequently, his political activities in South Africa, when read through the hindsight of his developing philosophy of satyagraha, are underlined (and even dismissed) in their moments of "elitist involvement," such as his association with the South African Indian traders.[55] Rather than allowing Gandhi's later mantle as the "mahatma" determine a teleological reading of his activities in South Africa, this section focuses instead on how Gandhi negotiated through the social and political contexts of that particular historical moment—given that, as he noted, satyagraha as an ethic developed through his involvement with the political questions emanating from the discrimination against Indians in South Africa (*Satyagraha*, 94).

The rest of this chapter takes on, then, the relatively modest task of detailing the narrative contours of Gandhi's remonstrance against the early anti-Indian legislative acts in Natal—namely, the debates generated by the Franchise Law Amendment Bill, introduced in 1894—and the colonial practice from 1895 on of imposing a poll tax on formerly indentured laborers. Although it is certainly not possible to isolate Gandhi's philosophy of satyagraha from his political activities, as the latter provided the testing ground for the former, my examination of Gandhi's letters and petitions in Natal positions him more as a representative of a purportedly collective Indian voice in Natal, instead of reading the documents as an index of his individual opinions alone. It is worth noting that even while Gandhi was involved in a protracted and voluminous correspondence with both the colonial and British governments, arguing for citizenship rights for South African Indians, he was also developing a strong anticolonial stance, one which, as evident in *Hind Swaraj*, repudiated the idea of parliamentary democracy itself.[56] Rather than privileging one set of writings over another—or weighing the merits of the individual voice versus the collective one, a contrast Gandhi himself was uncomfortable with[57]—I would like to point to the difference between the writings under study in this chapter and a document like *Hind Swaraj* not as a discrepant one, but as one that is instrumental in highlighting the polyvocal and layered nature of anticolonialism itself.

In her study of Gandhi's South Africa years, Swan points out that the hagiographic nature of much of the scholarship on Gandhi projects him as the harbinger of political consciousness to the South African Indians.[58] Such a view is perhaps endorsed by Gandhi's own comment that before his arrival "there was [*sic*] hardly any free and well-educated Indians in South Africa capable of espousing the Indian cause" (*Satyagraha*, 36). While pointing out the seeming political vacuum, however, Gandhi does not ignore the fact that Indian merchants had in fact presented their grievances through petitions. But in acknowledging this evidence of prior political activity, Gandhi presents it mainly in terms of its limitations: "It can be truly said that free Indians fought well against difficulties, seeing that they were thus seriously handicapped, and that they were ignorant of English, and that they had no experience of public work in India" (36). According to Gandhi, the petitions dispatched thus far were actually handicapped by the fact that the traders had failed to include the laborers in their efforts to redress the Indian situation. And while Gandhi suggests that this omission could be on account of an oversight, he also notes that it could have been occasioned by a feeling on the part of the traders that "matters might be made worse by [the laborers'] being allowed to join the movement" (36). In studying Gandhi's political involvement in Natal, it is precisely the question of including the indentured laborers that I would like to examine, for while Gandhi attempted to add a strategic edge to the political program of Natal Indians by affiancing it with metropolitan rhetoric, the uncertain treatment of indentured labor in that rhetoric complicated the basis of the cohesive Indian identity that Gandhi sought to consolidate. However, the Indian negotiations with imperial citizenship in Natal also highlight how the idioms of citizenship forwarded by Gandhi came to depend as much upon narrativizing a fading liberal metropolitan sensibility as upon including the ignored indentured laborers, a conjunction that proved vital yet problematic to the articulation of imperial citizenship.

The subordinate status of the Indians in South Africa was immediately evident to Gandhi as he stepped ashore in Durban. Abdullah Sheth, a prominent Indian businessman in the area, and the owner of the firm that had employed Gandhi, was present to receive him as he disembarked. But Gandhi did not feel welcome: "As the ship arrived at the quay and I watched the people coming on board to meet their friends, I observed that the Indians were not held in much respect. I could not fail to notice a sort of snobbishness about the manner in which those who knew Abdullah Sheth behaved towards him, and it stung me" (*Autobiography*, 108). Gandhi's initial experience in South Africa highlights the racial discrimination that exceeded statutory restrictions already imposed upon indentured and formerly indentured Indians. His observation of the "snobbishness" directed against Abdullah Sheth was but a prelude to his own experience of being forced to vacate a first-class railway compartment while traveling to Pretoria. Abandoned on a cold winter's night at the Maritzburg station by the railway guard, simply because he refused to remove himself to the van compartment, the impact of the Indians' situation in South Africa forced itself upon Gandhi, and as he famously narrates: "I began to think of my duty. Should I fight for my rights or go back to India, or should I go on to Pretoria without minding the insults, and return to India after finishing the case?" Deciding upon the former, Gandhi resolved to fight the "colour prejudice" and "try, if possible, to root out the disease and suffer hardships in the process" (114).

Gandhi's initiation into political life, however, was unremarkable enough in its beginnings: during his early months in Natal, he drafted letters, petitions, and memorandums on behalf of the Indian community, a task for which his legal training and knowledge of English—his London education—made him eminently suitable. With the increasing Indian presence in Natal, there was fear that Indians would be able to outvote the Europeans. Efforts were undertaken to disenfranchise Indians as early as 1880, but those attempts were stalled through the collective support of the governor of the colony, the Colonial Office in England, and the planters who, depending heavily upon immigrant labor from India, feared reprisal from the Indian government.[59] The threat of disenfranchisement, however, became more acute in 1894, when—despite the irrationality of the fear that Indians could outvote the Europeans—the mere fact that the Indian population outnumbered the European population hastened the introduction of the Franchise Amendment Bill, which would have prevented the further addition of Indians to the voters' rolls.

The Indians learned about the bill only when newspapers reported its second reading in the Legislative Assembly, the lower house of the Natal legislature. This news reached the Indian traders as they were hosting a farewell reception for Gandhi, who had completed his assignment and was actually scheduled to leave for India the next day. Gandhi records that he postponed his departure indefinitely upon the insistence of the traders, who prevailed upon him to lead the protest against the proposed legislation (*Autobiography*, 140). Since one of the bill's justifications was the "supposed unfitness of the Indians to vote,"[60] what followed was a series of circulars and petitions addressed to both houses of the Natal legislature, all of which cited the precedents set in India and England for Indian participation in political life, hence testifying to their political eligibility. The petitions to the Legislative Assembly not only emphasized the privileges enjoyed by Indians as subjects of the Crown through constant references to the Proclamation of 1858, but also voiced resentment at this seemingly default status being questioned or undermined. In a letter sent individually to all legislators in both houses, Gandhi posed the rhetorical question: "Do you really believe that no Indian British subject can ever acquire sufficient attainments for the purpose of becoming a full citizen of the Colony or of voting?"[61] After the bill was read for a third time in the Legislative Assembly, Gandhi appealed to the Governor of Natal, impressing upon him the

Indian hope that as representative of the Crown, he would surely "not sanction a measure that would seem to lay down that an Indian British subject of Her Majesty can never become fit to exercise the franchise."[62] England served as an example, as Gandhi reminded the governor that "even in England, any British subject having the proper qualifications is entitled to vote, irrespective of caste, colour, or creed."[63] In another petition to the Premier and the Colonial Secretary of Natal, Gandhi pointedly alluded to the Indian representation in the British Parliament: "the Bill seems to be so sweeping that even the Indian member of the British House of Commons, did he come here, would not be fit for becoming a voter."[64] The Indian member in question, of course, was Naoroji, indicating how Naoroji's election provided a reference point for articulations of imperial citizenship elsewhere. But this referentiality had varying effects: in a letter urging the Legislative Council, the upper house of the Natal legislature, to modify its stance on the bill, Gandhi cites, ironically enough, the House of Lords' rejection of the Irish Home Rule Bill.[65] While the citation indicates the uneven relation between Indian demands for imperial citizenship and the issue of Irish Home Rule, it also demonstrates the perceived need for narrating the imperial metropolis into the grid of colonial policymaking in South Africa, if only to protect a common citizenry against the heterogeneities of local colonial interests.

Since the right to vote was determined by property qualifications, Gandhi's arguments focused on protecting the rights of those Indians who, though already in possession of property, would lose the franchise if the bill passed; indentured laborers, consequently, did not explicitly appear within this argumentative framework. However, in appealing to the colonial and imperial authorities on behalf of the Indians who might soon be disenfranchised, Gandhi constituted the Natal Indians as a collective group, for while the colonists' fear of being outvoted by Indians applied to only a certain section of the Indian populace, a more diffuse racial antipathy was directed, as mentioned earlier, toward the Natal Indians as a whole. Mindful of the traders' impulse to extricate themselves from the generic label of "coolie," Gandhi nonetheless included the fate of the indentured laborers within the Indians' appeals, not the least because it was always abundantly evident that while the Europeans would be happy to do away with Indians in the colony, they would always want to make an exception in the case of indentured laborers.[66] Although, as discussed in the previous section, a general notion of imperial citizenship remained crucial to sustaining the case for indentured labor, Gandhi's political maneuvering also reveals how the figure of the indentured laborer became, in turn, equally crucial to forwarding Indian claims of imperial citizenship. What this interconstitutiveness throws into relief, though, is the gap between the universalist premise of liberal citizenship and its statutory requirements, the familiar gap that Joan Scott has described in another context as the "paradox" of democratic citizenship.[67] In Natal in the late nineteenth century, this paradox translated into a disjunction between the belief that Indians were entitled to citizenship rights by virtue of being subjects of the Crown, and the reality that they had to qualify for the egalitarian benefits of citizenship—a paradox that was embodied and mediated in many ways through the figure of the indentured laborer.

Although the Indian traders were dependent upon the laborers as a captive clientele, the interaction between the two groups did not readily constitute any collective identity, for it was also fractured by regional, linguistic, religious, and class differences.[68] As Gandhi recalls noting a few days after arriving in Natal:

> I could see that the Indians were divided into different groups. One was that of Musalman merchants, who would call themselves "Arabs." Another was that of Hindu, and yet another of Parsi, clerks. The Hindu clerks were neither here or there, unless they cast in their lot with the "Arabs." The Parsi clerks would call themselves Persians. These three classes had some social relations with one another. But by far the largest class was that composed of Tamil, Telugu and North Indian indentured and freed labourers ... The other three classes had none but business relations with this class. (*Autobiography*, 109)

The struggle against the franchise bill seemed to provide an opportunity to bridge these schisms, and it is to Gandhi's credit that, in a remarkable show of solidarity, over 10,000 Indians attached their signatures to a petition addressed to Lord Ripon, Secretary of State for the Colonies. The petition, drafted mostly by Gandhi, purported at its outset to represent the broad spectrum of the Indian population: "Some of Your Lordship's Petitioners are traders, who have come to the Colony and settled therein. Some again are those who, in the first instance, came from India under indenture, and have now, for some time (even thirty years), become free. Some are Indians under indenture, and some are educated in the Colony, and engaged in various pursuits of life."[69]

Presenting a unified voice against the impending legislation, the petition moves on to point out the bill's inconsistencies. One of the reasons advanced in the Natal Legislative Assembly to justify its decision to keep future Asians off the voters' rolls was that Asians were unfit to vote. Yet, the bill saw fit to retain the names of existing Asian voters on the list; the petition suggested that this implied a tacit concession to the Asian's ability to exercise his franchise. The main objection to this seeming inconsistency from the Indian perspective was that it created divisions among Indians of the same economic standing, between those who could vote and those whose voting rights were to be denied "based on accidental circumstances."[70] The petition pointed out that in contrast to an earlier version of the bill, which would have disenfranchised only certain Indians, the present version, by nullifying the possibility of Indians' ever being included in the voters' rolls, effectively disbarred all Indians: "now unfortunately, . . . all Indians, indentured, and freed, and free, are attempted to be put in the same scale."[71] While the Indians' apparent discomfiture at this leveling seems antithetical to the spirit of solidarity the petition opens with, it could be that Indian traders resented this leveling more because it implied a wholesale disenfranchisement of Indians by curbing the voting rights allowed thus far to a modicum of the Indian population. However, toward the end, the petition anticipates the Indian situation should the proposed legislation be enacted: "*if* Indian British subjects in a British colony are allowed to be treated *at all* on an unequal footing, a time will soon come when it will be impossible for Indians, having any idea whatever of self-respect, to remain in the Colony" (emphasis added).[72] The pointedly speculative undertone of this statement of course overlooks the entrenchment of exploitative labor conditions that had long since systematically failed to protect indentured Indians' interests as subjects of the Crown and placed them in an extremely disadvantaged social category. By narrativizing the existing plight of indentured Indians only as the impending predicament of propertied Indians, the petition effectively undermines the representativeness of the collective voice that it opened with— indeed, the collective voice that was being constituted through the petition.

In fact, the collective "Indian" identity that was being narratively constituted warrants further attention, for it is through its inflections that the dynamic of citizenship played itself out even after the immediate furor stirred by the franchise bill had subsided. On his visit to India in 1896, Gandhi published a pamphlet, the "Grievances of the British Indians in South Africa," popularly known as the "Green Pamphlet," to acquaint the Indian public with the state of affairs in South Africa and to gather its support for South African Indians. While Gandhi wrote the pamphlet expressly for an Indian audience, he was mindful of the wider audience whose scrutiny it would no doubt attract: as he noted later, the Green Pamphlet drew a "purposely subdued picture of the condition of Indians in South Africa" (*Autobiography*, 164). This mindfulness was not misguided, for the pamphlet did indeed incur the displeasure of Europeans in Natal, and Gandhi received a rather hostile reception on his return there. What is interesting in this mindfulness, though, is that even as the pamphlet takes care to detail the hardships faced by indentured laborers as well, underlining how difficult it is for them to even get a fair hearing, its tone regarding the plight of the indentured laborers is considerably more circumspect than when it draws attention to the injustice meted out to the "free Indians." While the several wrongs enacted against free Indians are spelled out, the description of the indentured laborers' circumstances is qualified by a remarkable passage that bears quoting at length:

> We, however, wish to guard ourselves against being understood to say that the life of the indentured Indians in Natal is harder than in any other country, *or that this is a part of the general grievances of the Indians in the Colony*. On the other hand, we know that there are estates in Natal where the Indians are very well treated. At the same time we do humbly submit that the lot of the indentured Indians is not all that it might be and that there are points which require attention (emphasis added).[73]

The reluctance to come out fully in support of the laborers, the anxious hedging on the question of their maltreatment, and the imminent disavowal of their cause—"this is [not] a part of the general grievances of the Indians in the Colony"—points to the ambivalence punctuating the inclusion of laborers within the collective Indian fold that was taking shape. In a document that was to bear colonial and metropolitan scrutiny, it was the relation between indentured labor and political claims that seemed to demand the most anticipatory caution.

Gandhi continues in the Green Pamphlet to argue for the citizenship rights of Indians on the basis of a universal logic, inasmuch as he points out that "we belong to the Imperial family and are children, adopted, it may be, [but] of the same august mother, having the same rights and privileges guaranteed to us as to the European children."[74] But the expansiveness of this appeal is undercut by observations such as the one that Natal Indian traders are needlessly harassed by the police, who cannot distinguish between traders and indentured laborers—a fact that surprises Gandhi, given that "nothing can be easier," since, as he notes, "the indentured Indian never is dressed in a fashionable dress."[75] In the preceding pages of the pamphlet, Gandhi had mentioned without comment the tacit understanding between Indians and the colonial authorities that merchants wearing a loose, flowing robe would not be accosted by the police. He even ruefully observed that because many Bengali and Tamil traders did not wear that kind of a robe (which was mostly worn by Gujarati traders), they were harassed by the police.[76] Yet his stance on the robe becomes somewhat contradictory. On the one hand, he critiques the fact that all traders are not given equal treatment due to the arbitrary importance attached to certain forms of dress, such as the robe. His commiseration with the traders who do not wear the robe is implicitly critical of the ways in which the question of dress should have any bearing on the equal treatment all traders deserve. However, rather than following this idea to what would have been its logical conclusion—a counteracting of the differentiating effects of dress—the Green Pamphlet endorses the idea of distinguishing merchants from indentured laborers by sartorial indicators, such as the robe.

An elaboration on Gandhi's views on the importance of matters sartorial, though of crucial import, is beyond the scope of this chapter, even though Gandhi's own sartorial appearance underwent several transformations during his time in South Africa. What is of interest here is how the question of dress—which became for Gandhi, as Emma Tarlo notes, "a strategy for exposing injustice" right from his South Africa days[77]—highlights the fraught relationship between traders and indentured laborers. It is worth noting that although Gandhi arrived in South Africa as an impeccably dressed barrister, paying much attention to the correctness of his attire, he recounted that toward the end of his stay in South Africa, he changed his clothing "so as to make it more in keeping with that of the indentured labourers" (*Autobiography*, 341). True, this transformation took place over a period of time, and it would be anachronistic to expect to see its effect in a document written as early as the Green Pamphlet. However, by 1896, Gandhi had already protested against the ways in which the matter of clothing reflected the discriminatory policies of the colonial government. When asked by the Natal court to remove his Indian turban in favor of an English hat in 1893, he wrote to the press arguing against such an order. It is interesting, then, that a justification for citizenship status such as that made in the "Grievances of the British Indians in South Africa" could not fully accommodate, narratively or conceptually, Gandhi's evolving sensitivity to the discriminatory effects of dress. Rather, with reference to indentured laborers, it yielded an uncharacteristically flat-footed response on Gandhi's part to the colonial sartorial code, and, in the larger context of citizenship, it indicates how the question of dress becomes instrumental in covering up the problems riddling citizenship when its universal logic cannot quite be actualized on a plane of corporeality. That it is the indentured laborers who should /could be arrested for violating vagrancy laws despite the fact that they were all part of the "same Imperial family," children of the "same august mother," seems to have been accounted for, from the Natal Indian perspective, by the simple fact of the inadequacy of attire.

Given that Gandhi presents a more studied treatment of dress in his autobiography, it would be tempting to argue for the autobiography's truth claim over the Green Pamphlet. However, that would miss the point of how a document written specifically to argue for citizenship, such as the Green Pamphlet, operates through a narrative logic that can only falter at the notion of political parity or corporeal inclusion. What is of even more interest is that the figure of the indentured laborer could not quite be excluded from the purview of an emergent political Indian sensibility either; rather, as Gandhi's writings indicate, the figure continually marks the framework of citizenship attempted by that sensibility, even as the indentured laborer evidently could not quite be accommodated within it.

It is important to note here that the ambiguity regarding the treatment of indentured laborers cannot readily be attributed to caste prejudice, because though the laborers were all poor and came to Natal for obvious economic reasons, they were from varying castes: along with the large numbers of lower-caste laborers, there was a significant representation from the upper and middle castes, especially from the Madras and Calcutta areas.[78] The unease occasioned by the laborers cannot be attributed solely to preexisting class biases, either, for indentured communities in Natal and elsewhere provided considerable class mobility; Gandhi himself presents the example of Joseph Royappen, who, born of indentured parents, acquired a thoroughly European style of living and went on to acquire a law degree from Cambridge (*Satyagraha*, 177). Rather, given that the Natal traders were fashioning themselves in terms of a metropolitan respectability that could buttress their appeals for citizenship, the existing relations between the indentured and nonindentured Indians must be reexamined in light of the protocols of late-Victorian ideas of citizenship, while not discounting the fact that the logic of citizenship provided a route for marking class and caste distinctions while appearing to subsume them. Despite the common belief, mentioned earlier, that one qualified as citizen simply by virtue of the status as subject of the Crown, the idea that citizenship rights had to be earned was also prevalent throughout the nineteenth century. In the debates preceding the Second Reform Act in England, even the argument from the radicals for so-called manhood suffrage did not extend to all adult males, but only to those who could prove their independence, as evidenced "through the property of one's self, one's will, and one's work."[79] The agitation for the Third Reform Act, too, did not witness a conflation of manhood suffrage with universal suffrage: even when the notion of enfranchising women was accommodated at a popular level, the vision was that the "'free-born Englishman' (and 'Englishwoman') who ought to be franchised were [those] able to 'stand on [their] own feet.'"[80] Gandhi approvingly cited an article that appeared in the *Times*, which clearly felt that it would be "wrong" for the Natal Government to "deny the rights of citizenship to British Indian subjects who, by years of thrift and good work in the Colony have *raised* themselves to the actual status of citizens" (emphasis added).[81] In fact, it was work, or at least the Indian potential for it, that Gandhi felt set the Indians apart in their claims from the "kaffirs," the derogatory term for native Africans. And while Gandhi remained politically distant from native Africans for much of his time in South Africa,[82] notions of work and industriousness allowed for a certain class mobility in his reckoning of the Indian situation in ways that also illustrate that it was not necessarily class but the question of indentured labor itself that became problematic. And this unease was due in no small measure to the rather complicated relation between nonindentured Indians and their purported industriousness.

The nineteenth-century emphasis on industriousness was in fact resonant of its larger preoccupation with character. Even as the precise index of character remained fairly malleable, there was wide consensus that one of its components was hard work. "Work, even the hardest," Samuel Smiles had declared in his immensely popular *Self-Help*, "is full of pleasure and materials for self-improvement."[83] Hard work, however, assumed rather puzzling dimensions with regard to the Indians in Natal. The case of hard-working, formerly indentured Indians who improved their lot provided a rosy picture of the aftermath of indentureship, thus sustaining arguments for indentureship itself. The industriousness of the traders, too, helped them consolidate their positions in Natal, "earning" them, as the *Times* had pointed out, their citizenship rights. However, this very industriousness made Indians an economic and political threat to the colony. That the hard-working hawkers, small-scale entrepreneurs, and wealthy traders proved to be good competitors was held against them,[84] despite the fact that, as the Indian traders had pointed out, "the foundation of English commerce lies in the fact of our being able to compete more successfully with other nations." In attempting to gain support from metropolitan quarters, the implicit audience for his petitions, Gandhi's representation of South African Indians had to negotiate the dilemma of a metropolitan bourgeois ideology that promoted a competitive industriousness but was also wary of what was deemed to be its potentially antisocial and unethical effects—a dilemma whose resolution demanded, as Patrick Brantlinger notes, that the "good bourgeois be both homo economicus *and* public spirited citizen" (emphasis in the original).[85]

While the expansive repercussion of this dilemma can be traced even in the consolidation of an ideology of separate spheres in nineteenth-century England—one that ensured that the ethical influence of the domestic sphere would counter the deleterious effects of the "ignoble" market—the specific effect of this dilemma manifested itself in late-nineteenth-century Natal, where Indians were berated not only for not observing the demarcation between workplace and home but also for being overly thrifty, too moderate in their habits, and parsimonious—all of which supposedly gave them an unfair economic edge over their European counterparts, making them "too competitive." Ironically, notions of thrift and moderation had, since at least the mid-century, been hailed as key metropolitan idioms underlining numerous attempts to reform the English poor, widely depicted as unclean, undisciplined masses overcrowding the urban centers. Commentators like Edwin Chadwick, equating profligacy with disease and moral decay, feared that the wayward and dissolute habits of the poor dangerously intruded upon bourgeois notions of respectability.[86] Tirelessly expounding the corrective value of thrift as a means of self-discipline and self-help, the hortatory Smiles even drew a clear connection between thrift and cleanliness: "cleanliness," he declared, is the best exponent of the spirit of Thrift."[87] In a strange reversal, the colonial argument against fairly successful Indians in Natal acquired a self-evident nature even in metropolitan discussions by maligning Indians for not only exhibiting the virtues of thrift, prudence, and temperance, but in doing so to a very great degree. The colonial displeasure at this excess was relayed through a depiction of Indians as "filthy," indicating the remarkable plasticity with which images of filth were deployed in the nineteenth-century imaginary.[88]

The colonial preoccupation with notions of cleanliness would have amplified Gandhi's own developing interest in the question of hygiene, which was to acquire for him a bio-moral import. "The reason for confession of sin," he noted in later years, "is precisely the reason that requires us to scrub and clean a dirty surface. What washing is for removing dirt on a material body, confession is for removing dirt on the spiritual plane."[89] At the quotidian level and even as early as his time in South Africa, Gandhi was particularly interested in ideas of hygiene and sanitation, and he often expressed regret at what he perceived to be Indian indifference to these matters. With reference to the issue of citizenship, this concern manifested itself in pronounced ways, with Gandhi expressing keen awareness of the fact that while Indians needed to be depicted as hardworking in order to distinguish them from the "backward kaffirs," their hard work also had to be tempered. In this, he tried to bring Indians within the folds of metropolitan sociality and respectability—including cleanliness.

Attempting to prevent the passage of the franchise bill, Gandhi set out, in an open letter addressed to both houses of the Natal legislature, to analyze the current situation through a discussion of the question, "Are the Indians desirable as citizens in the Colony?"[90] He took pains to point out that if hatred of the Indian "is based upon an ignorance of his general character and attainments, he may hope to receive his due at the hands of the Europeans in the Colony."[91] Detailing the significant role played by Indians in improving the economy of Natal, Gandhi noted: "It would seem that the Indian has helped to make this the Garden Colony of South Africa."[92] In elaborating on what the colony has gained by the Indian presence, however, he is careful to emphasize the nature of the Indian work ethic. Not without a certain self-righteousness, he observes that the Indian traders' economic success can be attributed to their "total abstinence from drink and its attendant evils," and that they "of course ... do not gamble, as a rule do not smoke, and can put up with little inconveniences."[93] Highlighting such qualities would no doubt have appealed to notions of bourgeois respectability, and in the "Open Letter" and elsewhere, Gandhi repeatedly employs this depiction of the South African Indian character. In fact, in what was a familiar rhetorical move characterizing Indian petitions until the beginning of the twentieth century, Gandhi quotes extensively from various European sources—including Sir George Birdwood, Bishop Heber, Sir Charles Trevelyan, and Victor Hugo—to corroborate his claims of the soundness of the Indian character in general. However, in what testifies to the shaky relationship between character and citizenship (and to the uncertain constitution of "character"), the fact that abstemious, thrifty, industrious Indians were maligned and potentially disenfranchised for these traits indicates how by the end of the nineteenth century, citizenship was as much about consumption as it was about those familiar constituents of character: hard work and self-restraint. In other words, it was not only one's respectability and industriousness but also one's role as consumer that was marshaled to profile political membership and entitlement.[94] Thus, what might be tabulated as moral probity on one register could very easily be seen as liability on another, and the prudent abstemiousness of hard-working Indians could at once constitute Indian eligibility for citizenship and also render it lacking. This was evidently not lost on Gandhi, cognizant of the fact that conventional testimonials of character alone were inadequate to the task: what was evidently needed was a more persuasive narrative logic that could steer through the complex and contradictory demands of character and citizenship. Interestingly, what recommended itself in its viability to establish a redemptive Indian sociability was the language of credit and creditworthiness.

As someone who viewed the maintenance of financial accounts as a key feature of public life, Gandhi was punctilious about bookkeeping, loath to enter even a single item under "sundries" (*Satyagraha*, 102). The fastidiousness with which he sought to balance accounts is evident in his detection of a slight error in the annual balance sheet of the Natal Indian Congress, which did not tally with the 723 subscriptions recorded in the association's ledger.[95] For Gandhi, the emphasis on accounting and bookkeeping was not so much about economic profit but rather, as it had been for his Victorian counterparts, about ethics and transparency, cognate to cleanliness itself: the "keeping of accounts is an independent duty," he notes, "the performance of which is essential to clean work" (103). In fact, Gandhi privileges the balance sheet as an important artifact of credibility, recalling how he often referred to that to argue on behalf of his clients (158). It is almost as if in the realm of representation, "clean credit" could absorb and compensate for the allegedly "unclean" Indian body.[96] Following the logic of accounting, of debit and credit, Gandhi points out that the common aspersions against Indians, such as abstemiousness or thrift—which could be viewed as debit—could quite literally be transformed into credit,[97] if one were to equate credit with creditworthiness, as prevalent in the relations between a debtor and a creditor. Since such transactions of economic intimacy, dependent as they were on the debtor's personal appraisal of the creditor, defined a goodly portion of economic exchange well into the nineteenth century,[98] credit relations in fact provided a crucial index of character. Maintaining that the "Indian's thrift" and "his moderate habits" actually ensured his creditworthiness, Gandhi is glad to be able to point out that "European firms in South Africa give hundreds of Indians large credit, practically on their word of honour, and have no cause to regret having done so."[99]

Gandhi's banking on this larger notion of credit as an index of public trust and social acceptance demonstrates the importance of credit and creditworthiness in an era of finance capital, in which the line between investment and speculation, between what was salubrious for the public and what could be potentially disruptive, had been particularly thin.[100] Credit, in other words, stood in for trust. And just as credit held a particular representational value in what was an abstract and unknowable system of finance, it also provided the narrative logic for representation in the context of citizenship, given that the promise of citizenship hinged, as the Natal Indians were to discover, on a formal equality that was at once comforting and misleading. But if creditworthiness allowed for a semblance of trust in the risky environs of a seemingly anonymous cash nexus, it is significant that "trade credit [itself] was determined not by known quantities of capital," but, as Margot Finn notes, "by perceived qualities of character."[101] For wealthy Natal Indians successful in securing credit on account of their financial reserves, however, this relation was to work more in reverse: they could reclaim their character through their credit. In this, credit begets character, which begets citizenship. Gandhi underlined this connection himself, even in later years enjoining South African Indian merchants to maintain good credit by ensuring that "liabilities are punctually paid," adding that "as with individuals, so with communities; as in pecuniary affairs, so in political matters."[102] Since economic credit was inextricably entwined with its social correlative, it was not enough for Indians to accrue economic credit through their commercial dealings. They had to accrue social credit as well, by being mindful of the health and economy of Natal and being good consuming members of the body politic. "We would [then] emerge," Gandhi noted, "a community rich in social virtues, stronger in the justness of our cause, and, to take up the analogy we have used at the outset [that of the balance sheet], with a far larger credit balance in our favour than we started with."[103] In fact, when recalling the European allegation against Natal Indians, Gandhi was to cast it in a telling rhetorical question: "How could cleanly open-handed Europeans with their multifarious wants compete in trade with such parsimonious and dirty people?" (*Satyagraha*, 42).

Noting how important it was for Indians to both pay heed to hygiene and overcome imputations of parsimony, Gandhi describes how over the years in South Africa lectures and public meetings were held on topics such as "domestic sanitation, personal hygiene, the necessity of having separate buildings for houses and shops and, for well-to-do traders, of living in a style befitting their position" (*Satyagraha*, 42). There seems to be little evidence, however, that similar arrangements were made for the instruction of laborers. It may be that the dispersed locations of laborers and their long working hours did not make such arrangements tenable. But when drafting the petitions surrounding the franchise bill, Gandhi also seems less inclined to account for the laborers in the way he does for the traders. Responding to charges of "untruthfulness" that were also leveled against the traders, for instance, Gandhi insists in the "Open Letter" that the imputations are "without foundation," and if the traders are perceived to be untruthful at all, it is because of the exigencies of business or, more often, the inaccuracies inherent in the process of translation (many traders did not speak English).[104] With regard to the indentured laborers, on the other hand, Gandhi rather readily accepts the charges of their untruthfulness. Despite positing material circumstances to explain the laborers' propensity to lie—namely, the "uncongenial surroundings" in the colony, and the facts that they receive no moral or religious instruction and that they might be severely punished by their masters were they to tell the truth—Gandhi remains content with presenting a somewhat pathological view of their prevarication. "The [indentured laborers] would lie without any reason, without any prospect of bettering themselves materially," he points out, even as he adds by way of defense: "Is there any class of people who would not do as they are doing under similar circumstances?"[105] A similar dynamic frames Gandhi's response to the general allegation of Indian disregard for hygiene as well. He concedes that he must, "to [his] great mortification, admit this charge partially,"[106] but while making the important point that these charges called for a "just and merciful operation of the sanitary law," he goes on to mitigate the charges by noting that the Indians' "personal habits, it would appear, are not dirty, except in the case of the indentured Indians, who are too poor to attend to personal cleanliness."[107]

In light of his studied attempts to account for Indian traders and establish their character, Gandhi's inability to even attempt something similar on behalf of the laborers is striking. It could be that by performing work that was deemed essential, the laborers did not pose a threat to the colony or compete with European interests, and therefore did not have to be accounted for. But the equanimity with which Gandhi accepts and reaffirms the allegations against the laborers invites further consideration. The disinclination to dispel allegations about the laborers' character or cleanliness by even pointing to their amenability to reform (which had been the attempt on the part of the colonial officials putting together the Natal Immigration Report, for instance) suggests that by being commodified in their labor, by not being allowed to "exceed the role of labor"[108]—in other words, they are unclean and untruthful because of the conditions of their labor—the indentured laborers come to bear the burden of the accusations leveled against Indians as a whole. By appearing admittedly as debit, they enable those like Gandhi to present a more plausible balance sheet of Indians in Natal, providing a narrative tenability for claims of citizenship.[109] Yet if the laborers provided the foil for Indians in general to appear as credit, the representational logic of the balance sheet could barely disguise the fact that it was the indentured laborers who accrued economic credit in a very real sense, and that too not so much for themselves as for the expatriate Indian community as a whole, and the colonial planters. As Gandhi emphasizes even in the "Open Letter," "Indian labourers are not only desirable but useful citizens of the Colony, and also absolutely essential to its well-being."[110] Precisely because this was so, the balance between the two aspects of credit—the social and the economic, the symbolic and the real—could be maintained only through reifying the commodification of indentured labor in the imperial economy, a commodification that translates here into a narrative mode that does not so much exclude the laborers as point to how they continually elude representation in terms that mark Indian eligibility for citizenship—terms that the laborers, in fact, make possible. Thus the "Open Letter" retains the figure of the "filthy" indentured laborer—unlike Fajalbhai Visram's petition, which did not even mention the laborers—beginning with a section devoted to the laborers, if only to highlight their dishonesty and lack of cleanliness. And the repeated emphasis on the laborers' usefulness in this letter and the various documents generated by the franchise bill and subsequent proposed legislation actually effaces the laborers in ways that absorb their quiddity and "use value," so to speak, rendering them necessary but anonymous and lacking both character and credit.[111]

That it is through rendering the laborers abstract that Natal Indians could hope to approximate the formal, abstracting claims of citizenship illustrates a relation between capital and citizenship that is at once parallel and inverse: if Indian traders emerge as citizens, it is because the laborers are commodified in their labor. The laborers are acknowledged in their presence and contribution, but disavowed in their personhood and citizenship. But in tracing how Gandhi's writings bear out this perverse logic, it is equally important, though, to foreground how Gandhi's South Africa years also marked a steady evolution in his own ideas regarding labor. As Gandhi recounts in his autobiography, he was so intrigued by John Ruskin's *Unto This Last* that he stayed up all night reading it on a train journey from Johannesburg to Durban. The aspect of Ruskin's treatise that appealed to him most were the principles, which, as Gandhi notes, emphasized "that a lawyer's work has the same value as the barber's inasmuch as all have the same right of earning their livelihood from their work. That a life of labour, i.e., the life of the tiller of the soil and the handicraftsman is the life worth living" (*Autobiography*, 274–75). Influenced by Tolstoy as well, Gandhi in later years elaborated more fully upon a philosophy of "bread labour" that weighed against the commodification of labor effected by industrial capitalism.[112] South Africa witnessed early attempts to approximate these ideals, and in setting up settlements at Phoenix and Tolstoy Farm, Gandhi emphasized the dignity of individual labor alongside an ethos of self-reliance.

Given this brief overview of Gandhi's steadily evolving ideas about the alienating and uneven effects of industrial capitalism, it is difficult to square them with the Natal petitions for citizenship—which, I have suggested, reify the commodification of indentured laborers. In fact, in his study on indentured laborers in Fiji, John D. Kelly cites Gandhi's inspirational example as one that helped the indentured Indians in Fiji counter the alienating effects of labor through modes of devotionalism.[113] Kelly's analysis, mostly drawing on evidence from Gandhi's later writings on labor, testifies to Gandhi's popularity among indenture communities across the empire. However, it must also be read alongside the contradictions and uneasiness that permeate Gandhi's representation of indentured laborers in Natal. Indeed, it has been pointed out that even as Gandhi championed the cause of labor and laborers, his representation of laborers, especially when it was compounded by caste (such as his representation of "untouchable" sanitation workers) often faltered, suffused as it was by a paternalism that drew criticism in later years from leaders like B. R. Ambedkar.[114] But the point of noting the contradictory or uneven nature of Gandhi's representation of laborers is not to show his failings. Rather, in light of his lifelong commitment to the cause of labor and laborers—he became one of the most vociferous critics of the system of indenture and played a vital role in getting it abolished in 1911—Gandhi's writings may be the most useful in illuminating the difficulties inherent in probing the question of labor and finding a representational index that does not reify the commodifying effects of that which it seeks to critique. In this, it is more productive to trace the difficulties and paradoxes that weigh on and through Gandhi's writings on citizenship in Natal, for not only do they underscore the uneven relations between capital, labor, and citizenship, but in their very unevenness they gesture to the possibilities—and compulsions—of formulating of citizenship, especially in an imperial context.

As Gandhi often noted, Indians, unlike the native African populace, "know the dignity and necessity of labour."[115] As indicated earlier, Gandhi's relations with the African community in Natal remained ambivalent at best, and the claims of imperial citizenship perhaps caused the greatest distance between Indian and African interests. During a "rebellion" by the Zulus in Natal in 1906, Gandhi mobilized an Indian corps on behalf of the British in a bid to demonstrate that "British Indians were not unworthy to be citizens of the Empire and were capable of recognizing their obligations if they also insisted on their rights."[116] Given that the perceived ability for hard work was what legitimated the Indian presence in Natal and helped insert it into a discourse of rights and entitlement in the first place, Gandhi's touting of Indian industriousness capitalized on colonial perceptions of "native laziness," overlooking the visible exploitation of native labor. Interestingly, the emphasis on Indian industriousness also effaced constitutive elements of indentured labor as well. Although Gandhi had to make amends for the abstemiousness of the Natal Indian traders, it was still the lifestyle of the law-abiding and temperate Indian that provided the most available template for the "model Indian," one who was, Gandhi pronounced, "as much civilized as a 'model' European."[117] There was little space for indentured laborers in this representation, given that gambling, alcoholism, and the use of narcotics were reportedly commonplace in indenture communities. Helping ameliorate the harshness of working conditions, pastimes like gambling and drinking constituted key sites through which facets of indentured identity and camaraderie were forged.[118] Not only did the emblematizing of the traders as "model Indians"—indeed, as model citizens—elide the possibilities of other nodes of indenture identity, but positing the traders as model citizens also compounded the commodification of female indentured labor. While the majority of indentured laborers were male, a significant number of them were female. Because of the extremely skewed gender distribution, however, women were subject not only to exploitative labor practices but also to sexual advances made by other indentured laborers and estate overseers. Labeling the women "promiscuous" and "immoral" was a convenient way for the colonial authorities to skirt the problems posed by the exploitative practices of indentured labor.[119] But because they were labeled as such, they fell beyond the representational framework of the model Indian, and the female indentured laborers are rarely mentioned in the petitions for the franchise, remaining doubly in shadow.

Unlike Gandhi's *Autobiography*, which includes a chapter-length description of his acquaintance with an indentured laborer, Balasundaram, who applied to Gandhi for help, the documents related to the franchise bill do not permit such individuation even by way of illustrating the problems faced by indentured laborers. Balasundaram is also the only laborer whose case is detailed in the Green Pamphlet although it presents the individual cases of several traders. The sole mention of Balasundaram, in fact, makes him emblematic of indentured laborers as a whole, reflecting how they evade representation otherwise. It is noteworthy that even Gandhi's retrospective references to the indentured laborers are filtered through a conjunction of character with idioms of cleanliness. Outlining how the program of satyagraha evolved in South Africa, he notes that "a satyagraha struggle is impossible without capital in the shape of character" (*Satyagraha*, 187), an observation that governs his description of the participation of Ramasundara, an indentured laborer, who in the early days of satyagraha was discovered to have been a "deserter," having abandoned his contract—a fairly common practice among laborers, given the harshness of their conditions. Of Ramasundara, Gandhi can only say, "The leaders of every clean movement are bound to see that they admit only clean fighters to it" (115). Yet, framed in and by their labor, the indentured laborers provide value, and despite his misgivings about Ramasundara, Gandhi cannot avoid mentioning him, noting that indentured laborers eventually "proved to be a most valuable acquisition to the movement . . . [and] made a large contribution towards winning the final victory" (115).

The final victory in question was the success of a mass strike that was organized as part of the satyagraha against the colonial government's repressive measures. The franchise bill eventually became law in 1896, through a clever bypassing of the Crown's caveats on the racial exclusion of its subjects. While Gandhi led the Indian contingent in continuing to oppose the legislation, in 1895 the Natal legislature proposed a bill that was aimed directly at the laborers, as it would have imposed a minimum ten-year period on indenture contracts and charged all formerly indentured laborers an annual poll tax of three pounds, should they choose to remain in the colony. Gandhi opposed the bill vehemently, arguing that it was "in direct opposition to the fundamental principles of the British Constitution."[120] The agitation against the poll tax continued for nearly two decades, gathering momentum alongside protests against fresh restrictions imposed on traders (including the Dealer's License Act) and on Indian immigration in general. During this period, Gandhi also moved from relying on petitions alone to enunciating an active program of satyagraha, wherein *satyagrahis*, generating a political force in observance of the principles of truth, love, and nonviolence, undertook measures such as courting arrest. Perhaps the most spectacular instance of satyagraha, one that for observers seemed to transform Gandhi's "elite politics" into a mass movement,[121] was the strike of 1913, which for the first time included indentured laborers. When the government reneged on its promise of repealing the poll tax, Gandhi made the objective of satyagraha the abolition of the tax, the payment of which he felt would ensure that freed laborers would waste "the best part of [their] life ... away in a state of bondage."[122] In carving out a language of freedom, however, the main constituency that this specific program of satyagraha came to depend on was the indentured laborers, but it depended on them in ways that took the conditions and operations of their labor for granted even as it sought more to protect the interests of those who had left it, the so-called free laborers.

It is impossible to describe here all the events of the strike, which started in the middle of October 1913. Its most significant feature was that several thousand—five or six thousand, in Gandhi's reckoning—indentured laborers went on strike in the mines and plantations, joining with Gandhi in a march, willing to court arrest if necessary. In *Satyagraha*, Gandhi describes the various stages of the march in some detail, including the details of their overnight camps and how much money they needed for rations. However, despite his close physical proximity with the indentured laborers, Gandhi's narration of the march does not individualize any of the indentured laborers or give them scope to emerge from an anonymous collectivity. In contrast to Gandhi's attempts to retrospectively commemorate individuals associated throughout the various stages of the proceedings, such as Daud Mahomed and Parsi Rustomji, if only to highlight their individual "merit" rather than "immortalize their names" (*Satyagraha*, 175), the sole merit of the laborers lies in the fact of their labor, the commodifying effects of which not only effaces them but also makes their refusal to work that much more potent for the purposes of Indian agitation.

By pointing out the absence in *Satyagraha* of the names of any of the individual laborers on the march, one cannot discount the possibility of an understandable oversight on Gandhi's part in recounting the details of an event ten years after it happened. But acknowledging this oversight also prompts an examination of what was deemed permissible in representing the laborers during the strike itself. In the weeks leading up to the strike, Gandhi warned the government of the "gravity of the step [Indians were] about to take," which, once taken, could make it "difficult to control the spread of the movement beyond the limits one may set."[123] Despite Gandhi's initial apprehensions about the response that the movement might provoke, given that many previous satyagrahis had demurred from undertaking to court arrest again, the agitation swelled beyond expectation, gaining momentum from the participation of indentured laborers. The swiftness with which laborers responded to the strike has not been fully ascertained or examined, the tendency being, as Swan notes, to attribute it "as an almost reflex response to the Gandhian imperative."[124] However, the fact that their presence in sheer numbers helped drive the point home to the colonial authorities is clear from the succession of telegrams Gandhi sent over the course of the strike and his march.

On October 22, 1913, he cabled G. K. Gokhale, prominent Indian reformer and activist and a mentor to Gandhi, who had visited South Africa the previous year and was keenly following the proceedings from India:

> Nearly hundred [in] gaol. Nearly two thousand labourers families indentured and free in Natal collieries on strike.[125]

On October 28, he cabled the Minister of the Interior in Natal:

> Hundreds of poor helpless and comparatively ignorant people will not listen to fancied and unfelt grievances serious in themselves, but based upon theory. I therefore appeal to minister to consider tax questions upon merits only.[126]

On November 4, he cabled Gokhale again:

> Five thousand on strike, of whom four thousand have to be fed, including three hundred women and six hundred children. Three hundred are in jail, and two hundred more have been arrested.[127]

The telegraphic format of course condenses the enormity of the strike and the immense participation it elicited into a question of numbers. But, as mentioned in the discussion about per capita income in the previous chapter, numbers also have a leveling effect in that they erase distinctions; in this case, they seem to blur the demarcations between indentured laborers and free Indians, Arab traders and coolies. They even allow for expressions of a unified national identity, as when Gandhi rhetorically asks: "Everyone has braved the rigours of weather, heat and cold and rain. To what end? For India."[128] The condensed nature of the telegrams, however, becomes metaphoric of the condensing of the laborers to numbers alone, for the unity crystallized in the numerical representation of the strike is punctured by the more extended description of its effects. The sense of urgency and success that the strike produced depended heavily on the narration of the hardships endured by the indentured laborers. "The courage that the indentured labourers have shown and the suffering they have gone through have been boundless,"[129] Gandhi notes. But when he seeks to draw public attention to those who were arrested, he focuses on the mistreatment meted out primarily to those prisoners who, despite being "men of good education," were "not given books to read" and who, despite protests, were addressed as "coolies" by the jailers.[130] Moreover, in contrast to the free or passenger Indians, such as Parsi Rustomji or P. K. Desai, who are named, the indentured laborers are mentioned on their own only in cables such as the one to Gokhale in which Gandhi notes, "we were astonished at the unlooked-for ability shown by indentured Indians without effective leadership to act with determination and discipline."[131] This is not to rest the argument on naming alone, but to point out that the prose of imperial citizenship in Natal produced a particular representational matrix: even when the laborers merit specific attention, they are always cast in doubt, suspended as they are somewhere between debit and credit, numbers and rhetoric, use value and exchange value, indenture and freedom.

The attempt to recover use value—the individual specificities of labor and, consequently, the personhood of laborers—has been posited on several fronts, namely through an attention to the material lives and cultural constructions of laboring populations.[132] In the case of imperial indentured labor, scholarship over the past decade has paved the way for such a recovery.[133] While the impetus of the argument here has been triggered by such retrievals, the analysis is also interested in a trajectory other than one of loss and recovery alone. It is invested more in the modes of retrieval that are made possible only through a discernment of the abiding irretrievability (of the laborers) that the narrative logic of citizenship relies upon, and indeed creates. By signaling how the intersecting operations of capital and citizenship combine to produce similar effects, but through contingent modes of representation, one can consider the kind of retrieval that effects, in Jean-Joseph Goux's terms, a "materialist reversal," wherein, with relation to capitalist exchange, the "value of commodities then discovers its actual material roots, since it is recognized as the representation of a *quantity of vital activity* which is 'exchanged' in the phenomenal form of commodities" (emphasis in the original).[134] What is not very clear in Goux's reference to Marx[135] is the process that instantiates this "materialist reversal." Goux ascribes it to the establishment of the exchange value itself, suggesting that it accompanies the moment of "idealist culmination."[136] The challenge, then, lies in recognizing this double moment, however briefly. If citizenship and capital are homologous to the degree that they both hinge on a certain abstraction, then it is the formulation and representative claims of citizenship that present an interpretive strategy in themselves, so that when encountering the formal abstraction of citizenship—upon reading the "citizen"—one simultaneously reads into this moment of "ideal culmination" its "materialist reversal" as well—an interpretive practice that lays bare the material components comprising/compromising the "universal." In the case of Indian claims for imperial citizenship in Natal, it is the uncertain and unclean figure of the indentured laborer that in its ubiquity continually prompts and underscores this ameliorative double movement, both away from and toward the idealist culmination. And if Gandhi's narrative strategy of focusing on the figure enables such a reading, it does so not only by insistently not excluding the laborers but by drawing attention to its continual failures to include them, by weighting the language of citizenship with its doubleness. Whether Gandhi was conscious of producing such an effect is certainly open to debate, but for someone who was cognizant and skeptical of the "truncating" and abstracting effects of citizenship,[137] his claims for imperial citizenship certainly reflect a canny adaptability to its fraught workings.

Soon after the end of the strike, in 1914, Gandhi wrote an obituary for a laborer who had participated in the march: "Hurbatsingh, an indentured Indian 70 years old, with no kith or kin, gave up his earthly life on Monday." "The whole Indian community," Gandhi writes, "mourns for him." Hurbatsingh, he continues, "who had not one relative in this wild, forbidding land has today 150,000 Indians living here as his kinsmen."[138] Apart from Balasundaram and Ramasundara mentioned earlier, Hurbatsingh may be the only laborer who merits such an extended description either in Gandhi's correspondence from that period or in *Satyagraha*. But even as Gandhi draws attention to the fact that Hurbatsingh's death merits attention because he was a satyagrahi, he also points out that Hurbatsingh was a formerly indentured laborer, one who was all the nobler because he joined the protest even though he was not liable for the poll tax. The continual marking of Hurbatsingh as an indentured laborer even though his indenture had long expired—or, conversely, the representation of indentured laborers through a formerly indentured laborer—indicates how the categories of "free" and "unfree" are muddied by the seeming indelibility of indenture. It is the mark of indenture, though, that ensures that Hurbatsingh will be embraced through a metaphor of familiality (he "has today 150,000 Indians living here as his kinsmen") that substitutes for the otherwise exclusionary potential of the claims of citizenship forwarded by Natal Indians, just as Gandhi's earlier references to the "imperial family" sought to counteract the exclusion of Indians from the ambit of imperial citizenship.[139] But the underlying grammar of the obituary Gandhi wrote also suggests that indentured labor cannot quite be accommodated even in the capacious terms of citizenship and community it alternately constitutes: "the whole Indian community" embraces an indentured laborer who was, after all, no longer indentured, and who was not even alive. In fact, living indentured laborers could hardly be admitted into the membership of one of the official Indian bodies that Gandhi helped organize, the Natal Indian Congress, whose membership fee of three pounds was incidentally the same amount that Gandhi had so vehemently deemed unreasonable in the form of the poll tax imposed on formerly indentured Indians.

Yet it was the mark of indenture that evidently provided the thrust for a collective broaching of the question of Indian status in South Africa, just as the mark of slavery was one that sustained indentured labor from an imperial perspective. As Gandhi described to a gathering in Madras in 1896: "adversity and identity of interests have united in a compact body the [South African] Indians from the three Presidencies, and they take pride in calling themselves Indians rather than Madrasees or Bengalees or Gujratees."[140] And in his attempt to forge a link between this diasporic community and the present gathering, Gandhi noted that members of the Madras audience would take interest in Natal affairs because of their own identity "as Indians."[141] They would surely understand, Gandhi said, the indignity suffered by the Natal Indians on account of being commonly labeled as "coolies," when "there is as much difference between partners of [here he referred to a prominent Natal Indian trading firm] and a 'coolie' as there is between anyone in this hall and a coolie."[142] Evidently, it is the nonidentification with the coolie, a figure who is hailed through negation, that forms the locus around which a collective identity coheres; more important, it is the nonidentifiability of the coolie that impels and sustains a political cohesiveness.[143] Not fully included or identifiable within Indian representation, yet determining its basis and contours, the thousands of Natal Indian indentured laborers stalk the Indian petitions and memoranda for citizenship, "undoing the opposition, the dialectic," as Derrida would note, between actual, effective presence and its other.[144]

Postcolonial writers and scholars, especially, have looked to the trope of spectrality as one that usefully raises, as Bishnupriya Ghosh notes, "ethical questions of exclusion and coercion,"[145] one that—by veering between presence and absence and blurring the boundaries between them—insistently questions what constitutes presence. Indeed, the exclusionary effects of liberal citizenship have haunted the literary imaginary of writers such as Mahasweta Devi, producing a subgenre of literature that Parama Roy coins "the bureaucratic gothic."[146] If the absent-presence of indentured laborers in the documents by and about Natal Indians highlights the spectral nature of citizenship, then it also draws attention to the operative logic that produces it: while the spectral is of key analytical—indeed, ethical—import, in attending to "spectral returns" alone, "the precise content of *what* is repeated may," as Martin Jay cautions, somewhat polemically, "get lost" (emphasis in the original).[147] It is worth noting that Gandhi is able to argue for Indians using the logic of the balance sheet and the rhetoric of creditworthiness because the economic credit subtended by the indentured laborers sustains and, importantly, is displaced by the traders' need for social and symbolic credit. In other words, if the indentured laborers are rendered spectral, that lays bare the continual displacement—not exclusion—that becomes indispensable to the South African Indian rhetoric of citizenship. To concede this is to consider how the indentured laborer bespeaks the doubleness of citizenship, highlighting what are its "equivocal claims to universality."[148] That the quiddity of indentured labor is absorbed or elided in the name of the "citizen" serves as an index to this equivocality, one that is otherwise reined in by the misleading possibilities and seemingly accessible requisites held out by the unfolding parameters of citizenship, be they standards of character, credit, or cleanliness. The spectral presence of the indentured laborer serves as a heuristic reminder not only of what is lost in the exclusionary process of liberal citizenship, but also of how it is lost, a line of questioning that can be equally redemptive, if not recuperative.[149]

The question of indentured labor in South Africa marked Gandhi's own foray into the political scene in India, one that has been seen to inaugurate a new phase of Indian nationalism. However, in extricating the narrative of imperial citizenship from that of Indian nationalism (a worthwhile project inasmuch as the triumphalist trajectory of the latter often subsumes the more discrepant logic of the former), I would like to point out the obvious fact that the claims of citizenship produced their own prescriptive model, and if the "ideal citizen" emerging in this chapter has been that of the bourgeois subject—particularly the law-abiding, temperate, self-made entrepreneur, given Gandhi's specific constituency—the following chapter draws attention to another aspect of nineteenth-century bourgeois subjecthood that framed claims to citizenship, one that seemed to veer away from the acquisitive capitalism of the entrepreneur: the professional.[150] When Gandhi was put on trial in Dundee on the charge of inciting indentured laborers to leave their province, he stated in his defence that he "had not gone beyond the principles and honor of the profession of which [he] was a part."[151] In light of the fact that a few years earlier, Gandhi had also published his views against professionalism (especially medicine and the law) as the product of a colonial modernity,[152] the site of professionalism draws attention to itself in terms of how it provided a vantage point for an educated colonial constituency, but also marked the limits of an imperial liberalism in ways that fomented the strongest critiques and consequent narrativizations of citizenship from and for a colonial constituency.

CHAPTER THREE

The Professional Citizen in/and the Zenana

Toward the end of her autobiographical memoir, *India Calling* (1934), Cornelia Sorabji, the first woman to study law at Oxford and the first Indian woman to become a lawyer, narrates an incident that took place at the border between the United States and Canada. On her way to address a gathering in Toronto in 1931, Sorabji was stopped by a Canadian immigration official, who refused to let her enter Canada on the ground that she did not possess the necessary visa. Upon Sorabji's remonstrance that she did not require such documentation, for she was "from British India, and [was] equally with Canadians of the British Empire,"[1] the official reportedly replied that Canada was not part of the empire. And though after some deliberation he was "willing to waive the question of Canada not being in the British Empire," he was still unwilling to let Sorabji enter Canada because, as he stated, "you are an alien and there is a law which prevents our letting you proceed" (*India Calling*, 292). The official's comment is certainly interesting, both on account of its contention about Canada's relation to the empire and in its conviction of Sorabji's purported alienness. What is even more telling, however, is Sorabji's narrative treatment of the incident: she prefaces it with the comment: "on my first visit [to Canada] an amusing thing happened" (291). A few pages later, she recounts meeting the immigration officer again on a subsequent trip to Canada, and cheerily reminding him of their previous encounter (296). While Sorabji concludes the episode at the Canadian border with the pointed remark "that was fun!" (296), the marked levity underlying the narration does only so much to cover up the glaring irony of the fact that Sorabji, who had been invited to Canada by the Canadian chapter of the Daughters of Empire, could so easily be rendered an "alien" at the imperial border. In its self-consciousness, though, this levity relays Sorabji's assuredness about her "equal" status, an assuredness that alone could afford a retelling that made the immigration officer's obduracy seem but comically myopic. It is almost as if under the retreating aegis of empire, it is Sorabji's narrative tone that seeks, if not anything else, to actualize the contours of an imperial citizenship at a time when its purported magnanimity was punctuated, more than before, by the racial and ethnic tensions generated by intra-colonial nationalisms.[2] But then, what was the basis of Sorabji's assurance of imperial citizenship, and what indeed had been the terms of her negotiation with its precepts as a female colonial subject?

Colonial Women, Female Professionalism, and the Imperial Metropolis

In addressing these questions, this chapter examines Sorabji's autobiography, *India Calling*, along with her unpublished diaries, legal reports, and correspondence with colonial authorities. It analyzes how Sorabji textualizes her status as imperial citizen by framing a narrative of professionalism through the rendition of her student years in England, her attempts to embark on a legal career in British India, and her experiences in the zenana, the interior dwelling quarters of the purdahnashin women whom she represented legally.[3] A pioneering female lawyer and a compellingly hybrid figure, who was avowedly "at home in two countries, England and India" (*India Calling*, ix), Sorabji has only now begun to attract critical attention, having remained a forgotten figure through much of India's postcolonial history. Indeed, the recent publications of new editions of *India Calling* speaks to Sorabji's increasing visibility. The terms of her recuperation, however, have been varied. Whereas in the introduction to one new edition of *India Calling*, Chandani Lokugé remarks that in certain sections of the memoir, Sorabji's "identity merges totally with that of the imperialists," in the introduction to another edition, Elleke Boehmer begins with the observation: "Cornelia Sorabji ... embodied some of the most potent contradictions of empire of her time."[4] In her examination of Sorabji's writings, Sonita Sarker notes that despite her "pro-British" credentials, Sorabji is "uncontainable [even] in obedient subjecthood to British ideology."[5] Given that Sorabji devoted her life to nation-building in India but remained loyal to the British Empire, that she was a pioneer in women's reform movements but was fiercely anti-suffragist, and that she was critical of the colonial state but also decried nationalist efforts, it is not surprising that she evades or confounds easy categorization—which may help explain her long absence from feminist, nationalist, and imperial histories.[6] In reading her life and work, in fact, Antoinette Burton usefully suggests that "analytical categories offered by either nationalist or feminist historiographies" are inadequate in understanding Sorabji,[7] a point that is reflected in Suparna Gooptu's careful biography, which provides ample consideration of how Sorabji's "political self reveals a complex and creative engagement with the process of social, cultural, and political transformations" of her time.[8] In fact, it would perhaps not be too far from the truth to surmise that if Sorabji's recalcitrance obscured her for so long, it is precisely that recalcitrance or "uncontainability" that accounts for her allure in recent scholarship: as a compellingly hybrid, transnational, even "trans-status subject,"[9] she eloquently emblematizes our literal and theoretical preoccupations with interrogating discrete frames of both critical analysis and geopolitical reference.

Even as her elusive life and career present her as a seductive case for critical study, it is worth drawing attention, however, to the ways in which Sorabji self-consciously presents herself as such: how she evades easy categorization by depicting herself as an elusive and liminal subject in a self-representation that becomes her mode of articulating citizenship in an imperial context. In other words, this chapter argues that the category of citizenship provides an alternative framework for locating the female subject in the face of overlapping nationalist, feminist, and imperial demands. While the "citizen" is by no means divorced from these frameworks—in fact is formulated through them—Sorabji's case is instructive in illuminating how a deracinated ideal of citizenship provides an important means of self-representation even as it operates, as illustrated in previous chapters, as the basis for claiming political rights. For Sorabji, who was avowedly apolitical, citizenship was not so much about claiming political rights as it was for Naoroji or Gandhi; for her, it was more about an ethos of duty and service. In fact, the conflation of citizenship with service characterized the growth of a civic sensibility in both India and England around the beginning of the twentieth century.[10] But even when the impetus to service was implicitly directed toward nation building—as was the case with Sorabji—it also provided for a self-fashioning that overstepped the increasing "nationalization" of the universal ideals of citizenship.

Thus it becomes important to highlight what has not received much attention: the idioms of Sorabji's presentation of herself as a female lawyer, her self-conscious narrativization of her professional career. Given that Sorabji devoted her whole life not only to the cause of providing legal services to Indian women, but also to *writing* about it,[11] I argue that the prodigious nature of Sorabji's writing about her work demands, despite the suggestive appeal of her multifaceted and even exorbitant biography, a closer scrutiny of the registers along which she narratively brings into existence a largely unprecedented professional career. While the import of her career as a lawyer has been taken note of—both Sarker and Burton point to the important implications of her representation of Indian women—Sorabji's narrative construction of her own professional identity and, more important, her framing of the notion of professionalism itself remain unexplored. A closer scrutiny of the narrativization of her professional career underscores the rhetorical strategies available to a colonial female professional in the late nineteenth century and the early twentieth, especially as she negotiated the demands of the colonial state and an emergent nationalist sensibility, both of which sought to harness women's work for their own purposes. This allows for a consideration of how "work," despite its evidently exploitative potential, also operates as an important "subject-constituting category" that provides women an important opportunity to negotiate their position amid networks of national, imperial, and patriarchal power.[12] In highlighting how Sorabji presents her legal career as a "calling" (hence, perhaps, the title of her memoir), the chapter foregrounds how for Sorabji, the invocation of calling does not so much convey a religious sensibility as it allows her to carve out a liminal place from which to present herself both as a professional and a citizen.

Responding to the influences of the Victorian period, which, as W. J. Reader points out, in many ways created "the professions as we know them,"[13] and belonging to a generation of women that had begun to "be professional" in India,[14] Sorabji represents "work" in ways that reveal how it instituted a differential relationship between women and the state—whether in England or in India. A reading of her experience as a female lawyer reveals how the category of work refracts and absorbs women's labor through the regularization and subordination of gender, class, or culture-specific identities. Professionalism, on the other hand, with its emphasis on expertise and an ethos of service,[15] offers the possibility, as Sorabji's writings indicate, of a more unmarked, egalitarian subject position.[16] In privileging expertise rather than the individual, professionalism in fact approximates the formless equality of liberal citizenship[17] in ways that fashion colonial claims to entitlement. Moreover, the ideal of selfless service suggested by professionalism—an ideal which, as Magali Larson points out, was insistently reiterated contra the institutionalization of professional privilege and remuneration in the industrialized stage of capitalism[18]—becomes particularly crucial for Sorabji. As the latter section of this chapter examines, it facilitates her rather self-interested representation of herself as a liminal and disembodied subject, which also becomes the only way she can claim the status of a citizen and negotiate with an imperial body politic as well as the citizenry of an emergent nationalist India, both of which defined themselves through a gendered logic.

Highly privileged as the concept of professionalism is, one is hesitant to underscore it as a mode of access to citizenship. But punctuating the narrative of professionalism with a recognition of its undeniable privilege also inaugurates the possibility of analyzing the imaginings and responsibilities that such a position demands—indeed, enables.[19] As the previous chapter pointed out, it was Gandhi's professional training and skill that provided the momentum for Indian agitation for political rights in South Africa, drawing attention, as well, to the plight of the indentured laborers. In Sorabji's case, the relationship between the professional and the "subaltern" becomes more pronounced,[20] for her articulation of a professional ideal could operate only through an inclusion of the marginalized purdahnashins who were otherwise marked as metaphoric of national imperatives and imperial duties but were hardly considered metonymic with nation or empire.[21] Key to a reading of *India Calling*, then, is an analysis of Sorabji's representation of the world of the Indian zenana, traditionally the inner dwelling quarters of women. While the zenana was a site of much interest in popular metropolitan and missionary narratives, this chapter underscores the ways in which it became crucial in liminalizing the narrative of professionalism, which had to otherwise contend with the gendered demands of both the empire and the emergent Indian nation.

Sorabji was born in 1866 in Nasik (a part of the Bombay presidency), and her biographical trajectory is marked by multiple points of affiliation. Her father, Rev. Sorabji Kharshedji, though of Zoroastrian lineage, had converted to Christianity in his youth; her mother, Franscina Sorabji, came from a tribal background and was raised as a Christian by her adoptive parents, an English army officer and his wife. While Sorabji's father worked as an agent of the Church Missionary Society in Nasik, her mother's involvement in the field of education culminated in her founding of the Victoria High School in 1876.[22] Significantly, while Sorabji points out that "there was an invisible circle drawn around [our family] ... which made it untypical of the Indian home of the period," she also notes that "from our earliest days we were also taught to call ourselves Indian" (*India Calling*, 7). Her parents' vision of India, however, emphasized a congruent relationship among its various constituencies, which, according to Sorabji, was ahead of its time. She observes: "Thus had our Parents conceived, and built upon, a unity which did not at the time exist in India: and which was also (and indeed till fifty years later) outside even the conception of the body which came, in the fulness of time, to represent Political India" (7–8). The implied disjunction between her parents' notion of India and what was to emerge from nationalist discourse speaks to the unease of the political embrace underlying the nationalist conception of "India." The tension in *India Calling*, in fact, lies in the fissures between Sorabji's imagining of India, and that of the nationalist imaginary. Her narrative is significant not only in highlighting an India-in-the-making, but also in gesturing to the implicit exclusions of what claimed to be eponymous of the nation. And it is precisely in these fissures that one can locate Sorabji's crafting of a narrative of female professionalism. Such a narrative allows a glimpse of alternative envisionings of nation—which, for Sorabji, who was to remain a staunch supporter of empire, were coterminous with and an effect of imperial citizenship, not inimical to it.

Having secured first place in the university examinations in India, Sorabji was entitled to a Government of India scholarship for pursuing higher studies in England. The scholarship, however, was denied on the ground of her being a woman, and she finally sailed for England in 1889, only after getting help from a number of English patrons and well-wishers to finance her education. Because of these previous connections, Sorabji gained easy access to the interior spaces of English life, and her reminiscences of England are tinged with a familial conviviality and an ensuing privilege. In what was to be a recurrent motif in her writing, Sorabji describes her journey to the imperial metropolis more in terms of an intimate homecoming. In *India Calling*, for instance, she remarks that the residence of Lord and Lady Hobhouse, her chief patrons, "whether in the town or country, was one of my 'English homes'" (126). In contrast to other Indians who primarily adopted the role of tourist-spectator in England,[23] Sorabji never presents herself in that way. However, even as she enjoyed a privileged status in England compared to the anonymous position occupied by most Indian travelers and students, the attention bestowed upon her spectacularized her credentials as an "Indian woman," a homogeneous construct that had sustained an imagining of Indian women as pitiable objects of metropolitan reform.[24] Thus while the label of "Indian woman" afforded metropolitan mobility and cachet, it also proved a liability, and Sorabji's stay in England veered between her attempts to negotiate her educational career and the corresponding English attempts to dictate it.

Sorabji's letters from England record how her patrons and guardians tried to influence her educational decisions. While her original plan was to study medicine, her letters show that Elizabeth Manning and Lady Hobhouse tried to convince her to pursue a career in education. Although Sorabji was not the first Indian woman to attempt to study medicine in England,[25] the notion of women—let alone Indian women—studying medicine had been a bone of contention in the decades preceding Sorabji's arrival. Although Parliament had finally passed legislation removing restrictions on medical education for women in 1876, female medical practitioners in England faced a hostile reception from the medical community and were limited in their career opportunities.[26] But the empire, especially India, promised a suitable outlet for female professionalization, as the customary seclusion of female patients from male physicians validated the demand for female doctors, thereby legitimizing the professional role of English female medical practitioners.[27] And even as English and American missionaries had been providing medical care to Indian women, the argument was forwarded that they catered only to lower-class or lower-caste Indian women. An invocation of the upper-class, higher-caste Indian woman sanctioned the opening of secular career opportunities for Englishwomen in India,[28] reflecting the uneven ways in which categories of class and caste were deployed to augment the rhetoric for English female professionalization.

Not surprisingly, Englishwomen could validate their newfound professional status most effectively by casting colonial women in a position of continual dependency or lag—hence the enduring currency of the pathetic figure of the Indian woman. But an already anglicized subject like Sorabji, who so clearly dispelled the ramifications of such a stereotype, must surely have challenged metropolitan benevolence, for not only could she not be reclaimed along predictable lines, but her very presence in England threatened to disrupt the gradualist narrative underlying Indian female proficiency, a narrative that held the highly competitive terrain of female professionalism tenuously in place. While in 1885, Lady Dufferin instituted a medical fund to provide medical aid for Indian women by supporting both the career opportunities of English female doctors in India and the training of Indian female physicians, she wrote from India to the mayor of London:

> Numbers of English lady doctors will find employment in India, as I am in hopes that posts will multiply here very much more quickly than we can find native women ready to fill them, and in fact the most sanguine of us know that it will be many years before the medical schools here can be expected to supply candidates for the larger appointments.[29]

In a letter to her parents, Sorabji records how Madeleine Shaw Lefevre, the departing principal of Somerville College (the college Sorabji was to attend in Oxford), had written to the Lady Dufferin Fund but was told by Lady Dufferin that she did "not think Indian girls ought to study out of their country, as the Grant Medical College [in India] is quite good enough for help."[30] Ironically, recipients of scholarships from the Dufferin Fund, such as Haimabati Sen, who received medical training in India, were disadvantaged in their professional advancement because of, among other reasons, the lack of a foreign degree.[31] Sorabji's benefactors' efforts to steer her away from a profession which was in the process of establishing Englishwomen as significant players in a hitherto male bastion (in contrast to the teaching profession, which had long been associated with women) needs to be contextualized, then, in light of an anxious politics of professionalization that articulated itself through a hierarchization of female subjects of empire.

Curiously enough, *India Calling* does not register any trace of Sorabji's being steered away from the study of medicine. The influencing of her career decisions by Lady Hobhouse and Elizabeth Manning finds voice only in her letters to her parents and is completely glossed over in the autobiography. In reading Sorabji's work, Burton has rightly called for a consideration of Sorabji's "archive" of writings, wherein her diaries, correspondence, and published material account for different but equally important sites of self-representation.[32] The implications of such a consideration can be extended further through an emphasis on the significant narrative disjunctions between these various sites, a feature of Sorabji's writings that has not received sufficient critical analysis but is important in pointing to the series of omissions and disavowals that evidently became the only permissible mode for narrating female professionalism. This is not to suggest that the letters written to her parents form the locus of an entirely unmediated experience; rather, I am inclined to mark the distinction between autobiographical memoirs written through protracted recollection, and letters and diaries—which, as Nancy Walker points out, in their relative immediacy "bring us closer ... to 'invisible presences' than can the autobiography or memoir."[33] The "presences" that impeded Sorabji's attempts to embark upon a professional career are indeed made "invisible" in her retelling four decades later. However, this erasure also makes visible the uncertainties clouding the professional opportunities for the female colonial subject as much as the precariousness of middle-class Englishwomen who aspired to the upper echelons of professional respectability, both of which are imbricated with the politics of empire.

Significantly, Sorabji not only eliminates any hint of her earlier medical aspirations from her autobiography, but she also situates her otherwise unexpected decision to study law within a longer and larger narrative of "imperial historicity,"[34] one that frames her as a significant player in the colonial theater of improvement. She narrates her decision to study law as an expected fruition of an imperial destiny etched in her childhood years. In *India Calling*, she mentions that she was attracted to the study of law from a very early age and recounts the case of a hapless "Guzerathi Hindu" dowager who had been cheated of her property by her manager and had come to Sorabji's mother for recourse (15). Commenting on the widow's plight, Franscina apparently said to young Cornelia: "There are many Indian women in trouble in that way. Would you like to learn how to help them?" In response to her own question, Franscina evidently suggested that her daughter should study law because, according to her, "that will show you the way to help in this kind of trouble" (17). Franscina's altruistic concern for Indian women, though eminently laudable, must also be located within the discourse of a "maternal imperialism" that reflected Englishwomen's desire to "socialize immature daughters to their adult rights and responsibilities."[35] While such a discourse obviously enabled Englishwomen to claim their own status as citizens of empire, and indeed of the English nation,[36] it provided a similar opportunity for colonial female subjects, such as the Sorabjis, to identify themselves with the imperial endeavor, rather than being identified as passive objects of imperial reform. That Sorabji was sensitive to the import of such a distinction from very early on is evident in her response to English attempts to manage her career and itinerary in England: as she noted rather irritably in a letter to her parents, "our fam.[ily] is generally helper not helped."[37] In later years, she was to elaborate more publicly upon the ramifications of that distinction by referring to the Queen's Proclamation of 1858 as one that guaranteed that "every individual was equal to every other individual, British to Indian, and Indian to Indian. Equality of opportunity was what [the Proclamation] gave to us."[38] The purported equality of opportunity allowed Sorabji to envisage an imperial citizenship that could sustain her otherwise unseemly role as a female lawyer; however, the benefits of such a citizenship could be narratively actualized only through an explicit protocol of silence that masked its otherwise discriminatory effects. For Sorabji, imperial citizenship is realized—or claimed—only through an indirect rhetoric of "maternal imperialism." While this rhetoric had been crucial to Englishwomen's efforts in consolidating an imperial status, it becomes doubly problematic for Sorabji. As someone who was hailed as an "Indian woman" in England, a figure that represented the focal point of metropolitan benevolence from which she did indeed benefit, Sorabji's taking recourse to the rhetoric of maternal imperialism rendered her narratively untenable. In presenting her as a (professional) imperial citizen, therefore, *India Calling* has to also present Sorabji as other than an Indian woman.[39]

Although *India Calling* is silent about Sorabji's earlier plans of studying medicine, it does state the many impediments she faced while studying law at Oxford. While pointing out the restrictions imposed on a female student of law, she repeatedly reports that, when questioned about her unusual career decision, she had only to narrate the early incident of the "Guzerathi Hindu" dowager to quell all skepticism (26). It is difficult, of course, to ascertain the credibility of the story of the "Guzerathi Hindu" widow. But if Franscina did indeed advise young Cornelia to study law, that advice would have been unprecedented in the 1870s (the date Sorabji gives for this episode), when there were no contemporary models of female lawyers, and the study of law by women was quite unheard of. Despite the relative advances made by women in the medical profession, the idea of female lawyers was still remote in the 1890s, when Sorabji undertook to study law in England. A petition by a group of women to be admitted to Lincoln's Inn had been rejected in 1873;[40] another petition to enroll a woman as a solicitor was rejected in 1876, the year when legal restrictions barring women from medical study were removed; and the proposal to provide employment to female clerks in 1883 was summarily dismissed.[41] It is beyond the scope of this chapter to comprehensively analyze the reasons for the relatively late female entry into law compared to medicine,[42] but one of the factors worth pondering is that while the idea of professionalism in general denoted an affinity with the state, that of the law in particular distinguished itself by its historical proximity to forms of political power.[43] According such proximity to women was no doubt deemed dangerous.[44] Such fears were compounded by the fact that over the years, the common argument for admission of female law students and their recognition as practitioners did increasingly rely upon their status as "equal subjects."[45] Not surprisingly, even as women began to receive legal training and engage in legal work in the closing decades of the nineteenth century, they were allowed to do so on the assumption that such work was disengaged from a professional career.[46] And while women were increasingly allowed access to legal education, professional bodies like the English Bar still prohibited female membership.[47] In fact, it could very well be argued that the reason why Sorabji's decision to study law did not cause much concern is that because she was the first woman to appear for the Bachelor of Civil Law exam in Oxford, her decision was seen as entirely idiosyncratic, and her legal study posed no threat to the professional aspirations of Englishmen, since women were called to the English Bar only after 1919. Ironically, while Sorabji was among the first women to study law in England, she could not enroll in the bar till 1923, a year after Ivy Williams had already become the first (English) woman to claim that honor.

Despite her fondness for England, Sorabji never planned to stay there after completing her education. She sailed back to India, as she writes, "at the end of my English period of training, determined to find a way of helping those whom I claimed as my portion" (*India Calling*, 55). Gaining entry to the legal profession in British India, however, was problematic because in order to practice in any High Court there, she had to be appointed as a *vakil* (attorney), and though she cleared the Ll.B. examination administered by Bombay University, her pioneering effort to be recognized as a vakil was denied on the ground that she could not "cite the precedent of a woman *vakil*" (64). As a memorandum of the Bombay High Court informed her: "The question of the admission of women as Vakils, raises, in their Lordship's opinion, the whole question of the admission of women to practice as Solicitors and Advocates of the High Court also."[48]

Yet, while the High Court deemed such a move "premature and undesirable," it was quick to recognize the value of the proposed legal services Sorabji offered. The memorandum continued:

> Their Lordships have come to the above conclusion the more regretfully, as they are well aware of and readily recognize the advantages of duly qualified women having direct access to, and taking instructions from, *pardanashin* and other women, who have at present to communicate with their legal adviser through more or less undesirable male intermediaries. Their Lordships, therefore, while they regret—their inability to admit Miss Cornelia Sorabji as a Vakil, rejoice to think there is nothing in the Rules or practice obtaining in this Presidency, to prevent her services being availed of by female litigants in the manner above indicated.[49]

If the judicial system of British India failed to acknowledge Sorabji's position as a female lawyer, it also acknowledged the value of her legal services precisely because she was a woman. In doing so, it demonstrated the gendered logic through which the modern state harnessed female professional labor only to naturalize the kind of provisional status that Sorabji was protesting against.[50] As the Law Member of the Viceroy's Council (who was also an acquaintance) wrote her: "There is much to be done: and I think *you* can do much: but I think you must do it, not as a professional or official person, but simply as a woman possessing the literary gift, and armed with a knowledge of law wh.[ich] few women have the chance of acquiring"[51] (emphasis in the original). In what was a reversal of the logic of commodification, the colonial administration and judiciary evidently sought to individualize Sorabji precisely to render her labor invisible, displacing her from the professional realm that purportedly operated otherwise. Hence the insistence, perhaps, that Sorabji present herself "not as a professional or official person." Foregrounding the official framing of Sorabji's identity as a legal practitioner is important, therefore, for it evidently institutionalized certain relations between gender, work, and empire that Sorabji sought specifically to undo.[52]

Relinquishing the possibility of gaining the requisite legal qualifications, Sorabji felt that her otherwise vulnerable status could be bolstered by campaigning for the Government of India to create the post of a female zenana official in the Court of Wards. Beginning in 1897,

Provincial Governments had passed the Court of Wards Act that enabled the government, in the event of the death of the male ruler of an estate, to take over the "management and administration of the estate of a minor heir pending majority" (*India Calling*, 18),[53] thus safeguarding the widow's interests against possible malfeasance on the part of male relatives. The act also provided for the health and education of the purdahnashin and her children, but it did not provide for a female official to supervise or represent them. It was precisely this lapse that presented an opportunity for Sorabji to offer her services, and she shrewdly pointed out that although the government had undertaken to administer the property of widowed purdahnashins, the act did nothing to facilitate access to the women, who were consequently unable to avail themselves of the act's benefits (119).

India Calling records the persistence with which Sorabji petitioned for the creation of a *permanent* post for a female zenana official. Her repeated use of words like "permanent" and "posterity" in relation to the post indicates a commitment to consolidating the position of female zenana officials in ways that exceeded the immediacy of her vested interests. However, it is significant that even while she wants the post of a female zenana official to be "officialized," she does not express too great a disconcertment at not being granted a definite position within the administrative machinery. Interestingly, and perhaps predictably, her scheme was opposed both by the government in England and colonial and native male constituencies in India, and she had to be satisfied when, in 1904, the Government of Bengal offered her the opportunity of executing her "scheme" in the Bengal provinces on a trial basis, with only a "retaining fee" (*India Calling*, 121–22). However, the autobiography does not depict Sorabji as too perturbed at receiving what she describes as but "a vague offer" (121–22). Professing a detachment from the trappings of office, she records that even if her proposal had been accepted in its entirety on a permanent basis, she herself had "thought [of] returning to [her] Native States and [her] roving *Sanad*:[54] but with a joyful heart, because now 'posterity' was provided for" [before being appointed by the colonial administration, Sorabji worked on an ad hoc basis in the princely Native states](122).

The comment in her autobiography, however, contrasts with an observation made much earlier when she was still in the process of establishing her status: "A woman doing an *untried* thing," Sorabji had written in the draft of a letter she was composing in 1899, "needs all the protection she can get from recognized authority. It was a *legal* status which I wanted: a traveling *sanda* [sic], a personal grant would not do. I must have some recognized title to work" (emphasis in the original).[55] Her comment in *India Calling* about being satisfied with only a "roving sanad" significantly reverses her earlier impetus to gain an official status and thus confirm her professional identity. This reversal is significant in that it evidences Sorabji's autobiographical refashioning of her "professional self": dependent on the colonial bureaucracy inasmuch as it afforded her the resources to implement her plans for zenana women, Sorabji narratively presents herself as more invested in officializing the post for posterity, rather than being "officialized" herself. Dissociating her professional imperative from an alignment with official colonial institutions of authority and hierarchy, she reiterates the desire for a "roving sanad," thus embracing an elusive mobility, both literally and metaphorically. The idealization of an idiom of mobility was not unusual, as the genre of travel writing had emerged by the early twentieth century as a marker of what Sidonie Smith describes as an "enabling independence" for bourgeois women. But if the idiom of mobility had gained currency because of its operation as a "sign of modernity,"[56] it is interesting that Sorabji deploys it precisely to mark its limits and fashion a new kind of professional subject, a professional citizen who bears, as will become evident, a somewhat angular relation to modernity and the modernizing state.[57] For Sorabji, mobility in fact becomes metaphoric for a professional identity that exceeds the calcifying categorizations reified by the irregular relation between work and citizenship that marked the rise of the modern professional woman both in the colony and the metropole. *India Calling* charts a professional citizenship that produces a disjunction between a professional identity and a professional "career," reflecting how the ethos of professionalism, rather than its structures (such as career and salary), provides an approximation of the abstract equality of citizenship, even though both professionalism and citizenship become inexorably particularized through calibrations of nation and empire.

That a disjunction between a professional identity and a professional career was necessary is evident from Sorabji's experiences with the colonial bureaucracy, which was not only reluctant to acknowledge her professional standing but which also tried to regularize her subject position through its particular recognition (or lack thereof) of her work.[58]

Despite the fact that by 1914 Sorabji was entrusted, by her own calculations, with the charge of 146 women and 132 children, a responsibility which required her to travel over an area of 255,648 square miles, she was still "degraded," as she points out, to a "second class label, in a position which at present connotes nothing in the way of position."[59] While the thrust of Sorabji's correspondence with the government was largely to protest her temporary status, in referring to the "second class label," she is also referring to the distinction made between government officers belonging to the Imperial Service and those belonging to the Provincial Service. Officers belonging to the Imperial Service were recruited in England by the Secretary of State, possessed English training and qualifications, and, as stated by Sorabji, enjoyed a "higher status."[60] The officers in the Provincial Service, on the other hand, were mostly Indians who were recruited in India by the local government and enjoyed lesser dignity of office as compared to their imperial brethren. Despite being trained and recruited in England in 1904, Sorabji was denied entry to the Imperial Service because, as she was told by the Secretary of State in 1913, "it [was] unnecessary and undesirable to make this concession to Indians in any case except where they serve side by side with Europeans in the same Department."[61] Because Sorabji did not work in any recognizable government department, she was denied this "higher status." However, as she argued in her letter to the government, "the higher Service would, as I have said, not be a concession, but a most natural consequence of my appointment from England, whether I were English or Indian."[62]

As a consequence of her disputed status vis-à-vis the Imperial Service and Provincial Service, Sorabji was involved in an ongoing and sometimes bitter wrangle about the difference in benefits between the two governmental cadres. Besides salary and pension, points of particular concern were whether Sorabji should be subject to the European Service Leave Rules or the Indian Service Leave Rules. As an official dispatch from the Bengal government pointed out on her behalf, the European Service Leave Rules befitted Sorabji more since she "was educated in England, visits England whenever she can obtain leave, and it is her intention to retire to England on the completion of her service."[63] While there was an implicit understanding in metropolitan quarters that Sorabji's usefulness could be attributed primarily to her anglicized upbringing and English training, the India Office in London made it clear that she would not be granted the benefit of European Service

Leave Rules. Ironically, this was an exclusion functioning more at a symbolic level, for the same directive gave her permission to take a furlough at an earlier date—even earlier than she could have hoped for if she had been considered eligible for European Service Leave Rules.[64]

While Sorabji's symbolic exclusion can be read in terms of its obvious racist undertone, it is significant that the grammar of racial discrimination was formulated at the intersection of her gender and official status, which conjoined to render her an anomaly within the official framework of empire. Not only was Sorabji not admitted into the Imperial Service despite possessing the requisite qualifications, but at times she was not deemed eligible for the Provincial Service either. Pointing out her inaccommodability within the bureaucratic structure altogether, the secretary of the Board of Revenue, Bengal, wrote her: "As the post held by you does not belong to any recognized service, it cannot be classified as either Provincial or Imperial. It is a special post for which special terms personal to you have been sanctioned by the Secretary of State."[65] The idea of a "special post" created by the Secretary of State on terms "personal" to Sorabji marks, in its condescending rhetoric, the inadmissibility of her official standing. While the idea of a "special post" reflects, as we have seen earlier, the double-handed way in which female professional labor was capitalized upon by the state, it also shows how the colonial bureaucracy used the vector of work to normalize a certain congruity between gender and citizenship. If Sorabji's position in the government was proof of her rights as a citizen of empire, at least as Indians framed imperial citizenship, then it is also through her perceived entitlements as imperial citizen that Sorabji, as an anglicized "Indian woman" doing a so-called "man's job" for the British government, is monitored (and dismissed) in her irregularity as "special."

Not surprisingly, then, *India Calling* constitutes a forum that not only acknowledges the significance of Sorabji's work, but does so in a way that does not necessarily have to produce a congruent subject position. Interestingly, rather than recording her prolonged negotiations with the government over her office, salary, pension, and other benefits—what came to be recognized as markers of a professional career—her autobiography completely erases the tedium of that very voluminous correspondence. Providing only a hint of her protracted and unsuccessful negotiations with the government, Sorabji dismisses it as a "silly matter," immediately reiterating that "nothing could mar the joy one had in the work itself" (*India Calling*, 181). One wonders, of course, if this rejection of an official status was the only way she could present her professional self, much like the way in which in an earlier era, Victorian women could foray into increasingly professionalized domains under the guise of philanthropy.[66] But this disavowal also enables a different mode for articulating Sorabji's professional identity. By wrenching her role from the contingencies of official approval, *India Calling* privileges instead a validation from the interior spaces of the zenana. In fact, it is the zenana that provides the possibilities, more than that offered by official discourse, for acknowledging Sorabji's professional worth—indeed, for her to present herself as an autonomous professional citizen.[67]

Although it is inevitable that Sorabji should choose the site of autobiography as one of self-legitimation, *India Calling* reads, quite contrarily, as a string of anecdotes about her purdahnashin clients, so much so that one hardly encounters Sorabji. Unlike the autobiographic accounts of other women who embarked upon public or professional lives from the mid-nineteenth century onward, Sorabji does not spend any time accounting for her entry into the "male public sphere," or in accommodating her "female domestic role" with the demands of her professional life.[68] And apart from the early section that recounts her early years with her family, her autobiography bears no trace of any affective relationship with kith and kin over the years, though she did maintain strong family ties throughout her life (she never married, though). Dipesh Chakrabarty observes that while there has been a proliferation of autobiographical accounts in India since the mid-nineteenth century, they have failed to reveal an "endlessly interiorized subject," for the accounts have been remarkably "public," when written by men, or immerse themselves in familial details, when written by women.[69] Sorabji's autobiography, though similarly refusing to offer any interiorized emotional self, does not, however, adhere to the recognizably gendered attributes postulated by Chakrabarty. Not only does Sorabji not write about her familial self, but she situates her "public" professional life within the privatized spaces of the zenana, blurring the hegemonic implications of a spatialized gender ideology. *India Calling* seeks, then, to construct a narrative self that is not specifically gendered, even though Sorabji was allowed to enter the zenana because she was a woman.

Such a narrative construction is made possible, though, through her writing of *India Calling* as a memoir. Deflecting attention from the self, the memoir as a form of self-writing[70] had emerged as a popular autobiographic mode among Victorian literary women, for it enabled them to narrate themselves through indirection.[71] Sorabji's retrospective deployment of this specific genre is understandable in that the memoir had proved immensely popular, for by putting more emphasis on the contexts of the writer's experience, it offered an insider's glimpse into hitherto unknown areas of experience.[72] Sorabji, who had long been writing for a late Victorian and Edwardian audience, was perhaps only too aware of popular reading tastes, a consideration her English editors also made sure she never lost sight of. The decision to write *India Calling* as a memoir in the 1930s was in fact highly strategic: it catered to the curiosity of an English metropolitan audience whose interest in the zenana had been piqued by the fact that the zenana had emerged as a catch phrase for reform, attracting the attention of imperial, nationalist, and feminist reformers alike.[73] Foregrounding the zenana would also have played a double role in that while as a narrator, Sorabji could assert her position in the zenana, her unnamed presence there would have suspended unseemly questions about her professional position. That this endeavor was both quite successful and necessary is evident from the fact that an English acquaintance, who had supposedly read *India Calling*, upon meeting Sorabji asked, in a rather disbelieving tone, "Are you a lawyer?"[74]

Liminalizing Citizenship

The zenana emerges as the only site that accepts, produces, and indeed demands a subject position that is not delineated by models of female identity coterminous with the production of imperial and nationalist modernities. In her role as Lady Legal Adviser to the Court of Wards, Sorabji adduces a mobility that becomes most valuable to the zenana women, but that would otherwise have been implausible within the restrictive tenets of domesticity, the other face of both colonial and nationalist modernities.[75] As she can remark of herself in *India Calling*, "I knew of no European or Indian woman, at that time, whom I could ask to adopt the life which I was living" (*India Calling*, 118). The comment of course reveals her attempt to reiterate her indispensability, an attempt that is understandable in light of her negotiations with colonial bureaucracy; it also reflects the identity she was invested in creating. Her description of how she was received by the families she dealt with presents her as an amorphous figure exceeding the known codes of religious, ethnic, or gender identities. As she is careful to report, an outspoken purdahnashin once exclaimed to her: "You are either mad or a *puja-in* [a religious woman], or why should you live like a man or a tiger, eating out of the hand of none: eating only what you kill!" (157). As well as noting the purdahnashins' repeated surprise at her position as a "Lady Commissioner," she also describes the incident in which, upon asking if her intervention in a religious practice to avert ill luck would have any effect, she was dismissively told: "Oh that should not matter. Luck and ill-luck concern the Believer alone" (133). Marked more by what she is not, Sorabji attains a disembodiment that questions what, or who, she is. She recounts that her palanquin bearers chant: "She spoke like the *Burra Lat Sahib* (Viceroy) . . . *And* [the guards] *obeyed*. Who can she be? . . . She wears garments of silk, but . . . eats only one bread a day," adding the refrain, "Who *can* she be?" (115; emphasis in the original). *India Calling* thematizes this rhetorical question, which, in its ritual insistence throughout the narrative, disembodies Sorabji in a way that mutes the question of particularity and renders her liminal—inasmuch as liminality serves, always, to test "the boundaries of our vital taxonomies."[76] Yet it is this disembodied liminality that endears Sorabji to the purdahnashins, who hail her as a guarantor of unbiased judgment and impartiality, the mark of a true professional. The zenana stories that constitute the bulk of *India Calling* relate her preeminence to her professional authority, skill, and expertise, all of which allow her to be Indian and English, and a woman, yet one who performs a "man's job." She can be all of these, or—given the narrative thrust of the zenana narratives—none. If the "liminar," as Victor Turner describes it, "is structurally or physically invisible in terms of his culture's standard definitions and classifications,"[77] then the unique effect that *India Calling* produces is that it liminalizes Sorabji by rendering her "invisible" in terms of identifiable categories, the ideal, indeed, of the abstract, universal citizen-subject that the liberal rhetoric of both nation and empire endorsed, but failed to actualize. Tellingly, even as she takes her place as citizen by deflecting the particularizing effects of the colonial regime, Sorabji's representation of the purdahnashin women hinges, nonetheless, on reifying such particularities.

If literalizing an abstract citizenship provides the most feasible option for Sorabji to announce her professionalism (and vice versa), then such a framework informs Sorabji's narration of the zenana women in ways that are problematic. The purdahnashin inhabitants of the zenana had been the focus of much narrative speculation over the course of the nineteenth century. Female travelers like Fanny Parks and Emily Eden[78] had offered tantalizing details of the seemingly enigmatic lives of these women, but Inderpal Grewal makes the important point that, in contrast to the description of the Oriental harem, where the women were seen as "promiscuous and duplicitous," the residents of the Indian zenana were seen "as passive and exploited as well as duplicitous."[79] With the advent of various missionary societies that took up the task of zenana education,[80] the zenana was subject to a similar depiction in missionary narratives as well. Because the missionary endeavors shared the belief with other secular reformers that the key to Indian reform lay in the reform of the woman at home, missionary efforts had to compete with others in staking their claims to the zenana. In claiming their territory, the missionary narratives about the zenana naturally concerned themselves with the importance of the religious work performed by the missions, so that phrases like "the door of the zenana opened and brought in the message of God"[81] provided a common narrative trajectory. Moreover, accounts like these seem more invested in individuating the tireless missionaries and their valiant labor, with the result that the Indian women feature almost as incidental objects of reform, coming into their own only when they accept the dispensation of Christianity. For instance, Mary Warburton Booth, affiliated with the Zenana Bible and Medical Mission, describes the transformation of a young girl she had been tending over the course of a few years: "There was nothing about her that told of her past; all the boldness had disappeared, for Lotus had grown into a beautiful Christian girl. She had once printed on a scrap of paper her own glad message, 'I will give my "hole" hart to God for ever,' and He Who understood all she meant, accepted her gift, and changed her altogether."[82]

Predictably, religion emerged as the main node of contact and narration of most missionary accounts of the zenana. Even in the writings of S. Armstrong-Hopkins, M.D., a female "medical missionary," the professional aspect of the encounter with zenana women is relegated to statements such as "Medicine and surgery and all that the English government can accomplish by establishing great hospitals throughout India are of comparatively little avail, and cannot fully meet the needs of these people ... I am glad to add that there is one remedy—one remedy—and only one. It is the blessed Gospel of Jesus Christ, and *it is sufficient*"[83] (emphasis in the original). However, although even this narrative tends, like the others, to describe the zenana women in terms of generalized, undifferentiated "types," the rendition of the author's official visits to the zenana in her capacity as a doctor (as when she visits the zenana of the Nawab of Hyderabad) yields an account that, perforce, presents her female patients as individuals. It is in this respect that *India Calling* distinguishes itself as a zenana narrative, for in emphasizing Sorabji's professional role above all others, it focuses solely on individuating the zenana women and their legal problems (thereby deflecting narrative attention from Sorabji as well). And in contrast to most zenana narratives, which alternate between horror at the abjection of the zenana women and a voyeuristic pleasure in their purported exoticism—the actual visit to the zenana is always held up as a much-awaited occasion—*India Calling* adopts a far more matter-of-fact approach to the zenana. To be sure, Sorabji often situates the zenana in the realm of the fantastic, especially when she highlights the peculiarity of her assignments, as when she had to fabricate a "kidnapping," legally represent an elephant, or rescue a princess from a fort while eluding bandits. Despite the high anecdotal value of her zenana narratives, though, Sorabji's repeated visits to the zenana (almost the entire narrative consists of those visits) render the zenana altogether too familiar. In contrast to other zenana narratives, in which the rare visit to the zenana is preceded by considerable narrative build-up, Sorabji even begins one zenana account with this prosaic opening: "And so I found myself inside the Zenana on a day when the Mother-in-law was on pilgrimage" (*India Calling*, 83). Moreover, even as she embarks on the litany of her zenana cases with an obligatory ethnographic overview of the details of the purdahnashins' daily lives—where they sleep, how they bathe, what jewelry they wear—*India Calling*'s narrative energies lie not so much in providing (voyeuristic) quotidian details about the zenana as in establishing, very quickly, the professional context of the narrative, which is more intent on highlighting the legal complexities of each case. As if to dispel any anticipations that her ethnographic overture may have produced, Sorabji follows her initial description of the purdahnashins by emphasizing that "it should be said at the outset that my women *clients* were widows" (78; emphasis added). And just a few pages later, she draws attention to her position as a lawyer in the zenana, the only opportunity she has to do so (82).

Since the zenana narratives serve to establish Sorabji's professional identity, they also provide an alternative framework for narrating the zenana women. Rather than typifying them in their abjection—Booth describes them moving about "as in a cage"[84]—Sorabji depicts them as rights-bearing subjects, noting that the purdahnashins were "still outside their rights" (*India Calling*, 192). Because the effort to give them access to their legal rights provides the fulcrum for Sorabji's professional narrative, it also provides the filter for representing the zenana women as "legal subjects." In addition to pointing out that Hindu women were guaranteed more rights than married Englishwomen prior to the Married Women's Property Act of 1882 (85), Sorabji highlights instances in which one zenana woman chose to defend herself in court (168), and another decided to buy out her incompetent husband's shares in the property (184). In recounting the case of a purdahnashin whose petition to secure the release of her estate from the Court of Wards so that she could manage it herself was refused, Sorabji points out the purdahnashin's remarkable familiarity with the legal process as it was manifested in the "mock legal games" she loved to play (59). Admittedly, none of these instances can be unqualifiedly hailed as marking the purdahnashins' exercising of their agency as legal subjects, least of all because Sorabji does not provide sufficient details about the contours and considerations affecting their decision making. Moreover, in all of this, Sorabji is undoubtedly the figure of authority in the zenana, and one cannot escape the patronizing tone marking her dealings with the purdahnashins: she refers to them as the "little widows," or "my bohurani." In narrating them through a legal register, though, Sorabji situates them within the narrative of law and history, rather than reifying their status as passive, ignorant beings dwelling in premodern, ahistorical splendor or wretchedness. As she wrote in her annual official report to the government: "If we can awake in [the purdahnashins] civic and national consciousness, if we can educate them to the service of their dependents, their district, their country . . . the Government will be leaving securities and safeguards in the wake of its new liberties and charters of self-rule."[85]

However, even as the narrative of law inscribes the widowed purdahnashins as modern subjects, it simultaneously underscores their dependence on the colonial state. In the absence of their husbands, it was the law or the colonial state that acquired the role of "surrogate husband," emphasizing its preeminence through a language of protection and control, the basic premise of the Court of Wards Act.[86] It is worth noting that while in her official reports to the government, Sorabji cannot but present herself as the emissary of the state, in *India Calling* she self-consciously distances herself from that role, presenting herself more as a disinterested mediator. But this is a disavowal operating again through avowed silence, as when she expresses her displeasure with the government's ruling on a case by noting, "I tell this story without comment" (*India Calling*, 213). However, even as Sorabji's narrative silence enables her to claim and disclaim the delimitations of imperial citizenship at strategic moments, she both speaks of and for the purdahnashins in ways that crystallize their dependence on the colonial state. At a highly charged historical moment, when colonial and nationalist modernities were battling over proprietary rights to the zenana, Sorabji wrests the purdahnashins' allegiance for the colonial state. For instance, she reports that a purdahnashin client was perturbed enough to discover that an Indian had been admitted into the Executive Council to exclaim: "I won't have other Hindustanis managing my property" (164). It is difficult, of course, to ascertain the credibility of the comment, and Sorabji could very well be ventriloquizing her own antinationalist views through the purdahnashin. But the quote is ironic in reflecting how Sorabji inscribes the purdahnashins in a highly gender-inflected role, even as she, as a "professional," was trying to adjudicate the terms of her own citizenship.

While *India Calling* narrates the purdahnashins through a legal register, with varying effects, it also relies heavily on a framework of public service to insert them into an emerging citizenry. Even as the logic informing Sorabji's self-representation differs from the one underpinning her representation of the purdahnashins, she draws the purdahnashins within a common rubric as when she writes to the government:

> Secluded women all over the country and to my personal knowledge all over Bengal, Behar, Orissa and Assam are constantly serving public needs, as owners of property, roads, bridges, hospitals, schools, public parks . . . Women pay taxes and take their share in the duties of Citizens: and more than their share in the relief of common ills, [and] in public services of all kinds. There are more honorary women Social Service Workers in India than men. And this must needs be so: but there are as yet in Calcutta, no public privileges to correspond,

no Libraries or Public Institutions: no Clubs especially for women, either residential for professional women like the Services Clubs or for amusement.⁸⁷

By introducing the purdahnashins as members of a civic collective in terms of their public service, Sorabji presents them in a novel light, which also speaks to the inherent exclusions of a liberal rhetoric of nationalism—or imperialism—that had failed to include them as such. But, for Sorabji, the domain of service not only presented an idiom for appropriating the claims of citizenship for those who were not even deemed subjects; it also further promised a circumvention of the delimiting qualities of state control and geopolitics, providing opportunities, as she notes, "to do what has not yet been attempted: to do what cannot be left to Government."⁸⁸

Sorabji's wariness of the "Government" did not only refer to the colonial state; rather, it was also a speculation on Indian nationalist politics that was vigorously shaping itself through an emphasis upon the realm of reform. By the 1920s, the imperative to work for women's reform constituted a key element of middle-class Indian women's domain of "work." In fact, as many as three national-level women's organizations situated women as prominent actors in the fields of Indian women's education, social status, and legal rights.⁸⁹ But the question of women's work and reform marked the imperative to an Indian modernity and was folded, as Mrinalini Sinha points out, "into a legitimate nationalist preoccupation"⁹⁰ that also perpetuated the iconicization of a modern Indian womanhood. Such an ideal often invoked the exalted image of women in India's distant Vedic past (one suffused with specifically Hindu-Aryan sensibilities), if only to sanction their entry into the contemporary realm of nationalist politics and the making of the "Indian modern."⁹¹ For Sorabji, the refraction of women's work through a nationalist framework with specific religious-cultural undertones was problematic because it seemed to detract from the purported disinterestedness of an idiom of service. As she was at pains to point out, "The essential thing was the individual Ward and her need, and one must work to that end, and that alone" (*India Calling*, 180). Not surprisingly, then, she was wary of the manner in which the question of "work," in terms of reform for and by women, had begun to be "politicized" through being implicated in a nationalist vocabulary. For her, "politics" was shorthand for the Indian nationalist and feminist movements that were both gaining momentum, often in tandem. Addressing a gathering in 1937, she was to observe:

> In 1919, Indian women were just beginning to take the lead in social service to which the necessities of the War had introduced us. And we were full of hope for the future ... In a moment, as it were, not only these workers but most professional women of Hindu origin were swept into aggressive politics. The destruction caused by these women—in conjunction with those who exploited them in the name of a perverted patriotism—was staggering: and what hit us hardest, was the depletion of our little band of workers.[92]

Her skepticism about an incipient Indian feminist agenda was marked by a similar disapproval of what seemed to her a distraction from substantive work.[93] Thus, despite the fact that by 1920 the idea of working toward reform for women, including working women, had galvanized large groups of middle-class Indian women to action, laying forth a definite feminist agenda, Sorabji is remarkably reticent about other women "workers." Interestingly, the only contemporary Indian woman other than the purdahnashin who is mentioned in *India Calling* is Rukhmabai,[94] whom Sorabji lauds for leading an "active professional life" while remaining "unemotional and untouched by the hysteria of politics or 'Women's rights.'" What seems most commendable about Rukhmabai is that she also managed to steer clear of jibes such as "Betrayer of your Country," which, as Sorabji points out, were "thrown at the steady workers who refused to be entangled with the moment's politics" (79). Sorabji's emphasis on "steady workers" and those who lead an "active professional life" suggests an anxiety to salvage a program of women's work not defined by the "hysteria of politics." Locating the "professional" as a refuge from the seemingly vested domain of politics also reveals a sensitivity to her own incompatibility with the precepts of a nationalist discourse that had not only informed the agenda for women's work in India, but claimed the agenda for nation-building itself. In this it is the liminal identity that Sorabji constructs through the zenana—which itself was a liminal space, caught as it was between modernity and tradition—that becomes important.

The plangency of Sorabji's emphasis on service was borne out by the tumultuous reaction to the 1927 publication of Katherine Mayo's *Mother India*. The work of an American writer, *Mother India* created a raging controversy in India, England, and the United States. By providing an account of the distressing condition of Indian women and highlighting the various ills inherent in the social and sexual practices of Indian men, Mayo had challenged the emerging Indian claim for self-rule by providing grist for the mill of imperialist propaganda.[95] Incidentally, Mayo quoted at some length from accounts of the purdahnashins by Sorabji, whom she knew.[96] While Mona Bose, the other Indian woman quoted by Mayo, publicly distanced herself from the statements published in *Mother India*, Sorabji did not embark upon any public display of renunciation. Sorabji's only published statement on the book (to my knowledge) was in the form of a newspaper review that was markedly moderate in contrast to the highly charged repudiation of Mayo's work in the Indian press. But Sorabji's refusal to denounce Mayo in the storm of criticism provoked by *Mother India* does not mean that she was entirely in consonance with Mayo's argument. Though she shared Mayo's proimperial tenor, she did not endorse Mayo's unconditional attack on the status of Indian women. In fact, her stance in *India Calling* suggests a more sympathetic approach to the purdahnashins' proclivity for traditional customs, one that was also appreciative, as described earlier, of the allowances enjoyed by Hindu women with regard to property rights and maintenance (*India Calling*, 84). Also, Sorabji's *Between the Twilights*, which Mayo quotes in her book, is considerably more nuanced in its approach to Indian conjugality. Mayo tries to bolster her argument by quoting Sorabji's description of the Indian wife: "She waits upon her husband when he feeds, silent in his presence, with downcast eyes. To look him in the face were bold indeed."[97] While Mayo ends her description there, Sorabji states just a few pages later in her own book: "I would not have you think the picture one of shadows. Often, and especially where love has entered the contract, 'tis a twilight study, softly lustrous."[98]

Moreover, while in highlighting the degradation of Indian women and the incompetence of Indians in ushering in reform, *Mother India* could easily be interpreted as presenting sufficient cause to refuse the Indian demand for self-rule, Sorabji, on the other hand, explicitly critiqued the idea of Indian self-rule but along very different lines. In contrast to Mayo, she was troubled not by the lack of reform, but the excessive reformist zeal of Indian nationalists, who, in their haste, threatened to exclude the majority of the population. Questioning the "homogeneous unity" assumed by the nationalist discourse, Sorabji's concern lay in the exclusionary nature of its agenda. Apprehensive that in its impetus toward improvement, the nationalist program was unmindful of the needs of the masses—the purdahnashins, the uneducated orthodoxy—she repeatedly argued for a more measured and varied pace of reform that would take their needs into account. As she states quite critically about the indigenous elite: "After all, the Emancipated have themselves been brought to the place where they stand, not by compulsory Legislation, but by personal conviction based on Education. Only, their progress has been rendered easy by the initial cleavage with ties of religion. Where these ties remain, is not a different rate of progression indicated?" (*India Calling*, 300). A sensitivity to the need for a different pace of progress could only be realized, Sorabji repeatedly suggested, not through the clamor for Indian self-rule, but through an acknowledgment of the benevolence of the British rule, which alone—in its relative self-assuredness—could afford a measured pace of reform.[99] Like Mayo, Sorabji effectively argued for an imperialist aegis, but from a different perspective.

While Sorabji was never implacable about the unyielding nature of the zenana, her emphasis on its very measured and gradual pace of progress also bespoke her own vulnerable status. Describing the ambivalence accompanying the fate of female doctors in British India, for instance, Sandhya Shetty articulates the terms of their dilemma with the observation that unveiling the purdahnashin for the "sake of her health," would have also eliminated the raison d'être of the female physician's professional status. Shetty asks succinctly: "was the fulfillment of the promise of visibility—[of] lifting purdah—*continually* deferred as a vital underlying principle of the profession's survival as a female domain?" (emphasis added).[100] This question echoes, perhaps, the terms of Sorabji's own predicament as Lady Legal Advisor to the Court of Wards, and its implications also ensured that her professional identity was read only in very particular ways by her contemporaries.

Sorabji's position regarding the zenana was quick to provoke the ire of Indian reformers: Kamaladevi Chattopadhyaya, prominent among female reform activists in India, wrote disparagingly that Sorabji, "the first Indian woman bar-at-law," supported "the purdah system because of her official position."[101] In fact, the space that the *Mother India* controversy had otherwise created for Indian women activists to speak for or against Indian female reform[102] effectively precluded Sorabji's views as a professional, conflating them entirely, as Chattopadhyaya's comment indicates, with her official position. It is precisely the implications of such a conflation that may have prompted Sorabji to delineate a professional identity that was severed from official moorings. But the untenability of such a proposition is evident in the fact that her position as an imperial loyalist in the employ of the government also claimed and contained her "professional departure" from an imperialist propaganda (even as it oftentimes failed to claim her). Though Sorabji had not planned it as such, her review of *Mother India* appeared in *The Englishman* within an explicitly polemical framework: the editors published her review as a counterpoint to a decidedly hostile review by an Indian sociologist which they had published two days earlier. Significantly, when reading *Mother India*, while Sorabji wrote to her English friend and confidante, Elena Rathbone, that it was "a great book truly,"[103] she also noted in her diary: "I wish I had time to write a series of sketches of Ind.[ian] Women to counteract wrong impressions."[104] Rather than privileging the veracity of one comment over the other, it is important to read the two in conjunction as an index to Sorabji's ambivalence on the issue, in which her own proprietary stance (as an Indian) toward the zenana played no small role. But the highly charged political scenario did not allow narrative space for such ambivalence: that Sorabji did not conjoin Indian female reform with a specifically nationalist cause, that she remained loyal to the imperial administration even as she critiqued the imperial assumptions about India, gave her very little position to "speak" from in the otherwise highly voluminous response that both sides generated in the controversy surrounding *Mother India*. The fact that Sorabji's relation with Mayo is riddled with a series of disjunctions between what she said about Mayo in private and what she wanted known in public[105] underlines Sorabji's highly complicated—and even impossible—position as an Indian female professional engaging in a certain kind of nation-building while remaining loyal to the British Empire (whose bureaucracy she was generally at odds with).

It is important to keep in mind that in response to *Mother India*, Indian female activists did not disagree significantly with Mayo's portrayal of the condition of Indian women. Rather, as Sinha points out in her far-reaching study of the *Mother India* controversy, Indian women "repeatedly challenged *Mayo's* right to speak for Indian womanhood even while they argued that there was an urgent need for the reform of women's position in India"[106] (emphasis in the original). And in arrogating this right for themselves, they appealed, as did Sarojini Naidu, a prominent figure of the nationalist movement, to "the glory of Indian womanhood."[107] In relating Naidu's success in mediating a position in the *Mother India* debate, in fact, Sinha describes how in the wake of the controversy, "modern" Indian women engaged in nationalist politics constructed a subject position by strategically "claim[ing] 'traditional' ideals of Indian womanhood *on behalf of the modernizing project of nationalism*" (emphasis in the original).[108] Not only did Sorabji invoke—through her support for zenana customs—traditional ideals to critique a nationalist modernity, but she herself was aloof from its highly inflected construct of the "Indian woman," which would otherwise have given her a legitimate point of entry into the field of nationalist politics that had emerged as the primary forum for addressing questions of women's reform. In noting Sorabji's exclusion from such a nationalist paradigm, I do not intend to ascribe it simply to an identity politics of essentialized subject-positions. It is not merely Sorabji's Parsee-Christian-English identity that marks her off from the nationalist narrative, for even western women like Annie Besant, Margaret Noble, Margaret Cousins, and Madeline Slade were variously, and at various points, incorporated within its folds. In fact, as Parama Roy insightfully suggests, it was the western woman who seemingly became "central to the project of imagining India/Hinduness,"[109] for it was her identity that was available, more than that of the Indian woman, "as relatively open, mobile, malleable"[110] for the purposes of nationalist discourse. Not only was Sorabji not western enough for such purposes, but unlike the aforementioned women, she was far too uninterested in imbibing ideals of traditional (identifiably Hindu) Indianness to be interpellated by the nationalist agenda.

The only position from which Sorabji did speak during the *Mother India* controversy, however, was that of the professional citizen. In her two-part review of *Mother India*, Sorabji had reiterated her emphasis on social service and proposed a Social Service Institute that would rectify the unfortunate turn of events by bringing together Indian and English women under a common umbrella.[111] While social service had promised a new professional opportunity for women in other countries as well,[112] Sorabji's emphasis on professionalized social-service workers marked an important political intervention into an increasingly polarized and racialized political milieu.[113] Proposing a Federation of

University Women in England as early as 1919, Sorabji had suggested that a "Labour Exchange of Professional Women for India" be added to the Employment Bureau, arguing that "the chief value of such an organization is that it would sit outside all political, official, or racial Labels, [and] that it would therefore have at this critical moment, a better opportunity for service than any conceivable body of workers in England or India."[114] The controversy over *Mother India* gave her further occasion to insistently delineate and qualify the role of the professional. Emphasizing that the role of "professional social worker" would maintain the important "connecting link between Professional Women [and] Prof.[essional] Institutions" while also making them "acceptable to the masses,"[115] Sorabji pointed out how the concerns of the orthodoxy—the purdahnashins—were otherwise overlooked by self-interested professional behavior: the condescending authority of British professionals determined to accentuate the backwardness of the zenana, or the reformist zeal of their Indian counterparts, who were only too willing to override zenana customs in an eagerness to prove their competence and "enlightenment."[116] Implying that the Social Service Workers' professional identity would not rely on such vested representations, Sorabji insisted that "in addition to professional qualifications the Social Worker should be equipped with a special knowledge of these differences,"[117] claiming that the "value of such knowledge, of use *professionally*" (emphasis added) would be the "[only] means of bridging differences between the forward moving and the backward peoples."[118] The image of the professional social-service worker, one who symbolized the professional ideal of expertise and disinterestedness—hence the constant emphasis on *professional* social service—offers a "countervailing source of rhetoric and action,"[119] in contrast to the impasse that Sorabji found herself in, in the wake of *Mother India*. The emphasis on the disinterested selflessness of professional service, of course, cannot quite be detached from Sorabji's self-interest, for it allowed her a certain rhetorical immunity, giving her, indeed, a position from which to "speak." A few years later, in her published interview with Gandhi, whom she deeply disagreed with, both on the basis and the modus operandi of his nationalist politics, she began, she says, "by reminding him that he was 'my learned friend' (he was educated for the bar as I was), and suggested that during the interview we should treat one another as fellow professionals, speaking our minds without fear of offenses given or taken."[120]

And as she comments in her autobiography, quite tongue-in-cheek: "a strict adherence to social service and social reform would have saved him [Gandhi] and his country" (*India Calling*, 274).

Not surprisingly, the League of Social Service that Sorabji did eventually form, with members in both India and England, finds prominent mention in *India Calling*, even as *Mother India* does not, and Sorabji specifically emphasizes the amity effected by the league, in sharp contrast to the "politics" of the day: "A small group of friends—Parsee, Bengali, Moslem (not in purdah) accompanied us," she says, "and helped us with the demonstrations. This co-operation which took no thought of communal distinction, or of the division between Orthodox and Progressive—was one of the happiest accidents of our adventure" (*India Calling*, 241). The collectivity that the League of Social Service embodied was obviously important as a blueprint for an independent India, whose imminence, Sorabji, despite her staunch imperial sentiments, was not one to deny. After the publication of *India Calling*, she noted: "We are now conscious of ourselves but only as a racial, religious, or communal unit. The work which lies bef.[ore] Us is to become conscious as *a social and civic unit*. No constitution however perfect could galvanize us into that consciousness"[121] (emphasis in the original). It was the deracinating and selfless ideal of professionalism that provided such a "constitution," distilling as it did an idiom of disembodied service through which alone, as Sorabji had commented, "Self-consciousness was slain and one realized the possibilities of the Body Corporate, if only the Body would allow allegiance to master rivalry and personal ambition."[122]

By extracting ideals of selfless service—the hallmark of professionalism—from corollary concerns of career gains and ambition, however, Sorabji situates the domain of professionalism outside the realm of capital, obviating its necessarily differentiating and deflecting effects.[123] In such a formulation, the "professional citizen" becomes the ideal citizen inasmuch as the ideal of service alone makes possible a cohesive body politic, "the body corporate." As Sorabji wrote in her review of *Mother India*, it was only a spirit of sacrifice and service that "will help and unite and energize" those in India, and as she asked, somewhat rhetorically: "who will lay aside ambition and go forth to the villages?"[124] Her concerns about a cohesive body politic were in fact historically quite resonant, for the question of the franchise, the most overt signification of citizenship, was being debated and decided along various separatist lines in a British India clamoring for its political rights. Sorabji's concern, in fact, seemed to parallel that of the Indian women activists, who in demanding women's right to vote had also vociferously denounced a communally split electorate, or an electorate divided against itself.[125] But Sorabji diverged from them on the question of the franchise altogether, deeming it a premature and distracting objective, given the enormity of work that still lay ahead. However, she echoed their concern, albeit differently, by pointing out during a lecture tour in the United States that the challenge of the hour in India was "to adjust the problem of representation in a common council of the realm," a task made doubly difficult by the absence of what she termed a "neutral national."[126]

The "neutral national" who was sensitive to the clamor of the masses would of course be the informed yet disinterested professional citizen, like Sorabji, but it is noteworthy that the niche for the professional citizen could be carved out only by highlighting the backwardness and orthodoxy of the masses, and the consequent need for a measured pace of reform. In this, Sorabji's tactical maneuver parallels that of the English female professionals or that of the colonial state, respectively. However, the nonparallel nature of her relation with both these constituencies ensures that her narrative of professionalism situates not just the masses, but itself as well, in an uneven relation with modernity. Significantly, *India Calling*, whose narrative energy is geared around upholding the letter of the law, ends by upholding another kind of law altogether. After carefully delineating her professional status in and through the zenana, Sorabji chooses to end her narrative with the following comment: "But there is no re-weaving it now. The Master Weaver, so I have heard, passes His hand over that which we bring Him—our poor workmanship—as we stumble into His presence in the dawn hour of the new day" (*India Calling*, 301). These final comments reify the sense of a calling that is not only explicit in the title of the memoir but that pervades the entire narrative, enabling it to seemingly transcend the quotidian rhetoric of nation or empire. In fact, Sorabji's recasting of her work as a calling shapes her professional identity by strategically divorcing it, as noted earlier, from a professional career. If the evocation of a calling plays a crucial role in reconnecting individuals with otherwise estranging identities of class and nation in times of crisis, when the "concept of work [itself] was losing meaning,"[127] then *India Calling*'s couching of Sorabji's professional role in terms of a calling invokes the premodern association of professionalism with a religious authority,[128] endowing it with an overriding spiritual significance. And while such an association is often seen to discredit more contemporary ideas of professionalism,[129] it becomes the idiom most available to mediate Sorabji's professional identity with the rhetoric of colonial and nationalist modernity. Ironically, however, while the idealized rhetoric of professional service forwarded by *India Calling* disallows Sorabji from mentioning the "ignoble" details of salary, pension, etc.—a barrister's fee, after all was supposed to be in the form of an honorarium[130]—immediately after the publication of *India Calling*, she notes in her diary the "unexpected additions" to her expenses that demanded that she start writing a "new series of sketches" as soon as she could.[131]

In fact, even as *India Calling* explicitly detaches the professional citizen from considerations of a career, the ineluctability of the monetary and institutional implications of a career are foregrounded, nonetheless, by the appendix, which lists Indian women who had received legal training by 1934, carefully noting those with just a university degree in law and those actually on the rolls, and taking care to point out how many were enrolled as barristers, pleaders, and vakils. Titled "Women in India Holding Legal Qualifications," with Sorabji's name heading the list, *India Calling*'s appendix undoes the disembodying idiom of selfless service that produces Sorabji as the professional citizen. While the text of *India Calling* insistently suggests that such citizenship can be approximated only through a narrative disembodiment, Sorabji's considerable deliberation in tabulating the female lawyers,[132] and her doing so but in the form of an appendix, serves as a continual reminder of what has to be disembodied, of what is continually elided. Sorabji emerges as but a liminal figure through this transaction, but there is no pathos to that liminality; rather, it is quite self-consciously invoked by the deliberately supplemental nature of the appendix. In fact, by invoking the premodern in the name of the modern; emphasizing a professional identity as the means to a career that cannot be named; highlighting her presence in the zenana, but only in its abstraction; writing an autobiography that she hardly inhabits; and locating herself in both the nation and empire, yet being marked by neither, Sorabji presents herself as irrevocably liminal. It is precisely the tension invoked by this liminality, though, that becomes a mode of adjudication, of citizenship.

By espousing the liminal in a colonial/national context, *India Calling* presents it as a viable mode for rescripting the political realities of imperial citizenship. And for Sorabji, the very textuality of the liminal makes it an important tool of negotiation. It is noteworthy that she writes prodigiously not only about the liminal world of the zenana, but, more important, about her professional service in it. If *India Calling* reconstellates the idiom of professional service only to render it and the professional liminal, then it functions as a passport of sorts for Sorabji—even though, historically, the category of imperial citizenship was becoming increasingly problematic. Though the Canadian immigration officer may have been reluctant to let Sorabji into Canada, the Montreal *Gazette* pronounced that "in *India Calling*, Miss Cornelia Sorabji has written the book on India for which we were all waiting,"[133] with the *National Review* of London noting appreciatively that "every British elector should read it."[134] (Incidentally, Sorabji was eventually let into Canada despite the officer's wrangling and had no problems entering it a year later.) In other words, Sorabji can rewrite herself as imperial citizen, precisely by writing. But the narrative silences of *India Calling*—omissions that can be discerned only through the filter of autobiography that heightens expectations of a "chronological unfolding of a life"[135]—also enact a liminal relation between representation and reality, drawing attention to the resonant particularities and limitations of Sorabji's position, if only through the disembodiment she consciously invokes. But the tension invoked by this liminality becomes, as mentioned earlier, another mode of articulating imperial citizenship, highlighting the necessarily contingent relation not only between colony and metropole, and narrative and silence, but also between the universal and the particular, the abstract and the embodied.[136] Although such a representation does not necessarily resolve the paradoxes of the category of citizenship, it renders it more supple by highlighting the liminal relation between its constitutive categories—a relation always in danger, like liminality itself, of being absorbed or normalized.[137]

CHAPTER FOUR

Bureaucratic Modernity, the Indian Civil Service, and Grammars of Nationalism

Often glorified as consisting of "the most powerful officials in the empire,"[1] the Indian Civil Service (ICS) formed the administrative backbone of the British Empire in India. Given the enormous political authority wielded by the ICS in the absence of any representative institutions, educated Indians eyed a position in it not only as a sign of gainful employment but as fruition of their claims to political rights. In 1868, Naoroji had pointed out that if British rule was to maintain its credibility, and if royal proclamations and parliamentary acts were not to be reduced to "a dead letter and a mockery," then it was imperative for entrance examinations for the ICS to be held simultaneously in India and England.[2] Naoroji's seemingly unexceptional demand for simultaneous examinations addressed what was actually an insidious clause that effectively excluded Indians from the Civil Service. Because entrance examinations were held only in England, and because it was difficult and expensive for applicants to travel to England only for the exam (in addition, many Indians faced religious injunctions against overseas travel), the Indian Civil Service remained exclusively British for much of the nineteenth century.

Consequently, admission into the ICS formed the basis of an emergent political consciousness, modeling a rhetoric of equality that allowed Indians to stage themselves as citizens. As Surendranath Banerjea, one of the first Indians to be admitted into the ICS, argued:

> What becomes of the Proclamation, what becomes of the generous words of our Sovereign, of the beneficient interpretation put upon them by her Viceroy, when viewed in the light of the proceedings of the Government of India? To tell the people of India that they are freely entitled to fill every office in the gift of the Crown, and that merit is to be the sole qualification, and then to point out to them that London is the only place, a place ten thousand miles distant, where

these examinations are to be held, is to be guilty, of impudent and impertinent hypocrisy.³

The call for simultaneous examinations in fact featured prominently among the demands made by the Indian National Congress, founded in 1885.⁴ But the Congress's demands for Indian admission into the ICS were to recede in significance after a few decades, and demands for admission into the administrative and legislative bodies of government were eventually deemed "moderate" by a newer generation of nationalist leaders, who were more strident in their demand fo complete political autonomy.⁵ In fact, what came to be termed Moderate nationalism in the first decade of the twentieth century has attracted relatively little historical attention in ways that seem to indicate, as has been noted, "that nothing important was happening" in the period leading up to Gandhi's arrival on the national scene in 1916.⁶ However, recent studies, like the one by Carey Watt, shed light on various modes of "nation-building" that were under way in the period termed Moderate nationalism. Watt emphasizes, for instance, that the Moderates, in addition to clamoring for admission into legislative and administrative bodies, also directed their efforts to "organized and institutionalized social service work" that drew in larger sections of the populace well before Gandhi's appearance on the national scene,⁷ the moment that is otherwise singularized as marking the beginning of a mass nationalist movement.

The Competition-Civilian and the "Competitionwallah"

This chapter examines the Indian Civil Service, focusing on the ways in which the Indian demand for admission into the ICS provided the grounds for formulating claims of formal equality as well as a civic self-fashioning. In highlighting what was termed a "Moderate" demand, however, my intent is not to provide an account of Moderate activities, nor is it to argue for Moderate preeminence. Rather, in reading *A Nation in Making* (1925), the autobiography of Surendranath Banerjea, prominent among Moderate leaders, I wish to examine the gendered idioms through which a "moderate" politics gets labeled as such. I also wish to trace the implications of the fact that modes of citizenship formulated during the "seed-time" of Indian nationalism—as characterized by the ICS agitation—also get elided by the overarching narrative of that nationalism. Given that the Moderate moment was marked, as Sanjay Seth has noted, in terms of its "incompleteness,"[8] this chapter reads *A Nation in Making* by way of configuring what gets constituted as "incomplete" in the nationalist narrative. It draws attention to how the nuances of Banerjea's narrative etch the discrepant relation between the citizen and the nation in ways that register the harnessing of the citizen by particular histories of nationhood.

The first section of the chapter draws attention to a key site of Moderate concern, the ICS, which provided the ground for thinking about the nation and its citizenry in ways that preceded and exceeded what was eventually constellated by Indian nationalist discourse. And it is precisely the fading of the ICS question that is of interest in the second section of the chapter, if only to arrest the idioms and impulses of citizenship that the ICS generated, before such notions lapsed into the self-evident trajectory of nationalism that contours the national field of affect as we understand it today.

The first section of this chapter begins with the Indian Civil Service as it was being reimagined in England in the mid-nineteenth century, not least because the ICS provided one of the early—and contested—sites for a review of liberal English notions of citizenship as well. Such a focus locates the ICS not just in terms of its unresponsiveness to demands for Indian admission—often the lens through which it is read—but also in terms of the problems assailing its very structure in mid-nineteenth century England, a fact that is ironed over by accounts that view the colonial state as a monolith if only to give urgency to ideas of native protest and resistance. The intent here is certainly not to discount that urgency. But suspending the antagonistic framework in which the ICS and the question of Indian claims are usually cast opens up, I suggest, a wider consideration of notions of modernity, citizenship, nationalism, and masculinity as they were grappled with in *both* India and England, in ways that usefully question Victorian claims to a modernizing state as well as the Indian nationalist articulations in response to it.

A study of the problems besetting the ICS in the mid-nineteenth century reveals the English too as but "reluctant debutantes" to a modernity that announced itself in part through an impulse toward bureaucratic reform.⁹ Naming the English "reluctant debutantes" might seem counterintuitive, for such reluctance has been mostly attributed to an emergent colonial middle class. Discussing the impetus toward educational and administrative reform in the latter decades of the nineteenth century in India—which marked the middle-class embrace of modernity in Bengal, for instance—Sumit Sarkar notes how the narrative of "bhadralok activism" was punctuated by "gaps and relapses ... doubts, [and] mordant autocritiques" that created a pause in what was otherwise a sense of "moving forward in harmony with time."¹⁰ It is this observation that frames Sarkar's insightful reading elsewhere of the curious figure of the "kalki avatar," or the compelling attributes of the barely literate priest, Ramakrishna, both of whom variously mediated ways for the late-nineteenth-century Bengali middle class to come to terms with the routinized and alienating effects of an impossible, yet inevitable, modernity.¹¹ Indeed, the unevenness of a colonial modernity can be gauged through the ensemble of gendered figures that it produced in the colonial imaginary, be it that of the feminized *grihalakshmi* (the virtuous, ideal housewife),¹² the masculinized reconstruction of the otherwise androgynous Krishna,¹³ or the childish (and womanish) Ramakrishna.¹⁴ What needs to be added to this picture, however, are the vexations attending the nineteenth-century *metropolitan* embrace of modernity, which was not only considerably dispersed in its provenance, as Ann Stoler has argued,¹⁵ but was also mediated by a proliferation of gendered tropes whose prevalence, especially in the realm of administrative rationality, remains unexamined. The gendered trope that is of interest to this study is that of the unmanly Englishman, the "competitionwallah."

In what has become axiomatic, the colonial theater was peopled mainly by "manly" Englishmen and "effeminate" natives, wherein the "unmanly" Englishman, marked in his consequent "un Englishness," was but an embarrassment, one who had to be mocked, excused, corrected, or simply wished away.¹⁶ As Mrinalini Sinha's excellent analysis of the gendered colonial dynamic referred to above also indicates, constructions of English hypermasculinity were impelled in no small measure by the anxiety of the Englishman who was unmanly.¹⁷ While such a figure serves as an implicit foil for analyses of English masculinity, this chapter focuses on the explicit crafting of such a figure, especially as he is incarnated as the "competitionwallah." A pejorative term that gained currency from the mid-nineteenth century onward, "competitionwallah" refers to the civilians (the term for ICS officers) who earned their place in the ICS by succeeding in a competitive examination process, in contrast to the earlier generation of civilians who had their paths paved through a network of patronage. Despite surmounting the rigors of examination, the competition-civilian was represented through imputations of inadequacy. Marked as ungentlemanly, physically weak, and bookish (both weak because bookish, and vice versa), the successful competition-civilian—branded as the "competitionwallah"—could not quite be accommodated within the structures of governance even though he was eminently qualified for it. In tracing the discursive figure of the competitionwallah in the archives of government reports and official correspondence—as well as literary and cultural representation, such as George Trevelyan's epistolary novel, *The Competition Wallah* (1866), and H. S. Cunningham's novel, *Chronicles of Dustypore* (1875)—I wish to focus on the competitionwallah as one exposing the problematic metropolitan dalliance with a bureaucratic modernity that revealed the limits as well as the possibilities of realizing the ideals and incentives of liberal citizenship.

While the mid-nineteenth century in India witnessed a transfer of power that marked the demise of the East India Company, the Indian Civil Service also underwent a significant overhaul in England in ways that reflected an ongoing liberal preoccupation with forms of governance. As John Stuart Mill, himself an employee of the East India Company, noted: "a government is to be judged by what it makes of the citizens, and what it does with them."[18] For Mill, a representative government was imminently preferable to a bureaucratic one in which "the work of government [is] in the hands of governors by profession; which is the essence and meaning of bureaucracy."[19] Careful not to dismiss bureaucratic governance, however, Mill hastened to add: "it is, at the same time, one of the most important ends of political institutions, to attain as many of the qualities of the one [representative government] as are consistent with the other [bureaucratic government]."[20] For Mill, a good government would try to secure "the great advantage of the conduct of affairs by skilled persons, bred to it as an intellectual profession, along with that of a general control vested in . . . by bodies representative of the entire people."[21] Good governance, in other words, called for a balance between representative democracy and a competent bureaucracy.

While the liberal dilemma of Victorian England was precisely how to maintain this balance, the purported cohabitation between these two forms of governance also meant that democratic discussions of a political nature hinged as much on matters pertaining to the expansion of the franchise as on regulating the nonelected element of government, the bureaucracy. In fact, despite his guarded rhetoric about the role of bureaucracy in government, Mill conceded: "no progress at all can be made towards obtaining a skilled democracy, unless the democracy are willing that the work which requires skill should be done by those who possess it."[22] While in a mark of what I take to be our own liberal predilection, the discussion of nineteenth-century citizenship has focused mostly on the expansion of the franchise and the efforts to produce the ideal citizen who could participate in the electoral process—both as voter and as representative—I would also like to draw, within the ambit of citizenship, the figure of the bureaucrat as well. Producing the good bureaucrat, in fact, became coincident with the pedagogic project of producing the good citizen, and—despite Victorian misgivings about the role of bureaucracy—as the protracted discussions regarding the composition of the ICS reveal, it was the ICS officer, the civilian, who in many ways emerged as the placeholder for the ideal citizen.[23]

The imperative to pay heed to the bureaucratic feature of government was evident in the *Report on the Organization of the Permanent Civil Service* (1854)—also known as the Northcote-Trevelyan Report—which made clear that "the Government of the country could not be carried on without the aid of an efficient body of permanent officers, . . . possessing sufficient independence, character, ability, and experience."[24] Emphasizing what was to be a "reciprocal relationship between selection and performance,"[25] the *Report* ushered in a rationalized mode of administration that privileged merit, competence, and efficiency, the terms of a bureaucratic modernity.[26] Because the deindividuating effect of bureaucracy makes it an easy target for revilement (as indeed it did in the nineteenth century), it is easy to lose sight of the fact that it was also the precepts of this bureaucratic modernity that provided one avenue for at least approximating ideals of liberal citizenship, inasmuch as it was a different set of criteria—"age, health, and moral fitness," rather than one's social antecedents—that was deemed to render an aspirant eligible for the responsibilities and benefits of public office. One way of ensuring such eligibility, it was felt, was by instituting competitive examinations as the means of entry into the Civil Service. The *Report*'s recommendation to do so highlights what Cathy Schuman describes as the "pedagogic economy" of the Victorian state, which in fact focused on examinations as an effective site for producing educated citizens.[27]

While the recommendation to introduce examinations was not fully implemented in all departments of the Civil Service until 1870, competitive examinations had in fact already been approved as the means of entry into the Indian Civil Service even before the publication of the *Report*, indicating how imperial exigencies heightened the imperative to nurture the civilian-citizen. As the 1854 report of a committee appointed to look into the introduction of examinations in the ICS pointed out: "Indeed, in the case of the Civil Servant of the Company a good general education is even more desirable than in the case of the English professional man; for the duties of a very young servant of the Company are more important than those which ordinarily fall to the lot of a professional man in England."[28] That the pedagogic objective of the ICS exam was to produce both the exemplary civilian and the worthy citizen is evident in the questions it was to ask candidates over the years. For instance, in an entrance examination later in the century, the English composition segment required candidates to elaborate on "the sense of honour in modern, medieval, and classical times" or to expand on "the features of the English character as shown in the contact of Englishmen, as a governing race, with a subject-race."[29]

The strategic institutionalization of English literary study over the nineteenth century and its overlap with colonial governance has been persuasively discussed in Gauri Viswanathan's splendid *Masks of Conquest*. What is of particular interest here is Viswanathan's instructive emphasis on the fact that educational measures, such as the introduction of English literary study in the colonies, emanated more from an embattled position of uncertainty on the part of the English than from what is commonly assumed as their "uncontested position of superiority and strength."[30] The ICS lends itself to a similar interpretation, in that the recommendation in 1853 of a rigorous and much-debated examination process shows that the ICS became the focus of urgent and far-ranging reform. The ICS registered the wider liberal objective to staff the public service "with a thoroughly efficient class of men."[31] However, if such a shift was to be actualized through an emphasis on the bureaucratic principles of, in Max Weber's words, "rational, technical specialisation, and training,"[32] then the fact that the ICS exam was to emphasize, following the 1854 report, a "good" but "*general*" (emphasis in the original) education—as indicated in its wide range of subjects—gives but one indication of the strained Victorian commitment to the terms of a bureaucratic modernity.[33]

However, that such a commitment was deemed necessary is evident in the discussions leading to the introduction of examinations in the ICS, well before such a system was fully implemented in all departments of the Civil Service in England. Until 1853, it was the East India Company's Court of Directors that nominated young men to what were called writerships, after which the nominees were required to pass a simple examination before embarking upon two years of training at Haileybury.[34] Not only did the apparent laxity of the Haileybury training assume almost farcical proportions,[35] but the patronage of the Court of Directors proved an embarrassment in a time of Whig Liberalism, when the emphasis was not only upon ensuring a high quality of administration, but also upon an "achieved as opposed to ascribed status."[36] That the ICS had become a feudalistic "family business," hinging on a nepotistic network of kindred ties, was undesirable. Introducing competitive examinations would, it was hoped, curtail aspersions against the credibility of public office and also mark a move toward administrative competence and efficiency, while squaring with liberal ideals.[37] As the 1854 report noted, "we think we can hardly be mistaken in believing that the introduction of that system will be an event scarcely less important to this country than to India."[38]

Despite its intent to signal a shift from inherited privilege, the introduction of entrance examinations was not egalitarian in effect. Although it intended to weed away undeserving and unproven candidates from the honors and responsibilities of the ICS, the ideal candidate it envisaged was someone who graduated with honors from Oxford or Cambridge, who in combining "character" with intelligence could alone recommend himself, it seemed, as suitable for shouldering the burden of imperial responsibility. The emphasis on "character," as mentioned in chapter 2, constituted a central aspect of Victorian political thought, and the question of the development of character went a long way in defining the role of the state.[39] However, whether character was prescriptive or descriptive and whether it was inherited or something to be acquired remained largely unresolved, in ways that reveal what can be described as "Britain's idiosyncratic modernization."[40] The uncertainty surrounding the idea of character manifested itself in ICS reforms as well. While envisioning a meritocracy, the ICS Commission was comfortable, nonetheless, in recognizing success only as defined by an Oxbridge education, inasmuch as that alone was deemed to guarantee the predisposition—character—required to pass the examination. Evidently, the examination system was intended not so much to offer the exalted offices of the Indian Civil Service to a wider section of the population as to legitimate the claims of a privileged elite that was already positioned to enter it.[41] The examination functioned, to use Bourdieu's formulation, as but a "mask of modernity," concealing "the social mechanism ordinarily associated with the most archaic societies."[42]

The mask worked well, though, for in its apparent "openness," the entrance examination attracted a wide constituency of aspiring English middle-class applicants, a constituency the ICS Commission was consequently at pains to disavow. Matters were further compounded by the fact that in abolishing the patronage of the Court of Directors, the examination system also technically paved the way for Indians to apply to join the ICS. Since any "natural born subject of Her Majesty" could take the examination, Lord Grenville announced that if Indians could travel to England and prove their qualifications, they could be appointed to ICS "without any prejudice to their place of birth."[43] Of course, as noted earlier in this chapter, it was difficult for Indians to travel to England. But this was a point upon which the authorities remained obdurate until late into the nineteenth century, despite several pleas to introduce simultaneous entrance examinations in India. Petitioners such as Naoroji insisted that candidates in India should be given the same or comparable[44] examinations as their counterparts in England and then proceed to England for training, but such a proposal was deemed unfeasible. A message from the Indian government to the secretary of state for India in 1888 stated: "The establishment of simultaneous competitive examinations in India and England would sacrifice the principle [of the ICS]. It would be entirely foreign to the intentions of the framers of the competitive system and be open to grave practical objections."[45] Ironically, it was an unmodern sanctity of place—the exams would not be the same if not held in England—that sought to uphold the purported benefits of a bureaucratic modernity.

As Macaulay had informed Parliament on June 24, 1853, the year the Government of India Act abolished company patronage of the ICS: "As soon as any young native of distinguished parts should, by the cultivation of English literature, have enabled himself to be victorious in competition over European candidates, he would, in the most honourable manner, by conquest, as a matter of right, and not as a mere eleemosynary donation, obtain access to the service."[46] Underlining Macaulay's intention that Indian success in the examination would showcase the fruition of the educational scheme for India he had outlined two decades earlier, the statement is evidence of the belief that education and ability could become the basis for a "matter of right." While the English were often to retract from this stance, the seductive power of the invitation to a supposedly level playing field remained in place for educated middle-class Indians until at least the end of the century. Thus, in complaining about the unfairness of the examination format, neither Naoroji nor Banerjea insisted upon the implicit inequities of a system that expected Indians to reproduce the best of an elite English education. Rather, they protested more about the impracticalities involved in a candidate's taking the risk to travel to England only to take an examination that he might then fail. In eschewing the semblance of any concessions made toward them with regard to educational requirements, Indians evidently looked to the competitiveness of the ICS examination as a "fair trial"[47] that provided them an opportunity to stake their claim, along with their English counterparts, to the responsibilities and privileges of governance—indeed to emerge as the exemplary citizen that the civilian was supposed to embody.

For the English middle class, too, the reformed ICS seemed to convey "a clear sense of rights and duties," creating a public sphere, as Thomas Osborne notes, "oriented in aspiration to state service."[48] But it was the very weight of such expectations that the ICS found difficult to bear, and the underlying class and racial coordinates regulating entry into the supposedly "open" competitive system spelled out the paradoxes beleaguering its liberal envisioning.

In the first examination, held in 1855, 70 percent of the successful candidates were Oxbridge graduates; for the first five years, the percentage of such graduates averaged 60 percent. But the seemingly steady flow of university graduates, let alone those from Oxbridge, began to diminish, and by 1864, only 10 percent of the successful candidates could boast an Oxbridge background.[49] Not only did the mid-1860s witness a steady increase in graduates from Scottish and Irish universities with the diminishing number of Oxbridge graduates, but the percentage of university graduates as a whole decreased until it roughly equaled that of candidates without university degrees.[50] Moreover, because the graduates of English public schools and universities were ill-equipped for the broad curricular scope of the examinations, it soon became widely accepted that in order to succeed, the applicant needed not a university degree, but study with a "crammer," informal coaching institutions that were usually run by clergymen or former civilians.[51] Middle-class families in trade aspiring for public recognition and respectability found it more pragmatic to send their sons to crammers than to incur the expense of a university education, for the crammers increased the probability of admittance into the ICS.[52] From the 1860s onward, a significant portion of candidates had attended one of the cramming institutions that had mushroomed in London as lucrative ventures designed specifically to train candidates to secure the maximum possible marks in the entrance examination.[53] The influence of the crammers was considered especially pernicious because they were patronized not only by candidates without university degrees, but also by graduates of public schools and Oxbridge, who found it worth their while to study with a crammer, thus nullifying, it was felt, the benefits of an expensive university (or public school) education and the gentlemanly qualities these institutions were believed to foster.[54]

Yet, given that the Indian Civil Service was open to all "naturally born subjects of Her Majesty," candidates who had studied with crammers could not be disqualified, nor could the displeasure at their increasing prominence be made too public. Thus, while Charles Wood—who had played a prominent role in advocating the abolition of patronage in 1853—publicly announced that "we wish to obtain the best cultivated young men ... without requiring that that knowledge should have been imparted at a commercial school, a university, or any other particular establishment," in a private letter to Charles Trevelyan, he was more honest: "It is difficult to say this in public, for I should have half a dozen wild Irishmen on my shoulders and as many middle class examination students, but that makes all the more reason for not giving in to anything which might lead to similar results."[55]

The dilemma of the composition of the ICS was reflected in the series of changes that were enacted during the nineteenth century regarding the age limit for admission into the ICS: between 1855 and 1859, it was twenty-three; between 1860 and 1865, twenty-two; between 1866 and 1877, twenty-one; and in 1876, it was nineteen or nineteen and a half. The fluctuating age limit encapsulates the various efforts to monitor the civilian profile during the century: the age limit had been higher to attract more university graduates; it was lowered to attract candidates who had at least graduated from public school, to make up for the diminishing percentage of Oxbridge candidates. While the lower age limit provoked resentment in India because it worked against Indian candidates, it was also designed to restrict the influence of crammers in England. And while the changes often sought to appeal to students from Oxbridge rather than provincial universities, the specific nature of the changes—including changes in the subjects on the examination and the weight given to them—also reflected a preference for candidates from English, rather than Irish or Scottish, universities.

Evidently, the ideal civilian-citizen was formulated across a number of registers, and the changing age limit did not just reflect the Victorian attempt to configure the correlation between age and maturity. In fact, it was difficult to find conclusive proof that the changes in age limit made any discernible difference in terms of civilian performance in India. Official opinion went so far as to concede that the changes in age limit in 1876, for instance, depended on factors other than the emotional and physical readiness of the candidate, and noted that the one feeling "expressed with the greatest unanimity was the desire that the Civil Service in India should be more largely recruited from the English Universities."[56] Although the desire for "Englishness" could be stated in fairly open terms in ways that also racialized admission into the Indian Civil Service, just what constituted Englishness remained equivocal, caught as the ICS was between the appeal of a meritocracy and what Lauren Goodlad describes as the enduring "gentleman's aura predicated on quasi-feudal appeals to social hierarchy."[57] But it was this modernization that remained suspended or necessarily incomplete—one that tacitly privileged "breeding" while openly preaching quantifiable "achievement"—that both provided the dynamic for Victorian myths of modernity and ensured its tenability.[58] In other words, what had to be written into the narrative of modernity that the ICS supplied was not only an anxiety engendered by the apparently leveling measure of the ICS, but also a dissatisfaction with its protocols. In this, it is the discursive construction of the competitionwallah that bears closer scrutiny.

The term "competitionwallah," or just "wallah," quickly gained currency in referring to the new civilians admitted to the ICS through the competitive examinations. It conjoined the notion of competition with the entrepreneurial connotations of the word "wallah," which among other things refers to a "seller." Probably of Anglo-Indian coinage,⁵⁹ the term evidently gained resonance in metropolitan circles as well, echoing as it did an anxiety at the ineffable—and surely incalculable—notion of breeding and character being transmuted through modes of capitalist exchange. In its derisiveness, the term also conveyed the prevalent disdain at the prospect of a market economy's creeping into the hallowed portals of governance.⁶⁰ However, even as the epithet gained currency, the competition-civilians themselves did not appreciably lower the standards of the Indian Civil Service. In fact, when the Government of India was asked to report on the performance of the new recruits in 1865, it did not have adequate proof of any shortcomings. And in 1874, when the Civil Service Commission asked the Secretary of State for India to furnish records of the "manner in which the civilians hitherto appointed have acquitted themselves when brought to the test of actual work," the response was at best noncommittal: "No such reports," the Under Secretary of State for India reported, "exist."⁶¹ The paucity of official evidence, however, was matched by the insistent production, even beyond official circles, of the ludicrous figure of the competition-wallah. One has to emphasize the insistence of this production, for the competition-civilians did not, as mentioned earlier, lower the standards of governance in any discernible way; however, that they were spectacularized in their inadequacy through the gendered figure of the "competitionwallah," testifies to how this figure bore the burden of, and indeed mediated, a modernity that could only be partial.

Writing to Charles Trevelyan about the new competition system in 1870, J. W. S. Wyllie of the Bombay Civil Service was unequivocal in his criticism of the competition-civilian. Wyllie notes that "integrity, physical and mental energy" are key requirements of a civilian, along with, of course, "the manners of a gentleman."⁶² Wyllie goes on to question the efficacy of the examination in ensuring such traits: "The contentment of the people is the life of the government, and the type of officer the people like is some one who shall listen to their long tales of grievance patiently, treat their notabilities with courtesy, and in his administrative action show vigor and promptitude tempered by cool judgment." "Where then is the guarantee," Wyllie asks, "for the people's satisfaction in the fact of their new master's having one day in London showed some proficiency in stringing together Greek iambics or flooring abstruse problems in pure mathematics?"⁶³

Wyllie's comments certainly indicate the fabled disconnect between colony and metropole, wherein it was widely believed that metropolitan policymaking could only dimly adjudge or approximate the exigencies that determined the actions of the officer in the colonies, "the man on the spot."[64] Wyllie's remarks also stem from dissatisfaction at the prospect of knowledge being reduced to examination results, which in itself was a prevalent critique of the new system.[65] But what may be most striking about his letter is the anxiety at the idea of governance being translated into intellectual accomplishment, an intellectualization that could emasculate the Indian Civil Service. Wyllie was certainly not the only one, and certainly not the first, to project intellectual labor as emasculating, even though the intellect itself was perceived to be a male domain. In fact, drawing out the convergent associations between intellectual occupations and an imputed femininity, James Eli Adams describes how the Victorian male writer, "the man of letters," felt compelled to strenuously mark out his vocation as an embodiment of a recognizable masculinity. The central premise in this reassertion of masculinity among male writers, Adams notes, was an emphasis upon a rigorous regime of bodily discipline.[66] That bodily discipline and the ensuing physical vigor featured prominently in ideals of manliness in Victorian England is evident in the prominence of areas such as athleticism in the school curriculum.[67]

Translated into an imperial context, such displays of manliness were deemed essential and led to inordinate attention being paid to skills such as horseback riding, for instance. As if on cue, Wyllie observes: "As to the necessity for physical energy in an Indian Civilian there can be only one opinion. A magistrate who cannot ride is simply not fit to be a magistrate . . . it does wound the people's pride to see their thousands *governed* by a man who scarcely passes muster among his own race" (emphasis in the original). With regard to the competition-civilians, then, his comment is quite predictable: "for so special a service as that of the British Crown in India one would rather imagine it desirable that the spirits and hearts of men, aye, their bodies too, if possible, should all be subjected to effective training."[68] Consequently, for the newer cadre of civilians, many of whom Wyllie views as the product of crammers, he reserves the terse comment: "I will not here allude to the ideal 'wallah' of Calcutta society; let it suffice that popular feeling has long ago endorsed the official verdict as to the deficiencies of the class in manners and athletic pursuits."[69] Not only not gentlemanly enough, but not manly enough either—though over the course of the Victorian period, the two were to become cognate[70]—the competitionwallah seemed doubly doomed, despite having triumphed over the intellectual rigors of the examination. But it was also necessary to produce the wallah as such, for it was the unmanly wallah alone who could afford nostalgic notions about training for the ICS in Haileybury and its vestiges of feudal privilege in an age of liberal reform. It was only in the context of his critique of the unmanly wallah, for instance, that Wyllie could launch into a lengthy reminiscence of the many benefits of Haileybury.[71] The unmanliness of the competitionwallah, though disavowed, also had to be invoked as it evidently had more to do with the fate of a fractured modernity in England than with Wyllie's concern for the welfare of Indian subjects.

G. O. Trevelyan's *The Competition Wallah* makes for interesting reading in this context, for it purports to voice the opinions of one who was subject to the opprobrium of the epithet: the competitionwallah himself. *The Competition Wallah* is a series of letters written from India by an imaginary civilian, Henry Broughton, who is introduced to a metropolitan audience by his friend, Charles Simkins. The letters were originally serialized in *Macmillan's Magazine* in 1864–65, with Trevelyan publishing them as a single volume the following year.[72] Broughton's letters provide a ringside view of civilian life in India, complete with details of the civilian's arrival, his journeys to rural outposts, and accounts of government balls at Calcutta. On certain levels, the letters even anticipate or respond to popular criticisms of the competionwallah. They point out, for instance, the acute loneliness of young civilians freshly arrived in India, who could not rely on the network of support that Haileybury alumni had (*Wallah*, 6–7). Self-conscious about aspersions of the civilians' lack of physical prowess, Broughton concedes that "to field sports the new civilians are not addicted to as a class" (9). As if in recompense, however, he devotes a full chapter to describing a hunting expedition he was party to in Nepal. Even in notching up a few points in the competitionwallah's favor, Broughton's narrative, it seems, cannot but be defensive.

In referring to the relatively modest background of the new breed of civilians, though, Broughton hails the moral temper they inject into the Indian Civil Service, in contrast to the debauched exploits of previous generations. In fact, Broughton lauds the ICS for providing a promising career for a new generation of deserving middle-class men with no influence or affluence to fall back upon. "In most cases," he notes, "the normal condition of a clever Englishman [in England] between the ages of twenty-two and thirty is a dreary feeling of dissatisfaction about his work and his prospects, and a chronic anxiety for 'a sphere'" (*Wallah*, 119). The ICS, in contrast, provides a career trajectory that is disciplining and fulfilling, in which it is impossible for the civilian to "have any misgiving concerning the dignity and importance of his work" (120). And as he waxes eloquent about the ICS, Broughton takes care to point out that its most creditable feature is that it is "open to every subject of the Queen, though his father be as poor as Job subsequently to the crash in that patriarch's affairs, and though he does not number so much as the butler of a member of Parliament among his patrons and connexions" (124). Broughton's sensitivity to the class-based exclusionary ideals of the ICS sensitizes him to the racial biases underlying the breaches of the Queen's Proclamation of 1858. Commenting on the racial snobbery of Englishmen in India, who bar Indians from traveling in first-class railway carriages, despite the "fraternity and equality which exist in theory between the subjects of our beloved Queen" (24), Broughton quips that the perceived disjunction between theory and practice in India could be explained by asking the rhetorical question: "How is that there are no tradesman's sons at Eton or Harrow?" (25). Seeking to justify the new system, Broughton also sets the tone for reviewing the relations between Indians and English. After all, as the prefatory comments to the volume indicate, the purpose of publishing *The Competition Wallah* lay in "inducing Englishmen at home to take a lively and effective interest in the native population of their Eastern dominions" (v).

Broughton's letters in fact present the competionwallah as the exemplary civilian-citizen, cognizant of the duties and ideals of citizenship: unlike English and other European settlers in India, competition-civilians, Broughton notes approvingly, "hearken to the voice of equity and humanity" (*Wallah*, 260) when dealing with Indians, especially in the post-proclamation era. Broughton becomes the voice of a liberal humanism as he reminds his readers that even every *ryot* is "equal in rights as citizen and man," difficult as it may be to keep track of the fact, given the ryot's "laziness, etc." (221).[73] Broughton's deep sense of "equity," albeit one that is forged through a mindfulness of "native difference," is aroused, the tenor of *The Competition Wallah* implies, not just by a compulsory adherence to official policy but by the competitioners' acute awareness of its notable lapses, including their designation as "competitionwallahs" in the first place.

It is no small coincidence that G. O. (George) Trevelyan should fictionally orchestrate a defense of the much-attacked reform of the Civil Service introduced by his father, Charles, or that he should narratively lend credibility to Macaulay's faith in a system of competition (Macaulay was his maternal uncle). Evidently, the defense of the competition recruit became in itself a family business. However, even as Broughton's letters implicitly defend the wallah, they fail to represent the wallah with convincing persuasion, so much so that *The Competition Wallah* has even been read by present-day scholars as a satire of the examination system.[74] In what may be the fullest reading of the text to date, John Clive reads *The Competition Wallah* in its more salutary tone. However, Clive views the text more in terms of its enumeration of the functions the competition-civilian performs in maintaining a balance of power after the events of 1857, saying little about Broughton's depiction of the wallah himself.[75] The critical ambiguity or reticence regarding the figure of the new civilian in *The Competition Wallah* may lie in the inability of the text to find an adequate representational framework for him. As a gentleman but not quite, or a civilian whose masculinity is evidently compromised by an intellectualization he must often disclaim, the new civilian, it seems, can be narrated primarily through reference to what he is not: only in contradistinction to debauched civilians of a previous generation or to contemporary European settlers or army men in India.

The lack of a representational framework that the competition-civilian could persuasively lay claim to by dint of what he embodied reveals an inability to render the hard-working, idealistic competitioner as the subject of narrative, let alone place him as civilian-citizen on an imperial stage. In fact, even until late in the second half of the nineteenth century, a period that witnessed an explosion of various forms of media, it was still the extravagant figure of the citizen as soldier, the soldier-hero, that commanded the narrative of empire,[76] perhaps echoing Thomas Carlyle's emphatic insistence on the need for heroes and hero worship in a world that "does *not* go by wheel-and-pinion 'motives,' self-interests, checks, balances," and on the existence of "something far other ... than the clank of spinning-jennies, and parliamentary majorities "[77] (emphasis in the original). The competition-civilian was indeed a product and embodiment of such a modern world and its democratic technologies. And while the seeming paradox of the "middle-class hero" was one that provided much of the impetus for the Victorian novel itself, the exigencies of the imperial theater in the mid-nineteenth century seem to have afforded little narrative scope for this new dispensation of the citizen, given that such a narrative was claimed with so much more assurance by the heroic figure of the soldier or the adventurer.[78]

Despite its professed sympathy for the reviled figure of the competition-civilian, even Trevelyan's *The Competition Wallah* is not without reservations about this figure. While Broughton espouses the egalitarian ideals of the competition system, he himself is the product of a privileged upbringing, having benefited from both a public school and Oxbridge education (as indeed had Trevelyan). The fact that Broughton's voice provides the controlling narrative places it at some distance from the constituency that he purports to defend. In fact, Simkins introduces Broughton by noting that he placed third in the entrance examination, "being beaten only," Simkins says, not without a snobbishness, "by a student from Trinity College, Dublin, and a gentleman educated at Eton, where he resided exactly three weeks, and a private tutor's, with whom he passed seven years" (*Wallah*, 3). The quandaries of the competition system, then, get played out in the narrative gap between the ideals of the system and its representation in Trevelyan's *The Competition Wallah*, a gap that highlights the difficulty in familiarizing—even from a sympathetic English perspective—the new civilian-citizen, the inheritor not of privilege but of the product of a democratic (and bureaucratic) modernity.

The representational predicament engendered by the figure of the competition-civilian—one that official discourse could not fully denounce, nor its defenders convincingly endorse—takes another interesting turn in H. S. Cunningham's *Chronicles of Dustypore: A Tale of Modern Anglo-Indian Life* (1875).[79] Written from an "official" perspective, inasmuch as Cunningham was posted to India as a high-ranking official, though not a member of the Indian Civil Service, *Chronicles* does not overtly take on the task of defending the competition-civilian and even echoes conventional opinion in depicting him in his "unmanliness." The novel's particular mode of depiction, however, ends up extending an unexpectedly salutary role to the new generation of civilians, if with uneven effect. *Chronicles* follows the lives of an English conclave in the fictitious Indian setting of Dustypore. The importance of the ics to this setting is brought home in the early pages of the novel, which describe the "tide of civil administration" (*Chronicles*, 3) sweeping Dustypore, taking it to new heights of sanitation and civic regulation. The internal fissures riving the administration, in fact, fictionalize the troubled legacy of the ics, the plight of the Dustypore Salt Board being a case in point. The Salt Board is entrusted with the important task of collecting revenues from salt in an area blessed with an abundance of it. It comprises, nonetheless, Haileybury civilians—suggestively named Strutt, Fotheringham, and Cockshaw—who hardly seem commensurate with the positions they occupy. While it was decreed by a viceregal proclamation that native monopolies over salt in the fictitious area of Rumble Chunder would continue to be respected by the government despite its annexation of the lands, the matter of ascertaining the rightful claimants to these monopolies continues to perplex the Salt Board, with the result that the case of the "Rumble Chunder Grant" assumes mythic proportions in Dustypore. An anonymous article in the *Edinburgh Review* notes rather caustically that Rumble Chunder was "a specimen of the gigantic messes which ensue, when second and third rate men have the management of first rate questions" (223). In what is obviously a barb at Fotheringham and his like, the article endorses the introduction of competitive examinations as a move necessary "to deal with the accumulated dullness with which years of licensed favouritism had crowded the ranks of the service" (224).

The arrival of Desvoeux, the "competitionwallah," promises to remedy matters. In contrast to the old civilians who, as Desvoeux airily comments, were "all the stupidest sons of the stupidest families in England for several generations," "we," Desvoeux announces, "are of the new *régime*, and are supposed to have wits, and we have a great deal of intelligence to get over" (*Chronicles*, 55). However, if the reader initially decides to settle on Desvoeux as the one to steer Dustypore through its administrative morass, the narrative quickly dissipates such reassurance. Even as *Chronicles* highlights the fortunes of the Salt Board, it is driven by a conventional marriage plot that is more invested in following the fortunes of young Maud Vernon, who ventures forth to India—as many women had done before her—to find a husband. As Maud gauges the various suitors in Dustypore, it is clear that Desvoeux, depicted as someone prone to gossip and having a professed disinclination for the outdoors—as when he says, "I should spoil my complexion and my gloves" (*Chronicles*, 101)—ranks very low on the scale of masculine eligibility. Tellingly, Maud decides to marry Sutton, a valiant and decorated soldier who heads the best irregular cavalry in that part of the country.

While the novel provides narrative closure for the marriage plot (Maud quickly marries Sutton), the fate of the Rumble Chunder Grant remains undecided. The marriage plot, on the other hand, in its valorizing of the soldier hero, gives latitude to criticize the competitionwallah and even excise him from the social scene of the novel; in fact, in the closing pages, there is no mention of Desvoeux. While we are given no indication of whether Desvoeux even remains in Dustypore, the apparent uncertainty regarding its administrative fate leaves one *wishing* him to stay. The desirability of his presence is in fact reinforced over the course of the novel too, for while serving as a foil for Sutton's eligibility, Desvoeux also questions the heroism that so commends Sutton. For one thing, the novel does not end with Maud's marriage: in fact, her marital life turns out not so marked by nuptial content after all. Soon after her marriage, she strikes a friendship with Desvoeux during her lonely vigils while Sutton is away on military campaigns. Although Maud's encounters with Desvoeux operate along lines of friendship rather than romance, they are not without a flirtatious banter, and the pleasure of his company soon leads Maud to admit to herself: "A hundred times, ... how good [Sutton] was, how true, how really great, how chivalrous in his devotion . . .—and yet—something more unheroic would perhaps have been sometimes a relief" (*Chronicles*, 268). Although these marital doubts are smoothed over by the end of the novel, they introduce enough skepticism of the soldier-hero, especially as viewed through the lens of bourgeois domesticity. Such a framing had in fact gained precedence in general, as is shown by the remarkable emphasis placed on the husbandliness of Sir Henry Havelock, the hero—from a British perspective—of the 1857 Mutiny, in narratives that continued to proliferate well after his death.[80] In the world of Dustypore, the need to temper heroism with domesticity is insinuated by the impropriety of Maud's desire for Desvoeux's company: the problem is not that she seeks the company of a man other than her husband, but that it is the competitionwallah's company that she seeks. That Maud does so, effectively reveals the failings of Sutton, the heroic soldier, as husband or bourgeois citizen.

Even though Desvoeux serves to provide both a foil for and a critique of Sutton, *Chronicles* is clearly more successful in finding a representational mode for the competition-civilian than Trevelyan's narrative rendition of that figure. It is interesting, though, that Desvoeux comes into his own as the figure of the dandy. Alongside the mention of his administrative competence, in fact, *Chronicles* makes abundant note of how "he talks great nonsense and abuses everybody" (50). The latitude of Desvoeux's witty nonchalance is matched only by his sartorial excess: "he was far too profusely set about with pretty things," it is pointed out, with "lockets and rings and costly knickknacks," and a handkerchief that was tied "with a more than Byronic negligence" (50). In his vanity and sartorial extravagance, Desvoeux brings to mind that other overdressed and vain civilian, William Thackeray's Jos Sedley, in *Vanity Fair*. However, even as *Chronicles* accords Desvoeux the distinction of being a dandy with far more linguistic finesse and intellectual sophistication than Jos Sedley, it is still odd that the civilian of the precompetition era (*Vanity Fair* was published in 1848) should provide the literary prototype for depicting a civilian of a later era, one who was admittedly "brilliant" and more worthy of the task than Jos.

But it may be only through the figure of the dandy that Desvoeux can make the best case for the competition-civilian. Admittedly, the linking of the competition-civilian with the dandy is not far-fetched, for in the wake of the democratization ushered in by the Second Reform Act and even the Third, it was as the dandy that the figure of the parvenu became the object of ridicule.[81] In terms of *Chronicles*, though, this linkage seems to suggest something more. The depiction of the competition-civilian as a dandy—a figure who, Regenia Gagnier notes, is remarkably protean in both refuting and reinforcing bourgeois moral values,[82] and who, as even *Chronicles* shows, is both antithetical and supplemental to that of the masculine soldier-hero[83]—introduces an open-endedness to the otherwise over-determined figure of the competition-civilian. In *Chronicles*, the crafted insouciance of the dandy becomes the other face of the competent industriousness of the middle-class competition-civilian, in ways that bring these unlikely figures together, blurring the boundaries between economic and cultural capital.[84] Such blurring assumes significance in light of the fact that the aim of the competitive examinations had been to assign an exchange value to the supposed inaccessibility of cultural capital:[85] to provide an accounting for it, to subject the inheritors of privilege to a market determinant. But in the context of the ICS, it was precisely this attempted calculability that also very literally engendered its difficulties, necessitating the production of a figure such as the "competitionwallah," who was to serve as proof and product of the intranslatability of cultural capital into more portable economic capital, and vice versa. The competition-civilian-as-dandy, however, frustrates the much maligned calculability assigned to the meritorious civilian; through his deliberate extravagance and epigrammatic wit, the dandy—despite, or through, his unmanliness—adduces a cultural capital whose inaccessibility the figure of the competitionwallah, in his inadequacy, was supposed to instructively convey.

The competition-civilian-as-dandy most pointedly reveals, in fact, the constitutive contradictions of a bureaucratic modernity. Such a figure gives us pause to consider how the disquiet that the new breed of civilians provoked was fueled not just by the class background of the new competition-recruits, or the antagonism expressed by old India hands, such as Wyllie, at the influx of a new breed of officers with no prior connection to India.[86] Rather, as a singular figure of heightened individuality, the dandy effectively points to how the anxieties surrounding the meritorious civilian also registered a pervasive unease at the consolidation of a bureaucratic machinery that would stifle cherished ideals of individualism and liberty, while also reducing the *aura* of governance to a bland matter of concentrated expertise. While the need for bureaucratic governance was inescapable by the 1860s, especially in the context of Britain's empire, in countering feudalistic notions of rule and patronage, the impulse toward bureaucratization also ran against liberal ideas of laissez faire individualism. Daniel Bivona is insightful in pointing out that the emergence of a bureaucratic modernity highlighted the "incompatibility between the individualist ideology [of British liberalism and its] desire to transform the world through power."[87] In fact, as Bivona observes, the increasing bureaucratization of British society was paralleled only by the "intensity with which its popular culture celebrated an anti-bureaucratic ethos of individual heroism."[88] While this paradox explains the enduring appeal of the lone imperial adventurer or soldier-hero, it also explains why the corresponding figure of the competitionwallah had to be created in response to a bureaucratic modernity whose importance, while decried, could not be denied. That the wallah was but a discursive figure, one whose inadequacy could never be demonstrated in official records, reflects more the anxieties that the competition-civilian provoked in his indispensability.

Interestingly, despite its obvious literary bearings, *Chronicles* was written by a high-ranking colonial official, who also authored the nonfictional *British India and Its Rulers* (1881). In the latter work, Cunningham praised the services of the meritorious, diligent competition-civilian in ensuring the administrative welfare of India and England's sway over it. Published a few years before the founding of the Indian National Congress—which stepped up demands for admission into the Indian Civil Service—*British India*'s favorable depiction of the implicitly English competition-civilian is evidently not without a sense of urgency provoked by the prospect of an articulate Indian middle class coming into visibility. However, Cunningham's earlier and more open-ended depiction of the competition-civilian in *Chronicles*—one rendered possible only through the appropriation of literary tropes such as the marriage plot and the figure of the dandy—reveals, if inadvertently, an urgency to also mediate the disquiet that the emergence of the middle-class English civilian-citizen had provoked. That *Chronicles* does so mostly through an economy of desire rather than fulfillment—Maud's desire for Desvoeux's amusing company, as well as the reader's desire for his administrative intervention—underlines the extent of that disquiet.

Indeed, the fact that it is the dandy—a figure who extravagantly contradicts middle-class industry, and who is embodied through the gap between appearance and essence[89]—who provides the narrative vehicle for Cunningham's extended depiction of the new generation of civilians effectively points to the various tensions coalescing in the discursive production of the "competitionwallah." It also hints at a crisis of representation otherwise, as the competition-civilian evidently eludes or exceeds narrative frames, as in Trevelyan's text. In the official reports, too, the competition-civilian appears primarily through the fluctuating requirements regarding age. Evidently, it was only as an exorbitant figure that the competition-civilian managed the aporias of a bureaucratic modernity, which marked the ideals and limits of Victorian liberalism. The plight of the new civilians reveals in fact the difficulties besetting the emergence of even the white, middle-class, English male as citizen, a category that Indians sought to lay claim to with such mixed results.

Banerjea's Nation in Making: Mourning Becomes the Nation?

The anxiety about the competition-civilian was prompted not only by the influx of students from English crammers—or Scottish and Irish universities—but by that of Indian students as well. Nowhere is this more evident than in the case of Surendranath Banerjea, one of the first Indians to be admitted into the ICS. Any narrative of the ICS from the Indian standpoint must consider the case of Banerjea, for his involvement with the ICS stoked the early flames of nationalist protest. Banerjea was not the first Indian to successfully compete in the ICS examination held in England: S. N. Tagore holds that distinction. Banerjea was not even a lifelong civilian, for he was expelled from the ICS soon after being admitted to it. In fact, being a civilian was only one of Banerjea's many roles, for he went on to undertake an astonishing range of activities after his expulsion. However, while his autobiography, *A Nation in Making*, devotes relatively little space to the ICS and mentions it chiefly in terms of his expulsion, this section of the chapter highlights how he appropriates the figure of the competition-civilian to fashion an idiom of citizenship that was key to his self-representation and the etching of a national body politic. Such a reading locates the formulation of citizenship forwarded by Banerjea—one that came to be marked "moderate" and failed—within wider and vexed contexts of a bureaucratic modernity that are otherwise elided by the chauvinisms of both national and imperial identities.

As *A Nation in Making* suggests, the question of Indian entry into the ICS was, in the early years, not explicitly associated with the arrogation of political prerogative precisely because it rested on an implicit assumption of it. For educated, middle-class Indians, the opening of the ICS to them represented, as it did for their counterparts in England, a lucrative and seemingly more egalitarian career choice. For many of them, in fact, it announced the coming of age of a generation of Western-educated neophytes eager to announce their progressive credentials. Banerjea pointedly represents his father, Durgacharan Banerjea, an eminent Calcutta physician, as an ardent devotee of the new wave of secular liberalism suffusing the Western-educated natives, "whose alienation from the faith of their fathers was complete and even militant."[90] In 1853, when Surendranath was barely five years old, his father, though hailing from an orthodox Kulin Brahmin family, had, in clear defiance of religious restrictions, drawn up a will directing that Surendranath be sent to England to complete his education. At that point, Surendranath's father seems to have formed no strong opinion as to what his son should study in England; the possibility of the ICS was first suggested to him by John Sime, the principal of Surendranath's college at Calcutta University, upon his graduation (*Nation*, 4). Coincidentally, the year when

Surendranath's father decreed that his son should study in England was also when the formal process of wresting control of admission into the ICS away from its Court of Directors began in England.

Surendranath passed the ICS's Open Competition Examination in 1869 and the Final Examination in 1871. Sripad Babaji Thakur, Romesh Chunder Dutt, and Behari Lal Gupta also succeeded at both levels, generating a somewhat misguided impression of the openness of the exams, one that the Civil Service Commission labored to both foster and disavow. Predictably, the fundamental paradoxes besetting the ICS became manifest in a controversy over Banerjea's age. Soon after the results of the Open Competition Examination were announced, which admitted Banerjea into candidacy for the Final Examination (normally held after two years of probation), his name, along with Thakur's, was removed from the list of successful candidates on account of age. According to the regulations at that point, a candidate had to be above nineteen but below twenty-one years of age. Born in 1848, Banerjea was within the age limit by normal reckoning. However, his matriculation form from Calcutta University stated that he was sixteen in 1863, thus putting him above the age limit in 1869. But, as Banerjea pointed out, the seeming inaccuracy in the form was not an error, but a result of his then calculating his age according to the "Indian method," by which a child is considered to be nine months old at the time of birth. Thus, in 1863, Banerjea had considered himself to be sixteen, which appeared to put him beyond the upper age limit in 1869 (*Nation*, 12).

The Civil Service Commission's refusal to accept Banerjea's explanation of the discrepancy invited a deluge of protest from prominent Calcutta residents like Ishwar Chandra Vidyasagar, Maharaja Jyotindra Mohun Tagore, and Raja Rajendra Lal Mitter, who testified to Banerjea's "English" age. His case seems to be the first instance when a specific action of the Civil Service Commission with regard to an Indian was subjected to widespread criticism. In fact, Banerjea's imminent disbarment provided a platform for crystallizing a political consciousness, for the question of professional advancement that became entwined with the ICS agitation also generated a language of entitlement.

Banerjea eventually won his case against the Civil Service Commission, and, after passing the Final Examination in 1871, he was appointed as Assistant Magistrate in Sylhet, then a part of Bengal (later a part of Assam). Here, too, his relations with the ICS proved contentious, and he was eventually dismissed over a relatively minor matter. *Nation* casts his dismissal from the ICS in the context of racial animosity, and it becomes quite evident that the perceived racial prejudice was one that played itself out along idioms of competency. As Banerjea recalls, he was so overwhelmed by the workload assigned to him that he was unable to process files in a timely fashion; as a result, a particular case concerning a theft was repeatedly postponed. As was evidently common procedure in such cases, to account for the delay, Banerjea signed an order declaring that the suspect was absconding. But the suspect had in fact not absconded, and when called upon to explain his action, Banerjea was unable to defend himself. The matter was referred to an all-European commission appointed for the purpose, and Banerjea was soon informed that the Government of India had recommended his dismissal from the ICS. Even though he went to England to plead his case, his career as a civil servant was effectively terminated (*Nation*, 28–29).

Banerjea's dismissal was, by all accounts, an inordinately severe punishment for an evidently trivial misdemeanor. As A. O. Hume, a former member of the ICS and a founder of the Indian National Congress, points out in an article appended to Banerjea's autobiography, contemporary European civilians judged guilty of graver misdeeds were let off with a lighter sentence (*Nation*, 408). Banerjea's decision to append Hume's explanatory account as a bookend to *Nation* illustrates the considerable weight of his ICS experience—though, as mentioned earlier, the ICS itself occupies relatively little narrative space. That Banerjea's imputed inefficiency (Hume points out that charges of "laziness" were attributed to him) was but symptomatic of a broader resentment is a notion that *Nation* consciously foregrounds: "My case excited very strong feeling in the Indian community," Banerjea points out, "and the general feeling amongst my countrymen was that, if I were not an Indian, I would not have been put to all this trouble" (29). Banerjea's expulsion from the ICS certainly reveals the mounting antagonism of the colonial state to the increasing demands for Indianization of the bureaucracy. While Banerjea was still in the ICS, a dispatch by the Secretary of State for India noted: "As it is necessary to admit natives of India to a share in the administration of the country in higher situations than has been the custom for many years, and as, for obvious reasons, we must not surrender into their hands so large a share of the administration . . . it follows that some limit to their admission to the higher offices, more especially the executive offices, is absolutely required."[91] In suggesting that his dismissal on charges of laziness was but a convenient manifestation of the resentment at the Indianization of the ICS, then, Banerjea certainly puts his finger on the spot. Yet, even as he was cognizant of the ideological charge of the language of incompetence (and laziness) that was used against him, a charge by no means unfamiliar in the colonial regime, it is noteworthy that it was along the very register of competence and industriousness, as the hard-working competition-civilian, that Banerjea chose to reinstate himself.

After the final unfavorable verdict from the India House in London, Banerjea attempted to qualify as a lawyer, and though he had already kept terms at the Middle Temple, the "Benchers" decided against calling him to the bar on account of his tainted reputation as a dismissed civilian. Banerjea's description of his failure to embark on any career is specifically couched in terms of thwarted professional aspiration, and his bitterness is tangible in a passage worth quoting at some length:

> In the iron grip of ruin I had already formed some forecast of the work that was awaiting me in life. I felt that I had suffered because I was an Indian, a member of a community that lay disorganized, had no public opinion, and no voice in the counsels of their government. I felt with all the passionate warmth of youth that we were helots, hewers of wood and drawers of water in the land of our birth. The personal wrong done to me was an illustration of the helpless impotency of our people . . . In the midst of impending ruin and dark, frowning misfortune, I formed the determination of addressing myself to the task of helping our helpless people in this direction. (*Nation*, 33)

The movement from hurt outrage at colonial discrimination to a determined resolve to give shape to a political consciousness is by no means an unfamiliar pattern; it has already been evident in Gandhi's narration of his experience at the Pietermaritzburg station. Of interest here, though, is the particular vector along which a political consciousness is formulated. If, as the Indian clamor for admission into the ICS demonstrates, the proof of the rights of citizenship for the educated Indian middle class came to lie most visibly in a professional career, then it is ironic that Banerjea took up the task of educating his countrymen for citizenship as a career in itself.

Significantly, of all the figures in the period under study in this book, Banerjea is the one who pushes the discussion of citizenship into the closest proximity with that of nationhood and nation-building, inasmuch as his emphasis on a political and civic self-fashioning coalesces around building a national public sphere, what Partha Chatterjee describes as a "'national' civil society."[92] Interestingly, though, Banerjea's narration of his efforts at nation-building subscribes to the rubric of the ICS career he was denied. His description in *Nation* of the days immediately following his momentous decision to dedicate himself to constructing an Indian public sphere is strikingly similar to his earlier description of his intensive preparation—cramming—for the Final Examination of the ICS. As an ICS candidate in London in 1871, he had spent, he notes, "laborious days when [he] could think and dream of nothing else, except of [his] books and examinations" (*Nation*, 22). After his dismissal from the ICS in 1874, he devoted himself to a similarly rigorous schedule of study in his lodgings near Hampton Court, where, as he recalls, "from ten o'clock in the morning after breakfast till dinner time at eight o'clock in the evening, I was incessantly at work, reading books that I thought would inspire me with the fervour and equip me with the capacity for which was to be my life-work" (33). This obvious narrative paralleling could well be a compensatory gesture on Banerjea's part to prove that he indeed was capable of the workload that the ICS demanded. But, as becomes clear, the narrative not only emphasizes the volume of Banerjea's work but also his mode of approaching it, in ways that indicate it was not so much the ICS itself but its forging of the civilian-citizen through an emphasis on merit, organized training, and expertise that provided an important node for self-representation as well as a narrative teleology for conceptualizing the nation and its citizenry.

Nation derives its narrative dynamic, in fact, from the astonishing variety of activities that Banerjea takes on in his varied career as a nation-builder: teaching at the Metropolitan Institution from 1875 on; founding the Ripon College in Calcutta (*Nation*, 38); founding the Indian Association in 1876, to inculcate middle-class Indian interest in public affairs; and, in 1879, becoming proprietor of the *Bengalee*, a weekly newspaper which he eventually converted into a daily. The details of the preparation for and the implementation of these various activities also make clear that it is a secular logic of bureaucratic modernity that authorizes Banerjea's representation of himself as nation-builder. The successive chapter headings in *Nation*—"The Indian Association," "Reactionary Government and Its Consequences," "Journalism," "The Contempt Case: Imprisonment," "Political Activities, 1883–85"—reflect the progression of Banerjea's career, indicating how what marks his making of the nation is his tireless, directed labor in what, following Benedict Anderson's *Imagined Communities*, we have come to understand as homogeneous, empty time that marks both the nation and its citizen in a liberal trajectory of development. Banerjea, Sumit Sarkar tells us, never bothered to visit Ramakrishna.[93] Nor did he evidently have much time for his family, either. In what is now marked as a characteristic of Indian male autobiographies of the period, *Nation* hardly mentions its author's domestic, personal life,[94] and even the fleeting glimpses one gets of his family members are telling in their context. Banerjea describes, for instance, how he attended the inaugural meeting of the Indian Association, of which he was the founder, only a few hours after the death of his son. "This is not the only time I have had to perform a public duty under the weight of a great personal bereavement" (*Nation*, 42), he notes. Quite true. In 1911, he addressed the annual meeting of the Indian National Congress barely three days after the death of his wife. Keeping to scheduled meetings while also encountering death laces Banerjea's narrative with multiple temporalities, the implications of which I will take up later.

The linear overlay of Banerjea's narrative, however, is heavily informed by the autobiographical form itself, particularly in its liberal, nineteenth-century incarnation. It is within this autobiographical tradition of an "orderly evolution" that Javed Majeed rightly locates Banerjea's autobiography.[95] What I would like to emphasize here, though, is the bureaucratic self-fashioning that such narrativization entails, and this is not so much because of Banerjea's former status as bureaucrat. Rather, keeping in mind Nicholas Dames's astute reading of the structural linearity provided by the organizing trope of a "career" in nineteenth-century narratives of self-representation, it is worth pointing out, as Dames does, that the narrative and structural logic of a career owed much to both bureaucratic rationality and experience, the latter often garnered in the colonies.[96] Therefore, while *Nation* invokes a linear structure that reflects, as Majeed notes, "Banerjea's autobiography as a narrative of orderly growth both for himself and India,"[97] I would like to underscore how this gradualism also points to a particular mode of bureaucratic self-fashioning, one apparently integral to the early formulation of a national public sphere and the citizen's place in it. What happens, though, when such a framework falls upon itself?

While the intellectual diligence with which Banerjea takes up his new career invokes the emphasis on knowledge and preparation marked by the advent of the competition-civilian, Banerjea is careful to couple it with an emphasis on his bodily rigor, as if to refashion himself against the stereotype of both the unmanly competitionwallah and the non-masculine Bengali. In announcing himself to the nation-to-be, Banerjea takes care to note the stereotype of the weak, ineffectual Bengali that had entrenched itself in other parts of the country. While such perceptions of the Bengali were not entirely novel, they received a fillip in the late nineteenth century through colonial ascriptions of Bengali effeteness—which, Sinha points out, marked one response to the threat allegedly posed by middle-class, educated Bengalis to British paramountcy.[98] As if to disprove the imputed unacceptability of the Bengali as a potential nation-builder, *Nation* refers to a national tour Banerjea had undertaken, over the course of which he was received, as he described elsewhere, "with open arms and treated as a brother by my countrymen from the banks of the Beas to the briny waters that wash the coast of Madras."[99] His unflagging energy during the tour is matched only by his unflagging enthusiasm in narrating it in his autobiography, pointing out as he does that the tour of the Northern Provinces began during the "hottest time of the year" and that despite warnings that he was "incurring a grave risk," he was determined to undertake the tour: "risk or no risk, I had made up my mind and there was no going back" (*Nation*, 45).

Evidently, it was through an emphasis on somatic eligibility that Banerjea merged himself with a national body politic in ways that displaced his particularized identity as a Bengali Hindu. That such a displacement was important to him is evident in his presidential address to the Indian National Congress in 1895. "Let it not be said," he asserts, "that this is the Congress of one social party rather than that of another." Rather, he says: "It is the Congress of United India, of Hindus and Mahomedans, of Christians, of Parsees, and of Sikhs . . . here we have all agreed to bury our social and religious differences, and recognize the one common fact that being subjects of the same Sovereign and living under the same Government and the same political institutions, we have common rights and common grievances."[100] However, since it is a corporeal register through which Banerjea is able to fuse himself with the abstract citizenry he narratively constitutes, his attempts to create a national body politic also shift the focus to the body itself, often playing itself out literally, through his own body.

In this, the full text of Banerjea's presidential address merits some bemusement. He begins with a reprimand to the members who had procrastinated on formulating a constitution. He goes on to chide the Congress for its inaction in trying to mobilize public opinion in England in favor of holding simultaneous examinations for the ICS in India. He then admonishes his audience: "it is no use recording a Resolution here once a year, and then going to sleep over it for rest of the twelve months."[101] Interestingly, his autobiography has nothing to say about the content of his presidential address. Instead, it expends considerable energy in drawing out the physical preparation and exertion the address demanded:

> For two hours every day, and from day to day, I was absorbed in this work, ... and the speech grew until it became, I fear, one of the biggest ever delivered from the presidential chair of the Congress. After two hours' hard work at the speech I used to have my regular constitutional walk on the riverside for three-quarters of an hour, when the whole of what I had written would be thought over, repeated and corrected, and the corrections embodied in the manuscript. This work was continued for six weeks without interruption ... I delivered the whole of my speech without referring to any notes, except perhaps when there was a long string of figures. The delivery took over four hours, and I think I was able, during the whole of that time, to keep up, undiminished and without flagging, the attention of a vast assembly of over five thousand people. (*Nation*, 140)

In highlighting Banerjea's preparation rather than the contents of the speech, *Nation* seems to offer his bodily regimen as an equally eloquent political statement in the making of the nation. The autobiography not only successfully somaticizes professional eligibility (horseback riding, after all, had been a prerequisite for entry into the ICS) but citizenship as well, compensating for the alleged physical failings of the competition-civilian, either Indian or English.

The preeminence of the body in fact contours the narrative framework of the memoir, whose first few pages feature Banerjea's observation: "I was taught when still quite a boy the need of taking regular and daily exercise" (*Nation*, 4–5). Written in the restorative environs of Simultolla, a popular health resort that Banerjea was to retire to in later years, *Nation* engages with the cultivation and maintenance of the (male) body, highlighting what had in fact emerged as a prominent feature of Indian male self-fashioning in the late nineteenth century.[102] In its emphasis on physical culture, though, *Nation* veers between underlining its importance in terms of building physical strength and a more holistic notion of bodily health, a distinction that Gandhi in later years was also often ambivalent about.[103] While Banerjea reports admiringly that his older brother Jitendranath, who exercised "with great ardour," was "the strongest man among the Bengalees" (5), he also concludes with an observation that emphasizes health over strength: "the physical co-operating with the moral, must form a homogenous whole," he notes rather piously, "checking and restraining whatever is evil in human nature, improving and elevating what is good in us" (395). Of course, physical strength was not always divorced from a moral charge; rather, muscularity often became a constitutive relay for mental and ethical fortitude. As Vivekananda wrote to a disciple: "What I want is muscles of iron and nerves of steel, inside which dwells a mind of the same material as that of which the thunder-bolt is made."[104] *Nation*, however, is more uncertain about this correlation, and this ambivalence about the significance of the regimented male body that was to become such a heavily loaded signifier in the impetus to nationalism is telling: precisely what was such a body to signify? If it signified, as has been abundantly noted, a remasculinization of the male colonized body hitherto signified as effete and incapable, such that this could be the body ready to take on the mantle of the citizen,[105] then what has not been duly noted is that the terms of that resignification—both of the body and of citizenship—were by no means self-evident. Banerjea's obsessive preoccupation with bodily culture relays a defensiveness not just in the face of English aspersions against Indian masculinity or Indian apprehensions of Bengali effeminacy, but also in the face of the renegotiated male body being claimed and commandeered by a nationalist momentum that was considerably fractured. Banerjea's emphasis on the healthy and strong body is not just about giving "weight" to an incipient national body (politic); rather, it becomes irrefragably charged with questions about the identity of this body in relation to empire, history, and modernity itself.

As Bal Gangadhar Tilak observed in 1907, "two new words have recently come into existence with regard to our politics, and they are *Moderates* and *Extremists*"[106] (emphasis in the original). The Extremists, impatient with the absence of demands other than for Indian inclusion in the ICS or legislative councils—demands that were viewed as only moderate in their scope and constitutionalism—advocated a more vigorous, even violent, style of political action. In contrast to the Moderate demand for reform or added representation, the Extremists alleged that they would settle for nothing less than complete autonomy or self-rule, *swaraj*.[107] While many Moderate leaders, including Banerjea, shared the objective of self-government, they were not willing to depart from a gradualist approach based on the idea of reform, a fundamental difference that was to split the Congress at the session in Surat in 1907, where Banerjea even had shoes and other sundry objects thrown at him while addressing the assembly (*Nation*, 210). Recalling the split as a "painful wrench," Banerjea rationalizes: "The Congress, however great an organization, was after all a means to an end. That end was self-government. We decided to sacrifice the means for the end" (307). The opposing factions were reconciled in 1916, but it was a shaky reconciliation, and the Congress was soon to be divided on the question of the Montagu-Chelmsford Report, which, prepared in 1918, recommended measures to be undertaken toward the eventual attainment of self-government in India.[108] While the Extremists declared the measures recommended by the report "entirely unacceptable"[109] (305), Banerjea, though disappointed, voiced the Moderate belief that the report nonetheless marked a "speedy inauguration of the beginnings of responsible government" (306).

Banerjea's emphasis on the "beginnings of responsible government"—an emphasis that extended beyond his amenability to the Montagu-Chelmsford Report alone—reflects his (liberal) reliance on a gradualist pace for reform, in contrast to the pronounced immediacy of the Extremist insistence on self-government "now." Although never quite content with the colonizer's "not yet," either, for Banerjea, an overstepping of a gradual pace of reform was to succumb, nonetheless, to the untenability of a belief in the "strange magical transformation [of] the masses" into self-aware, knowing citizens.[110] Yet it was this "strange magical transformation," one effected by what Dipesh Chakrabarty aptly describes as a suspension of a "stagist" historicism,[111] that animated anticolonial nationalism, absorbing the betrayals of colonial liberal policy and demanding the fullness of citizenship in a form that also firmly arraigned it within the territorial delineaments of the nation. In other words, what was obscured as too gradual—rejected in the name of a temporality—was also an alternate anticolonial conception of spatiality and its affective contours. While Banerjea was not alone in arguing during the First World War that fighting for the British Empire was the responsibility of imperial citizens (*Nation*, 300), his advocacy after

1918 of an "imperial system," wherein the "ideal of every true citizen of the Empire" would be embodied in an "imperial civic spirit [that would] have its roots in local patriotism" (373), limned a cosmopolitan coevality that often went against the grain of popular nationalist sentiment, though it was not entirely idiosyncratic.[112] Yet, in this, Banerjea was not just out of joint with discussions of citizenship along nationalist lines, he was also out of joint with discussions of citizenship within a broader framework of empire. His envisioning of an imperial citizenship partly intersected with that of someone like Lionel Curtis, who advanced the notion of an imperial state (Banerjea even corresponded with him).[113] However, although Curtis advocated an imperial state, he was remarkably hesitant about the terms under which the colored subjects of empire would be included in it, if at all. Curtis's stance only underlined the incongruity, from an imperialist perspective, of Banerjea's espousal of imperial citizenship as an Indian subject—an incongruity only doubled by Banerjea's increasing "no-place" in the narrative through which Indian nationalism eventually sought to instantiate the figure of the citizen.

It is significant that while the differences between the Moderates and the Extremists have been variously explained by factors of class (the former are depicted as representing an elitist bourgeoisie), age, education, and regional identity, it was a very gendered trope that became the one most apt to articulate this distinction. As Tilak, associated prominently with the newer dispensation, noted: "Three P's—pray, please and protest—will not do unless backed by solid force."[114] Lajpat Rai, among others, corroborated the stand against this perceived mendicancy by imputing to it a distinctly nonmasculine charge: "the message which the people of England wanted to send to you through me was the message that in our utterance, in our agitations and in our fight and struggle for liberty, we ought to be more manly than we have been heretofore."[115] The Moderates were obviously not "manly" enough, but their lack of manliness was imputed not just on the basis of their political program but on the very substance of what had previously determined the legitimacy of the demand for political rights: the question of a professional career. Aurobindo Ghose, who published one of the early Extremist attacks on the older generation of Congress leaders, remarked: "the actual enemy [of the nationalist movement] is not any force exterior to ourselves, but our own crying weakness, our cowardice, our selfishness, our hypocrisy."[116] Much of this, it was widely felt, could be attributed to the Moderates, especially their professional standing—which evidently made them incapable or unwilling to embark on a more widespread and effective program of protest, such as noncooperation. As the *Bande Mataram*, a nationalist publication, caustically noted, the Congress was nothing more than "half-a-dozen lawyers, meeting in a casual way at the Local Bar Library."[117]

The seemingly self-serving attributes of a professional career (something that Sorabji tried so hard to fashion otherwise) rendered the Moderates redundant, or at least dispensable, against the backdrop of a more powerful idiom of masculinity that had come to capture the nationalist imagination: that of the self-denying *sanyasi*. Reifying the common association between asceticism and renunciation, the sanyasi had been reincarnated, in Bengal at least, in the works of Bankimchandra and Vivekananda. The figure assumed considerable political valence in broader debates determining the course of nationalist activity. As Lajpat Rai asked, rhetorically: "Is it not a matter of shame for us that this National Congress in the last twenty-one years should not have produced at least a number of political sannyasis that could sacrifice their lives for the political regeneration of the country?"[118] It was such a renunciatory figure, the *Bande Mataram* implied in a jibe at the Moderates, that alone could "enable a fallen nation to shake off its weakness, turn cowards into heroes and selfish men into self-denying martyrs."[119] The idiom of renunciation thus generated a more virile masculinity that replaced the mendicant constitutionalism of the Moderates, though mendicancy in itself was historically never removed from the figure of the renunciator.[120] The renunciatory figure had evidently been reconfigured in a way that visibly co-opted the ground for heroism. The self-denying sacrifice espoused by the Extremists, one that was spectacularized by the "blood sacrifice" of young revolutionaries undertaking daring campaigns against colonial authorities, lent itself readily to heroic narrative, producing a remarkable intertextuality in which the "freedom fighters" came to be inspired by the exploits of fictional freedom fighters (who in turn were inspired by them),[121] leaving the professional or competition-civilian as represented by the likes of Banerjea, once again without a viable narrative.[122]

It is worth invoking the bureaucratic figure of the competition-civilian here, for in describing the split between Moderates and Extremists, Banerjea mentions that "the Moderates were classed by their political opponents as allies of the bureaucracy, and bracketed with them in their denunciations" (*Nation*, 307). Significantly, over the course of *Nation*, Banerjea steadily dissociates himself from the colonial bureaucracy, even though the narrative impetus for the memoir is provided, as mentioned earlier, by a bureaucratic self-fashioning. It is not hard to imagine why Banerjea would situate himself at a remove from the colonial bureaucracy, which, in the absence of representative institutions, largely stood in for the intransigent colonial state. It is also very probable that in writing *Nation* in 1925, Banerjea specifically sought to distance himself from the bureaucracy precisely because he had come to be associated with it in Extremist parlance. After all, Moderate demands had not only emanated from a bureaucratic modernity but also were bureaucratic in nature, inasmuch as they sought reform of the bureaucracy and greater Indian representation in it as their urgent demand.[123] It is significant, however, that in distancing himself from the bureaucracy, Banerjea draws attention to the drawbacks of bureaucracy itself, and not just its colonial incarnation:

> Bureaucracy is always unequal to a new situation or to an unexpected development. So long as things go on in the normal groove, bureaucracy, deriving its light and leading from precedent and from ancient dust-laden files, feels happy and confident. But when the clouds appear on the horizon and when there is the ominous presage of stormy weather ahead, the bureaucratic mind feels restive; the files afford no guidance . . . (195)

By depicting the bureaucracy in what can be described as its "systematic functionality,"[124] Banerjea renders it insensible to the turns of history, to the challenges posed by imminently more vibrant demotic aspirations. In doing so, he participates in a critique that also becomes a necessary response—and one that is by no means singular—to the paradoxical relationship between bureaucracy and democracy. After all, it is precisely the rationality of bureaucratic knowledge, the systemized "knowledge of the files,"[125] that lends the bureaucracy what Weber describes as its necessarily "permanent character," enabling it to perform its functions in keeping with a "societally exercised authority," rather than "feudal orders based upon personal piety."[126] But this also renders the bureaucracy seemingly inert—or, as Weber puts it, "unshatterable"—with the result that "democracy as such is opposed to the rule of bureaucracy in spite of its unavoidable yet unintended promotion of bureaucratization."[127] Depicting the bureaucracy in its stifling insensibility, Weber's logic suggests, becomes one way of continually renewing our faith in democracy (and in government).

Banerjea's highlighting of the bureaucracy in precisely those terms reflects some of that logic and can perhaps be explained by reasons other than a critique of colonial practices alone: bracketing off the bureaucracy does not so much reaffirm faith in the British as it vivifies a more vibrant self-government, in whose "beginnings" Banerjea was so invested. Upon taking on the portfolio of Local Self-Government in Bengal in 1918—after an election that was highly unpopular among the Extremists, who felt that Banerjea was giving in too readily to minor electoral concessions granted to Indians in a show of the progressive realization of responsible government—Banerjea threw himself into ensuring the enactment of the Calcutta Municipal Act, which extended the municipal franchise among Indians, including women. While the passing of the Municipal Act marked what Banerjea considered a milestone, it received, according to him, a fairly lukewarm response from the Extremist press. Recalling his involvement with the act, in fact, Banerjea notes: as "officials and bureaucrats, [we were] associated with a machinery that was designed to perpetuate a fraud and whitewash a delusion ... In vain did we protest we were not officials" (*Nation*, 349). While his disclaimer tries to carve a more nuanced position vis-à-vis what was perceived to be his bureaucratic role, and his collaboration with the colonial state,[128] the logic of its underlying anxiety also indicates why Banerjea himself gets written out of the ensuing narrative of nationalism. After all, for Aurobindo, the failure of the early Congress lay precisely in its interest in appealing "to the British for more places in the civil service instead of arousing a sense of patriotism."[129] Evidently, while early formulations of citizenship and anticolonial critique were forged through the site of bureaucratic modernity, its technologies, *Nation* implicitly suggests, were rendered incompatible with what was projected as the more organic "spirit" of the nation—one that could be invoked through nativist heroes and atavistic pasts, not (Indian) competition-civilians.[130]

However, as Manu Goswami points out in her study of the territorialization of Indian nationhood in the late nineteenth and early twentieth centuries, despite its pitting of what was posited as the "'synthetic' organic unity of indigenous institutions" against the "'analytical, mechano-centric' character of Western society,"[131] Indian nationalism of the period "had profound statist implications"[132] that invoked the centralized (bureaucratic) model of the developmental state. Goswami's insightful delineation of how populist ideals of *swaraj* were imbricated with premeditations of statehood illustrates how, as David Lloyd notes in a broader context, "it is a peculiarity of nationalism that of all modes of potentially counterhegemonic formations none is more thoroughly reinscribed by the formations it ostensibly opposes."[133] It is telling that the structure of the ICS, including its Indian members, was retained in the Indian Administrative Service that was created after independence.[134] And it is perhaps something of the "peculiarity" that Lloyd mentions that the narrative of Indian nationalism mediates, in part, by locating the Moderates—in all their "bureaucratic" affiliation—along a teleology of nationalism, where they represent an "inadequate" phase that is acknowledged only in the certainty of its supersession. Ironically, the narrative grounds itself in a gradualism that it seeks to critique.

In one of the few historiographies of Moderate nationalism, Seth thoughtfully draws attention to the "curious mixing of metaphors" that characterizes the nationalist narrative, one in which the Moderates are at once the "founding fathers" of Indian nationalism but represent its "childhood" phase.[135] A temporal paradox, indeed, the anomalies of which are ironed over by a gendered injunction: at the infamous 1907 Surat Congress, for instance, Tilak had declared, "They *fear* a civilised government. It is *unmanly*. If you are not prepared to brave the dangers, be quiet, but don't ask *us* to retrograde"[136] (emphasis added). The unmanly "Moderate" becomes, like the "competitionwallah," a product of the necessary unevenness of bureaucratic modernity that he also helps mediate.

Given the implicit teleology of Indian nationalism, it is worth remembering here that, despite the linearity informing Banerjea's overt selection and ordering of events in *Nation*, the narrative also works against this assigned chronology. Banerjea emphasizes in the preface:

> The need for Reminiscences such as these has become all the more pressing in view of recent developments in our public life, when unfortunately there is a marked, and perhaps a growing, tendency among a certain section of our people to forget the services of our early nation-builders—of those who have placed India on the road to constitutional freedom. (*Nation*, unnumbered page)

And, as becomes evident, *Nation* presents not just an accounting of Banerjea's life but that of his Moderate contemporaries as well, the "early nation-builders" who were already being superseded in the unfolding narrative of the nation.

Noting the extraordinary interest Banerjea takes in narrating his contemporaries, Bhikhu Parekh suggests that "Banerjea felt uneasy talking about himself and could only do so in the name and under the protective shelter of an impersonal entity."[137] It is true that Banerjea's narrative—replete with phrases like "of him also I should like to say a word or two" (*Nation*, 119)—seems only too ready to interrupt its flow by offering vignettes of his contemporaries. Parekh reads this compulsive interest in other people's lives as a device to narrate oneself through indirection, a move that, he notes, characterizes an "Indian" unease with the genre of autobiography.[138] But the fact that most of those whom Banerjea mentions in his autobiography were already dead at the time of his writing—a fact that also renders the autobiography an obituary—indicates, I would suggest, another node of compulsion: it infuses the narrative with a temporality that interrupts the linearity of the autobiography, illuminating the disjunctions of the nation whose disparate making Banerjea registers.

At a robust rate of what would be one death for every fifteen pages, *Nation* names—indeed, individually mourns—no fewer than thirty people, including Ambika Charan Majumdar, Pherozeshah Mehta, Badruddin Tyabji, and Kashinath Telang, all drawn from different parts of the country but constituting a national body politic that had apparently run its "moderate" course. "All of them are now," Banerjea writes, "alas, dead and gone" (*Nation*, 49). The obituary, Judith Butler notes, functions as the instrument by which "grievability is publicly distributed"; by establishing the protocols of who is to be mourned, the obituary itself becomes "an act of nation-building."[139] In this, it is significant that through what was the relative novelty of his very public rendition of grief,[140] Banerjea pointedly casts the incipient nation in terms of its relation to the dead. The insistence of his grief, in fact, makes the nation by reminding it of its multiple births and its stillborn citizens: it militates against the imputed teleology of the nationalist narrative, perversely peopling it with those who are otherwise rendered "inadequate" or "incomplete" in the fullness of the nationalist "now."[141]

While simply naming the departed constitutes an act of mourning, *Nation* also dwells on what is to be mourned. Noting the death of Ananda Mohan Bose, for instance, Banerjea writes: "Mr. Ananda Mohan Bose, with his great intellectual and moral gifts did not combine that physical robustness which sets them off to the best advantage, nor, I have to add regretfully, did he take that great care of his health" (*Nation*, 38). An emphasis on the neglected health and premature death of his contemporaries is a concomitant to many of *Nation*'s elegies, even as Banerjea glosses over the deaths and even the lives of his wife and son. The solicitousness of Banerjea's grief for his friends, in fact, makes room for a certain intimacy in an autobiography that ostensibly locates itself in the nonfamilial, nonprivate realm. The continual interjection of grief-stricken lamentations in *Nation* infuses its "public" domain with intimations of the "private," speaking not only to the multiple registers through which the "private" is autobiographically constituted,[142] but also to how the nation-space—as Banerjea formulates it—is riven with temporal contingencies and affective dissonances, even when marked in terms of a bureaucratic logic. To point this out is to consider the necessary disjunctions underlying associative principles of rational civil society, which, in Banerjea's case, can evidently hail the citizen only through multiply refracted temporalities. Indeed, it is through his recurrent emphasis on the bodies of the departed that Banerjea inserts himself as "citizen" by reworking the nation and its dead in a continual arithmetic of body, time, and space that extends the corporeal beyond the temporal—thereby accommodating those rendered outmoded, like Banerjea. *Nation*'s exigencies of mourning thus call attention to the fundamental disjunctions undergirding his ideation of citizenship. In fact, to overlook *Nation*'s implied incompatibilities would be to attribute perhaps too much to the seemingly settled norms of liberal citizenship, whose implied singularity, otherwise, provokes responses that often displace its potential salutariness. It is significant that the affective economy of Banerjea's unrequited mourning not only renders insufficient the singular birth of the nation, but also punctuates the purportedly seamless transition of the citizen-body from competition-civilian to Hindu ascetic.[143]

In blurring the boundaries between autobiography and obituary, in narrating himself through the deaths of others, Banerjea writes, then, an exemplary text of mourning as he underscores the fact that mourning is a precondition for life, that it constitutes an epistemological necessity.[144] The unrequited nature of his mourning, however, makes his narrative a failure of sorts, inasmuch as the "success" of mourning depends on the negation of its condition.[145] Derrida succinctly notes: "in order to succeed, [mourning] would well have to *fail*, fail *well*"[146] (emphasis in the original). It is not only the logic of mourning that singularizes the thematic of failure in the text, but also Banerjea's own failed status as civilian, national "hero," or even imperial citizen. However, if *Nation* allows also for the narrative restitution of Banerjea and the citizenship he lays claim to, then the various formulations of imperial citizenship also take on a symbolic import for the many others who remain unnamed or unmourned, or who are accommodated within the postcolonial nation only as "failure." It is a reminder of this failure, though, that produces a "mindfulness" that, as Wendy Brown notes, "conjures the power of the past while resisting any preordained implications of that power for the making of a more just future."[147] As Banerjea concedes in his final paragraph, "we cannot remain wedded to the past . . . move on we must . . . with a loving concern for the present and with deep solicitude for the future" (*Nation*, 403). The haunting corporeality of the text does not necessarily unsettle this historicity by trafficking with the past; rather, in mourning what is being construed as the "past" or as "failure," it becomes another way to insistently urge alternate possibilities—of history, of nation, of citizenship.

If Banerjea's story of the nation becomes also a requiem, it provides a meditation on the ethics of citizenship itself—one that measures the proximity between death and debt, one that alerts us to the politics of presence and absence. It registers the failure that marks imperial citizenship itself: the failed promises by the colonial/imperial state that provide its narrative dynamic, as well as the imminent failure of imperial citizenship in the face of the triumphalist and unitary narrative of the nation. Imperial citizenship in many ways underlines how narrative often fails the citizen. Yet it is this failure that impels, as in the case of Banerjea, an insistent questioning of what is embodied and abstracted in the code of citizenship, what congeals in the name of the nation-to-be. If Banerjea as imperial citizen can inhabit only a nation that never was, then imperial citizenship becomes a template for what is realized in the name of the nation and the citizen—and what remains unrealizable in the prose of citizenship that remains but fugitive.

Afterword

While Banerjea's articulation of citizenship remains suffused with a sense of loss or failure, the idea of imperial citizenship did gain ground in various guises in the early decades of the twentieth century. Even as official policies of imperial citizenship discussed by various colonial officials, functionaries, and visionaries failed to take off, and even as legislation like the British Nationality and Status of Aliens Act of 1914 failed to bear fruit for Indians, the concept of imperial citizenship itself continued to gain prominence as the rallying point for a political vocabulary, inasmuch as it provided the ground for articulating liberal universalist ideals of citizenship. For instance, the Imperial Indian Citizenship Association, founded in Bombay in 1914, functioned as a watchdog for the rights of Indians across the British Empire, concerning itself with the "Indian question" particularly in South Africa, East Africa (especially Kenya), and Fiji.¹ As one of the association's founding members noted: "To our Indian fellow-countrymen, our message is one of fearless pursuit of civic rights and absolute equality shorn of every humiliating disability on any racial or economic ground."² But even as the association sought to act as a clearinghouse, disseminating information about Indian grievances across the empire and stepping up appeals to relevant authorities both in India and the settler-colonies, it also had the objective of making the case for imperial citizenship before Indians living in India itself: "It is no longer possible," one of the group's reports pointed out, "for the Colonies and Dominions to legislate for these Indians without provoking the closest scrutiny on the part of the Indian public."³

Indeed, the discussion on citizenship was quite an active one in India, in ways that linked civic rights with political autonomy, and civil liberties with the franchise.⁴ In his 1919 *Rights of Citizens*, S. Satyamurthy provided a treatise on modern citizenship, emphasizing that "the State is no longer a sovereign power which commands" but "a group of individuals having in their control forces which they must employ to create and to manage public service."⁵ Interestingly, Satyamurthy appended to his work a resolution adopted by the Indian National Congress and the All-India Muslim League, which emphasized that "the Statute [the Government of India Act of 1919] to be passed by the Parliament should include the declaration of the rights of the people of India as British citizens: that all Indian subjects naturalized or resident in India are equal before the law."[6] Notably, the resolution made no mention of the Queen's Proclamation of 1858. The fact that it evidently did not need to do so, in 1918, is no small indication of the ongoing naturalization of a vocabulary of rights, one that also exceeded the question of sovereign promise or imperial benevolence. But as this book has shown, the naturalization of the new vocabulary took place in disparate venues and through diverse routes, which often extended beyond the realm of the juridico-political. Tracing the multiple strands of citizenship and their complex affective and imaginative ideations—indeed, even associating them with the project of citizenship—makes clear that the history of citizenship has multiple bearings and points of provenance, which not only exceed the compartmentalization of citizenship into discrete civil, political, and social units,[7] but also call for an entwining of legal history with social process, political negotiations with their cultural and affective imaginings. It points to how the category of citizenship is hardly self-evident. Prying citizenship apart from the nation-state in fact allows for a capacious reading of these histories of citizenship.[8] It keeps alive the ties between citizenship as defined—and denied—by the state and its intimate links with notions of civil liberty and civil society.[9] At the very least, keeping alive the alterity of citizenship—its contingent pasts and possible futures—helps us gauge how, when, and why citizenship is claimed by the nation-state, an understanding necessary for continually negotiating with a political entity whose salience remains inescapable.

S. V. Puntambekar pointed out in 1928: "A citizen is a civilized being. It is a great advance on the old idea of a legal citizen that we now study a citizen's life in all its aspects, political, social, religious, economic and cultural."[10] Remarkably prescient in terms of our current reformulations of the ambit of citizenship, Puntambekar went on to outline citizenship in its "Indian" incarnation: "Indian citizenship deals with a citizen's full life in India, his past, present, and future as influenced by Indian environment, tradition, and the currents of her civilisation."[11] For Puntambekar, not only does the template of citizenship make it possible to claim an epistemology as Indian, but its universal ideals also allow for the envisioning of a bounded territoriality as "India": "No doubt India presents some disintegrating tendencies in her caste system, her various creeds, her different languages," Puntambekar points out, "but it is a peculiar fact that all her castes, creeds or groups conceive India as one."[12] If it is the universalist assumption of citizenship that instantly unites a disparate and disjointed populace into a common teleology—to fill the space of the nation with all who are "Indians"—in an alchemy Puntambekar describes as a "peculiar fact," then it is also noteworthy that for him, India emerges as "a separate geographical unit marked out by nature,"[13] one that is "not the result of British conquest and rule, but ... is essentially a persistent Hindu conception moulding the life of the people throughout her history."[14] In its conflation of the nation (and its potentially incendiary myth of origins) with citizenship, this observation should be located alongside the formulations of citizenship posited by others like Satyamurthy or the Imperial Indian Citizenship Association, if only to get a sense of the competing discourses of citizenship in terms of the distinct national imaginaries—cartographic or psychic—that they variously tapped and formulated. The irony of the universal ideal of citizenship, of course, is that it chooses the highly particularized category of the nation-state to announce its universality. In this, arresting precisely the inevitability of the form of nationhood—and its particular imaginary—maintains, if cautiously, the contingencies of the universal.

In giving weight to the genealogy that such an endeavor demands, it behooves us to note the failings of imperial citizenship: to become official policy; to meet the demands put forth by some of the figures under study in this book; and, by the 1930s, to effectively encapsulate the political demands of the Indian people. This is just as well. Nonetheless, to study the various formulations of imperial citizenship accords a historical thickness to the envisioning of India as "India"; it acknowledges a debt that has evidently remained invisible. Acknowledging that debt expands the understanding of citizenship beyond the trajectory of the nation; it also allows for a reckoning of failure itself as something other than only lack or limitation. If colonial subjects repeatedly articulated their positions as citizens in ways that were marked by failure in the expansive context of empire, then not only does the nation emerge in the face of this failure but, importantly, it defines it as such. And to excavate this failure—indeed, to read and write failure into citizenship in general—is not necessarily a redundant exercise: it reconfigures citizenship as process, something that the triumphalism of nationalist discourse often obscures. "Any political language," Judith Butler notes in a more theoretical strain, "must be one of failure, for the failure to fill the place ... is precisely the future promise of universality, its status as a limitless and unconditional feature of all political articulation."[15] To register how imperial citizenship narrativizes failure, is a failed narrative, or fails narrative is not, then, without dividend. At the very least, it deflects the complacency engendered by the premise of universal citizenship, in its plenitude and rationality.

Indeed to go back to an earlier moment—and back to British Columbia, an outpost of the British Empire that this book started with—it is worthwhile to dwell, by way of an epilogue, on the incident of the *Komagata Maru*. Entering Vancouver Harbour in May 1914, the *Komagata Maru* carried approximately 350 Sikh passengers, who had incurred heavy expenses in chartering the ship in order to travel a continuous route to Canada (in an attempt to prevent Indians from entering Canada, the Canadian authorities had enacted a seemingly innocuous law that allowed entry only to those who arrived in Canada by a continuous route, thereby rendering it almost impossible for Indians to travel to Canada). Although the *Komagata Maru* had followed a continuous route and did not, therefore, violate immigration rules, the passengers were denied entry to Canada. After a long standoff, during which the passengers were allegedly denied representation or any means of communication with acquaintances ashore, the ship was ordered to return to India, denied even the chance to stock provisions for the long journey back across the Pacific. Eventually, the Canadian government relented in allowing the ship to replenish its supplies, but only in preparation for the passengers to leave Canada even before they entered it. After an arduous journey, during which the ship had to seek help from the British consul in Kobe, the *Komagata Maru* finally reached Calcutta in September 1914.[16]

Predictably, this incident aroused resentment and recrimination, with the Imperial Indian Citizenship Association including the details of the case even as late as in its 1927 collection of reports, "The question at issue is not," the report quoted an observer, "whether Canada has a legal right to exclude anybody but whether British citizenship carries with it the right of free entrance to any part of the Empire."[17] But, according to the observer, an even more pointed question raised by the case of the *Komagata Maru* was if "any race [has] a moral right to consider any part of the world's surface as its own special reserve."[18] In examining the various possibilities that the multiple formulation of citizenship by colonial subjects of empire opened up—as well as the boundaries and limitations that these formulations hinged upon—and in debating whether imperial citizenship was a failure or doomed to fail, it may well be meet to use the fate of imperial citizenship as an instance to ask what the "success" of citizenship might mean, or at least to concede the continuing relevance of such a question.

Notes

Introduction

1. "Memorandum from Hindu Friend Society of Victoria, British Columbia, to Colonial Office, April 28, 1911, in Oriental and India Office Collections (henceforth OIOC), *Imperial Conference, 1911*, 281.

2. Petition on behalf of Moolchand Shivcharan Dass, October 30, 1905, in National Archives of India (henceforth NAI), "Alleged Unlawful Deportation from Australia of a Native of India," 90.

3. Banerjea, *Bengalee*, January 14, 1893.

4. For a description of the political status of the subject who does not partake of any sovereign authority but is a "subject of the Prince," see Balibar, "Citizen Subject," 47. With respect to Britain, this notion of the subject had precedence in common law, according to which "subjects are called [the king's] liege subjects, because they are bound to obey and serve him, and he is called their liege lord because he should maintain and defend them" (Jones, *British Nationality Law and Practice*, 32–33).

5. This is to say that as subjects of the Crown, Indians were variously marked by what Partha Chatterjee describes as the "rule of colonial difference" that suspended the application of universalist principles of representative self-government (*The Nation and Its Fragments*, 18).

6. The provisions of the Australian Immigration Restriction Act had been relaxed to allow Indian "merchants, students, and tourists" to visit Australia. Cited in a letter from Secretary to the Government of India, Department of Revenue and Agriculture, to all Local Governments and Administrations, October 18, 1904, in NAI, "Australian Immigration Restriction Act (Amendment Act), no. 17 of 1905," 297.

7. Benhabib, *The Claims of Culture*, 172.

8. Banerjea, *A Nation in Making*, 116.

9. Ibid., 117.

10. Ibid., 116. Banerjea, like many of the figures of study in this book, often uses "England" or "English" interchangeably with "Britain" or "British." When I use "England" or "English" in this book to maintain consistency with the quoted material—or for geographical reasons—I do so with an awareness of the hegemonic relation of Englishness to other constituent nodes of British identity. For a good discussion of the relation of Englishness to British identity, see Baucom, *Out of Place*.

11. See McClintock, "'No Longer in a Future Heaven,'" 89.

12. Chatterjee, *The Nation and Its Fragments*, 25–26.

13. Exceptions to this are the scholarship on formulations of citizenship from the late nineteenth century through the early twentieth with regard to Indian women's enfranchisement and emergence as citizens. See A. Roy, *Gendered Citizenship*; T. Sarkar, "Enfranchised Selves"; and Sinha, *Specters of Mother India* and "Suffragism and Internationalism."

14. For example, in her important study of colonial India, Nair points out that "there cannot be 'rights-bearing subjects' where there are no citizens" and that the "ideology that promised citizenship and the nation state, [was] namely nationalism" (*Women and Law in Colonial India*, 38–39). Conversely, for a reading of how the study of citizenship can be preempted on account of its Enlightenment legacy, see S. Sarkar, *Writing Social History*, 107.

15. Berlant, *The Queen of America Goes to Washington City*, 20.

16. Jones, *British Nationality Law and Practice*, 6.

17. Benhabib, *The Claims of Culture*, 161.

18. Ibid., 16. Such a formulation is being pursued from various disciplinary perspectives. See Canning and Rose, Introduction; McClelland and Rose, "Citizenship and Empire," 277; Sommers, "Citizenship and the Place of the Public Sphere"; Schaffer and Smith, *Human Rights and Narrated Lives*; and R. Smith, *Stories of Peoplehood*.

19. Sassen, "The Repositioning of Citizenship," 56.

20. On this point, see Spivak's "Diasporas Old and New."

21. The phrase is borrowed from the title of Ong, *Flexible Citizenship*.

22. Sassen, "The Participation of States and Citizens in Global Governance," 16.

23. Ibid., 27. See also Kerber, "The Meanings of Citizenship."

24. See, for example, Anderson and Guha, Introduction; and Hasan, Sridharan, and Sudarshan, *India's Living Constitution*.

25. For an insightful account of the ways in which the absence of a code of imperial citizenship actually helped further claims of imperial unity across the British Empire, see Gorman, "Wider and Wider Still?"

26. The emphasis on what it takes to "become" a citizen reflects how citizenship is always, as Etienne Balibar describes, a "moving historical site that is both sociological and symbolic: a meeting point between processes of transformation of the division of labor, of population movements, of revolutions in manners, and dynamics of emancipation or solidarity" (*We the People of Europe*, 77). For different elaborations on this point, see Isin, *Being Political*, 275–76. See also B. Turner, "Contemporary Problems in the Theory of Citizenship," 2.

27. Chakrabarty, *Provincializing Europe*, 8.

28. See Gibbins, "J. S. Mill, Liberalism, and Progress"; and Malachuk, *Perfection, the State, and Victorian Liberalism*.

29. Recent books on various aspects of Victorian liberalism include: A. Anderson, *The Powers of Distance*; Dellamora, *Friendship's Bonds*; Goodlad, *Victorian Literature and the Victorian State*; and Thomas, *Cultivating Victo-*

rians. This is by no means an exhaustive list; it is meant only to indicate the renewed scholarly interest in Victorian liberalism.

30. Goodlad, *Victorian Literature and the Victorian State*, 21.

31. Bailkin, "The Place of Liberalism," 84.

32. These sites have recently been the focus of engaging scholarly studies. See Cólon, *The Professional Ideal in the Victorian Novel*; Ruth, *Novel Professions*; and Schuman, *Pedagogical Economies*.

33. Antoinette Burton, "Who Needs the Nation?" 140. See also Hall, "Thinking the Postcolonial"; Schwarz, "The Expansion and Contraction of England"; Sinha, "Britain and Empire"; and Tabili, *"We Ask for British Justice."*

34. This is to say that the emphasis on Indians' roles as interlocutors does not necessarily assume a coherent, uniform subject position that renders predictable the terms of their appellation as "colonial," or delimits their appellation to that rubric alone.

35. One cannot point, of course, to a single, unified liberal ideology of the nineteenth century. For a discussion of the many strands and versions of liberalism in its social, economic, and political registers, see Bellamy, Introduction. My reference to nineteenth-century liberalism in this book speaks not to a particular political or economic strain of liberalism, but to its larger engagement with questions—and trajectories—of representation and self-determination, especially as it formulated itself on the basis of a formal equality.

36. See Robb, *Liberalism, Modernity, and the Nation*. For accounts of the nineteenth-century Indian negotiation with liberalism as a political doctrine, see Bayly, "Rammohan Roy and the Advent of Constitutional Liberalism in India"; and Moore, *Liberalism and Indian Politics*.

37. Sinha, *Specters of Mother India*, 16.

38. Such a move would fall under the broad rubric of what Chakrabarty describes as "provincializing Europe," but my emphasis rests more on his recent reiteration that "universalistic thought [is] always and already modified by particular histories" (Chakrabarty, "Preface to the 2007 Edition," in *Provincializing Europe*, xiv; see also *Provincializing Europe*, 69–71; and Dube, "Presence of Europe," 865). It is this irreducibly "modified" nature of the Enlightenment discourse of citizenship that I trace by focusing on registers that are readily considered more familiar to it.

39. Wallerstein, "Citizens All?" 652.

40. See Kazanjian, *The Colonizing Trick*; Stovall and Van Den Abbeleele, *French Civilization and Its Discontents*; and Goldberg, *Racist Culture*.

41. Joan Wallach Scott, *Only Paradoxes to Offer*, 18.

42. The "claim to universality," Judith Butler notes, "always takes place in a given syntax, through a certain set of cultural conventions in a recognizable venue" ("Restaging the Universal," 35). Any claim to the universal, therefore, can be iterated only through the particular, in ways that qualify the universality of the claim while also rendering it possible (hence

its doubleness). In emphasizing the narrativity of citizenship, I would like to follow through with how a materialist reading of citizenship reveals its doubleness not as a theoretical presupposition alone, but also as an effect of the narrative registers that make a universalist claim possible while also modeling—sometimes inadvertently—its necessary exclusions. This speaks more to the implicit exclusions of the particular narrative registers (the social values and the categories they deploy) that enable the formulation of citizenship than it does to the compromised nature of universality alone, but both need to be taken into account.

43. Sinha, "Suffragism and Internationalism," 483. See also her *Specters of Mother India*, 14–15, and "The Lineage of the 'Indian' Modern."

44. Marx, following Rousseau, notes that the political man, the citizen, is "only abstract," not "man in his sensuous, individual and *immediate* existence" ("On the Jewish Question," 46). Marx uses much the same logic in describing what makes capitalist exchange possible: "But clearly, the exchange relation of commodities is characterized precisely by its abstraction from their use-values." As he points out just a little earlier, use-value is "conditioned by the physical body of the commodity itself" (*Capital*, 126–27). For a discussion of the homology between capital and citizenship, see Kazanjian, *The Colonizing Trick*.

45. Some of the influential critiques from varying feminist perspectives include Pateman, *The Sexual Contract*; Scott, *Only Paradoxes to Offer*; and Young, *Inclusion and Political Democracy*.

46. See Lowe, *Immigrant Acts*.

47. White, "The Value of Narrativity in the Representation of Reality," 1. For a more recent discussion that expands the scope of this argument, see White, "Historical Fiction, Fictional History, and Historical Reality."

48. See, for example, Brooks and Gewitz, *Law's Stories*.

49. Mehta, *Liberalism and Empire*, 7.

50. Ibid., 49.

51. Mill, "Considerations on Representative Government," 453. For a discussion of the role India played in Mills's intellectual career, see Zastoupil, *John Stuart Mill and India*.

52. See Mehta, *Liberalism and Empire*, 74–76.

53. Stepan, "Race, Gender, Science, and Citizenship," 29.

54. It is worth considering here the case that Amanda Anderson makes in a different but related context for examining the stance of cultivated detachment that was important in Victorian authors' negotiations with modernity. Anderson persuasively argues for the significance of this avowed objectivity as a focus of study, even as such a stance has been unpopular in contemporary "materialist, feminist, poststructuralist, and identity-based criticism," which explicitly prefers "opposing ideals" of "situatedness, embodiedness, particularity, and contingency" (*The Powers of Distance*, 7). I am mindful here, too, of Elaine Hadley's cautionary reminder that the critical detachment that Anderson delineates was itself part of a larger politi-

cal project that was woefully inadequate in delivering its promises ("On a Darkling Plain," 99). My interest is not in the Victorian stance of critical detachment, but in studying the colonial approximations of a formal equality, I emphasize the importance of tracing the narrative move toward a disembodied abstraction. However, I take such a move to be contingent, strategic, and ultimately failed—although worthy of study inasmuch as it is necessitated by the very limitations of the Victorian liberal project that Hadley rightly points out.

55. For an example of the wide-ranging importance of this kind of scholarship with reference to South Asia, see Mills and Sen, *Confronting the Body*.

56. Frederick Cooper's reminder that the "critique of universalism and the critique of particularism ... both remain at too high a level of abstraction to explain how any framing developed in the course of interaction or struggle or to help us reframe issues in the future and discuss responsibility for future action" is apropos (*Colonialism in Question*, 138). Recent studies that similarly engage in the discrepant negotiations with other aspects of Enlightenment thought include Sorkin, *The Religious Enlightenment*; and Mufti, *Enlightenment in the Colony*.

57. Sunder Rajan, *Scandal of the State*, 22. See also Scott, "Universalism and the History of Feminism"; Werbner and Yuval-Davis, Introduction; Chakrabarty, "Subject of Law and Subject of Narratives," 112; and Sinha, *Specters of Mother India*, 12.

58. As Ernesto Laclau observes, the "universal does not have a concrete content of its own" but "is the always receding horizon resulting from the expansion of an indefinite chain of equivalent demands" ("Universalism, Particularism, and the Question of Identity," 101).

59. N. Singh, *Black Is a Country*, 40.

60. I am grateful to one of the readers for Duke University Press for urging me to develop this point.

61. Laclau, "Subject of Politics, Politics of the Subject," 152.

62. The idea of citizenship as capture is apropos, given what I take to be its fugitive nature. The following description gives one example of this fugitivity: the citizen is "neither the individual nor the collective, just as he is neither an exclusively public being nor a private being" (Balibar, "Citizen-Subject," 51).

63. Not only is the gothic characterized by its fascination with extremities of being, but it is also ridden with "a contextual and proprietary" concern about the corporeal, about how and where bodies should be placed (Mighall, *A Geography of Victorian Gothic Fiction*, 142). It is the gothic concern with corporeality that brings it in proximity with discussions of citizenship. Following George Haggerty, I use "gothic" in the lower case as I am referring to a mode of narrative, rather than to a specific aesthetic movement (Haggerty, *Queer Gothic*, 205).

64. For a rich reading of how the gothic provided an apt metaphor for

the upheavals of the French Revolution, see Paulson, "Gothic Fiction and the French Revolution." The reading does not, however, extend the connection to ensuing formulations of citizenship.

65. Here I refer particularly to the imbrication of gothic discourse with questions of representation: the ability of the gothic to convey "the crucial problematic of the presentation of that which had previously been thought presentable" (Mishra, *The Gothic Sublime*, 16).

66. T. Sarkar, "Enfranchised Selves: Women, Culture and Rights in Nineteenth-Century Bengal," 122.

67. Gorman, "Wider and Wider Still?" 16.

68. Kaviraj, "The Imaginary Institution of India," 1.

69. Duara, "Historicizing National Identity," 152.

70. Benjamin, "Theses on the Philosophy of History," 256.

71. Vernon, "Notes Towards an Introduction," 9. Conversely, arguing that because English law was unwritten, the onus was on defenders to "preserve the law, not interpret it," Ian Baucom provides an excellent reading of the ways in which notions of "Englishness" were constructed through the legislations regarding nationality and immigration (*Out of Place*, 9). Both perspectives are crucial in considering how Indians negotiated with laws regarding British nationality and subjecthood.

72. For an elaboration of this distinction, see Balibar, "Citizen Subject," 47.

73. For an elaboration of the varied understandings of citizenship, see McClelland and Rose, "Citizenship and Empire, 1867–1928," 284–88.

74. Gorman describes the official and quasi-official attempts—made primarily by four metropolitan thinkers—to institute a common citizenship across the empire; see Gorman, *Imperial Citizenship*.

75. Lister, *Citizenship*, 70.

76. See Hall, "The Nation Within and Without," 180; and Gilbert, *The Citizen's Body*, chap. 1.

77. Hall, McClelland, and Rendall, Introduction, 58.

78. McClelland, "'England's Greatness, the Working Man,'" 72.

79. Rendall, "The Citizenship of Women and the Reform Act of 1867," 169.

80. Rendall, "Citizenship, Culture, and Civilisation," 129.

81. Quoted in Hall, "The Nation Within and Without," 222.

82. Woollacott, "Australian Women's Metropolitan Activism," 209.

83. Fletcher, "Women of the Nations, Unite!" 112.

84. See Burton, *Burdens of History*; and Grewal, *Home and Harem*, chap. 2.

85. Burton, *Burdens of History*, 175.

86. George, *The Politics of Home*, 38.

87. The importance of taking the diasporic nature of empire into account is taken up further in chapter 2. It is variously formulated in Axel, *The*

Nation's Tortured Body; Ho, "Empire through Diasporic Eyes"; and Mohanram, *Race, Diaspora, and the British Empire*.

88. Except in extended surveys, such as Visram, *Ayahs, Lascars, and Princes*; and Fisher, Lahiri, and Thandi, *A South-Asian History of Britain*.

89. OIOC, *Proclamation, by the Queen in Council, to the Princes, Chiefs, and People of India*, 117–18.

90. See Hunt, *The French Revolution and Human Rights*, 13.

91. Butler, "Restaging the Universal," 40.

92. See Kendle, *The Colonial and Imperial Conferences 1887–1922*.

93. Quoted in "Position of British Indians in the Dominions," in OIOC, *Imperial Conference, 1911*, 829.

94. "British Nationality and Status of Aliens Act, 1914," 32. The principle of *jus soli*, "right of the soil," that the act embodies formed the basis of British nationality law until 1981.

95. "British Nationality and Status of Aliens Act, 1914," 34. Those born in the territory of British India were non-European natural-born British subjects, but through naturalization could be treated as natural-born European subjects. See Parry, *Nationality and Citizenship Laws of the Commonwealth and of the Republic of Ireland*, 169.

96. OIOC, *Conference of Prime Ministers and Representatives of the United Kingdom, The Dominions, and India, held in June, July, and August, 1921*, 74.

97. "Empire Men of the Moment: India at the Imperial Conference," *Daily News*, June 16, 1921.

98. For Richard Jebb's interest in an official policy of imperial citizenship, see Gorman, *Imperial Citizenship*, chap. 2.

99. Richard Jebb, letter to the editor, *Morning Post*, June 29, 1921.

100. Jones, *British Nationality Law and Practice*, 232. See also Parry, *Nationality and Citizenship Laws of the Commonwealth and of the Republic of Ireland*, xv and 82–87.

101. Parry, *Nationality and Citizenship Laws of the Commonwealth and of the Republic of Ireland*, xv.

102. Dummett and Nicol, *Subjects, Citizens, Aliens and Others*, 2.

103. Paul, *Whitewashing Britain*, 20.

104. See, for instance, Ranajit Guha, "Chandra's Death." For a specific elaboration of this point with relation to law, see Upendra Baxi, "The State's Emissary," 252; and Radhika Singha, *A Despotism of Law*, xiv.

105. In addition to Sunder Rajan, *Scandal of the State*, examples include Tharu, "Citizenship and Its Discontents"; and Kapur, *Erotic Justice*.

106. Kaviraj, "The Imaginary Institution of India," 2.

107. Ibid., 6.

108. Ibid., 29.

109. Dummett and Nicol, *Subjects, Citizens, Aliens and Others*, 81.

110. Ibid., 83.

111. Gorman, *Imperial Citizenship*, 18.

112. Quoted in "Constitution of the Empire," in 010C, *Imperial War Conference, 1917*, 368.

113. See Pandey, "Can a Muslim Be an Indian?"

114. Boehmer, *Empire, the National, and the Postcolonial, 1890–1920*; and Bose, *Organizing Empire*.

115. Goswami, *Producing India*, 5.

116. Bhabha, "DissemiNation."

117. See Argov, *Moderates and Extremists in the Indian Nationalist Movement*.

118. Seth, "Rewriting Histories of Nationalism," 98.

119. Ibid., 115.

120. I owe this formulation to James Vernon, who points out that a historiography privileging only the discourse of the "real" entails "a denial of desire, a denial of ambiguity and doubt, . . . and a denial of the pleasures of the past and its alterity" ("Narrating the Constitution," 213).

121. Bhabha, "DissemiNation," 295.

122. Ibid., 293.

123. Ibid., 291.

124. Ibid., 303.

125. See Brennan, "The National Longing for Form."

126. Azim, *The Colonial Rise of the Novel*, 10.

127. Jameson, "Third-World Literature in the Era of Multinational Capitalism."

128. Bahri makes due note of the "overrepresentation of postcolonial literature in the novel form" (*Native Intelligence*, 201). See also Edwards, "The Genres of Postcolonialism," 2.

129. Jahan Ramazani, *The Hybrid Muse: Postcolonial Poetry in English* (Chicago: University of Chicago Press, 2001), 4, quoted in Edwards, "The Genres of Postcolonialism," 2.

130. See Chaudhuri, "*The Flute, Gerontion*, and Subalternist Misreadings of Tagore."

131. Bakhtin uses the idea of the chronotope to describe the alignment and "connectedness" of "temporal and spatial relationships that are artistically expressed in literature" (*The Dialogic Imagination, Four Essays*, 84).

132. See, for instance, Cheah's reading of the "despair of postindependence novels" in *Spectral Nationality*, 240.

133. Robbins uses the term "discrepant cosmopolitanism" in his elaboration of cosmopolitanism as a "density of overlapping allegiances rather than the abstract emptiness of nonallegiance" ("Comparative Cosmopolitanisms," 253). Grewal presents a similarly weighted account of the "postcolonial cosmopolitan" (*Transnational America*, 38).

134. Aravamudan, "In the Wake of the Novel," 27.

135. See Mukherjee, *Realism and Reality*, 65. Priya Joshi is illuminating in showing that the "antirealist" fiction of a writer like G. W. M. Reynolds

"resonated with the subconscious needs [of Indians] as readers in a subordinate political context" (*In Another Country*, 29).

136. Butler, "Restaging the Universal," 24.

137. Holden, "Other Modernities," 94. Here it is important, though, to keep in mind Sangari's caveat about reading nonmimetic narrative modes (she points to those of writers such Salman Rushdie and Gabriel García Márquez) as necessarily coinciding with the project of postmodernism ("Politics of the Possible," 27).

138. Holden, "Other Modernities," 98.

139. The term is from Reinhard Lupton, *Citizen-Saints*, 211.

1. Of the Indian Economy and English Polls

1. As Naoroji stated in a speech to the National Liberal Club in London, "the word England, or Britain, is always used by me as embracing the United Kingdom" (*Poverty and Un-British Rule in India*, 343). Naoroji implicitly assumes Englishness to be representative of British identity, and his interchangeable use of "England" and "Britain," as evident in this chapter, reflects the perceived centrality of English cultural identity. Henceforth in this chapter, all references to *Poverty* will be cited parenthetically in the text.

2. Pal, *The Rise and Growth of Economic Nationalism in India*, 16.

3. Chandra, "The Cultural Complement of Economic Nationalism," 106.

4. Goswami, *Producing India*, 209.

5. Ibid., 221.

6. Klaver, *A/Moral Economics*, xv–xvi.

7. Poovey, *A History of the Modern Fact*, 312.

8. Ibid., 313.

9. B. Anderson, *Imagined Communities*, 166.

10. Appadurai, *Modernity at Large*, 120.

11. Viswanathan, *Outside the Fold*, 158.

12. See Heinzelman, *The Economics of the Imagination*; and McCloskey, *The Rhetoric of Economics*.

13. The positivist slant to racial theorizing was propelled by the professionalization of disciplines such as anthropology. See Stocking, *Victorian Anthropology*, 246. Emphasizing the interplay between general understandings of race and scientific articulations of it points to what was a "variety of racial attitudes" prevalent in the period, which also helps explain the pervasive hold of racial beliefs (Lorimer, "Race, Science, and Culture," 13).

14. See the Introduction.

15. Brantlinger, *Rule of Darkness*, 227.

16. Schmitt, *Alien Nation*, 10.

17. A. Smith, *An Inquiry into the Nature and Causes of the Wealth of*

Nations, 477. For a discussion of this point, see Andriopoulos, "The Invisible Hand," 747.

18. See, for example, Baldick, *In Frankenstein's Shadow*, 121–41; and Moretti, *Signs Taken for Wonders*, chap. 3.

19. The phrase is from Teresa Goddu, who notes that "many texts that are not predominantly gothic [in form] use gothic effects at key moments to register cultural contradictions" (*Gothic America*, 10).

20. Malchow, *Gothic Images of Race in Nineteenth-Century Britain*, 127.

21. Brantlinger, *Rule of Darkness*, 227. Brantlinger also links this anxiety with a growing interest in occultism.

22. Hurley, *The Gothic Body*, 5.

23. Robert Mighall, *A Geography of Victorian Gothic Fiction*, 127.

24. Naoroji, *The Grand Little Man of India*, 2: 216.

25. Masani, *Dadabhai Naoroji*, 71. See also Ralph, *Naoroji*.

26. In addition to setting up a number of political organizations to promote the Indian cause, he joined the Liverpool Literary and Philosophic Society, the Royal Asiatic Society of Great Britain, and the Ethnological Society, among others.

27. Halberstam, *Skin Shows*, 20.

28. References to India's poverty were central in early petitions to the British government entreating a modicum of self-governance for India, but those references were not necessarily accompanied "by any equivalent concern for the poor" (Seth, "Rewriting Histories of Nationalism," 104).

29. Naoroji, *Essays, Speeches, Addresses and Writings on Indian Politics of the Hon'ble Dadabhai Naoroji*, 99 (emphasis in the original). Henceforth in this chapter, all references to *Essays* will be cited parenthetically in the text.

30. Ruskin, "Veins of Wealth," 187.

31. Stokes, *The English Utilitarians and India*, 39–40.

32. Macaulay, "Government of India," 141.

33. Unlike M. G. Ranade, his contemporary, Naoroji did not repudiate the principles of political economy; rather, as an analysis of his critique reveals, he was against what he felt to be a deviation from its principles. For the liberal conception of empire along principles of classical political economy, see Winch, *Classical Political Economy and Colonies*.

34. Rao, *The National Income of British India 1931–32*, 2.

35. The phrase "functional equivalence" is from Mary Poovey, who describes how it signified the shift in political economy from early modern ideas of political and economic order that otherwise derived from theologically sanctioned ideals (*Making a Social Body*, 29).

36. Gilbert, *The Citizen's Body*, 34.

37. Southwood Smith, quoted in Graeme Davison, "The City as a Natural System," 361–62.

38. Ibid.

39. Mighall, *A Geography of Victorian Gothic Fiction*, 67.

40. Warwick, "Lost Cities," 79.
41. Osborne, "Security and Vitality," 114.
42. Ibid., 115.
43. Poovey, *Making a Social Body*, 40.
44. Gallagher, "The Body versus the Social Body in the Works of Thomas Malthus and Henry Mayhew," 92. The argument is extended further in Gallagher, *The Body Economic*, chap. 2.
45. The nature of that critique also suggests the extent to which political economy itself was, as Gallagher notes, one of the "competing 'organicisms' of the opening decades of the nineteenth century" (*The Body Economic*, 4).
46. See Ganguly's *Dadabhai Naoroji and the Drain Theory* for an account of the commentators on the subject whom Naoroji drew from.
47. Edwin Chadwick, too, was concerned about this aspect of faulty draining, and, as Osborne describes, he advocated a "principle of exchange," with "sewage from the cities being used, through a network of sewage farms, to fertilize the agriculture that in turn fed the cities" ("Security and Vitality," 105).
48. The phrase is from Prakash, *Another Reason*, 130.
49. See Arnold, *Colonizing the Body*. For an analysis of the implications of Chadwick's reading in terms of its depiction of the English poor, see Childers, "Observation and Representation."
50. Prakash, *Another Reason*, 132.
51. See Arata's discussion of *Dracula* in his *Fictions of Loss in the Victorian Fin de Siècle*.
52. Naoroji's comment echoes the shift in medical practice in the latter half of the nineteenth century, abandoning bloodletting as an acceptable mode of medical treatment. See S. Adams, "The Medicinal Leech."
53. Bending, *Representation of Bodily Pain in Late Nineteenth Century English Literature*, 168.
54. Ibid., 127.
55. Sharpe, *Allegories of Empire*, 64.
56. Ibid.
57. Brantlinger also notes that the prolific literary representations of the grisly events of the rebellion also served to mystify its real causes, "treating the motives of the rebels as wholly irrational, at once childish and diabolic" (*Rule of Darkness*, 222).
58. *The Times*, November 18, 1865, quoted in Christine Bolt, *Victorian Attitudes to Race*, 77.
59. Quoted in Bolt, *Victorian Attitudes to Race*, 93.
60. See Metcalf, *Ideologies of the Raj*, 45.
61. For a reading of the gendered contours of the debate surrounding the Ilbert Bill, see Sinha, *Colonial Masculinity*, chap. 1.
62. Sharpe, *Allegories of Empire*, 67.
63. See Dasgupta, *A History of Indian Economic Thought*, 80–83.

64. The alienation of their labor, and the consequent draining of its products, is mentioned only once in *Poverty* (251).

65. I will take up the representation of the Victorian middle-class male in terms of "gentlemanliness" in chapter 4.

66. Spivak, "Can the Subaltern Speak?" 305.

67. Mani, "Contentious Traditions."

68. Ranade, *Essays on Indian Economics*, 83–84.

69. Malchow, *Gothic Images of Race in Nineteenth-Century Britain*, 76–78.

70. See Chowdhury, *The Frail Hero and Virile History*, 20.

71. Rai, *Rule of Sympathy*, 57.

72. A. Smith, *The Theory of Moral Sentiments*, 9.

73. Gallagher, *The Body Economic*, 60.

74. Jaffe, *Scenes of Sympathy*, 22.

75. In 1886, both Naoroji and Lalmohun Ghose had unsuccessfully run for Liberal seats in Holborn and Deptford, respectively. Although Naoroji was elected as a Liberal to represent Central Finsbury in 1892, he lost the seat in the 1895 election. Another Indian, Mancherjee Bhownagree, was elected in that year as a Conservative to represent Bethnal Green Northeast. In a forthcoming book, Michael Fisher draws attention to D. O. Sombre, partly of Indian descent, who was elected to Parliament in 1841.

76. McClelland, "'England's Greatness, the Working Man,'" 71.

77. See Burton, "Tongues Untied"; Mukherjee, "'Narrow-majority' and 'Bow-and-agree'"; Schneer, *London 1900*; and Visram, *Asians in Britain*.

78. Hall, "The Nation Within and Without," 180.

79. "Liberal Candidate for Holborn," *Holborn Guardian*, June 26, 1886. In July 1889 the *Holborn Guardian* was renamed *The Holborn and Finsbury Guardian*, which is cited later in this chapter.

80. *The Times*, June 26, 1886.

81. S. Sen, "Chameleon Games," 5.

82. Quoted in Curtis, *Anglo-Saxons and Celts*, 102.

83. *Punch*, no. 14 (1849), quoted in Lebow, *White Britain and Black Ireland*, 40. For an account of the growing Irish agitation during the course of the century, see O'Day, *Irish Home Rule 1867–1921*.

84. *Blackwood's Magazine*, May 1846, 573. Quoted in Lebow, *White Britain and Black Ireland*, 62.

85. Quoted in Lebow, *White Britain and Black Ireland*, 63.

86. Curtis, *Apes and Angels*, 38.

87. See Smart and Hutcheson, "'Negative History' and Irish Gothic Literature," 105–6. The essay provides an insightful reading of how the gothic provides a narrative frame for writing nineteenth-century Irish history.

88. Dutt, *Open Letters to Lord Curzon on Famines and Land Assessments in India*, 17.

89. Lebow, *White Britain and Black Ireland*, 36.

90. It should be pointed out here that Naoroji had written some notes

on Ireland. However, these are untraceable in the Naoroji Papers in the National Archives of India, where they are catalogued, tellingly, under the heading "Miscellaneous." One cannot resist reading this absent presence of the Ireland documents as symptomatic of the "ghostly persistence" of Ireland in Naoroji's metropolitan career. The phrase "ghostly persistence" is from David Punter. I discuss Punter's use of this phrase in n112 of this chapter.

91. Recent readings of various anticolonial alliances have realigned conventional categories of postcolonial analysis. See Boehmer, *Empire, the National, and the Postcolonial, 1890–1920*; and L. Gandhi, *Affective Communities*.

92. Bahri, *Native Intelligence*, 76.

93. For an analysis of the construction of middle-class identities in nineteenth-century England, see Davidoff and Catherine Hall, *Family Fortunes*; and Gagnier, *Subjectivities*.

94. Quoted in Brasted, "Indian Nationalist Development and the Influence of Irish Home Rule, 1870–1886," 43.

95. Joyce, *Visions of the People*, 53.

96. Ibid., 51.

97. "Finsbury Politics," *The Holborn and Finsbury Guardian*, June 18, 1892.

98. "Central Finsbury Election," *The Holborn and Finsbury Guardian*, July 2, 1892.

99. Seeley, *The Expansion of England*, 44.

100. Quoted in Mehrotra, *The Commonwealth and the Nation*, 7.

101. Quoted in Mehrotra, *The Commonwealth and the Nation*, 9.

102. See Corbett, "Public Affections and Familial Politics," 878.

103. Cook, *Imperial Affinities*, 79.

104. After gaining entrance into the House of Commons, the Irish Home Rulers had appointed themselves parliamentary custodians of unrepresented imperial constituencies. Irish members such as F. H. O'Donnell had initiated sustained discussion of Indian topics at a time when India merited surprisingly little parliamentary debate, and Naoroji, who had been introduced to O'Donnell in 1875 and also knew Michael Davitt (the founder of the Irish Land League), was briefly considered for possible nomination from one of the Irish constituencies. See Cumpston, "Some Early Indian Nationalists and their Allies in British Parliament, 1851–1906," 285.

105. See Candy, "The Inscrutable Irish-Indian Feminist Management of Anglo-American Hegemony, 1917–1947"; and Viswanathan, "Ireland, India, and the Poetics of Internationalism."

106. Cook, *Imperial Affinities*, 120.

107. Brasted, "Indian Nationalist Development and the Influence of Irish Home Rule, 1870–1886," 49.

108. Naoroji, "Presidential Address at the Second Meeting of the Indian National Congress, Calcutta," in *The Grand Little Man of India*, 1:2.

109. Richard Davis, "The Influence of the Irish Revolution on Indian Nationalism," 57.

110. See Bose and Ward, "India's Cause Is Ireland's Cause"; and Silvestri, "'The Sinn Féin of India.'"

111. This is to say Indians were circumspect in representing the Irish as "Irish": interestingly, they had been able to absorb the Irish as "Indian" with dexterous magnanimity—be it historically, as in the refiguration of Margaret Noble as Sister Nivedita (see P. Roy, *Indian Traffic*, chap. 4), or novelistically, as in Rabindranath Tagore's *Gora*. See Candy, "The Inscrutable Irish-Indian Feminist Management of Anglo-American Hegemony, 1917–1947," for a reading of Indian depictions of Annie Besant as the "Irish Brahmani."

112. The potato famine, for instance, was largely ignored by professional historians in the nineteenth century. The reference to the "ghostly persistence" of Irish suffering is from David Punter, who notes that Irish history itself was constantly under threat of erasure (quoted in Smart and Hutcheson, "'Negative History' and Irish Gothic Literature," 113).

113. "The Battle of London—I. Amongst the Candidates and Electors with a Note-Book," *Pall Mall Gazette*, June 23, 1886, 11–12.

114. "Mr. Naoroji's Debut," *Pall Mall Gazette*, June 25, 1886, 6.

115. "Notes by 'Invisible,'" *Holborn Guardian*, June 19, 1886, 2.

116. "Notes by 'Invisible,'" *Holborn Guardian*, June 26, 1886, 6.

117. Vernon, *Politics and the People*, 260.

118. "Mr. Naoroji's Debut," *Pall Mall Gazette*, June 25, 1886, 6.

119. Ibid.

120. For the significance of the role of the "Gentleman Leader" in England, see Vernon, *Politics and the People*, 258.

121. For an extended discussion of the role of visuality (and what was "invisible") in Victorian culture, see Flint, *The Victorians and the Visual Imagination*.

122. For the social demographics of Central Finsbury, see Pelling, *Social Geography of British Elections 1885–1910*, 49.

123. "Lord Salisbury in Edinburgh," *The Times*, December 1, 1888.

124. "Letters to the Editor," *The Manchester Guardian*, December 1, 1888, 7.

125. *Daily News*, December 3, 1888, 6.

126. "Letters to the Editor," *Pall Mall Gazette*, December 4, 1888, 14.

127. *Edinburgh Evening Dispatch*, December 1, 1888.

128. Burton, "Tongues Untied," 644.

129. *Edinburgh Evening Dispatch*, December 1, 1888.

130. *The Manchester Guardian*, December 1, 1888, 7. For the intricacies of this belief, see Trautmann, *Aryans and British India*. Although the "Aryan" character of Indians enjoyed currency in metropolitan circles, it did not affect any legislative decisions regarding the equal status of Indians; see Leopold, "British Applications of Aryan Theory of Race to India, 1850–1870," 592.

131. "Occasional Notes," *Pall Mall Gazette*, December 1, 1888, 4.

132. Ibid.

133. "The Week," *Leeds Mercury*, December 8, 1888, 4.

134. Bolt, *Victorian Attitudes to Race*, 181. See also Lorimer, *Colour, Class, and the Victorian*.

135. See Luhrman, *The Good Parsi*.

136. Leopold, "British Applications of Aryan Theory of Race to India, 1850–1870," 591.

137. See Naoroji, *The Parsi Religion*.

138. Naoroji, *The Manners and Customs of the Parsees*, 5.

139. Burton, "Tongues Untied," 644; Mukherjee, "'Narrow-majority' and 'Bow-and-agree.'"

140. Rich, *Race and Empire in British Politics*, 5.

141. Lorimer, "Race, Science, and Culture," 32.

142. Wiegman, *American Anatomies*, 30. See also Lorimer, "Race, Science, and Culture," 21.

143. "The Week," *Leeds Mercury*, December 8, 1888, 4.

144. Brody, *Impossible Purities: Blackness, Femininity, and Victorian Culture*, 10.

145. "Finsbury Politics," *The Holborn and Finsbury Guardian*, June 18, 1892, 6.

146. Manifesto published by the Women's Franchise League, n.d., w-135, Naoroji Papers, National Archives of India (NAI).

147. Halberstam, *Skin Shows*, 21.

148. Ibid.

149. "Lord Dufferin on India," *The Times*, December 3, 1888.

150. S. R. Mehrotra, *The Emergence of the Indian National Congress*, 398.

151. "Lord Dufferin on India," *The Times*, December 3, 1888.

152. C. A. Bayly, "Ireland, India, and the Empire," 392.

153. Dufferin to Kimberley, February 3, 1885, quoted in T. G. Fraser, "Ireland and India," 87.

154. "Mr. Naoroji, M.P., on Political Aspects," *The Holborn and Finsbury Guardian*, August 23, 1892, 6.

155. *The First Indian Member of the Imperial Parliament*, 27.

156. "The Return of Mr. D Naoroji for Central Finsbury," *Holborn and Finsbury Guardian*, July 23, 1892, 6. Despite the evident interchangeability of "liberal" and "Liberal" in this statement, I would like to emphasize that my use of "Liberal" (as opposed to "liberal") in this chapter has referred only to the Liberal party, which adhered to many principles of liberalism but can in no way be taken to embody it in its entirety.

157. *The First Indian Member of the Imperial Parliament*, 27.

158. Ibid., 109.

2. South Africa, Indentured Labor, and Credit

1. "The Return of Mr. D. Naoroji for Central Finsbury," *The Holborn and Finsbury Guardian*, July 23, 1892.

2. Pocock, "The Ideal of Citizenship since Classical Times," 36. The

principle of *civis Romanus sum* was specifically invoked in 1850 by Lord Palmerston to defend his actions in the Don Pacifico case.

3. *The Holborn and Finsbury Guardian*, July 23, 1892.

4. See Tinker, *A New System of Slavery*; and Saunders, *Indentured Labour in the British Empire, 1834–1920*.

5. Included in Letter by R. G. Herbert to Under Secretary of State for India, May 25, 1871, in NAI, "Kidnapping of Women by Recruiters for Emigrants."

6. For a detailed study of how laborers for Natal were recruited, see Metcalf, "'Hard Hands and Sound Healthy Bodies.'"

7. Kelly, *A Politics of Virtue*, 67.

8. See Kale, *Fragments of Empire*, 8–9.

9. *The Natal Mercury*, April 28, 1859, quoted in Joy Brain, "Indentured and Free Indians in the Economy of Colonial Natal," 200.

10. See Bhana, *Indentured Indian Emigrants to Natal 1860–1902*.

11. *The Natal Mercury*, July 14, 1866, quoted in Meer et al., *Documents of Indentured Labour*, 111.

12. Kelly, *A Politics of Virtue*, 84.

13. Prakash, *Bonded Histories*, 6.

14. Statement by Balakistna, April 13, 1871, in NAI, "Complaints of Return Coolies from Natal," 81.

15. Statement by Mooneswamy, April 13, 1871, in ibid.

16. Affidavit of Veraputheran, September 25, 1871, in NAI, "Emigration Proceedings," 201.

17. Report by A. Mesham, Acting Resident Magistrate, Inanda, October 6, 1871, in ibid., 199.

18. Letter from Sir T. W. C. Murdoch to R. G. W. Herbert, February 24, 1872, in ibid., 197.

19. Letter from Secretary of State for India, May 10, 1872, in ibid., 211.

20. NAI, "Natal Immigration Report for 1879," 101.

21. Ibid.

22. NAI, "Report of the Protector of Immigrants, Natal, for 1891–92," 95.

23. See Collini, "The Idea of Character in Victorian Political Thought," 40.

24. Watt, *Serving the Nation*, 49.

25. See McClelland, "'England's Greatness, the Working Man.'"

26. Bhana, "Indian Trade and Trader in Colonial Natal," 236.

27. Swanson, "'The Asiatic Menace,'" 404.

28. OIOC, "Papers Relating to the Grievances of Her Majesty's Indian Subjects in the South African Republic," 389.

29. Swanson, "'The Asiatic Menace,'" 408.

30. Ibid., 400. The petition is not dated, but a counterpetition was sent in response to it by "Arab" merchants in 1885.

31. Shah, *Contagious Divides: Epidemics and Race in San Francisco's Chinatown*, 74.

32. Stepan, *The Idea of Race in Science*, 111. See also Rich, *Race and Empire in British Politics*.

33. See Swanson, "'The Asiatic Menace,'" 410.

34. See Crook, "'Schools for the Moral Training of the People,'" 27.

35. OIOC, "Papers Relating to the Grievances of Her Majesty's Indian Subjects in the South African Republic," 390.

36. Ibid., 413.

37. Pyrah, *Imperial Policy in South Africa*, 3.

38. Huttenback, *Racism and Empire*, 21.

39. Quoted in Huttenback, *Racism and Empire*, 144.

40. Huttenback, "Indians in South Africa, 1860–1914," 278.

41. OIOC, "Papers Relating to the Grievances of Her Majesty's Indian Subjects in the South African Republic," 422.

42. Ibid., 423.

43. Ibid., 422–23.

44. Hall, *White, Male and Middle-Class*, 257.

45. Seedat, Introduction, 87.

46. "Letter to the Office of the Protector of Indian Immigrants," January 18, 1892, in Meer, "Pre-Gandhian Indian Politics in Natal—1891–1892," 101.

47. "Letter from Colonial Secretary's Office, Natal," January 22, 1892, in ibid.

48. Swan, *Gandhi*, 41.

49. Ibid., 43.

50. J. Brown, *Gandhi*, 23. See also Pyarelal, *Mahatma Gandhi*, 225–37; and Hay, "The Making of a Late-Victorian Hindu."

51. Mohandas K. Gandhi, "On My Way Home Again to India," April 9, 1892, *Collected Works of Mahatma Gandhi*, 1:64. Henceforth in this chapter, this title will be abbreviated as CWMG.

52. J. Brown, *Gandhi*, 31.

53. Mohandas K. Gandhi, *An Autobiography*, 51. Henceforth in this chapter, all references to *Autobiography* will be cited parenthetically in the text.

54. Mohandas K. Gandhi, "Satyagraha in South Africa," in CWMG 29:92. This work was translated into English by Valji G. Desai (with Gandhi's approval) and published in 1928 as a book with the same title. *Satyagraha* is included in CWMG, vol. 29. All references to *Satyagraha* in this chapter are to the CWMG edition and, henceforth in this chapter, will be cited parenthetically in the text.

55. Arnold, *Gandhi*, 50.

56. Mohandas K. Gandhi, *Hind Swaraj*, in CWMG 10:16. *Hind Swaraj* was written in 1909 and published in two parts in that year, and as a booklet in 1910. All references to the work in this chapter are to the CWMG edition.

57. This is evident, for instance, in his avowed reluctance to write an autobiography privileging an "I." As he notes in the introduction to his autobiography, rather than attempting a "real autobiography," he wanted

"simply to tell the story of [his] numerous experiments with truth" (*Autobiography*, 14). For a discussion of Gandhi as autobiographer, see Parekh, *Colonialism, Tradition and Reform*, 257–66.

58. Swan, *Gandhi*, xiv.
59. Huttenback, "Indians in South Africa, 1860–1914," 277.
60. Mohandas K. Gandhi, "The Indian Vote," September 29, 1893, in CWMG 1:78.
61. Mohandas K. Gandhi, "Questions for Legislators," July 1, 1894, in CWMG 1:101.
62. Mohandas K. Gandhi, "Deputation to Natal Governor," July 3, 1894, in CWMG 1:103.
63. Ibid., 102.
64. Mohandas K. Gandhi, "Deputation to Natal Premier," June 29, 1894, in CWMG 1:99.
65. Mohandas K. Gandhi, "Petition to Natal Council," July 4, 1894, in CWMG 1:105.
66. Mohandas K. Gandhi, "The Grievances of the British Indians in South Africa," August 1896, CWMG 2:17.
67. Scott, *Only Paradoxes to Offer*, 7.
68. For an account of the diverse composition of the Indian population in Natal, see Bhana and Brain, *Setting Down Roots*, 21–76. While Brahmin recruits were less desirable because they were considered less suitable for hard labor, the high demand for labor in Natal, Metcalf notes, ensured that the labor pool contained a significant portion of upper caste laborers as well ("'Hard Hands and Sound Healthy Bodies,'" 230).
69. Mohandas K. Gandhi, "Petition to Lord Ripon," July 17, 1894, in CWMG 1:116.
70. Ibid., 123.
71. Ibid., 125.
72. Ibid., 128.
73. Mohandas K. Gandhi, "The Grievances of the British Indians in South Africa," 24.
74. Ibid., 34–35.
75. Ibid., 12.
76. Ibid., 9.
77. Tarlo, *Clothing Matters*, 67.
78. Bhana, *Indentured Indian Emigrants to Natal, 1860–1902*, 114.
79. Biagini, *Liberty, Retrenchment, and Reform*, 272.
80. Ibid., 294.
81. Mohandas K. Gandhi, "Grievances of the British Indians in South Africa," 18.
82. See Bhana and Vahed, *The Making of a Political Reformer*, 41–42; and Bhana, *Gandhi's Legacy*, 21–22.
83. Smiles, *Self-Help; With Illustrations of Character, Conduct, and Perseverance*, 49.

NOTES 215

84. Vahed, "Control and Repression," 23.

85. Brantlinger, *Fictions of State*, 33.

86. Chadwick, *Report on the Sanitary Condition of the Labouring Population of Great Britain*, 200.

87. Smiles, quoted in Crook, "'Schools for the Moral Training of the People,'" 29.

88. For a discussion on the highly ambivalent Victorian response to the notion of filth, especially in terms of its association with both poverty and prosperity, see Herbert, "Filthy Lucre."

89. Mohandas K. Gandhi, "Letter to D. V. Rama Rao," May 29, 1926.

90. Mohandas K. Gandhi, "Open Letter," December 1894, in CWMG 1:144.

91. Ibid., 143.

92. Ibid., 145.

93. Ibid., 147.

94. See Trentmann, "Bread, Milk, and Democracy."

95. Mohandas K. Gandhi, "Balance-Sheet of Natal Indian Congress," September 1901, in CWMG 3:203–4.

96. I would like to thank David Sorkin and the 2005-6 fellows at the Institute for Research in the Humanities of the University of Wisconsin, Madison, for encouraging me to pursue this connection further.

97. My discussion of the rhetorical logic of debit and credit is indebted to Mary Poovey's argument tracing the emergence of double-entry bookkeeping. See Poovey, "Accommodating Merchants." Poovey's *Genres of the Credit Economy* further elaborates on that argument. Because of the recent publication of this book, however, I have been unable to incorporate its suggestions.

98. Finn, *The Character of Credit*, 282.

99. Mohandas K. Gandhi, "Grievances of the British Indians in South Africa," 41.

100. See Arondekar, Schmitt, and Henry, Introduction, 9.

101. Finn, *The Character of Credit*, 47.

102. Mohandas K. Gandhi, "The Balance-Sheet," July 2, 1903, in CWMG 3:354.

103. Ibid., 355.

104. Mohandas K. Gandhi, "Open Letter," December 1894, in CWMG 1:159.

105. Ibid., 158.

106. Ibid., 147.

107. Ibid., 147–48.

108. The formulation is from Kale, *Fragments of Empire*, 10.

109. The logic underlying Gandhi's acknowledgment of the laborers' filthiness shows that what is rejected as filthy is also, as Cohen and Johnson describe it—referring to Peter Stallybrass and Allon White—central to "culture's self-constitution" (Introduction, xvi).

110. Mohandas K. Gandhi, "Open Letter," December 1894, in CWMG 1:148.

111. The term "use-value" here refers to Marx's description of "use-value" as the specificities of "human labour power, in the physiological sense" that are abstracted in the production of exchange value (*Capital* 1:136).

112. Mohandas K. Gandhi, "Duty of Bread Labour," in CWMG 41:211.

113. Kelly, "Fiji Indians and 'Commoditization of Labor,'" 109–11. In this essay, Kelly also examines how Gandhi linked labor with notions of service and sacrifice.

114. See Coward, "Gandhi, Ambedkar, and Untouchability," 54; Prashad, *Untouchable Freedom*, 135–42; and Hardiman, *Gandhi in His Time and Ours*, 132.

115. Mohandas K. Gandhi, "Grievances of the British Indians in South Africa," 12.

116. Mohandas K. Gandhi, untitled enclosure included in "Letter to Private Secretary to Lord Elgin," November 20, 1906, in CWMG 6:198. *Autobiography* provides a tellingly ambivalent description of his involvement in the rebellion. In this later account, Gandhi is struck by the injustice of British actions against the Zulus, but he uses the description of his involvement as a member of the Indian Ambulance Corps more as a turning point to describe his decision to dedicate his life to public service: the Zulus remain racialized, and mostly absent, figures in the description (*Autobiography*, 313–14).

117. Mohandas K. Gandhi, "The Indian Franchise: An Appeal to Every Briton in South Africa," December 16, 1895, in CWMG 1:260.

118. Vahed, "Indentured Masculinity in Colonial Natal, 1860–1910," 247. For a reading of the ways in which Gandhi's position on temperance generally overlooked the lifestyle of the lower castes, thereby advocating a cause that was more or less elite, see Fahey and Manian, "Poverty and Purification"; and Hardiman, "From Custom to Crime."

119. Beall, "Women under Indenture in Natal," 107. See also B. Lal, "Kunti's Cry."

120. Mohandas K. Gandhi, "Petition to Natal Assembly," May 5, 1895, in CWMG 1:177.

121. See Arnold, *Gandhi*, 50.

122. M. K. Gandhi, "Petition to Natal Council," June 26, 1895, in CWMG 1:213.

123. Gandhi, "Letter to Secretary of Interior," September 28, 1913, in CWMG 12:215.

124. Swan, *Gandhi*, 246. For an account of the various registers through which Gandhi's later interaction with the "masses" operated, see Amin, "Gandhi as Mahatma."

125. Mohandas K. Gandhi, "Cable to Gokhale," October 22, 1913, in CWMG 12:244.

126. Mohandas K. Gandhi, "Telegram to Minister of Interior," October 28, 1913, in *CWMG* 12:255.

127. Mohandas. K. Gandhi, "Cable to Gokhale," November 4, 1913, in *CWMG* 12:257.

128. Mohandas K. Gandhi, "Letter to Indians," before November 11, 1913, in *CWMG* 12:262.

129. Ibid.

130. Mohandas K. Gandhi, "Letter to 'Natal Advertiser,'" after December 22, 1913, in *CWMG* 12:285.

131. Mohandas K. Gandhi, "Cable to G. K. Gokhale," January 2, 1914, in *CWMG* 12:315.

132. See Lowe, *Immigrant Acts*; and Taussig, *The Devil and Commodity Fetishism*.

133. See Carter, *Voices from Indenture*; and Niranjana, *Mobilizing India*.

134. Goux, *Symbolic Economies*, 62–63.

135. Ibid. Here Goux is referring to Marx's premise that in order to facilitate the production of a more uniform exchange-value, the use-value of commodities (the physiological specificities that go into a commodity's making) is necessarily leveled into something that is "equal," or, as Marx puts it, "abstract" (*Capital*, 1:136–37).

136. Goux, *Symbolic Economies*, 62–63.

137. Parekh, *Gandhi's Political Philosophy*, 116.

138. Mohandas K. Gandhi, "Immortal Hurbatsingh," January 7, 1914, in *CWMG* 12:321.

139. Gandhi's references to the familial differ from Naoroji's allusions to the bourgeois family discussed in the previous chapter, as Gandhi uses the references to support his vision of what Parekh describes as "a non-statal polity," one that built up "a strong sense of local strength and solidarity," providing "meaningful interpersonal relationships" (*Gandhi's Political Philosophy*, 116).

140. Mohandas K. Gandhi, "Address in Madras," October 26, 1896, in *CWMG* 2:95.

141. Ibid., 94.

142. Ibid., 97.

143. In her study on Indian indentureship in Trinidad, Niranjana traces the problematic relation of the figure of the coolie, especially the female coolie, with Indian nationalism (*Mobilizing India*, 79–83).

144. Derrida, *Specters of Marx*, 39–40.

145. Ghosh, "On Grafting the Vernacular," 201.

146. P. Roy, "Figures of Famine," 8. I am grateful to the author for sharing this unpublished work with me.

147. Jay, *Cultural Semantics*, 162.

148. Butler, "Competing Universalities," 179.

149. For an extremely useful discussion attentive to the problems

underlying notions of retrievability, see Spivak, "Subaltern Studies"; and Sharpe, *Ghosts of Slavery*.

150. For an analysis of these two aspects of nineteenth-century middle-class identity, see Goodlad, "A Middle Class Cut into Two," 158.

151. Mohandas K. Gandhi, "Trial at Dundee," November 11, 1913, in CWMG 2:263.

152. Mohandas K. Gandhi, *Hind Swaraj*, 32–33.

3. The Professional Citizen in/and the Zenana

1. Sorabji, *India Calling: The Memories of Cornelia Sorabji* (London: Nisbet, 1934), 294. All references to *India Calling* are to this edition; henceforth in this chapter, all references to it will be cited parenthetically in the text.

2. For an examination of this infringement with relation to Indians in Canada, see Mongia, "Race, Nationality, Mobility."

3. Purdah literally means "curtain," and purdahnashin refers to women who lived behind the curtain. Purdahnashins were mostly upper-class women from Hindu or Muslim families, who led sequestered lives and were prohibited from venturing beyond the inner quarters of their homes.

4. Lokugé, Introduction, xxii; Boehmer, Introduction, ix.

5. Sarker, "Unruly Subjects," 278.

6. The silence surrounding Sorabji and the problems inherent in reading her "difficult" position echo the caution sounded by Sangari and Vaid, who point out the dangers of the tendency of feminist movements to valorize a "positive and inspirational history" along categories of "nation" or "woman" (Introduction, 18).

7. Burton, *At the Heart of Empire*, 114.

8. Gooptu, *Cornelia Sorabji, India's Pioneer Woman Lawyer*, 195–96.

9. The phrase is borrowed from the title of Sarker and De, *Trans-Status Subjects* (see Sarker, "Unruly Subjects").

10. Watt, *Serving the Nation*, 50.

11. Besides writing for *The Nineteenth Century and After*, the British literary magazine, Sorabji also published the following monographs: *Love and Light behind the Purdah* (1901), *Between the Twilights: Being Studies of Indian Women by One of Themselves* (1908), *The Purdahnashin* (1917), and *India Recalled* (1936).

12. Sunder Rajan, *Scandal of the State*, 170.

13. Reader, *The Rise of the Professional Classes in Nineteenth-Century England*, 2. See also Carr-Saunders and Wilson, *The Professions*; and Corfield, *Power and the Professions in Britain 1700–1850*.

14. See Gedge and Choksi, *Women in Modern India*; and Forbes, *Women in Modern India*, 161–67.

15. Perkin, *The Rise of Professional Society*, 363. See also Carr-Saunders and Wilson, *The Professions*, 421–22.

16. For an elaboration and critique of this point in relation to professionalism, see Swindells, *Victorian Writing and Working Women*, 25–26. Conversely, for a discussion of how professional expertise helped construct a middle-class masculinity in mid-Victorian England, see Priti Joshi, "Edwin Chadwick's Self Fashioning."

17. Access to professional knowledge, of course, remains highly stratified. For an elaboration and critique of this point, see Robbins, *Secular Vocations*, 33–34.

18. Larson, *The Rise of Professionalism*, 62.

19. See Robbins's argument on the question of academic and professional privilege (*Secular Vocations*, 205–6).

20. I use subaltern within quotation marks, for while the purdahnashins were wealthy and privileged in their own right, they were scripted out of the representative norms of colonial and nationalist modernities.

21. The distinctions between seeing women as metaphoric and not metonymic of a nation is from Elleke Boehmer, quoted in McClintock, "'No Longer in a Future Heaven,'" 90.

22. See Sorabji, "*Therefore.*"

23. See Burton, "Making a Spectacle of Empire."

24. Burton, *At the Heart of Empire*, 111. For a broader discussion of this dynamic, see Grewal, *Home and Harem*, 60; Burton, *Burdens of History*; and Nair, "Uncovering the Zenana."

25. For a record of Indian women studying medicine in England in the later years of the nineteenth century, see Lahiri, *Indians in Britain*.

26. For the complexities of this debate, see Poovey, *Uneven Developments*, especially chap. 6. Also see M. Lal, "The Politics of Gender and Medicine in Colonial India."

27. Jayawardena, *The White Woman's Other Burden*, 76. See also Burton, "Contesting the Zenana"; Forbes, "Medical Careers and Health Care for Indian Women"; and Shetty, "(Dis)Locating Gender."

28. Forbes, "Medical Careers and Health Care for Indian Women," 518.

29. Quoted in M. Lal, "The Politics of Gender and Medicine in Colonial India," 50.

30. Sorabji, letter to parents, September 21, 1889, MSS EUR F165/1, Sorabji Papers, in the Oriental and India Office Collection of the British Library. Henceforth in this chapter, this collection will be abbreviated as Sorabji Papers.

31. Sen received the Vernacular Licentiate in Medicine and Surgery in 1894 from the Campbell Medical School, in Calcutta. Many thanks to Geraldine Forbes for clarifying this. Despite Sen's academic success, she had difficulty in finding employment not only because she lacked a foreign degree, but also because of her "race, gender, an inferior degree, and lack of

experience" (Forbes, Introduction, 27). She did, however, practice medicine for forty years in the districts in Bengal.

32. Burton, *Dwelling in the Archive*, 84.

33. Walker, "'Wider Than the Sky,'" 275.

34. The phrase is from Sarker, "Unruly Subjects," 271.

35. Ramusack, "Cultural Missionaries, Maternal Imperialists, Feminist Allies," 120.

36. See Burton, *Burdens of History*, chap. 2.

37. Sorabji, letter to parents, December 31, 1889, MSS EUR F165/1, Sorabji Papers.

38. *India*, November 22, 1930 [pamphlet no. 70, series 1930–31, New York: Foreign Policy Association, 1931], in MSS EUR F165/179, Sorabji Papers.

39. Containing a glossary of "Hindustani" words, *India Calling* was written primarily for a metropolitan audience, as her correspondence regarding its publication indicates. See MSS EUR F165/96, Sorabji Papers.

40. Mossman, *The First Women Lawyers*, 116.

41. Sachs and Wilson, *Sexism and the Law*, 172.

42. See Albisetti, "Portia Ante Portas."

43. Reader, *The Rise of the Professional Classes in Nineteenth-Century England*, 23.

44. Albisetti, "Portia Ante Portas," 844.

45. See Sachs and Wilson, *Sexism and the Law*, 14–40.

46. Ibid., 172. Eliza Horme completed a law degree at the University of London in 1888, but although she engaged in legal work, it was as a "conveyancer and patent agent," at the "boundaries of professional jurisdiction" (Mossman, *The First Women Lawyers*, 120).

47. Abel-Smith and Stevens, *Lawyers and the Courts*, 192.

48. Memorandum from Her Majesty's High Court of Judicature, Bombay, July 16, 1897, MSS EUR F165/118, Sorabji Papers.

49. Ibid.

50. For a related argument with reference to British women's involvement in the Second World War, see Rose, *Which People's War?* chap. 4.

51. Letter from T. Raleigh to Cornelia Sorabji, March 21, 1901, MSS EUR F165/119, Sorabji Papers. Raleigh was the Law Member of the Viceroy's Council from 1901 to 1904.

52. Sorabji's efforts to gain admittance into the legal system in British India were as protracted as they were frustrating for her. For a detailed account, see Mossman, *The First Women Lawyers*, 191–232.

53. The Provincial Government of Bengal, Behar, and Orissa was the first to pass the law, followed by the governments of Madras (1902), Bombay (1905), and the United Provinces (1912).

54. Sanad literally means a grant or charter. Sorabji's use of the word refers to the special license she got from several Native States to serve as counsel and plead in their courts for specific cases. Ironically, this was in contrast to the refusal by the Bombay and Allahabad High Courts to ac-

commodate her, and the many reservations on the part of the colonial state in granting her official standing.

55. Sorabji, letter to editor, April 28, 1899, MSS EUR F165/118, Sorabji Papers.

56. S. Smith, *Moving Lives*, xi.

57. As the chapter will discuss, the angular relation between modernity and professionalism is borne out by Sorabji's writing, particularly her viewing of her work as a calling. At this point, however, I would also like to point to wide-ranging discussions of professionalism that emphasize its preindustrial roots and impulses. See Isin, *Being Political*, 234.

58. For details of her correspondence with the colonial bureaucracy on this issue, see Gooptu, *Cornelia Sorabji, India's Pioneer Woman Lawyer*, 93–130.

59. Sorabji, letter to the Secretary to the Board of Revenue, October 14, 1914, MSS EUR F165/126, Sorabji Papers.

60. Ibid., 45.

61. Ibid., 39.

62. Ibid., 39.

63. Letter from J. H. Kerr, Secretary to the Government of Bengal, to Secretary to the Government of India, Department of Revenue and Agriculture, November 27, 1912, MSS EUR F165/121, Sorabji Papers. The dispute about Sorabji's leave stemmed from the different privileges accorded to the Imperial Service and the Provincial Service and the fact that Sorabji was considered ineligible for Imperial Service benefits, such as the European Service Leave Rules. As Kerr's letter explains, "since her appointment is not mentioned in article 297 of the Civil Service Regulations, her long leave will be regulated by the provisions of Chapter XIV which deal with the Indian Services." Because the Indian Service Leave Rules were more stringent, Kerr adds: "The Governor in Council feels that the application of the Indian Service Rules in this case would cause considerable hardship, and he strongly recommends that Miss Sorabji be admitted to the benefit [of European Service Leave rules]."

64. Letter from Secretary of State to Governor General of India in Council, August 15, 1913, MSS EUR F165/121, Sorabji Papers.

65. Letter from A. Marr, Secretary to the Board of Revenue, Bengal, to Cornelia Sorabji, January 6, 1914, MSS EUR F165/126, Sorabji Papers.

66. For the tensions between philanthropy and professionalism in Victorian England, see Eliot, *The Angel out of the House*; and Prochaska, *Women and Philanthropy in Nineteenth-Century England*.

67. For a formulation of the professional expert as "autonomous citizen," see Larson, "The Production of Expertise and the Constitution of Expert Power," 30.

68. See the autobiographies of Reddy (*Autobiography of Mrs. S. Muthulakshmi Reddy*) and H. Sen (*The Memoirs of Dr. Haimabati Sen*), who were roughly contemporaneous with Sorabji as pioneering female professionals.

A similar negotiation with an "interior" domestic and emotional life, which in many ways strategically counterbalanced a more professional role, can also be seen in the accounts of professional women writing in England in the late nineteenth century; see Sanders, *The Private Lives of Victorian Women*. For an analysis of the relations between domesticity and professionalism in nineteenth-century England, see also Cohen, *Professional Domesticity in the Victorian Novel*; and Peterson, *Traditions of Victorian Women's Autobiography*.

69. Chakrabarty, "Postcoloniality and the Artifice of History," 9.

70. Smith and Watson, *Reading Autobiography*, 198.

71. Corbett, *Representing Femininity*, 100–101.

72. Ibid.

73. Burton, *Dwelling in the Archive*, 10.

74. Sorabji, diary entry for May 25, 1935, MSS EUR F165/97, Sorabji Papers.

75. For an account of the highly restrictive practices disciplining the European female presence in the colonies, see George, *Politics of Home*. For an elaboration of this point specifically with regard to Sorabji, see Fleming, "Between Two Worlds" 94.

76. Squier, *Liminal Lives*, 4.

77. Turner, *Dramas, Fields, and Metaphors*, 232. In a different context, John McBratney examines how the liminal space between colony and metropole plays an important role in Rudyard Kipling's literary depiction of Britons born in India (*Imperial Subjects, Imperial Space*). In McBratney's analysis, the liminal can be invoked only in the fictitious space of Anglo-Indian childhood. It is interesting, then, that for Sorabji, the liminal becomes a narrative tool for negotiating the extra-fictitious, "adult" world of imperial politics.

78. Eden, *Up the Country*; and Parks, *Wanderings of a Pilgrim in Search of the Picturesque*.

79. Grewal, *Home and Harem*, 51.

80. See Roy and Roy, *Zenana Mission*.

81. A.D., *Until the Shadows Flee Away*, 131. Though the volume is undated, the references indicate that it was published after 1912.

82. Booth, "*Take This Child*," 75.

83. Armstrong-Hopkins, *Within the Purdah*, 9.

84. Booth, "*Take This Child*," 91.

85. Sorabji, "Annual Report of the Lady Assistant to the Court of Wards," August 1920, MSS EUR F165/133, Sorabji Papers.

86. This formulation is from Basu, who, in her study of women's property rights in the Indian nation-state, points out how the courts act as "husbands" and "reinforce and validate the patriarchal power of husbands" (*She Comes to Take Her Rights*, 216–17).

87. Sorabji, letter to Mr. McWatters, Hasting House, Calcutta, March 18, 1929, MSS EUR F165/163, Sorabji Papers.

88. Sorabji, "On the Possibilities Appertaining to a Social Service Institute," September 29–30, 1927, MSS EUR F165/163, Sorabji Papers.

89. The organizations were the Women's Indian Association (WIA), the National Council of Women in India (NCWI), and the All India Women's Conference (AIWC). For an account of the emergence of these organizations, see Forbes, *Women in Modern India*; and Kumar, *The History of Doing*.

90. Sinha, "Reading *Mother India*," 7. See also Ray, "The Freedom Movement and Feminist Consciousness in Bengal, 1905–1929."

91. See Chakravarti, "Whatever Happened to the Vedic Dasi?" Sinha also points out that despite being interpellated within a nationalist framework, Indian feminists were also successful in working against its particularized ideals in an effort to "claim an abstract and universal modernity" ("Refashioning Mother India," 626). Sorabji, however, did not participate in the Indian feminist effort, for it was still geared around ideals of national autonomy, which were inimical to her political beliefs.

92. Sorabji, "Women in Changing India," Notes for "Tea Time Talks," November 4, 1937, MSS EUR F165/155, Sorabji Papers.

93. "The feminist movement proper, such as it is," Sorabji points out, "has indeed been organized in India by Westerners, and, within the past ten years, with amazing success. But meetings, resolutions, eloquent speeches, much advertisement—these are apt to make up the sum of our feminism. It is a puffball—not an edible mushroom. The situation is likely to be more complicated than those can imagine who know only what may be called 'the-out-of-doors side' of India, and hence take no account of the multitudes behind the purdah" ("'Indian Women of the Outside': The Emancipated Who, with No Book of Rules, Have Attained New Spheres of Freedom,"*Asia*, April 1924) 302, MSS EUR F165/155, Sorabji Papers).

94. Rukhmabai was Sorabji's contemporary in England, studying medicine at the London School of Medicine for Women. She received her medical degree from Edinburgh in 1893. She was a cause célèbre during the 1880s in both India and England on account of the legal controversy surrounding her much-noted divorce.

95. For details of the controversy, see Sinha, Introduction. See also Sinha, *Specters of Mother India*, chaps. 2 and 3.

96. Mayo quotes directly from Sorabji's *Between the Twilights*.

97. Mayo, *Mother India*, 127.

98. Sorabji, *Between the Twilights*, 131.

99. For a reading of this stance in terms of a "gynechronology," see Sarker, "Unruly Subjects," 274.

100. Shetty, "(Dis)Locating Gender," 211.

101. Chattopadhyaya, *Indian Women's Battle for Freedom*, 51.

102. See Sinha, "Reading *Mother India*," 18–19.

103. Sorabji, letter to Elena Rathbone, August 24, 1927, MSS EUR F165/157, Sorabji Papers.

104. Sorabji, diary entry for September 14, 1927, MSS EUR F165/ 89, Sorabji Papers.
105. Sinha, *Specters of Mother India*, 145.
106. Sinha, "Reading *Mother India*," 20.
107. Ibid., 21.
108. Sinha, "Gender in the Critique of Colonialism and Nationalism," 262.
109. P. Roy, *Indian Traffic*, 92.
110. Ibid., 123.
111. Sorabji, "Mother India: A Note of Hope," *The Englishman*, September 1, 1927, MSS EUR F165/161, Sorabji Papers.
112. See Walkowitz, "The Making of a Feminine Professional Identity."
113. See Sinha, "Suffragism and Internationalism."
114. Sorabji, "Problem Relating to India for Consideration of the Federation of University Women in England," February 14, 1919, MSS EUR F165/158, Sorabji Papers.
115. Sorabji, letter to Elena Rathbone, October 12, 1927, MSS EUR F165/157, Sorabji Papers.
116. Sorabji, "On the Possibilities Appertaining to a Social Service Institute," MSS EUR 165/163, Sorabji Papers.
117. Ibid.
118. Ibid.
119. Elliot uses this phrase to describe the larger function of professionalism in "political and economic systems" (*The Sociology of the Professions*, 149).
120. Sorabji, "Gandhi Interrogated," 453.
121. Sorabji, note in diary, n.d. 1935, MSS EUR F165/97, Sorabji Papers.
122. Sorabji, "'Wein and Women': Describing the International Conference of Women at Vienna 1930," MSS EUR F165/167, Sorabji Papers.
123. As Lowe has pointed out, the workings of capitalism situate it in a complex and contradictory relation with the ideals of democratic citizenship (*Immigrant Acts*, chaps. 1 and 7).
124. Sorabji, "'Mother India': The Incense of Service: What Sacrifice Can We Make?" *The Englishman*, August 31, 1927, MSS EUR F165/161, Sorabji Papers.
125. See Sinha, "The Lineage of the 'Indian' Modern."
126. Sorabji, Notes for "India and Nationalism" [a lecture presented at the Institute of Politics, Williamstown, Mass., August 26–27, 1930], August 26, 1930, MSS EUR F165/179, Sorabji Papers.
127. Goldman, *Max Weber and Thomas Mann*, 110.
128. Carr-Saunders and Wilson, *The Professions*, 290.
129. Robbins, *Secular Vocations*, 24.
130. Carr-Saunders and Wilson, *The Professions*, 13.
131. Sorabji, "Diary Entry," December 30, 1934, MSS EUR F165/96, Sorabji Papers. See Larson, *The Rise of Professionalism*, for a discussion of the

NOTES   225

profound paradoxes engendered by professionalism's uneasy conjunction of "anti-capitalist principles" with an inevitable "market orientation" (63); Ruth insightfully argues that this paradox in fact constitutes the "dialectic" of professionalism ("Between Labor and Capital," 279).

132. See MSS EUR F165/169, Sorabji Papers, for Sorabji's correspondence with various Indian universities to determine the number of Indian women graduating with a degree in law.

133. *Gazette* (Montreal), January 26, 1935, MSS EUR F165/197, Sorabji Papers.

134. *National Review*, March 1935, MSS EUR F165/97, Sorabji Papers.

135. Kaplan, "Resisting Autobiography," 122.

136. While this point has been variously discussed with reference to citizenship, for an illuminating analysis, see Menon, *Recovering Subversion*.

137. Squier, *Liminal Lives*, 4.

4. Modernity and the Indian Civil Service

1. Dewey, *Anglo-Indian Attitudes*, 3.

2. Naoroji, "Admission of Educated Natives into the Indian Civil Service," in *Essays, Speeches*, 76.

3. Banerjea, *Bengalee*, January 14, 1893.

4. See Masselos, *Indian Nationalism*; and S. Sarkar, *Modern India*, 88–100.

5. See Argov, *Moderates and Extremists in the Indian Nationalist Movement*.

6. Watt, *Serving the Nation*, 5.

7. Ibid., 6–7.

8. Seth, "Rewriting Histories of Nationalism," 98.

9. The phrase "reluctant debutante" is from Murshid, *Reluctant Debutantes*.

10. S. Sarkar, "Renaissance and Kaliyuga: Time, Myth and History in Colonial Bengal," in *Writing Social History*, 190–91.

11. See S. Sarkar, "Kaliyuga, Chakri, and Bhakti: Ramakrishna and His Times," in *Writing Social History*, 282–357; and "The Kalki-Avatar of Bikrampur." See also Chatterjee, "A Religion of Urban Domesticity."

12. See Chatterjee, "The Nationalist Resolution of the Woman's Question."

13. See Kaviraj, *The Unhappy Consciousness*, 72–106. For an extended discussion of the reformulation of native masculinity in response to colonial modernity, see Nandy, *The Intimate Enemy*.

14. P. Roy brings this out in her reading of Ramakrishna in *Indian Traffic*, 92–127.

15. Stoler, *Race and the Education of Desire*.

16. The reference here is to the title of Sinha, *Colonial Masculinity: The*

"Manly Englishman" and the "Effeminate Bengali" in the Late Nineteenth Century. For a psychoanalytical reading of the fear of unmanning in the colonies, see Lane, *The Ruling Passion*, especially chap. 1.

17. Sinha, *Colonial Masculinity*, 103-05. See also Collingham, *Imperial Bodies*.
18. Mill, "Considerations on Representative Government," 229.
19. Ibid., 289.
20. Ibid., 291.
21. Ibid.
22. Ibid., 292.
23. Admittedly, the ICS officer occupied the upper echelons of the bureaucracy, but the ideal qualities that he represented were also the ideal qualities of bourgeois citizenship, revealing the implicit exclusions of that citizenship, as well as the extent to which the empire fashioned English envisionings of citizenship.
24. Northcote and Trevelyan, *Report on the Organization of the Permanent Civil Service*, 3; henceforth Northcote-Trevelyan Report.
25. I take this formulation from Vincent's description of the Northcote-Trevelyan Report in *Culture of Secrecy*, 33.
26. Agar, *The Government Machine*, 49.
27. Schuman, *Pedagogical Economies*, 13.
28. "Report on the Indian Civil Service," November 1854, in the Oriental and India Office Collection of the British Library (henceforth OIOC), *The Selection and Training of Candidates for the Indian Civil Service*, 300. This report was presented by Charles Wood, and the committee's other members included Thomas Macaulay and Benjamin Jowett.
29. OIOC, *Open Competition for the Civil Service of India, June 1884*, 14.
30. Viswanathan, *Masks of Conquest*, 10.
31. Northcote-Trevelyan Report, quoted in Schuman, *Pedagogical Economies*, 78.
32. Weber, "Parliament and Government in Germany Under a New Political Order," in *Political Writings*, 156.
33. As Weber points out, England "preserved" itself from the "bureaucratization that was the fate of all states in the Continent" (*Political Writings*, 328). See also Goodlad, *Victorian Literature and the Victorian State*, xii.
34. Compton, "Open Competition and the Indian Civil Service, 1854-1876," 265. See also Cohn, "Recruitment and Training of British Civil Servants in India, 1600-1860"; Cross, "Selection and Training of the Candidates for the Indian Civil Service"; and Moore, "Abolition of Patronage in the Indian Civil Service."
35. Beames, *Memoirs of a Bengal Civilian*, 63. See also Gilmour, *The Ruling Caste*, 42.
36. Dewey, "The Education of a Ruling Caste," 267.
37. Rather than an all-powerful bureaucracy that stifled legislation—like the one in Russia, for instance—the liberal objective in England was, as

Montgomery notes, to "secure the efficient execution of policies by competent and impartial officers" (*Examinations*, 21).

38. "Report on the Indian Civil Service," in OIOC, *The Selection and Training of Candidates for the Indian Civil Service*, 301.

39. Collini, "The Idea of Character in Victorian Political Thought," 35.

40. Goodlad, *Victorian Literature and the Victorian State*, 24.

41. Schuman, *Pedagogical Economies*, 10.

42. Bourdieu, *The State Nobility*, 376.

43. Quoted in Misra, *The Bureaucracy in India*, 75.

44. Naoroji, "Admission of Educated Natives into the Indian Civil Service," in *Essays, Speeches*, 77.

45. "Despatch from Government of India to Right Hon. Viscount Cross, Secretary of State for India, October 9, 1888," in OIOC, *Correspondence Relating to the Report of the Indian Public Service Commission*, 9.

46. Quoted in H. Singh, *Problems and Policies of the British in India*, 14–15.

47. Naoroji, "Admission of Educated Natives into the Indian Civil Service," in *Essays, Speeches*, 78.

48. Osborne, "Bureaucracy as a Vocation," 307.

49. Dewey, "The Education of a Ruling Caste," 268.

50. Spangenburg, *British Bureaucracy in India*, 22–23 (tables 1 and 2).

51. For a discussion of the use of "crammers" for the ICS examinations, see Cohn, "Recruitment and Training of British Civil Servants in India, 1600–1860," 127.

52. Spangenburg, *British Bureaucracy in India*, 21.

53. Ibid., 24.

54. Dewey, "The Education of a Ruling Caste," 272. For an elaboration of the significance of the "gentlemanly ideal" in Victorian England, see Mason, *The English Gentleman*, 162; and Goodlad, *Victorian Literature and the Victorian State*, 129. For an elaboration of the association of this ideal with a public school or Oxbridge training, see Wilkinson, *Gentlemanly Power*; and Newsome, *Godliness and Good Learning*. The renewed emphasis on gentlemanliness was a Victorian legacy, which can be explained in part by the educational legacy of Thomas Arnold, the headmaster of Rugby from 1828 to 1841. Redirecting aristocratic implications of gentlemanliness from previous centuries, Arnold sought to formulate the Victorian "Christian gentleman," one who combined "middle-class morality [with] gentry-class style" (Wilkinson, *Gentlemanly Power*, 10). In an era of radical social readjustment, the new gentlemanly ideal was cherished because it was seen to provide, in Arnold's words, a mediating "classless class of well-bred men" (quoted in Goodlad, *Victorian Literature and the Victorian State*, 129).

55. Quoted in Compton, "Open Competition and the Indian Civil Service 1854–1876," 271.

56. "Despatch from Under Secretary of State for India to the Secretary,

Civil Services Commission, July 24, 1889," in OIOC, *Correspondence Relating to the Report of the Indian Public Service Commission*, 85.

57. Goodlad, *Victorian Literature and the Victorian State*, 26.

58. For an elaboration of this logic, see Marx, *Grundrisse*, 162.

59. Britons who had settled in India or were raised there were referred to as Anglo-Indians. In contrast to Haileybury civilians whose families had long connections with India, the competition-civilian would have been a newcomer to the Anglo-Indian community in India. The possible Anglo-Indian coinage of "competitionwallah" suggests the resentment at this figure as an inexperienced interloper who could not lay claim to any "India connections." While Anglo-Indian opinion was quite distinct—and often even opposed—to metropolitan policy-making, the case of the competition-civilian seems to have brought Anglo-Indian and metropolitan anxieties into concert. According to the *Hobson-Jobson*, the venerable compendium of Anglo-Indian words and phrases, "competitionwallah," a mixture of English and Hindustani, was probably coined by a Haileybury civilian. While the term became readily popular in India, it was a familiar one in metropolitan circles as well, especially after the publication of Trevelyan's *The Competition Wallah* in 1864.

60. This disdain was manifested, for instance, in Anthony Trollope's criticism of the proposal to introduce Civil Service examinations in his 1858 novel, *Three Clerks*.

61. Letter from Under Secretary of State, India Office, to Secretary, Civil Service Commissioners, September 7, 1874, in OIOC, *The Selection and Training of Candidates for the Indian Civil Service*, 283. The original query was from T. Walrond, Secretary, Civil Service Commission, August 5, 1874, in ibid., 282–83.

62. Wyllie, *A Letter to the Hon'ble Sir C.E. Trevelyan, K.C.B.*, in National Library, Kolkata (henceforth NL), 1.

63. Ibid., 2.

64. The phrase comes from the title of Long, *The Man on the Spot*.

65. Schuman, *Pedagogical Economies*, 4.

66. J. Adams, *Dandies and Desert Saints*, 2.

67. See Mangan, "Social Darwinism and Upper-Class Education in Late Victorian and Edwardian England." The emphasis on physical culture also reflected Victorian notions of holistic health, in which the healthy body was in concert with moral and spiritual well-being: *mens sana in corpore sano*. See Haley, *The Healthy Body and Victorian Culture*.

68. Wyllie, *A Letter to the Hon'ble Sir C.E. Trevelyan, K.C.B.*, in NL, 5.

69. Ibid., 6–7.

70. See Bristow, *Empire Boys*.

71. Wyllie, *A Letter to the Hon'ble Sir C.E. Trevelyan, K.C.B.*, in NL, 8.

72. Trevelyan, *The Competition Wallah*, v. Henceforth in this chapter, all references to *Wallah* will be cited parenthetically in the text.

73. A ryot is a cultivator of the land.

74. Compton, "Open Competition and the Indian Civil Service 1854–1876," 272.

75. Clive, "Peter and the Wallah."

76. Streets, *Martial Races*, 120.

77. Carlyle, *On Heroes, Hero-Worship and the Heroic in History*, 171.

78. As Collingham notes, memoirs of English ICS civilians later in the century often emphasized the civilians' bodily rigor and intellectual labor by way of reworking the civilian into a "heroic" figure (*Imperial Bodies*, 140).

79. Cunningham, *Chronicles of Dustypore*, 3. Henry Stewart Cunningham was posted to India as a judge and a member of the Famine Commission. Henceforth in this chapter, all references to *Chronicles* will be cited parenthetically in the text.

80. Dawson, *British Adventure, Empire, and the Imagining of Masculinities*, 83.

81. Collingham, *Imperial Bodies*, 120.

82. Gagnier, *Idylls of the Marketplace*, 68.

83. See J. Adams, "The Hero as Spectacle," 222. A longer version of this article appears in Adams, *Dandies and Desert Saints*, chap. 1.

84. My arrival at this formulation has been aided by James Adams's reading of the dandiacal implications of the Carlylean hero (*Dandies and Desert Saints*, 38).

85. Schuman, *Pedagogical Economies*, 10.

86. While the subtitle of Cunningham's novel, *A Tale of Modern Anglo-Indian Society*, may implicitly define resentment toward the competition-wallah as a specifically Anglo-Indian phenomenon, this would only have been a move to deflect attention from the support that sentiment received in the supposedly more liberal metropolis, albeit for different reasons.

87. Bivona, *British Imperial Literature, 1870–1940*, 10.

88. Ibid., 18. This would also explain Kipling's status as a chronicler par excellence of British India. In depicting the dailyness of the administrator's life in the final two decades of the century (such as in *Plain Tales from the Hills*), Kipling is singular in humanizing the administrator, though he does not manage to do so without adding a touch of the heroic. For a reading of Kipling's depiction of English administrators, see Bivona, chap. 3.

89. See Glick, "The Dialectic of Dandyism."

90. *A Nation in Making*, 2. Henceforth in this chapter, all references to *Nation* will be cited parenthetically in the text. For a biography of Banerjea, see B. Banerjea, *Surendranath Banerjea and the History of Modern India*.

91. "Despatch from H.M.'s Secretary of State for India No. 34, April 1872," in NL, *Notes Connected with the Collection of Papers Relating to the Appointment of Natives of India*.

92. Chatterjee, however, uses the term more to describe the limitations of this liberal sphere of nationalist politics that prevailed before the onset of the mass nationalist movement ("On Civil and Political Society in Postcolonial Democracies," 175).

93. S. Sarkar, *Writing Social History*, 304.

94. See Chatterjee, *The Nation and Its Fragments*, 138.

95. Majeed, *Autobiography, Travel, and Postnational Identity*, 179.

96. Dames, "Trollope and the Career," 249.

97. Majeed, *Autobiography, Travel, and Postnational Identity*, 180.

98. Charges of Bengali effeteness were often extended to refer to the politically articulate Indian middle class as well (Sinha, *Colonial Masculinity*, 16). However, as Sinha also points out with reference to native admission into the Indian Civil Service, by the mid-1880s, British domination of the ICS came to be constructed in counterpoint not to an "Indian" identity but to "fragmented and competing provincial native identities" (*Colonial Masculinity*, 132). Given the relative success of Bengalis in gaining admission to the ICS, the construction of the "effeminate Bengali" or Bengali babu evidently played out along similar lines as that of the English competition-wallah (*Colonial Masculinity*, 104). Criticism of the Bengali babu garnered support from other native communities as well.

99. Banerjea, "Indian Unity," 46.

100. Banerjea, "Congress Presidential Address, Poona, 1895," 15.

101. Ibid., 119.

102. Rosselli, "The Self-Image of Effeteness." For an elaboration of this in a North Indian context, see Gupta, *Sexuality, Obscenity, Community*.

103. Alter, *Gandhi's Body*, 19.

104. Quoted in Majumdar, *Militant Nationalism in India and Its Socioreligious Background*, 61.

105. Chowdhury, *The Frail Hero and Virile History*, 113.

106. Tilak, *Bal Gangadhar Tilak: His Writings and Speeches*, 55.

107. See S. Sarkar, *Modern India*, 125–37; McLane, *Indian Nationalism and the Early Congress*; and Wolpert, *Tilak and Gokhale*.

108. The Moderates regrouped to form the Liberal Party. See H. Banerjee, *Political Activity of the Liberal Party in India*; and Saxena, *Indian National Movement and the Liberals*.

109. Banerjea attributes this comment to Tilak. The response to the report, however, was not as evenly divided as *Nation* will have us believe. See Metcalf and Metcalf, *A Concise History of India*, 166; and Sitaramayya, *The History of the Indian National Congress*, 255–65.

110. Banerjea, "Self-Government for India," in *Speeches and Writings of Hon. Surendranath Banerjea*, 131.

111. Chakrabarty, *Provincializing Europe*, 10.

112. See, for instance, Nandy's discussion of Rabindranath Tagore's unease, in a different context, with the implied congruency of nationalism, anti-imperialism, and patriotism (*The Illegitimacy of Nationalism*, 89). See also Viswanathan's reading of Tagore's unpopular "internationalism" ("Ireland, India, and the Poetics of Internationalism," 8).

113. See Gorman, "Lionel Curtis, Imperial Citizenship, and the Quest for Imperial Unity," 92.

NOTES 231

114. Tilak, *Bal Gangadhar Tilak*, 45.
115. Quoted in Majumdar, *Militant Nationalism in India and Its Socio-religious Background*, 66.
116. Quoted in McLane, *Indian Nationalism and the Early Congress*, 157.
117. "Congress and Democracy," in Mukherjee and Mukherjee, *"Bande Mataram" and Indian Nationalism (1906–08)*, 32. For a reading of the limited nature, however, of Aurobindo's nationalist rhetoric, see Southard, "The Political Strategy of Aurobindo Ghosh."
118. Quoted in Majumdar, *Militant Nationalism in India and Its Socio-religious Background*, 71.
119. "Ideals Face to Face," in Mukherjee and Mukherjee, *"Bande Mataram" and Indian Nationalism (1906–08)*, 85.
120. Chowdhury, *The Frail Hero and Virile History*, 122.
121. Nandy, *The Illegitimacy of Nationalism*, 28.
122. For a reading of how the heroism of "militant nationalists" inspired popular narrative in India, see Bose, *Organizing Empire*, chap. 3. For a discussion of how they were rendered popular through the proliferation of visual technology, see Pinney, *"Photos of the Gods,"* chap. 6.
123. Seth, "Rewriting Histories of Nationalism," 101.
124. Bivona, *British Imperial Literature, 1870–1940*, 17.
125. Dandeker, *Surveillance, Power and Modernity*, 9.
126. Weber, "Bureaucracy," 228–29.
127. Ibid., 228. Mill shared some of these reservations about the bureaucracy ("Considerations on Representative Government," 289). For an account of the critique of what is seen to be determinism in Weber's account of the bureaucracy, which he famously referred to as an "iron-cage," see Dandeker, *Surveillance, Power and Modernity*, 16–17. For an alternate reading of the bureaucracy, see Osborne, "Bureaucracy as a Vocation."
128. For an account of the difficult transition from bureaucratic to representative state institutions, see Misra, *The Bureacracy in India*, 321–23.
129. McLane, *Indian Nationalism and the Early Congress*, 157.
130. In other words, the Indian nationalist movement needed "popular heroes." My thanks to Dipesh Chakrabarty for discussing this latter point with me.
131. Goswami, *Producing India*, 275.
132. Ibid., 273.
133. Lloyd, "Nationalisms against the State," 182.
134. See Vithal, "Evolving Trends in the Bureaucracy."
135. Seth, "Rewriting Histories of Nationalism," 99.
136. Tilak, *Bal Gangadhar Tilak*, 379.
137. Parekh, *Colonialism, Tradition, and Reform*, 257.
138. Ibid., 251–52.
139. Butler, *Precarious Life*, 34.
140. As Chatterjee points out, a public condolence meeting held to mourn the death of Bankimchandra in 1894, for instance, was criticized

because of its contravention of the Hindu observance of mourning that calls for seclusion. Writing in defense of the condolence meeting, however, the young poet Rabindranath Tagore argued for the necessity of such an event on progressive grounds, reasoning that a public show of mourning, especially for those in public life, was necessary to consolidate an emergent public sphere ("On Civil and Political Society in Postcolonial Democracies" 166).

141. L. Gandhi's suggestion to consider what is rendered "immature" in anti-imperial politics is also important here (*Affective Communities*, 12).

142. My reading here is aided by Kaviraj's analysis of an autobiographical text (by Sibnath Sastri) roughly contemporaneous with that of Banerjea's ("The Invention of Private Life," 110–12).

143. For a discussion of the ways in which the male Hindu body becomes the necessary embodiment of the ideal citizen, see Wakankar, "Body, Crowd, Identity," 52.

144. See Eng and Kazanjian, *Loss*.

145. Mourning, Freud tells us, distinguishes itself from melancholia because melancholia involves a failure to libidinally withdraw from the object of loss, whereas mourning can be "relied upon being overcome after a certain lapse of time" ("Mourning and Melancholia," 244).

146. Derrida, *The Work of Mourning*, 144.

147. W. Brown, "Of Specters and Angels," 173.

Afterword

1. Natarajan, Foreword, iii. The foreword is to a collection of fifteen bulletins—each one titled *Indians Abroad*—periodically issued by the Imperial Indian Citizenship Association, starting in 1923.

2. Pettit, Introduction, *Indians Abroad*. The expectation of just rewards for Indian contribution to the First World War also furthered this scrutiny.

3. Ibid., 1.

4. See Dutta, "From Subject to Citizen."

5. S. Satyamurthy, *Rights of Citizens*, 2.

6. Ibid., appendix B.

7. The reference here is to Marshall's influential formulation of citizenship in *Citizenship and Social Class, and Other Essays*.

8. See Hazareesingh, "The Quest for Urban Citizenship."

9. See Chandhoke, "Vocabularies of Resistance, Vocabularies of Rights."

10. Puntambekar, *An Introduction to Indian Citizenship and Civilisation*, 1.

11. Ibid.

12. Ibid., 13.

13. Ibid., 14.

14. Ibid.

15. Butler, "Restaging the Universal," 32.
16. The details of the incident are in Anna Ross, "The Sad Story of the *Komagata Maru*," quoted in Vaiz, *Indians Abroad*, 669–71.
17. Ibid., 670.
18. Ibid., 671.

Bibliography

Private Papers

Naoroji, Dadabhai, Papers. National Archives of India (NAI), New Delhi
Sorabji, Cornelia, Papers. MSS EUR F165. Oriental and India Office Collection (OIOC), British Library, London

Government Reports and Papers

UNITED KINGDOM

Oriental and India Office Collection (OIOC), British Library, London

Conference of Prime Ministers and Representatives of the United Kingdom, The Dominions, and India, held in June, July, and August, 1921. Summary of Proceedings and Documents. London: His Majesty's Stationery Office, 1921. In *Parliamentary Papers*, IOR V/4/Session 1921, Vol. 14.

Correspondence Relating to the Report of the Indian Public Service Commission Including the Question as to the Limit of Age for the Indian Civil Service. London: Her Majesty's Stationery Office, 1890. In IOR L/PJ/6/291 File 2267.

Imperial Conference, 1911. Papers Laid Before the Conference. London: His Majesty's Stationery Office, 1911. In *Parliamentary Papers*, IOR V/4/Session 1911, Vol. 54.

Imperial War Conference, 1917: Extracts from Minutes of Proceedings and Papers Laid Before the Conference. London: His Majesty's Stationery Office, 1917. In *Parliamentary Papers*, IOR V/4/Session 1917/18, Vol. 23.

"Papers Relating to the Grievances of Her Majesty's Indian Subjects in the South African Republic." In *Parliamentary Papers*, IOR V/4/Session 1895, Vol. 62.

Proclamation, by the Queen in Council, to the Princes, Chiefs, and People of India (Published by the Governor-General at Allahabad, November 1st, 1858). London: George E. Eyre and William Spottiswoode, 1858. In *Parliamentary Papers*, IOR V/4/Session 1876, Vol. 56.

The Selection and Training of Candidates for the Indian Civil Service. London:

George E. Eyre and William Spottiswoode, 1876. In *Parliamentary Papers*, IOR v/4/Session 1876, Vol. 55.

INDIA

National Archives of India, New Delhi (NAI) (All references are to publications of the Government of India)

"Alleged Unlawful Deportation from Australia of a Native of India." In *Proceedings of the Department of Commerce and Industry, February 1906*, no. 11.
"Australian Immigration Restriction Act (Amendment Act), No. 17 of 1905." In *Proceedings of the Department of Commerce and Industry, April 1906*, no. 3.
"Complaints of Return Coolies from Natal." In *Proceedings of the Department of Agriculture, Revenue, and Commerce: Emigration. August 1871*, no. 10.
"Emigration Proceedings." In *Proceedings of the Department of Agriculture, Revenue, and Commerce, May 1872.*
"Kidnapping of Women by Recruiters for Emigrants." In *Proceedings of the Department of Agriculture, Revenue, and Commerce: Emigration. August 1871*, no. 6.
"Natal Immigration Report for 1879." In *Home, Revenue, and Agricultural Department Proceedings, January 1881.*
"Report of the Protector of Immigrants, Natal, for 1891–92." In *Proceedings of the Revenue and Agricultural Department, January 1893.*

National Library, Kolkata (NL)

Notes Connected with the Collection of Papers Relating to the Appointment of Natives of India. Calcutta: Superintendent of Government Printing, 1886. G.P. 351.3 [1] (54) In 2ncp.
Wyllie, J. W. S. *A Letter to the Hon'ble Sir C. E. Trevelyan, K.C.B. on the Selection and Training of Candidates for H.M.'s Indian Civil Service.* Calcutta: Home Secretariat Press, 1870. G.P. 351.3 [1] (54) W979.

Newspapers and Periodicals

Bengalee
Daily News (London)
Edinburgh Evening Dispatch
The Englishman
Holborn Guardian

The Holborn and Finsbury Guardian
Leeds Mercury
The Manchester Guardian
Morning Post
Pall Mall Gazette
The Times

Other Published Sources

A. D. *Until the Shadows Flee Away: The Story of C.E.Z.M.S. Work in India and Ceylon*. London: Church of England Zenana Missionary Society, n.d.

Abel-Smith, Brian, and Robert Stevens. *Lawyers and the Courts: A Sociological Study of the English Legal System 1750–1965*. Cambridge: Harvard University Press, 1967.

Adams, James Eli. *Dandies and Desert Saints: Styles of Victorian Masculinity*. Ithaca, N.Y.: Cornell University Press, 1995.

———. "The Hero as Spectacle: Carlyle and the Persistence of Dandyism." In *Victorian Literature and the Victorian Visual Imagination*, edited by Carol T. Christ and John Jordan, 213–29. Berkeley: University of California Press, 1995.

Adams, Stephen. "The Medicinal Leech: A Page from the Annelids of Internal Medicine." *Annals of Internal Medicine* 109, no. 5 (1988): 399–405.

Agar, Jon. *The Government Machine: A Revolutionary History of the Computer*. Cambridge: MIT Press, 2003.

Albisetti, James. "Portia Ante Portas: Women and the Legal Profession in Europe, ca. 1870–1925." *Journal of Social History* 33, no. 4 (2000): 825–57.

Alter, Joseph. *Gandhi's Body: Sex, Diet, and the Politics of Nationalism*. Philadelphia: University of Pennsylvania Press, 2000.

Amin, Shahid. "Gandhi as Mahatma: Gorakhpur District, Eastern UP, 1921–22." In *Subaltern Studies: Writings on South Asian History and Society*, vol. 3, edited by Ranajit Guha, 1–61. New Delhi: Oxford University Press, 1984.

Anderson, Amanda. *The Powers of Distance: Cosmopolitanism and the Cultivation of Detachment*. Princeton, N.J.: Princeton University Press, 2001.

Anderson, Benedict. *Imagined Communities: The Rise and Spread of Nationalism*. London: Verso, 1983.

Anderson, Michael R., and Sumit Guha. Introduction. *Changing Concepts of Rights and Justice in South Asia*, edited by Michael R. Anderson and Sumit Guha, 1–13. New Delhi: Oxford University Press, 1998.

Andriopoulos, Stefan. "The Invisible Hand: Supernatural Agency in Political Economy." ELH 66, no. 3 (1999): 739–58.

Appadurai, Arjun. *Modernity at Large: Cultural Dimensions of Globalization*. Minneapolis: University of Minnesota Press, 1996.

Arata, Stephen. *Fictions of Loss in the Victorian Fin de Siècle: Identity and Empire*. Cambridge: Cambridge University Press, 1996.
Aravamudan, Srinivas. "In the Wake of the Novel: The Oriental Tale as National Allegory." *Novel* 33, no. 1 (September 1999): 5–31.
Argov, Daniel. *Moderates and Extremists in the Indian Nationalist Movement: 1883–1920*. Bombay: Asia Publishing House, 1967.
Armstrong-Hopkins, A. *Within the Purdah: Being the Personal Observations of a Medical Missionary in India*. New York: Eaton and Mains, 1898.
Arnold, David. *Colonizing the Body: State Medicine and Epidemic Disease in Nineteenth-Century India*. Berkeley: University of California Press, 1993.
———. *Gandhi*. London: Pearson Education, 2001.
Arondekar, Anjali, Cannon Schmitt, and Nancy Henry. Introduction. "Victorian Investments," edited by Anjali Arondekar, Cannon Schmitt, and Nancy Henry, special issue, *Victorian Studies* 45, no. 1 (2002): 7–16.
Axel, Brian Keith. *The Nation's Tortured Body: Violence, Representation, and the Formation of a Sikh "Diaspora."* Durham, N.C.: Duke University Press, 2001.
Azim, Firdous. *The Colonial Rise of the Novel*. London: Routledge, 1993.
Bahri, Deepika. *Native Intelligence: Aesthetics, Politics, and Postcolonial Literature*. Minneapolis: University of Minnesota Press, 2003.
Bailkin, Jordanna. "The Place of Liberalism." *Victorian Studies* 48, no. 1 (autumn 2005): 83–91.
Bakhtin, Mikhail. *The Dialogic Imagination, Four Essays*. Edited by Michael Holquist. Translated by Caryl Emerson and Michael Holquist. Austin: University of Texas Press, 1981.
Baldick, Chris. *In Frankenstein's Shadow: Myth, Monstrosity, and Nineteenth-Century Writing*. Oxford: Clarendon Press of Oxford University Press, 1987.
Balibar, Etienne. "Citizen Subject." In *Who Comes After the Subject?* edited by Eduardo Cadava, Peter Connor, and Jean-Luc Nancy, 33–57. New York: Routledge, 1991.
———. *We, the People of Europe: Reflections on Transnational Citizenship*. Translated by James Swenson. Princeton, N.J.: Princeton University Press, 2004.
Banerjea, Surendranath. "Congress Presidential Address, Poona, 1895." In *Speeches and Writings of Hon. Surendranath Banerjea*, 11–99. 1st edition Madras: G. A. Natesan, n.d.
———. "Indian Unity." In *Speeches of Surendranath Banerjea*, 31–50. Calcutta: Indian Association, 1970.
———. *A Nation in Making: Being the Reminiscences of Fifty Years of Public Life*. London: Oxford University Press, 1925.
———. "Self-Government for India." In *Speeches and Writings of Hon. Surendranath Banerjea*, 126–42. Madras: G. A. Natesan, n.d.

Banerjee, Bani. *Surendranath Banerjea and History of Modern India, 1848–1925*. New Delhi: Metropolitan, 1979.
Banerjee, Hasi. *Political Activity of the Liberal Party in India*. Calcutta: K. P. Bagchi, 1987.
Basu, Srimati. *She Comes to Take Her Rights: Indian Women, Property, and Propriety*. Albany: State University of New York Press, 1999.
Baucom, Ian. *Out of Place: Englishness, Empire, and the Locations of Identity*. Princeton, N.J.: Princeton University Press, 1999.
Baxi, Upendra. "The State's Emissary: The Place of Law in Subaltern Studies." In *Subaltern Studies: Writings on South Asian History and Society*, vol. 7, edited by Partha Chatterjee and Gyanendra Pandey, 246–64. Delhi: Oxford University Press, 1992.
Bayly, C. A. "Ireland, India, and the Empire: 1780–1914." *Transactions of the Royal Historical Society*, 6th ser., 10 (2000): 377–97.
———. "Rammohan Roy and the Advent of Constitutional Liberalism in India, 1800–30." *Modern Intellectual History* 4, no. 1 (2007): 25–41.
Beall, Jo. "Women under Indenture in Natal." In *Essays on Indentured Indians in Natal*, edited by Surendra Bhana, 89–115. Leeds, England: Peepal Tree Press, 1990.
Beames, John. *Memoirs of a Bengal Civilian*. London: Chatto and Windus, 1961.
Bellamy, Richard. Introduction. *Victorian Liberalism: Nineteenth-Century Political Thought and Practice*, edited by Richard Bellamy, 1–14. London: Routledge, 1990.
Bending, Lucy. *Representation of Bodily Pain in Late Nineteenth Century English Literature*. Oxford: Oxford University Press, 2000.
Benhabib, Seyla. *The Claims of Culture: Equality and Diversity in the Global Era*. Princeton, N.J.: Princeton University Press, 2002.
Benjamin, Walter. "Theses on the Philosophy of History." *Illuminations*, edited by Hannah Arendt, 253–64. New York: Shocken, 1968.
Berlant, Lauren. *The Queen of America Goes to Washington City: Essays on Sex and Citizenship*. Durham, N.C.: Duke University Press, 1997.
Bhabha, Homi. "DissemiNation: Time, Narrative and the Margins of the Modern Nation." In *Nation and Narration*, edited by Homi Bhabha, 291–322. London: Routledge, 1990.
Bhana, Surendra. *Gandhi's Legacy: The Natal Indian Congress 1894–1994*. Pietermaritzburg, South Africa: University of Natal Press, 1997.
———. *Indentured Indian Emigrants to Natal 1860–1902: A Study Based on Ships' Lists*. New Delhi: Promilla, 1991.
———. "Indian Trade and Trader in Colonial Natal." In *Enterprise and Exploitation in a Victorian Colony: Aspects of the Economic and Social History of Colonial Natal*, edited by Bill Guest and John Sellers, 235–63. Pietermaritzburg, South Africa: University of Natal Press, 1985.
Bhana, Surendra, and Joy Brain. *Setting Down Roots: Indian Migrants in South Africa 1860–1911*. Johannesburg: Witwatersrand University Press, 1990.

Bhana, Surendra, and Goolam Vahed. *The Making of a Political Reformer: Gandhi in South Africa, 1893–1914*. New Delhi: Manohar, 2005.

Biagini, Eugenio. *Liberty, Retrenchment, and Reform: Popular Liberalism in the Age of Gladstone 1860–80*. Cambridge: Cambridge University Press, 1992.

Bivona, Daniel. *British Imperial Literature, 1870–1940: Writing and the Administration of Empire*. Cambridge: Cambridge University Press, 1998.

Boehmer, Elleke. *Empire, the National, and the Postcolonial, 1890–1920: Resistance in Interaction*. Oxford: Oxford University Press, 2002.

———. Introduction. *India Calling: The Memories of Cornelia Sorabji*, edited by Elleke Boehmer, ix–xv. Nottingham, England: Trent Editions, 2004.

Bolt, Christine. *Victorian Attitudes to Race*. London: Routledge and Kegan Paul, 1971.

Booth, Mary Warburton. *"Take This Child."* London: Marshall Brothers, n.d.

Bose, Purnima. *Organizing Empire: Individualism, Collective Agency, and India*. Durham, N.C.: Duke University Press, 2003.

Bose, Sarmila, and Eilis Ward. "India's Cause Is Ireland's Cause." In *Elite Links and Nationalist Politics*, edited by Michael Holmes and Denis Holmes. Dublin: Folens, 1997.

Bourdieu, Pierre. *The State Nobility: Elite Schools in the Field of Power*. Translated by Lauretta Clough. Stanford, Calif.: Stanford University Press, 1989.

Brain, Joy. "Indentured and Free Indians in the Economy of Colonial Natal." In *Enterprise and Exploitation in a Victorian Colony: Aspects of the Economic and Social History of Colonial Natal*, edited by Bill Guest and John Sellers, 198–233. Pietermaritzburg, South Africa: University of Natal Press, 1985.

Brantlinger, Patrick. *Fictions of State: Culture and Credit in Britain, 1694–1994*. Ithaca, N.Y.: Cornell University Press, 1996.

———. *Rule of Darkness: British Literature and Imperialism, 1830–1914*. Ithaca, N.Y.: Cornell University Press, 1988.

Brasted, Howard. "Indian Nationalist Development and the Influence of Irish Home Rule, 1870–1886." *Modern Asian Studies* 14, no. 1 (1980): 37–63.

Brennan, Timothy. "The National Longing for Form." In *Nation and Narration*, edited by Homi Bhabha, 44–70. London: Routledge, 1990.

Bristow, Joseph. *Empire Boys: Adventures in a Man's World*. London: Harper Collins Academic, 1991.

"British Nationality and Status of Aliens Act, 1914." In *The Public General Acts Passed in the Fourth and Fifth Years of the Reign of His Majesty, King George the Fifth, Being the Fourth Session of the Thirtieth Parliament of the United Kingdom of Great Britain and Ireland*. London: King's Printer of Acts of Parliament, 1914.

Brody, Jennifer. *Impossible Purities: Blackness, Femininity, and Victorian Culture*. Durham, N.C.: Duke University Press, 1998.
Brooks, Peter, and Paul Gewirtz, eds. *Law's Stories: Narrative and Rhetoric in the Law*. New Haven: Yale University Press, 1996.
Brown, Judith. *Gandhi: Prisoner of Hope*. New Haven, Conn.: Yale University Press, 1989.
Brown, Wendy. "Specters and Angels: Benjamin and Derrida." *Politics out of History*, 138–73. Princeton, N.J.: Princeton University Press, 2001.
Burton, Antoinette. *At the Heart of Empire: Indians and the Colonial Encounter in Late-Victorian Britain*. Berkeley: University of California, 1998.
———. *Burdens of History: British Feminists, Indian Women, and Imperial Culture, 1865–1915*. Chapel Hill: University of North Carolina Press, 1994.
———. "Contesting the Zenana: The Mission to Make Lady Doctors for India 1874–1885." *Journal of British Studies* 35 (July 1996): 368–97.
———. *Dwelling in the Archive: Women Writing House, Home, and History in Late Colonial India*. New York: Oxford University Press, 2003.
———. "Making a Spectacle of Empire: Indian Travelers in Fin-de-Siècle London." *History Workshop Journal* 42 (1996): 127–46.
———. "Tongues Untied: Lord Salisbury's 'Black Man' and the Boundaries of Imperial Democracy." *Comparative Studies in Society and History* 42, no. 3 (2000): 632–61.
———. "Who Needs the Nation? Interrogating 'British' History" [1997]. In *Cultures of Empire: A Reader: Colonisers in Britain and the Empire in the Nineteenth and Twentieth Centuries*, edited by Catherine Hall, 137–53. Manchester: Manchester University Press, 2000.
Butler, Judith. "Competing Universalities." In *Contingency, Hegemony, Universality: Contemporary Dialogues on the Left*, edited by Judith Butler, Ernesto Laclau, and Slavoj Žižek, 137–81. London: Verso, 2000.
———. *Precarious Life: The Powers of Mourning and Violence*. London: Verso, 2004.
———. "Restaging the Universal: Hegemony and the Limits of Formalism." In *Contingency, Hegemony, Universality: Contemporary Dialogues on the Left*, edited by Judith Butler, Ernesto Laclau, and Slavoj Žižek, 11–43. London: Verso, 2000.
Candy, Catherine. "The Inscrutable Irish-Indian Feminist Management of Anglo-American Hegemony, 1917–1947." *Journal of Colonialism and Colonial History* 2, no. 1 (2001): 1–28.
Canning, Kathleen, and Sonya O. Rose. Introduction. *Gender, Citizenships, and Subjectivities*, edited by Kathleen Canning and Sonya O. Rose, 1–18. Oxford: Blackwell, 2002.
Carlyle, Thomas. *On Heroes, Hero-Worship and the Heroic in History*. [1841]. New York: AMS Press, 1969.
Carr-Saunders, A. M., and P. A. Wilson. *The Professions*. London: Frank Cass, 1964.

Carter, Marina. *Voices from Indenture: Experiences of Indian Migrants in the British Empire*. London: Leicester University Press, 1996.

Chadwick, Edwin. *Report on the Sanitary Condition of the Labouring Population of Great Britain*. [1842]. Edited by M. W. Flinn. Edinburgh: Edinburgh University Press, 1965.

Chakrabarty, Dipesh. "Postcoloniality and the Artifice of History: Who Speaks for 'Indian' Pasts?" *Representations* 37 (winter 1992): 1–29.

———. *Provincializing Europe: Postcolonial Thought and Historical Difference*. Princeton, N.J.: Princeton University Press, 2000.

———. "Subject of Law and Subject of Narratives." In *Habitations of Modernity: Essays in the Wake of Subaltern Studies*, 101–14. Delhi: Permanent Black, 2002.

Chakravarti, Uma. "Whatever Happened to the Vedic Dasi?" In *Recasting Women: Essays in Colonial History*, edited by Kumkum Sangari and Sudesh Vaid, 27–87. New Delhi: Kali for Women, 1989.

Chandhoke, Neera. "Vocabularies of Resistance, Vocabularies of Rights." In *Mapping Histories: Essays Presented to Ravinder Kumar*, edited by Neera Chandhoke. London: Anthem Press, 2000.

Chandra, Sudhir. "The Cultural Complement of Economic Nationalism." *The Indian Historical Review* 12, nos. 1–2 (1985–86): 106–20.

Chatterjee, Partha. *The Nation and Its Fragments: Colonial and Postcolonial Histories*. Delhi: Oxford University Press, 1999. First published 1993 by Princeton University Press.

———. "The Nationalist Resolution of the Women's Question." In *Recasting Women: Essays in Colonial History*, edited by Kumkum Sangari and Sudesh Vaid, 233–54. New Delhi: Kali for Women, 1989.

———. "On Civil and Political Society in Postcolonial Democracies." In *Civil Society: History and Possibilities*, edited by Sudpita Kaviraj and Sunil Khilnani, 165–77. Cambridge: Cambridge University Press, 2001.

———. "A Religion of Urban Domesticity: Sri Ramakrishna and the Calcutta Middle Class." In *Subaltern Studies: Writings on South Asian History and Society*, vol. 8, edited by Partha Chatterjee and Gyanendra Pandey, 40–68. New Delhi: Oxford University Press, 1992.

Chattopadhyaya, Kamaladevi. *Indian Women's Battle for Freedom*. New Delhi: Abhinav, 1983.

Chaudhuri, Rosinka. "*The Flute*, *Gerontion*, and Subalternist Misreadings of Tagore." *Social Text* 78 (spring 2004): 103–22.

Cheah, Pheng. *Spectral Nationality: Passages of Freedom from Kant to Postcolonial Literatures of Liberation*. New York: Columbia University Press, 2003.

Childers, Joseph. "Observation and Representation: Mr. Chadwick Writes the Poor." *Victorian Studies* 37, no. 3 (spring 1994): 405–32.

Chowdhury, Indira. *The Frail Hero and Virile History: Gender and the Politics of Culture in Colonial Bengal*. Delhi: Oxford University Press, 1998.

Clive, John. "Peter and the Wallah: From Kinsfolk to Competition." In *History and Imagination: Essays in Honor of H. R. Trevor-Roper*, 311–25. New York: Holmes and Meier, 1981.

Cohen, Monica. *Professional Domesticity in the Victorian Novel: Women, Work, and Home.* Cambridge: Cambridge University Press, 1998.

Cohen, William, and Ryan Johnson. Introduction. *Filth: Dirt, Disgust, and Modern Life*, edited by William Cohen and Ryan Johnson, vii–xxxvii. Minneapolis: University of Minnesota Press, 2005.

Cohn, Bernard. "Recruitment and Training of British Civil Servants in India, 1600–1860." In *Asian Bureaucratic Systems Emergent from the British Imperial Tradition*, edited by Ralph Braibanti, 87–140. Durham, N.C.: Duke University Press, 1966.

Collingham, Elizabeth. *Imperial Bodies: Physical Experience of the Raj, 1800–1947.* Cambridge: Polity, 2001.

Collini, Stefan. "The Idea of Character in Victorian Political Thought." *Transactions of the Royal Historical Society* 35 (1985): 29–50.

Colón, Susan E. *The Professional Ideal in the Victorian Novel: The Works of Disraeli, Trollope, Gaskell, and Eliot.* New York: Palgrave, 2007.

Compton, J. M. "Open Competition and the Indian Civil Service 1854–1876." *English Historical Review* 83, no. 327 (April 1968): 265–84.

Cook, S. B. *Imperial Affinities: Nineteenth Century Analogies and Exchanges between India and Ireland.* New Delhi: Sage, 1993.

Cooper, Frederick. *Colonialism in Question: Theory, Knowledge, History.* Berkeley: University of California Press, 2005.

Corbett, Mary Jean. "Public Affections and Familial Politics: Burke, Edgeworth, and the 'Common Naturalization' of Great Britain." ELH 61, no. 4 (1994): 877–97.

———. *Representing Femininity: Middle-Class Subjectivity in Victorian and Edwardian Women's Autobiographies.* New York: Oxford University Press, 1992.

Corfield, Penelope. *Power and the Professions in Britain 1700–1850.* London: Routledge, 1995.

Coward, Harold. "Gandhi, Ambedkar, and Untouchability." In *Indian Critiques of Gandhi*, edited by Harold Coward, 41–66. Albany: State University of New York Press, 2003.

Crook, Tom. "'Schools for the Moral Training of the People': Public Baths, Liberalism, and the Promotion of Cleanliness in Victorian Britain." *European Review of History* 13, no. 1 (2006): 21–47.

Cross, Charles, Jr. "Selection and Training of the Candidates for the Indian Civil Service: 1870–1880." Ph.D. diss., Vanderbilt University, 1983.

Cumpston, Mary. "Some Early Indian Nationalists and their Allies in British Parliament, 1851–1906." *English Historical Review* 76 (1961): 278–97.

Cunningham, H. S. [1875]. *Chronicles of Dustypore: A Tale of Modern Anglo-Indian Society.* London: Smith, Elder, 1877.

Curtis, L. P. *Anglo-Saxons and Celts: A Study of Anti-Irish Prejudice in Victorian England.* Bridgeport, Conn.: University of Bridgeport Press, 1968.

———. *Apes and Angels: The Irishman in Victorian Caricature.* Washington: Smithsonian Institution Press, 1971.

Dames, Nicholas. "Trollope and the Career: Vocational Trajectories and the Management of Ambition." *Victorian Studies* 45, no. 2 (winter 2003): 247–78.

Dandeker, Christopher. *Surveillance, Power and Modernity: Bureacracy and Discipline from 1700 to the Present Day.* Cambridge: Polity, 1990.

Dasgupta, Ajit. *A History of Indian Economic Thought.* London: Routledge, 1993.

Davidoff, Leonore, and Catherine Hall. *Family Fortunes: Men and Women of the English Middle Class 1780–1850.* Rev. ed. London: Routledge, 2002.

Davis, Richard. "The Influence of the Irish Revolution on Indian Nationalism: The Evidence of the Indian Press, 1916–22." *South Asia* 9, no. 2 (1986): 55–68.

Davison, Graeme. "The City as a Natural System." In *In Pursuit of Urban History*, edited by Derek Fraser and Anthony Sutcliffe, 349–70. London: Edward Arnold, 1983.

Dawson, Graham. *British Adventure, Empire, and the Imagining of Masculinities.* London: Routledge, 1994.

Dellamora, Richard. *Friendship's Bonds: Democracy and the Novel in Victorian England.* Philadelphia: University of Pennsylvania Press, 2004.

Derrida, Jacques. *Specters of Marx: The State of the Debt, the Work of Mourning, and the New International.* Edited by Stephen Cullenberg and Bernd Magnus. Translated by Peggy Kamuf. New York: Routledge, 1994.

———. "Louis Marin." In *The Work of Mourning.* Translated and edited by Pascale-Anne Brault and Michael Naas. Chicago: University of Chicago Press, 2001.

Dewey, Clive. *Anglo-Indian Attitudes: The Mind of the Indian Civil Service.* London: Hambledon, 1993.

———. "The Education of a Ruling Caste: The Indian Civil Service in the Era of Competitive Examination." *English Historical Review* 88 (April 1973): 262–85.

Duara, Prasenjit. "Historicizing National Identity, or Who Imagines What and When." In *Becoming National*, edited by Geoff Eley and Ronald Grigor Suny, 151–78. New York: Oxford University Press, 1996.

Dube, Saurabh. "Presence of Europe: An Interview with Dipesh Chakrabarty." *South Atlantic Quarterly* 101, no. 4 (fall 2002): 859–68.

Dummett, Ann, and Andrew Nicol. *Subjects, Citizens, Aliens and Others: Nationality and Immigration Law.* London: Weidenfeld and Nicolson, 1990.

Dutt, R. C. *Open Letters to Lord Curzon on Famines and Land Assessments in India.* London: Kegan Paul, Trench, Trubner, 1900.

Dutta, Nilanjan. "From Subject to Citizen: Towards a History of the Indian Civil Rights Movement." In *Changing Concepts of Rights and Justice in South Asia*, edited by Michael R. Anderson and Sumit Guha, 274–88. Delhi: Oxford University Press, 1998.

Eden, Emily. *Up the Country: Letters Written to her Sister from the Upper Provinces of India*. [1866]. 2 vols. Reprint. London: Virago, 1983.

Edwards, Brent Hayes. "The Genres of Postcolonialism." *Social Text* 78 (spring 2004): 1–16.

Eliot, Dorice Williams. *The Angel out of the House*. Charlottesville: University Press of Virginia, 2002.

Elliot, Philip. *The Sociology of the Professions*. London: Macmillan, 1972.

Eng, David, and David Kazanjian, eds. *Loss: The Politics of Mourning*. Berkeley: University of California Press, 2003.

Fahey, David M., and Padma Manian. "Poverty and Purification: The Politics of Gandhi's Campaign for Prohibition." *The Historian* 67, no. 3 (fall 2005): 489–506.

Finn, Margot. *The Character of Credit: Personal Debt in English Culture*. Cambridge: Cambridge University Press, 2003.

The First Indian Member of the Imperial Parliament: Being a Collection of the Main Incidents Relating to the Election of Mr. Dadabhai Naoroji to Parliament. Madras: Addison, 1892.

Fisher, Michael H., Shompa Lahiri, and Shinder S. Thandi. *A South-Asian History of Britain: Four Centuries of Peoples from the Indian Sub-Continent*. Oxford/Westport, Conn.: Greenwood World Publishing, 2007.

Fleming, Leslie. "Between Two Worlds: Self-Construction and Self-Identity in the Writings of Three Nineteenth Century Indian Christian Women." In *Women as Subjects: South Asian Histories*, edited by Nita Kumar, 81–107. Charlottesville: University Press of Virginia, 1994.

Fletcher, Ian Christopher. "'Women of the Nations, Unite!': Transnational Suffragism in the United Kingdom, 1912–14." In *Women's Suffrage in the British Empire: Citizenship, Nation, and Race*, edited by Ian Christopher Fletcher, Laura E. Nym Mayhall, and Philippa Levine, 105–20. London: Routledge, 2000.

Flint, Kate. *The Victorians and the Visual Imagination*. Cambridge: Cambridge University Press, 2000.

Forbes, Geraldine. "Medical Careers and Health Care for Indian Women: Patterns of Control." *Women's History Review* 3, no. 4 (1994): 515–30.

———. Introduction. *The Memoirs of Dr. Haimabati Sen: From Child Widow to Lady Doctor*, translated Tapan Raychaudhuri, edited by Geraldine Forbes, 9–45. New Delhi: Roli Books, 2000.

———. *Women in Modern India*. Vol. 4, section 2 of *The New Cambridge History of India*. Cambridge: Cambridge University Press, 1996.

Fraser, T. G. "Ireland and India." In *'An Irish Empire'? Aspects of the British Empire*, edited by Keith Jeffrey, 77–93. Manchester: Manchester University Press, 1996.

Freud, Sigmund. "Mourning and Melancholia." [1915]. In *The Standard Edition of the Complete Psychological Works of Sigmund Freud*, edited by James Strachey, 14:237–60. London: Hogarths, 1957.
Gagnier, Regenia. *Idylls of the Marketplace: Oscar Wilde and the Victorian Public*. Stanford, Calif.: Stanford University Press, 1996.
———. *Subjectivities: A History of Self-Representation in Britain, 1832–1920*. New York: Oxford University Press, 1991.
Gallagher, Catherine. *The Body Economic: Life, Death and Sensation in Political Economy and the Victorian Novel*. Princeton, N.J.: Princeton University Press, 2006.
———. "The Body versus the Social Body in the Works of Thomas Malthus and Henry Mayhew." In *The Making of the Modern Body: Sexuality and Society in the Nineteenth Century*, edited by Catherine Gallagher and Thomas Laqueur, 83–106. Berkeley: University of California Press, 1987.
Gandhi, Leela. *Affective Communities: Anticolonial Thought, Fin-de-Siècle Radicalism and the Politics of Friendship*. Durham, N.C.: Duke University Press, 2006.
Gandhi, Mohandas K. *An Autobiography: The Story of My Experiments with Truth*. Translated by Mahadev Desai. Boston: Beacon, 1951.
———. *Collected Works of Mahatma Gandhi*. Vols. 1–100. Delhi: Ministry of Information and Broadcasting, 1958–94.
———. "Letter to D. V. Rama Rao, May 29, 1926." In *The Moral and Political Writings of Mahatma Gandhi*, edited by Raghavan Iyer, 2:201–2. Oxford: Clarendon Press of Oxford University Press, 1986.
Ganguly, Birendranath. *Dadabhai Naoroji and the Drain Theory*. Bombay: Asia Publishing House, 1965.
Gedge, Evelyn, and Mithan Choksi, ed. *Women in Modern India: Fifteen Papers by Indian Women Writers*. Bombay: D. B. Taraporewala Sons, 1929.
George, Rosemary Marangoly. *Politics of Home: Postcolonial Relocations and Twentieth-Century Fiction*. Cambridge: Cambridge University Press, 1996.
Ghosh, Bishnupriya. "On Grafting the Vernacular: The Consequences of Postcolonial Spectrology." *boundary 2* 31, no. 2 (2004): 197–218.
Gibbins, John. "J. S. Mill, Liberalism, and Progress." In *Victorian Liberalism: Nineteenth-Century Political Thought and Practice*, edited by Richard Bellamy, 91–109. London: Routledge, 1990.
Gilbert, Pamela. *The Citizen's Body: Desire, Health, and the Social in Victorian England*. Columbus: Ohio State University Press, 2007.
Gilmour, David. *The Ruling Caste: Imperial Lives in the Victorian Raj*. New York: Farrar, Strauss and Giroux, 2003.
Glick, Elisa. "The Dialectic of Dandyism." *Cultural Critique* 48, no. 1 (2001): 129–63.
Goddu, Teresa. *Gothic America: Narrative, History, and Nation*. New York: Columbia University Press, 1997.

Goldberg, David Theo. *Racist Culture: Philosophy and the Politics of Meaning.* Oxford: Oxford University Press, 1993.
Goldman, Harvey. *Max Weber and Thomas Mann: Calling and the Shaping of the Self.* Berkeley: University of California Press, 1988.
Goodlad, Lauren. "A Middle Class Cut into Two: Historiography and Victorian National Character." ELH 67, no. 1 (2000): 143–78.
———. *Victorian Literature and the Victorian State: Character and Governance in a Liberal Society.* Baltimore, Md.: Johns Hopkins University Press, 2003.
Gooptu, Suparna. *Cornelia Sorabji, India's Pioneer Woman Lawyer: A Biography.* New Delhi: Oxford University Press, 2006.
Gorman, Daniel. *Imperial Citizenship: Empire and the Question of Belonging.* Manchester: Manchester University Press, 2007.
———. "Lionel Curtis, Imperial Citizenship, and the Quest for Imperial Unity." *The Historian* 66, no. 1 (September 2004): 67–96.
———. "Wider and Wider Still? Racial Politics, Intra-Imperial Immigration and the Absence of Imperial Citizenship in the British Empire." *Journal of Colonialism and Colonial History* 3, no. 3 (2002): 1–24.
Goswami, Manu. *Producing India: From Colonial Economy to National Space.* Chicago: University of Chicago Press, 2004.
Goux, Jean-Joseph. *Symbolic Economies: After Marx and Freud.* Ithaca, N.Y.: Cornell University Press, 1990.
Grewal, Inderpal. *Home and Harem: Nation, Gender, Empire, and the Cultures of Travel.* Durham, N.C.: Duke University Press, 1996.
———. *Transnational America: Feminisms, Diasporas, Neoliberalisms.* Durham, N.C.: Duke University Press, 2005.
Guha, Ranajit. "Chandra's Death." In *Subaltern Studies: Writings on South Asian History and Society*, vol. 5, edited by Ranajit Guha, 135–64. Delhi: Oxford University Press, 1987.
Gupta, Charu. *Sexuality, Obscenity, Community: Women, Muslims, and the Hindu Public in Colonial India.* Delhi: Permanent Black, 2001.
Hadley, Elaine. "On a Darkling Plain: Victorian Liberalism and the Fantasy of Agency." *Victorian Studies* 48, no. 1 (autumn 2005): 92–102.
Haggerty, George. *Queer Gothic.* Urbana: University of Illinois Press, 2006.
Halberstam, Judith. *Skin Shows: Gothic Horror and the Technology of Monsters.* Durham, N.C.: Duke University Press, 1995.
Haley, Bruce. *The Healthy Body and Victorian Culture.* Cambridge: Harvard University Press, 1978.
Hall, Catherine. "The Nation Within and Without." In *Defining the Victorian Nation: Class, Race, Gender and the Reform Act of 1867*, edited by Catherine Hall, Keith McClelland, and Jane Rendall, 179–233. Cambridge: Cambridge University Press, 2000.
———. "Thinking the Postcolonial, Thinking the Empire." In *Cultures of Empire: Colonizers in Britain and the Empire in the Nineteenth and Twentieth Centuries*, edited by Catherine Hall, 1–33. Manchester: Manchester University Press, 2000.

———. *White, Male and Middle-Class: Explorations in Feminism and History.* New York: Routledge, 1992.
Hall, Catherine, Keith McClelland, and Jane Rendall. Introduction. *Defining the Victorian Nation: Class, Race, Gender, and the Reform Act of 1867*, edited by Catherine Hall, Keith McClelland, and Jane Rendall, 1–70. Cambridge: Cambridge University Press, 2000.
Hardiman, David. "From Custom to Crime: The Politics of Drinking in Colonial South Gujarat." In *Subaltern Studies: Writings on South Asian History and Society*, vol. 4, edited by Ranajit Guha, 165–228. New Delhi: Oxford University Press, 1985.
———. *Gandhi in His Time and Ours: The Global Legacy of His Ideas.* New York: Columbia University Press, 2003.
Hasan, Zoya, E. Sridharan, and R. Sudarshan, eds. *India's Living Constitution: Ideas, Practices, Controversies.* Delhi: Permanent Black, 2002.
Hay, Stephen. "The Making of a Late-Victorian Hindu: M. K. Gandhi in London 1888–1891." *Victorian Studies* 33, no. 1 (autumn 1989): 75–98.
Hazareesingh, Sandeep. "The Quest for Urban Citizenship: Civic Rights, Public Opinion, and Colonial Resistance in Early-Twentieth Century Bombay." *Modern Asian Studies* 34, no. 4 (2000): 797–829.
Heinzelman, Kurt. *The Economics of the Imagination.* Amherst: University of Massachusetts Press, 1980.
Herbert, Christopher. "Filthy Lucre: Victorian Ideas of Money." *Victorian Studies* 44, no. 2 (2002): 185–213.
Ho, Engseng. "Empire through Diasporic Eyes: A View from the Other Boat." *Comparative Study of Society and History* 46, no. 2 (2004): 210–46.
Holden, Philip. "Other Modernities: National Autobiography and Globalization." *Biography* 28, no. 1 (winter 2005): 89–103.
Hunt, Lynn. *The French Revolution and Human Rights: A Brief Documentary History.* New York: St. Martin's, 1996.
Hurley, Kelley. *The Gothic Body: Sexuality, Materialism, and Degeneration at the Fin de Siècle.* Cambridge: Cambridge University Press, 1996.
Huttenback, Robert. "Indians in South Africa, 1860–1914: The British Imperial Philosophy on Trial." *English Historical Review* 63 (1966): 273–91.
———. *Racism and Empire: White Settlers and Coloured Immigrants in the British Self-Governing Colonies 1830–1910.* Ithaca, N.Y.: Cornell University Press, 1976.
Isin, Engin F. *Being Political: Genealogies of Citizenship.* Minneapolis: University of Minnesota Press, 2002.
Jaffe, Audrey. *Scenes of Sympathy: Identity and Representation in Victorian Fiction.* Ithaca, N.Y.: Cornell University Press, 2000.
Jameson, Fredric. "Third-World Literature in the Era of Multinational Capitalism." *Social Text* 15 (autumn 1986): 65–88.
Jay, Martin. *Cultural Semantics: Keywords of Our Time.* Amherst: University of Massachusetts Press, 1998.

Jayawardena, Kumari. *The White Woman's Other Burden: Western Women and South Asia during British Colonial Rule*. London: Routledge, 1995.

Jones, J. Mervyn. *British Nationality Law and Practice*. Oxford: Clarendon Press of Oxford University Press, 1947.

Joshi, Priti. "Edwin Chadwick's Self Fashioning: Professionalism, Masculinity, and the Victorian Poor." *Victorian Literature and Culture* 33, no. 2 (2004): 353–70.

Joshi, Priya. *In Another Country: Colonialism, Culture, and the English Novel in India*. New York: Columbia University Press, 2002.

Joyce, Patrick. *Visions of the People: Industrial England and the Question of Class, 1848–1914*. Cambridge: Cambridge University Press, 1991.

Kale, Madhavi. *Fragments of Empire: Capital, Slavery, and Indian Indentured Labor Migration in the British Caribbean*. Philadelphia: University of Pennsylvania Press, 1998.

Kaplan, Caren. "Resisting Autobiography: Out-Law Genres and Transnational Feminist Subjects." In *De/Colonizing the Subject: The Politics of Gender in Women's Autobiography*, edited by Sidonie Smith and Julia Watson, 115–38. Minneapolis: University of Minnesota Press, 1992.

Kapur, Ratna. *Erotic Justice: Law and the New Politics of Postcolonialism*. London: Glass House, 2005.

Kaviraj, Sudipta. "The Imaginary Institution of India." In *Subaltern Studies: Writings on South Asian History and Society*, vol. 7, edited by Partha Chatterjee and Gyanendra Pandey, 1–39. New Delhi: Oxford University Press, 1992.

———. "The Invention of Private Life: A Reading of Sibnath Sastri's *Autobiography*." In *Telling Lives in India: Biography, Autobiography, and Life History*, edited by David Arnold and Stuart Blackburn, 83–114. Bloomington: Indiana University Press, 2004.

———. *The Unhappy Consciousness: Bankimchandra Chattopadhyay and the Formation of Nationalist Discourse in India*. Delhi: Oxford University Press, 1995.

Kazanjian, David. *The Colonizing Trick: National Culture and Imperial Citizenship in Early America*. Minneapolis: University of Minnesota Press, 2003.

Kelly, John D. "Fiji Indians and 'Commoditization of Labor.'" *American Ethnologist* 19, no. 1 (1992): 97–120.

———. *A Politics of Virtue: Hinduism, Sexuality, and Countercolonial Discourse in Fiji*. Chicago: University of Chicago Press, 1991.

Kendle, John. *The Colonial and Imperial Conferences 1887–1922*. London: Longmans, Green, 1967.

Kerber, Linda. "The Meanings of Citizenship." *The Journal of American History* 84, no. 3 (1997): 833–54.

Klaver, Claudia. *A/Moral Economics: Classical Political Economy and Cultural Authority in Nineteenth-Century England*. Columbus: Ohio State University Press, 2003.

Kumar, Radha. *The History of Doing: An Illustrated Account of Movements for Women's Rights and Feminism in India 1800–1990*. London: Verso, 1993.

Laclau, Ernesto. "Subject of Politics, Politics of the Subject." *differences* 7, no. 1 (1995): 146–64.

———. "Universalism, Particularism, and the Question of Identity." In *The Identity in Question*, edited by John Rajchman, 93–108. London: Routledge, 1995.

Lahiri, Shompa. *Indians in Britain: Anglo-Indian Encounters, Race, and Identity, 1880–1930*. London: Frank Cass, 2000.

Lal, Brij. "Kunti's Cry: Indentured Women in Fiji Plantations." *The Indian Economic and Social History Review* 22, no. 1 (1985): 55–71.

Lal, Maneesha. "The Politics of Gender and Medicine in Colonial India: The Countess of Dufferin's Fund, 1885–1888." *Bulletin of the History of Medicine* 68, no. 1 (1994): 29–66.

Lane, Christopher. *The Ruling Passion: British Colonial Allegory and the Paradox of Homosexual Desire*. Durham, N.C.: Duke University Press, 1995.

Larson, Magali Sarfatti. "The Production of Expertise and the Constitution of Expert Power." In *The Authority of Experts: Studies in History and Theory*, edited by Thomas Haskell, 28–80. Bloomington: Indiana University Press, 1984.

———. *The Rise of Professionalism: A Sociological Analysis*. Berkeley: University of California Press, 1977.

Lebow, Richard Ned. *White Britain and Black Ireland: The Influence of Stereotypes on Colonial Policy*. Philadelphia: Institute for the Study of Human Issues, 1976.

Leopold, Joan. "British Application of Aryan Theory of Race to India, 1850–1870." *English Historical Review* 89, no. 352 (July 1974): 578–603.

Lister, Ruth. *Citizenship: Feminist Perspectives*. Rev. ed. New York: New York University Press, 2003.

Lloyd, David. "Nationalisms against the State." In *The Politics of Culture in the Shadow of Capital*, edited by David Lloyd and Lisa Lowe, 173–98. Durham, N.C.: Duke University Press, 1998.

Lokugé, Chandani. Introduction. *India Calling: The Memories of Cornelia Sorabji, India's First Barrister*, edited by Chandani Lokugé, xii–xxxvi. New Delhi: Oxford University Press, 2001.

Long, Robert D. *The Man on the Spot: Essays in British Empire History*. Westport, Conn.: Greenwood, 1995.

Lorimer, Douglas. *Colour, Class, and the Victorians: English Attitudes towards the Negro in the Mid-Nineteenth Century*. New York: Holmes and Meier, 1978.

———. "Race, Science, and Culture: Historical Continuities and Discontinuities, 1850–1914." In *The Victorians and Race*, edited by Shearer West, 12–33. Aldershot: Scolar, 1996.

Lowe, Lisa. *Immigrant Acts: On Asian American Cultural Politics.* Durham, N.C.: Duke University Press, 1996.
Luhrman, Tanya. *The Good Parsi: The Fate of a Colonial Elite in a Postcolonial Society.* Cambridge: Harvard University Press, 1996.
Macaulay, Thomas Babington. "Government of India: A Speech Delivered in the House of Commons on the 10th of July, 1833." In *The Works of Lord Macaulay Complete*, edited by Lady Trevelyan, 8: 111–42. London: Longmans, Green, 1897.
Majeed, Javed. *Autobiography, Travel, and Postnational Identity: Gandhi, Nehru, and Iqbal.* Basingstoke, England: Palgrave Macmillan, 2007.
Majumdar, Beman Behari. *Militant Nationalism in India and Its Socioreligious Background.* Calcutta: General Printers and Publishers, 1966.
Malachuk, Daniel S. *Perfection, the State, and Victorian Liberalism.* New York: Palgrave, 2005.
Malchow, H. L. *Gothic Images of Race in Nineteenth-Century Britain.* Stanford, Calif.: Stanford University Press, 1996.
Mangan, J. A. "Social Darwinism and Upper-Class Education in Late Victorian and Edwardian England." In *Manliness and Morality: Middle Class Masculinity in Britain and America 1800–1940*, edited by J. A. Mangan and James Walvin, 135–159. Manchester: Manchester University Press, 1987.
Mani, Lata. "Contentious Traditions: The Debate on Sati in Colonial India." In *Recasting Women: Essays in Colonial History*, edited by Kumkum Sangari and Sudesh Vaid, 88–126. New Delhi: Kali for Women, 1989.
Marshall, T. H. *Citizenship and Social Class, and Other Essays.* Cambridge: Cambridge University Press, 1950.
Marx, Karl. *Capital.* Vol. 1. Translated by Ben Fowkes. London: Penguin, 1976.
———. *Grundrisse: Foundations of the Critique of Political Economy.* Translated by Martin Nicolaus. London: Penguin, 1973.
———. "On the Jewish Question." In *The Marx-Engels Reader*, edited by Robert C. Tucker, 26–52. 2nd ed. New York: Norton 1978.
Masani, R. P. *Dadabhai Naoroji: The Grand Old Man of India.* London: Allen and Unwin, 1939.
Mason, Philip. *The English Gentleman: The Rise and Fall of an Ideal.* London: Andre Deutsch, 1982.
Masselos, Jim. *Indian Nationalism: An History.* New Delhi: Sterling, 1991.
Mayo, Katherine. *Mother India.* [1927]. Edited by Mrinalini Sinha. Ann Arbor: University of Michigan Press, 2000.
McBratney, John. *Imperial Subjects, Imperial Space: Rudyard Kipling's Fiction of the Native-Born.* Columbus: Ohio University Press, 2002.
McClelland, Keith. "'England's Greatness, the Working Man.'" In *Defining the Victorian Nation: Class, Race, Gender and the Reform Act of 1867*, edited by Catherine Hall, Keith McClelland, and Jane Rendall, 71–118. Cambridge: Cambridge University Press, 2000.

McClelland, Keith, and Sonya O. Rose. "Citizenship and Empire, 1867–1928." In *At Home with the Empire: Metropolitan Culture and the Imperial World*, edited by Catherine Hall and Sonya O. Rose, 275–97. Cambridge: Cambridge University Press, 2006.

McClintock, Anne. "'No Longer in a Future Heaven': Gender, Race, and Nationalism." In *Dangerous Liaisons: Gender, Nation, and Postcolonial Perspectives*, edited by Anne McClintock, Aamir Mufti, and Ella Shohat, 89–112. Minneapolis: University of Minnesota Press, 1997.

McCloskey, Deirdre. *The Rhetoric of Economics*. Madison: University of Wisconsin Press, 1998.

McLane, John R. *Indian Nationalism and the Early Congress*. Princeton, N.J.: Princeton University Press, 1977.

Meer, Fatima. "Pre-Gandhian Indian Politics in Natal—1891–1892." In *The South African Gandhi: An Abstract of the Speeches and Writings of M. K. Gandhi, 1893–1914*, edited by Fatima Meer. Durban: Madiba Publishers, 1995.

Meer, Y. S., et al., eds. *Documents of Indentured Labour: Natal 1851–1917*. Durban, South Africa: Institute of Black Research, 1980.

Mehrotra, S. R. *The Commonwealth and the Nation*. New Delhi: Vikas, 1978.

———. *The Emergence of the Indian National Congress*. New Delhi: Vikas, 1971.

Mehta, Uday S. *Liberalism and Empire: A Study in Nineteenth Century British Liberal Thought*. Chicago: University of Chicago Press, 1999.

Menon, Nivedita. *Recovering Subversion: Feminist Politics beyond the Law*. Urbana: University of Illinois Press, 2004.

Metcalf, Barbara, and Thomas Metcalf. *A Concise History of India*. Cambridge: Cambridge University Press, 2002.

Metcalf, Thomas. "'Hard Hands and Sound Healthy Bodies': Recruiting 'Coolies' for Natal, 1860–1911." In *Forging the Raj: Essays on British India in the Heyday of Empire*, edited by Thomas Metcalf, 218–49. New Delhi: Oxford University Press, 2005.

———. *Ideologies of the Raj*. Vol. 3, part 4 of *The New Cambridge History of India*. Cambridge: Cambridge University Press, 1994.

Mighall, Robert. *A Geography of Victorian Gothic Fiction: Mapping History's Nightmares*. Oxford: Oxford University Press, 1999.

Mill, John Stuart. "Considerations on Representative Government." [1861]. In *On Liberty and Other Essays*, 205–470. Edited by John Gray. Oxford: Oxford University Press, 1991.

Mills, James H., and Satadru Sen, eds. *Confronting the Body: The Politics of Physicality in Colonial and Post-Colonial India*. London: Anthem, 2004.

Mishra, Vijay. *The Gothic Sublime*. Albany: State University of New York Press, 1994.

Misra, B. B. *The Bureaucracy in India: An Historical Analysis of Development up to 1947*. New Delhi: Oxford University Press, 1977.

Mohanram, Radhika. *Race, Diaspora, and the British Empire.* Minneapolis: University of Minnesota Press, 2007.
Mongia, Radhika Viyas. "Race, Nationality, Mobility: A History of the Passport." In *After the Imperial Turn: Thinking with and through the Nation*, edited by Antoinette Burton, 196–214. Durham, N.C.: Duke University Press, 2003.
Montgomery, R. J. *Examinations: An Account of Their Evolution as Administrative Devices in England.* Pittsburgh: University of Pittsburgh Press, 1967.
Moore, R. J. "Abolition of Patronage in the Indian Civil Service." *The Historical Journal* 7, no. 2 (1964): 246–57.
———. *Liberalism and Indian Politics: 1872–1922.* London: Cox and Wyman, 1966.
Moretti, Franco. *Signs Taken for Wonders: Essays in the Sociology of Literary Forms.* Translated by Susan Fischer, David Forgacs, and David Miller. London: Verso, 1983.
Mossman, Mary Jane. *The First Women Lawyers: A Comparative Study of Gender, Law and the Legal Professions.* Portland, Oregon: Hart, 2006.
Mufti, Aamir. *Enlightenment in the Colony: The Jewish Question and the Crisis of Postcolonial Culture.* Princeton, N.J.: Princeton University Press, 2007.
Mukherjee, Haridas, and Uma Mukherjee, eds. *"Bande Mataram" and Indian Nationalism (1906–08).* Calcutta: Firma K. L. Mukhopadhyay, 1957.
Mukherjee, Meenakshi. *Realism and Reality: The Novel and Society in India.* Delhi: Oxford University Press, 1985.
Mukherjee, Sumita. " 'Narrow-majority' and 'Bow-and-agree': Public Attitudes Towards the Elections of the First Asian MPs in Britain, Dadabhai Naoroji and Mancherjee Merwanjee Bhownagree, 1885–1896." *Journal of the Oxford University Historical Society* 2 (Michaelmas 2004): 1–20.
Murshid, Ghulam. *Reluctant Debutantes: Response of Bengali Women to Modernization 1849–1905.* Rajshahi, Bangladesh: Rajshahi University, 1983.
Nair, Janaki. "Uncovering the Zenana: Visions of Indian Womanhood in Englishwomen's Writings 1813–1940." *Journal of Women's History* 2, no. 1 (1990): 8–34.
———. *Women and Law in Colonial India.* New Delhi: Kali for Women, 1996.
Nandy, Ashis. *The Illegitimacy of Nationalism: Rabindranath Tagore and the Politics of Self.* New Delhi: Oxford University Press, 1994.
———. *The Intimate Enemy: Loss and Recovery of Self under Colonialism.* Delhi: Oxford University Press, 1983.
Naoroji, Dadabhai. *Essays, Speeches, Addresses and Writings on Indian Politics of the Hon'ble Dadabhai Naoroji.* Edited by Chunilal Lallubhai Parikh. Bombay: Caxton Printing Works, 1887.
———. *The Grand Little Man of India, Dadabhai Naoroji: Speeches and Writings.* Edited by A. M. Zaidi. Vol. 1. New Delhi: S. Chand, 1984. Vol. 2. New Delhi: Indian Institute of Applied Political Research, 1988.

———. "*The Manners and Customs of the Parsees*": A Paper Read Before the Liverpool Philomathic Society, March 13, 1861. Bombay: Union Press, 1864.

———. *The Parsi Religion*. London: Swan Sonnenschein, 1889.

———. *Poverty and Un-British Rule in India*. London: Swan Sonnenschein, 1901.

Natarajan, K. A. Foreword. In *Indians Abroad*, edited by S. A. Vaiz. Bombay: Imperial Indian Citizenship Association, 1927.

Newsome, David. *Godliness and Good Learning: Four Studies on a Victorian Ideal*. London: John Murray, 1961.

Niranjana, Tejaswini. *Mobilizing India: Women, Music, and Migration between India and Trinidad*. Durham, N.C.: Duke University Press, 2006.

Northcote, Stafford Henry, and Charles Trevelyan. *Report on the Organization of the Permanent Civil Service together with a Letter from the Rev. B. Jowett*. London: George E. Eyre and William Spottiswoode, 1854.

O'Day, Alan. *Irish Home Rule 1867–1921*. Manchester: Manchester University Press, 1998.

Ong, Aihwa. *Flexible Citizenship: The Cultural Logics of Transnationality*. Durham, N.C.: Duke University Press, 1999.

Osborne, Thomas. "Bureaucracy as a Vocation: Governmentality and Administration in Nineteenth-Century Britain." *Journal of Historical Sociology* 7, no. 3 (1994): 289–313.

———. "Security and Vitality: Drains, Liberalism and Power in the Nineteenth Century." In *Foucault and Political Reason: Liberalism, Neoliberalism, and Rationalities of Government*, edited by Andrew Barry, Thomas Osborne, and Nikolas Rose, 99–121. Chicago: University of Chicago Press, 1996.

Pal, Bipan Chandra. *The Rise and Growth of Economic Nationalism in India: Economic Policies of Indian National Leadership*. New Delhi: People's Publishing House, 1966.

Pandey, Gyanendra. "Can a Muslim Be an Indian?" *Comparative Studies in History and Society* 41, no. 4 (October 1999): 608–29.

Parekh, Bhikhu. *Colonialism, Tradition and Reform: An Analysis of Gandhi's Political Discourse*. New Delhi: Sage, 1989.

———. *Gandhi's Political Philosophy: A Critical Examination*. Notre Dame, Ind.: University of Notre Dame Press, 1989.

Parks, Fanny. *Wanderings of a Pilgrim in Search of the Picturesque, During Four-and-Twenty Years in the East; with Revelations of Life in the Zenana*. [1850]. 2 vols. Karachi, Pakistan: Oxford University Press, 1975.

Parry, Clive. *Nationality and Citizenship Laws of the Commonwealth and of the Republic of Ireland*. London: Stevens and Sons, 1957.

Pateman, Carole. *The Sexual Contract*. Stanford, Calif.: Stanford University Press, 1988.

Paul, Kathleen. *Whitewashing Britain: Race and Citizenship in the Postwar Era*. Ithaca, N.Y.: Cornell University Press, 1997.

Paulson, Ronald. "Gothic Fiction and the French Revolution." *ELH* 48, no. 3 (1981): 532–54.
Pelling, Henry. *Social Geography of British Elections 1885–1910*. London: Macmillan, 1967.
Perkin, Harold. *The Rise of Professional Society: England since 1880*. London: Routledge, 1989.
Peterson, Linda H. *Traditions of Victorian Women's Autobiography: The Poetics and Politics of Life Writing*. Charlottesville: University Press of Virginia, 1999.
Pettit, Jehangir Bomanjee. Introduction. *Indians Abroad: Bulletin 6, Kenya*. Bombay: Imperial Indian Citizenship Association, July 1923.
Pinney, Christopher. *'Photos of the Gods': The Printed Image and Political Struggle in India*. London: Reaktion, 2004.
Pocock, J. G. A. "The Ideal of Citizenship since Classical Times." In *Theorizing Citizenship*, edited by Ronald Beiner, 29–52. Albany: State University of New York Press, 1995.
Poovey, Mary. "Accommodating Merchants: Accounting, Civility, and the Natural Laws of Gender." *differences* 8, no. 3 (1996): 1–20.
———. *Genres of the Credit Economy: Mediating Value in Eighteenth- and Nineteenth-Century England*. Chicago: University of Chicago Press, 2008.
———. *A History of the Modern Fact: Problems of Knowledge in the Science of Wealth and Society*. Chicago: University of Chicago Press, 1998.
———. *Making a Social Body: British Cultural Formation 1830–1864*. Chicago: University of Chicago Press, 1995.
———. *Uneven Developments: The Ideological Work of Gender in Mid-Victorian England*. Chicago: University of Chicago Press, 1988.
Prakash, Gyan. *Another Reason: Science and the Imagination of Modern India*. Princeton, N.J.: Princeton University Press, 1999.
———. *Bonded Histories: Genealogies of Labor Servitude in Colonial India*. Cambridge: Cambridge University Press, 1990.
Prashad, Vijay. *Untouchable Freedom: A Social History of a Dalit Community*. New Delhi: Oxford University Press, 2000.
Prochaska, F. K. *Women and Philanthropy in Nineteenth-Century England*. Oxford: Clarendon Press of Oxford University Press, 1980.
Puntambekar, S. V. *An Introduction to Indian Citizenship and Civilisation*. Vol. 1. Benares, India: Nand Kishore and Bros., 1928.
Pyarelal. *Mahatma Gandhi*. Vol. 1, *The Early Phase*. Ahmedabad, India: Navjivan, 1965.
Pyrah, G. B. *Imperial Policy and South Africa, 1902–10*. Oxford: Clarendon Press of Oxford University Press, 1955.
Rai, Amit. *Rule of Sympathy: Sentiment, Race, and Power, 1750–1850*. New York: Palgrave, 2002.
Ralph, Omar. *Naoroji: The First Asian M.P.* Antigua, West Indies: Hansib Caribbean, 1997.

Ramusack, Barbara. "Cultural Missionaries, Maternal Imperialists, Feminist Allies: British Activists in India, 1865–1945." In *Western Women and Imperialism: Complicity and Resistance*, edited by Nupur Chaudhuri and Margaret Strobel. Bloomington: Indiana University Press, 1992.

Ranade, M. G. *Essays on Indian Economics: A Collection of Essays and Speeches*. Madras: G. A. Natesan, 1906.

Rao, V. K. R. V. *The National Income of British India 1931–32*. London: Macmillan, 1940.

Ray, Bharati. "The Freedom Movement and Feminist Consciousness in Bengal, 1905–1929." In *From the Seams of History: Essays on Indian Women*, edited by Bharati Ray, 174–218. New Delhi: Oxford University Press, 1995.

Reader, W. J. *The Rise of the Professional Classes in Nineteenth-Century England*. London: Weidenfeld and Nicolson, 1966.

Reddy, Muthulakshmi. *Autobiography of Mrs. S. Muthulakshmi Reddy*. Madras: 1964.

Reinhard Lupton, Julia. *Citizen-Saints: Shakespeare and Political Theology*. Chicago: University of Chicago Press, 2005.

Rendall, Jane. "Citizenship, Culture, and Civilisation: The Languages of British Suffragists, 1866–74." In *Suffrage and Beyond: International Feminist Perspectives*, edited by Caroline Daley and Melanie Nolan, 127–50. New York: New York University Press, 1994.

———. "The Citizenship of Women and the Reform Act of 1867." In *Defining the Victorian Nation: Class, Race, Gender and the Reform Act of 1867*, edited by Catherine Hall, Keith McClelland, and Jane Rendall, 119–78. Cambridge: Cambridge University Press, 2000.

Rich, Paul B. *Race and Empire in British Politics*. Cambridge: Cambridge University Press, 1990.

Robb, Peter. *Liberalism, Modernity, and the Nation*. New Delhi: Oxford University Press, 2007.

Robbins, Bruce. "Comparative Cosmopolitanisms." In *Cosmopolitics: Thinking and Feeling beyond the Nation*, edited by Bruce Robbins and Pheng Cheah, 246–64. Minneapolis: University of Minnesota Press, 1998.

———. *Secular Vocations: Intellectuals, Professionalism, Culture*. London: Verso, 1993.

Rose, Sonya O. *Which People's War? National Identity and Citizenship in Britain 1939–45*. Oxford: Oxford University Press, 2003.

Rosselli, John. "The Self-Image of Effeteness: Physical Education and Nationalism in Nineteenth-Century Bengal." *Past and Present* 86 (February 1980): 121–48.

Roy, Anupama. *Gendered Citizenship: Historical and Contextual Explorations*. New Delhi: Orient Longman, 2005.

Roy, Benoy Bhusan, and Pranati Roy. *Zenana Mission: The Role of Christian Missionaries for the Education of Women in 19th Century Bengal*. Delhi: Indian Society for Promoting Christian Knowledge, 1998.

Roy, Parama. "Figures of Famine." Unpublished manuscript.

———. *Indian Traffic: Identities in Question in Colonial and Postcolonial India*. Berkeley: University of California Press, 1998.

Ruskin, John. "Veins of Wealth." In *Unto this Last and Other Writings* [1862], edited by Clive Wilmer, 180–89. London: Penguin, 1985.

Ruth, Jennifer. "Between Labor and Capital: Charlotte Brontë's Professional Professor." *Victorian Studies* 45, no. 2 (winter 2003): 279–303.

———. *Novel Professions: Interested Disinterest and the Making of the Professional in the Victorian Novel*. Columbus: Ohio State University Press, 2006.

Sachs, Albie, and Joan Hoff Wilson. *Sexism and the Law: A Study of Male Beliefs and Legal Bias in Britain and the United States*. Oxford: Martin Robertson, 1978.

Sanders, Valerie. *The Private Lives of Victorian Women: Autobiography in Nineteenth Century England*. New York: St. Martin's, 1989.

Sangari, Kumkum. "Politics of the Possible: or the Perils of Reclassification." In *Politics of the Possible: Essays on Gender, History, Narrative, Colonial English*, 1–28. New Delhi: Tulika, 1999.

Sangari, Kumkum, and Sudesh Vaid. Introduction. *Recasting Women: Essays in Colonial History*, edited by Kumkum Sangari and Sudesh Vaid, 1–26. New Delhi: Kali for Women, 1989.

Sarkar, Sumit. "The Kalki-Avatar of Bikrampur: A Village Scandal in Early Twentieth Century Bengal." In *Subaltern Studies: Writings on South Asian History and Society*, vol. 6, edited by Ranajit Guha, 1–53. New Delhi: Oxford University Press, 1989.

———. *Modern India: 1885–1947*. New Delhi: Macmillan, 1983.

———. *Writing Social History*. New Delhi: Oxford University Press, 1997.

Sarkar, Tanika. "Enfranchised Selves: Women, Culture and Rights in Nineteenth-Century Bengal." In *Gender, Citizenships and Subjectivities*, edited by Kathleen Canning and Sonya O. Rose, 120–39. Oxford: Blackwell, 2002.

Sarker, Sonita. "Unruly Subjects: Cornelia Sorabji and Ravinder Randhawa." In *Trans-Status Subjects: Gender in the Globalization of South and Southeast Asia*, edited by Sonita Sarker and Esha Niyogi De, 267–88. Durham, N.C.: Duke University Press, 2002.

Sassen, Saskia. "The Participation of States and Citizens in Global Governance." *Indiana Journal of Legal Studies* 10, no. 1 (2003): 5–28.

———. "The Repositioning of Citizenship: Emergent Subjects and Spaces for Politics." *CR: The New Centennial Review* 3, no. 2 (2003): 41–66.

Satyamurthy, S. *Rights of Citizens*. Madras: Cambridge Press, 1919.

Saunders, Kay, ed. *Indentured Labour in the British Empire, 1834–1920*. London: Croom Helm, 1984.

Saxena, Abha. *Indian National Movement and the Liberals*. Allahabad, India: Chugh, 1986.

Schaffer, Kay, and Sidonie Smith, eds. *Human Rights and Narrated Lives: The Ethics of Recognition*. New York: Palgrave, 2004.

Schmitt, Cannon. *Alien Nation: Nineteenth-Century Gothic Fictions and English Nationality*. Philadelphia: University of Pennsylvania Press, 1997.

Schneer, Jonathan. *London 1900: The Imperial Metropolis*. New Haven: Yale University Press, 1999.

Schuman, Cathy. *Pedagogical Economies: The Examination and the Victorian Literary Man*. Stanford, Calif.: Stanford University Press, 2000.

Schwarz, Bill. "The Expansion and Contraction of England." In *The Expansion of England: Race, Ethnicity and Cultural History*, edited by Bill Schwarz, 1–9. London: Routledge, 1996.

Scott, Joan Wallach. *Only Paradoxes to Offer: French Feminists and the Rights of Man*. Cambridge: Harvard University Press, 1996.

———. "Universalism and the History of Feminism." *differences* 7, no. 1 (1995): 1–14.

Seedat, Hassim. Introduction to "Pre-Gandhian Indian Politics in Natal—1891–1892," by Fatima Meer. In *The South African Gandhi: An Abstract of the Speeches and Writings of M. K. Gandhi, 1893–1914*, edited by Fatima Meer, 87–89. Durban, South Africa: Madiba Publishers, 1995.

Seeley, J. R. *The Expansion of England: Two Courses of Lectures*. London: Macmillan, 1899.

Sen, Haimabati. *The Memoirs of Dr. Haimabati Sen: From Child Widow to Lady Doctor*. Edited by Geraldine Forbes. Translated by Tapan Raychaudhuri. New Delhi: Roli, 2000.

Sen, Satadru. "Chameleon Games: Ranjitsinhji's Politics of Race and Gender." *Journal of Colonialism and Colonial History* 2, no. 3 (2001): 1–42.

Seth, Sanjay. "Rewriting Histories of Nationalism: The Politics of 'Moderate Nationalism' in India, 1870–1905." *The American Historical Review* 104, no. 1 (1999): 95–116.

Shah, Nayan. *Contagious Divides: Epidemics and Race in San Francisco's Chinatown*. Berkeley: University of California Press, 2001.

Sharpe, Jenny. *Allegories of Empire: The Figure of Woman in the Colonial Text*. Minneapolis: University of Minnesota Press, 1993.

———. *Ghosts of Slavery: A Literary Archaeology of Black Women's Lives*. Minneapolis: University of Minnesota Press, 2003.

Shetty, Sandhya. "(Dis)Locating Gender: Space and Medical Discourse in Colonial India." In *Eroticism and Containment: Notes from the Flood Plain*, edited by Carol Siegel and Ann Kibbey, 188–230. New York: New York University Press, 1994.

Silvestri, Michael. "'The Sinn Féin of India': Irish Nationalism and the Policing of Revolutionary Terrorism in India." *Journal of British Studies* 39 (October 2000): 454–86.

Singh, Hira Lal. *Problems and Policies of the British in India*. New York: Asia Publishing House, 1963.

Singh, Nikhil Pal. *Black Is a Country: Race and the Unfinished Struggle for Democracy*. Cambridge: Harvard University Press, 2004.

Singha, Radhika. *A Despotism of Law: Crime and Justice in Early Colonial India*. New Delhi: Oxford University Press, 1998.

Sinha, Mrinalini. "Britain and Empire: Toward a New Agenda for Imperial History." *Radical History Review* 72 (1998): 163–74.

———. *Colonial Masculinity: The "Manly Englishman" and the "Effeminate Bengali" in the Late Nineteenth Century*. Manchester: Manchester University Press, 1995.

———. "Gender in the Critiques of Colonialism and Nationalism: Locating the 'Indian Woman.'" In *Feminists Revision History*, edited by Ann-Louise Shapiro, 246–75. New Brunswick, N.J.: Rutgers University Press, 1994.

———. Introduction to *Mother India*, by Katherine Mayo, 1–64. Edited by Mrinalini Sinha. Ann Arbor: University of Michigan Press, 2000.

———. "The Lineage of the 'Indian' Modern: Rhetoric, Agency, and the Sarda Act in Late Colonial India." In *Gender, Sexuality and Colonial Modernities*, edited by Antoinette Burton, 207–22. New York: Routledge, 1999.

———. "Reading *Mother India*: Empire, Nation, and the Female Voice." *Journal of Women's History* 6, no. 2 (summer 1994): 6–44.

———. "Refashioning Mother India: Feminism and Nationalism in Late-Colonial India." *Feminist Studies* 26, no. 3 (fall 2000): 623–44.

———. *Specters of Mother India: The Global Restructuring of an Empire*. Durham, N.C.: Duke University Press, 2006.

———. "Suffragism and Internationalism: Enfranchisement of British and Indian Women under an Imperial State." *The Indian Economic and Social History Review* 36, no. 4 (1999): 460–84.

Sitaramayya, Pattabhi. *The History of the Indian National Congress (1885–1935)*. Madras: Working Committee of the Congress, 1935.

Smart, Robert A., and Hutcheson, Michael. "'Negative History' and Irish Gothic Literature: Persistence and Politics." *Anglophonia* 15 (2004): 105–18.

Smiles, Samuel. *Self-Help; With Illustrations of Character, Conduct, and Perseverance*. Rev. ed. Chicago: Belford, Clarke, 1885.

Smith, Adam. *An Inquiry into the Nature and Causes of the Wealth of Nations*. [1776]. Edited by Edwin Cannan. Chicago: University of Chicago Press, 1976.

———. *The Theory of Moral Sentiments*. [1759]. Edited by D. D. Raphael and A. L. Macfie. Oxford: Oxford University Press, 1976.

Smith, Roger. *Stories of Peoplehood: The Politics and Morals of Political Membership*. Cambridge: Cambridge University Press, 2003.

Smith, Sidonie. *Moving Lives: 20th-Century Women's Travel Writing*. Minneapolis: University of Minnesota Press, 2001.

Smith, Sidonie, and Julia Watson. *Reading Autobiography: A Guide for Interpreting Life- Narratives*. Minneapolis: University of Minnesota Press, 2001.

Sommers, Margaret. "Citizenship and the Place of the Public Sphere: Law, Community, and Political Culture in the Transition to Democracy." *American Sociological Review* 58, no. 5 (October 1993): 587–620.
Sorabji, Cornelia. *Between the Twilights: Being Studies of Indian Women by One of Themselves.* London: Harper, 1908.
———. "Gandhi Interrogated." *Atlantic Monthly*, April 1932, 453–58.
———. *India Calling: The Memories of Cornelia Sorabji.* London: Nisbet, 1934.
———. *India Recalled.* London: Nisbet, 1936.
———. *Love and Light behind the Purdah.* London: Freemantle, 1901.
———. *The Purdahnashin.* Calcutta: Thacker, Spink, 1917.
———. *"Therefore": An Impression of Sorabji Kharshedji Langrana and His Wife Franscina.* Oxford: Oxford University Press, 1924.
Sorkin, David. *The Religious Enlightenment: Protestants, Jews, and Catholics from London to Vienna.* Princeton, N.J.: Princeton University Press, 2008.
Southard, Barbara. "The Political Strategy of Aurobindo Ghosh: The Utilization of Hindu Religious Symbolism and the Problem of Political Mobilization in Bengal." *Modern Asian Studies* 14, no. 3 (1980): 353–76.
Spangenburg, Bradford. *British Bureaucracy in India: Status, Policy and the I.C.S. in the Late Nineteenth Century.* Columbia, Mo.: South Asia Books, 1976.
Spivak, Gayatri. "Can the Subaltern Speak?" In *Marxism and the Interpretation of Culture*, edited by Lawrence Grossberg and Cary Nelson, 271–313. Urbana: University of Illinois Press, 1988.
———. "Diasporas Old and New." In *Class Issues: Pedagogy, Cultural Studies, and the Public Sphere*, edited by Amitava Kumar, 87–116. New York: New York University Press, 1997.
———. "Subaltern Studies: Deconstructing Historiography." In *Subaltern Studies: Writings on South Asian History and Society*, vol. 4, edited by Ranajit Guha, 330–63. Delhi: Oxford University Press, 1985.
Squier, Susan Merrill. *Liminal Lives: Imagining the Human at the Frontiers of Biomedicine.* Durham, N.C.: Duke University Press, 2004.
Stepan, Nancy. *The Idea of Race in Science: Great Britain 1800–1960.* London: Macmillan, 1982.
———. "Race, Gender, Science, and Citizenship." *Gender and History* 10, no. 1 (April 1998): 26–52.
Stocking, George W., Jr. *Victorian Anthropology.* New York: Free Press, 1987.
Stokes, Eric. *The English Utilitarians and India.* Oxford: Clarendon Press of Oxford University Press, 1959.
Stoler, Ann. *Race and the Education of Desire: Foucault's History of Sexuality and the Colonial Order of Things.* Durham, N.C.: Duke University Press, 1995.

Stovall, Tyler, and Geirges Van Den Abbeleele, eds. *French Civilization and Its Discontents: Nationalism, Colonialism, Race*. Lanham, Md.: Lexington Books, 2003.

Streets, Heather. *Martial Races: The Military, Race and Masculinity in British Imperial Culture 1857–1914*. Manchester: Manchester University Press, 2004.

Sunder Rajan, Rajeswari. *Scandal of the State: Women, Law, and Citizenship in Postcolonial India*. Durham, N.C.: Duke University Press, 2003.

Swan, Maureen. *Gandhi: The South African Experience*. Johannesburg: Ravan, 1985.

Swanson, Maynard W. "'The Asiatic Menace': Creating Segregation in Durban, 1870–1900." *The International Journal of African Historical Studies* 16, no. 3 (1983): 401–21.

Swindells, Julia. *Victorian Writing and Working Women: The Other Side of Silence*. Cambridge: Polity, 1985.

Tabili, Laura. *"We Ask for British Justice": Workers and Racial Difference in Late Imperial Britain*. Ithaca, N.Y.: Cornell University Press, 1994.

Tarlo, Emma. *Clothing Matters: Dress and Identity in India*. Chicago: University of Chicago Press, 1996.

Taussig, Michael. *The Devil and Commodity Fetishism*. Chapel Hill: University of North Carolina Press, 1980.

Thackeray, William Makepeace. *Vanity Fair: A Novel without a Hero*. [1848]. New York: Penguin, 2001.

Tharu, Susie. "Citizenship and Its Discontents." In *A Question of Silence: The Sexual Economies of Modern India*, edited by Mary E. John and Janaki Nair, 216–42. New Delhi: Kali for Women, 1998.

Thomas, David Wayne. *Cultivating Victorians: Liberal Culture and the Aesthetic*. Philadelphia: University of Pennsylvania Press, 2004.

Tilak, Bal Gangadhar. *Bal Gangadhar Tilak, His Writings and Speeches*. Madras: Ganesh, 1919.

Tinker, Hugh. *A New System of Slavery: The Export of Indian Labour Overseas, 1830–1920*. Oxford: Oxford University Press, 1973.

Trautmann, Thomas. *Aryans and British India*. Berkeley: University of California Press, 1997.

Trentmann, Frank. "Bread, Milk, and Democracy: Consumption and Citizenship in Twentieth-Century Britain." In *The Politics of Consumption: Material Culture and Citizenship in Europe and America*, edited by Martin Daunton and Matthew Hilton, 129–64. Oxford: Berg, 2001.

Trevelyan, G. O. *The Competition Wallah*. London: Macmillan, 1866.

Turner, Bryan. "Contemporary Problems in the Theory of Citizenship." In *Citizenship and Social Theory*, edited by Bryan Turner, 1–18. London: Sage, 1993.

Turner, Victor. *Dramas, Fields, and Metaphors: Symbolic Action in Human Society*. Ithaca, N.Y.: Cornell University Press, 1974.

Vahed, Goolam. "Control and Repression: The Plight of Indian Hawkers and Flower Sellers in Durban, 1910–1948." *The International Journal of African Historical Studies* 32, no. 1 (1999): 19–48.

———. "Indentured Masculinity in Colonial Natal, 1860–1910." In *African Masculinities: Men in Africa from the Late Nineteenth Century to the Present*, edited by Lahoucine Ouzgane and Robert Morrell, 239–56. New York: Palgrave, 2005.

Vaiz, S. A., ed. *Indians Abroad*. Bombay: Imperial Indian Citizenship Association, 1927.

Vernon, James. "Narrating the Constitution: The Discourse of the 'Real' and the Fantasies of Nineteenth-Century Constitutional History." In *Re-reading the Constitution: New Narratives in the Political History of England's Long Nineteenth Century*, edited by James Vernon, 204–29. Cambridge: Cambridge University Press, 1996.

———. "Notes Towards an Introduction." In *Re-reading the Constitution: New Narratives in the Political History of England's Long Nineteenth Century*, edited by James Vernon, 1–21. Cambridge: Cambridge University Press, 1996.

———. *Politics and the People: A Study in English Political Culture, c. 1815–1867*. Cambridge: Cambridge University Press, 1993.

Vincent, David. *Culture of Secrecy: Britain, 1832–1998*. New York: Oxford University Press, 1998.

Visram, Rozina. *Asians in Britain: 400 Years of History*. London: Pluto, 2002.

———. *Ayahs, Lascars, and Princes: Indians in Britain 1700–1947*. London: Pluto, 1986.

Viswanathan, Gauri. "Ireland, India, and the Poetics of Internationalism." *Journal of World History* 15, no. 1 (2004): 7–30.

———. *Masks of Conquest: Literary Study and British Rule in India*. New York: Columbia University Press, 1989.

———. *Outside the Fold: Conversion, Modernity, and Belief*. Princeton, N.J.: Princeton University Press, 1998.

Vithal, B. P. R. "Evolving Trends in the Bureaucracy." In *State and Politics in India*, edited by Partha Chatterjee, 208–31. New Delhi: Oxford University Press, 1997.

Wakankar, Milind. "Body, Crowd, Identity: Genealogy of a Hindu Nationalist Ascetics." *Social Text* 45 (winter 1995): 45–73.

Walker, Nancy. "'Wider Than the Sky': Public Presence and Private Self in Dickinson, James, and Woolf." In *The Private Self: Theory and Practice of Women's Autobiographical Writings*, edited by Shari Benstock, 272–304. Chapel Hill: University of North Carolina Press, 1988.

Walkowitz, Daniel. "The Making of a Feminine Professional Identity: Social Workers in the 1920s." *The American Historical Review* 95, no. 4 (1990): 1051–75.

Wallerstein, Immanuel. "Citizens All? Citizens Some! The Making of the Citizen." *Comparative Study of Society and History* 45, no. 4 (2003): 650–79.
Warwick, Alexandra. "Lost Cities: London's Apocalypse." In *Spectral Readings: Towards a Gothic Geography*, edited by Glennis Byron and David Punter. Basingstoke, England: Macmillan, 1999.
Watt, Carey. *Serving the Nation: Cultures of Service, Association, and Citizenship in Colonial India*. New Delhi: Oxford University Press, 2005.
Weber, Max. "Bureaucracy." In *From Max Weber: Essays in Sociology*, edited and translated by H. H. Gerth and C. Wright Mills, 196–244. New York: Oxford University Press, 1946.
———. *Political Writings*. Edited by Peter Lassman and Ronald Speirs. Cambridge: Cambridge University Press, 1994.
Werbner, Pnina, and Nira Yuval-Davis. Introduction. *Women, Citizenship and Difference*, edited by Nira Yuval-Davis and Pnina Werbner, 1–38. London: Zed, 1999.
White, Hayden. "Historical Fiction, Fictional History, and Historical Reality." *Rethinking History* 9, nos. 2–3 (June–September 2005): 147–57.
———. "The Value of Narrativity in the Representation of Reality." In *On Narrative*, edited by W. J. T. Mitchell, 1–25. Chicago: University of Chicago Press, 1980.
Wiegman, Robyn. *American Anatomies: Theorizing Race and Gender*. Durham, N.C.: Duke University Press, 1995.
Wilkinson, Rupert. *Gentlemanly Power: British Leadership and the Public School Tradition*. London: Oxford University Press, 1964.
Winch, Donald. *Classical Political Economy and Colonies*. Cambridge: Harvard University Press, 1965.
Wolpert, Stanley. *Tilak and Gokhale: Revolution and Reform in the Making of Modern India*. Berkeley: University of California Press, 1962.
Woollacott, Angela. "Australian Women's Metropolitan Activism: From Suffrage, to Imperial Vanguard, to Commonwealth Feminism." In *Women's Suffrage in the British Empire: Citizenship, Nation, and Race*, edited by Ian Christopher Fletcher, Laura E. Nym Mayhall, and Philippa Levine, 207–23. London: Routledge, 2000.
Young, Iris. *Inclusion and Political Democracy*. New York: Oxford University Press, 2000.
Zastoupil, Lynn. *John Stuart Mill and India*. Stanford: Stanford University Press, 1994.

Index

All-India Muslim League, 192
Anderson, Benedict, 30, 178
Anglo-Indians, 67, 162, 222 n. 77, 228 n. 59, 229 n. 86
Anticolonialism, 4, 5, 18, 60, 186; alternate concept of, 182; Gandhi and, 89; in narrative of Indian nationalism, 26; nationalist resistance and, 28, 182; political alliances based on, 209 n. 91; polyvocal nature of, 89; *swadeshi* and, 36. *See also* Indian nationalism, nationalists
Antivivisectionists, 48–49
"Arab traders," 91, 110
Armstrong-Hopkins, S., 135
Aryanism, 201 n. 30; ideal of womanhood as, 139; as notion of ascendancy, 67–68
Aurobindo, 183, 231 n. 117
Australia, 1–2, 19–20, 83
Australian Immigration Restriction Act of 1905, 197
Autobiography, 12, 32–33; Banerjea and, 35, 151, 173–75, 178–80, 188–89; Gandhi and, 88, 97, 105, 213–14 n. 57; of professional women, 221 n. 60; Sorabji and, 34, 117, 123–24, 128, 131–32, 146, 148–49
Autobiography of My Experiments with Truth, 88–97, 105, 107, 214 n. 57, 216 n. 116

Bankimchandra (Chatterjee), 184
Bengal, 51, 64, 128, 130, 131, 138, 153, 174, 184, 186, 220 n. 31

Bengalee, 177
Bengali, 72, 96, 113, 146, 179, 181, 230 n. 98
Besant, Annie, 144, 210 n. 111
Between the Twilights, 141, 218 n. 11, 222 n. 96
Bhabha, Homi, 29–30
Bhadralok, 51, 153
Bharat Mata, 54
Bhownagree, Mancherjee, 208 n. 75
"Black man" controversy, 33, 38, 55, 66–69, 72
Body politic, 2, 33, 44, 60, 70; Banerjea and, 173, 179, 188; educated Indians in, 51; feminization of, 53; Gandhi's views on, 103; ideas of health and, 46–47; indentured labor and, 45, 52; Indian, 36, 38, 55, 74; Sorabji's views on, 120, 146
Bombay High Court, 126
Bombay Presidency Association, 56–57
Booth, Mary Warburton, 135, 137
Bose, Anandamohan, 188
Bose, Mona, 141
Bourgeoisie, 11, 115; character and, 34; citizenship and, 226 n. 23; in *The Competition Wallah*, 69–70; domesticity as, 169; English masculinity and, 51; familial ideals of, 8, 61, 63–64, 217 n. 139; identity as, 84–85; Indian nationalists and, 36, 183; metropolitan values of, 99; nation and, 22; respectability as, 100–101; women and, 129. *See also* Middle class

Bright, John, 30
British common law, 126
British Empire, 1, 4, 5, 8, 10, 12, 24–25, 33, 40, 75–76, 116–17, 143, 150, 182, 191, 194, 198 n. 25; as family, 3, 61–66; liberalism and, 134, 206 n. 33; race and, 63
British Nationality and Status of Aliens Act, 24, 191, 203 n. 94
British nationality law, 5, 25, 203 n. 94
British Parliament, 38, 44, 92. *See also* Parliament
Bureaucracy, 8, 16, 226 n. 37; Banerjea's representation of, 185–86; colonial, 23, 129, 131, 221; critical responses to, 231 n. 127; democracy and, 185; gendered labor and, 129, 133, 143; Indianization of, 175; J. S. Mill's views on, 154–55; liberal attitude toward, 155; Moderates and, 184–85, 187; transition from, 231 n. 128; Weber's description of, 185–86, 226 n. 33
Bureaucratic modernity, 34–35, 155–58, 167, 171–73, 177, 185–87
Bureaucratic self-fashioning, 178, 185
Bureaucrats, 155
Burton, Antoinette, 8, 67, 69, 117, 119, 123, 202 nn. 84–85, 208 n. 77, 219 nn. 23–24, 219 n. 27, 220 n. 36, 222 n. 73
Butler, Judith, 23, 32, 188, 194, 199 n. 42

Calcutta Municipal Act, 186
Canada, 1–3, 19, 83, 116, 149, 194, 218 n. 2
Capital: abstracting effects of, 12, 70; bodily health and, 48; citizenship and, 12, 76, 80, 105, 111–12, 200 n. 44, 224 n. 123; cultural form of, 170–71; Gandhi's views on, 106; labor and, 71, 76; Naoroji's references to, 48, 51, 53, 55; slavery and, 78. *See also* Commodification of labor; Marx, Karl
Caribbean, 76

Carlyle, Thomas, 166, 229 n. 84
Caste, 73, 92, 97–98, 106, 122, 193, 214 n. 68, 216 n. 18
Central Finsbury, 33, 51, 62, 66, 68, 70, 73, 208 n. 75, 220 n. 122
Chadwick, Edwin, 47, 99, 207 n. 47
Chakrabarty, Dipesh, 7, 132, 182, 199 n. 38, 201 n. 57, 231 n. 30
Chamberlain, Joseph, 23–24, 62
Character, 80, 98–99, 114; citizenship and, 101, 103; cleanliness and, 34, 76, 102–8; credit and, 76, 102–3, 105; franchise and, 83, 100; ICS reforms and, 155–58, 162; indentured laborers and, 78, 81, 104, 108; of Indians, 101–2, 104; in liberal ideology, 7
Chattopadhyaya, Kamaladevi, 142
Chronicles of Dustypore, 34, 154, 167–70, 172
Chronotope, 30–31, 204 n. 131
Church Missionary Society, 120
Circulation, 8; of economy, 33, 46, 48; in gothic narrative, 46; as template for health, 45–47
Civil Service Commission, 34, 162, 174. *See also* Entrance examinations; Indian Civil Service
Civil society, 177, 189, 192, 232 n. 140
Class: citizenship and, 42, 53, 98; exclusionary effects of, 2, 11, 42, 53, 159, 165; franchise and, 19; Moderates and, 183; Naoroji and, 68; South African Indians and, 87, 93, 97–98; upper, 65, 72, 122, 218; working, 22, 56, 62, 65–66, 71. *See also* Bourgeoisie; Middle class
Classical political economy, 33, 36, 37, 40, 46. *See also* Political economy
Cleanliness, 8, 34, 76, 83, 100, 104–5, 108, 114; credit and, 102–3
Commodification of labor, 105–7, 127. *See also* Capital
Commodity: labor as, 78; Marx's description of, 200 n. 44, 217 n. 135. *See also* Marx, Karl

Commonwealth, 62–63; of Nations, 5
Competition Wallah, The, 35, 154, 164–67, 228 n. 17
Competitionwallah, 151, 153–54, 161–62, 164, 166, 168–72, 179, 187, 228 n. 59, 230 n. 98
Constitution: British, 1, 8, 18, 25, 85, 108; Indian, 4
Constitutionalism, 181, 184
Coolies, 44–45, 77–78, 80, 82–83, 92, 110–11, 113–14, 217 n. 143. *See also* Indentured labor
Cosmopolitanism, 31, 183, 204 n. 133
Court of Wards, 127–28, 133, 137–38, 152
Cousins, Margaret, 144
"Crammer," 160, 161, 163, 172, 227 n. 51
Credit: 8, 16, 34, 76, 111; citizenship and, 103; cleanliness and, 102–3; narrative logic of, 101–2, 104–5, 114, 215 n. 97
Crown: allegiance to, 18, 26; subjects of, 1, 3, 15, 24–25, 27, 78, 80, 85, 91, 93–94, 98, 195 n. 5, 197 n. 5
Cunningham, Henry Stewart, 34, 154, 167, 171–72, 229 n. 79, 229 n. 86
Curtis, Lionel, 183, 230 n. 113

Dandy, 170–72
Davitt, Michael, 64, 209 n. 104
Declaration of the Rights of Man and Citizen, 23
Diaspora, 21, 22, 75–76, 84, 113, 202 n. 87
Dominions, 17, 19, 22–25, 27, 191
Dracula, 48
Drain: economic theory of, 33, 45–48, 51–54, 60, 207 n. 46, 208 n. 64; in Victorian Britain, 46, 207 n. 47
Dufferin, Lady, 122–23
Dufferin, Lord, 71–72
Duncan, Colonel, 65
Durban Indian Committee, 86–87
Dutt, R. C., 36, 60, 174

East India Company, 22–23, 42, 154, 156–58
Eden, Emily, 135
Elections: in Holborn, 38, 56, 58, 66; in Central Finsbury, 73
English Bar, 126, 176
Englishness, 36, 40, 54, 85, 161; British identity and, 197 n. 10, 205 n. 1; cricket and, 58; gentleman status and, 51–53, 66, 208 n. 65, 227 n. 54; masculinity and, 50–51, 153, 219 n. 16; middle-class values and, 61; nationality law and, 202 n. 71
Enlightenment, 4, 14, 27, 30, 32, 198 n. 14, 199 n. 38, 201 n. 56
Entrance examinations, 7, 150, 151, 155–58, 160, 161, 168, 170, 177, 180, 227 n. 37, 227 n. 51. *See also* Civil Service Commission; Indian Civil Service
Equality: abstract basis of, 2, 11–15, 34, 129; citizenship claims based on, 9, 11, 13, 23, 33, 52, 77, 88, 125, 150, 165, 191–92; formal, 2, 3, 8–9, 13, 16–17, 27, 35, 102, 199 n. 35, 201 n. 54; liberal rhetoric of, 62, 119
Exchange value, 111–12, 170, 206 n. 111, 217 n. 135
Extremism, 181–186. *See also* Indian nationalism, nationalists

Family: bourgeois notions of, 8, 61, 63, 217 n. 139; empire as, 3, 61–66; Gandhi's reference to, 95, 97, 113, 123, 217 n. 139; relation to monarch based on, 17, 57
Fiji, 76, 106, 191
Franchise, 13, 136, 145, 155, 176, 191, 198 n. 13; in Britain, 19, 21, 27; municipal, 186; Naoroji and 62, 70–71; in Natal, 27, 34, 89, 91, 107; Sorabji and, 147; women and, 12, 19, 70–71, 107, 198 n. 13. *See also* Suffrage; Suffragists
Franchise Amendment Bill, 91–94, 100–103, 108
"Free Indians," 81, 84, 89, 95, 109, 110

Free trade, 38, 42, 53
French Revolution, 27, 202 n. 64
Froude, James, 62

Gender: body politic described in terms of, 53; colonial modernity and, 153; in construction of competitionwallah, 162; in depictions of Moderate nationalism, 141, 183, 187; in indentured labor communities, 107; logic of citizenship and, 11, 13, 19, 131; nationalist logic of, 120; in political discourse, 3; Sorabji's narrative negotiation of, 132, 134, 138; women's labor and, 119, 127, 131. *See also* Indian feminist movement; Women's reform
Gentleman, 51–53, 66, 208 n. 65, 227 n. 54
Gentleman leader, 66, 210 n. 120; ICS officer as, 154, 160–63, 166–67; Naoroji as "English," 66–67
Ghose, Aurobindo, 183, 117 n. 231
Ghose, Lalmohun, 208 n. 75
Gladstone, William, 58–59, 63, 65–66, 73
Gokhale, G. K., 110–11
Goldstein, Vida, 20
Gothicity, 31, 33, 38, 41, 46, 54, 60–61; citizenship as, 16, 32, 201 n. 63, 201 n. 65; England's relation to India as, 54; fin-de-siècle elements of, 32, 37, 39, 40, 55; "imperial gothic," 39–40; in Irish history, 208 n. 87; revolt of 1857 as, 49–50; *sati* described as, 52
Government, representative, 3, 7, 13, 154
Government of India Act (1919), 192
Green Pamphlet, 95–97, 108
Grihalakshmi, 153
Gupta, Behari Lal, 174

Haileybury, 157, 164, 168, 228 n. 59
Health: Banerjea's views on, 180–81, 189; of body politic, 46–47, 181; citizenship and, 45; economy and, 38, 44–48, 53–54; of purdahnashin, 128, 142; racial exclusion and, 82; Victorian notions of, 22 n. 67
Hind Swaraj, 89, 213 n. 56
Hindu Friend Society, 1–3
Historiography, 36, 118, 187, 214 n. 120
Holborn, 33, 41, 57, 63–66, 218 n. 75
House of Commons, 25, 41, 55, 57, 92, 209 n. 104
Hume, A. O., 175
Hunt, James, 50
Hygiene, 82, 100, 103–4

Ilbert Bill, 50, 207 n. 61
Immigration, 79, 104, 109, 116, 149, 194, 197 n. 6, 202 n. 77
Imperial citizenry, 33, 38, 53–55
Imperial Conferences, 23–24, 28
Imperial Indian Citizenship Association, 191, 193–94, 232 n. 1
Imperial metropolis, 20, 41, 55, 75, 76, 84–85, 92, 117, 121
Imperial Service, 130–31, 221 n. 63
Imperial unity, 19, 63, 67, 69, 198 n. 25
Indentured labor, 8, 10, 21, 33, 34, 78, 80–81, 85–87, 99, 120; citizenship and, 76–77, 79, 90; commodification of, 105; Gandhi's representation of, 92, 93, 95–97, 103–4, 106–14. *See also* Coolies
India Calling, 32, 34, 116–17, 120, 121, 123–26, 128–29, 131–42, 146–49, 218 n. 1, 220 n. 39
Indian Administrative Service, 187
Indian Association, 177–78
Indian Civil Service: 10, 17, 22, 34, 80, 150–52, 154, 156, 158, 160–64, 167, 230 n. 98; admission into, 172. *See also* Competitionwallah
Indian Famine Commission, 60
Indian feminist movement, 118, 130, 140, 223 n. 91, 223 n. 93. *See also* Women's reform
Indian National Congress, 22, 64, 71–73, 151, 172, 175, 178–80, 182–84, 192
Indian national identity, 73, 110

Indian national income, 36, 43, 144
Indian nationalism, nationalists, 35, 186–87, 217 n. 143; bourgeoisie and, 36, 183; concept of "India" and, 121; discourse of, 17, 121, 140, 141, 144, 194; demands of, 22; economic analysis of, 36; identity as, 73, 110; imaginary of, 55; imperial citizenship and, 115, 183; Irish allied with, 64; leaders of, 10, 17, 28, 36, 151; as mass movement, 151; politics of, 53, 63; popular feelings of, 64; narrative of statehood and, 29; resistance and, 28; response to modernity and, 152; teleology of, 17, 26–27, 29, 152; women's reform and, 139, 140, 144, 223 n. 91. *See also* Anticolonialism; Nationalism
Ireland, 58–63, 70, 209 n. 91
Irish, 55, 57, 159, 160–61, 208 n. 83, 208 n. 87, 210 nn. 111–12; Indian anticolonialism and, 60, 64, 71, 209 n. 104; Irish Home Rule, 10, 22, 23, 39, 58, 60–65, 92; popular representations of, 38, 58–60

Jamaica, 50
Jus soli, 203 n. 94

Komagata Maru, 194–95

Labor: capital and, 71, 76; citizenship and, 76; commodification of, 105–7, 127; as commodity, 78. *See also* Indentured labor
Law: purdahnashins and, 137, 222 n. 86; women's study of, 125–27, 148, 220 n. 46
League of Social Service, 146
Lefevre, Madeleine Shaw, 123
Liberal Association of Holborn, 57
Liberal government, 83
Liberalism, 7–9, 172, 198 n. 29, 209 nn. 35–36, 211 n. 156; bourgeois identity as, 75; bureaucracy and, 154–57, 159; character and, 80; citizenship and, 3, 5, 11, 19, 27, 68, 70–72, 74, 93, 114–15, 119, 152, 154–55, 189, 191, 199 n. 38; colonialism and, 12–13, 42–43, 73, 115; developmental trajectory of, 178, 182; empire and, 134, 206 n. 33; imperial metropolis as, 17, 90, 229 n. 86; imperial unity and, 69; laissez faire ideas as, 171; nationalism and, 139; universalist basis of, 11–13, 15, 85
Liberal party, 57, 61, 230 n. 108; Naoroji as candidate of, 41, 58, 60
Liberals, 208 n. 75, 221 n. 156
Liminality: citizenship as, 133–34, 149; idioms of, 16, 31, 34; nation as, 30; Parsees as, 68; professionalism as, 120, 149; Sorabji's representation as, 119–20, 134, 140, 148, 222; zenana as, 140, 149
Loyalty, 26–28, 57, 84

Macaulay, Thomas Babington, 42–43, 158–59, 166, 226 n. 28
Magna Carta, 1, 22–23
Majumdar, Ambika Charan, 188
Malthus, Thomas, 36
Marx, Karl, 33, 40, 48, 112, 200 n. 44, 216 n. 111, 217 n. 135, 228 n. 58. *See also* Capital; Commodification; Commodity
Masculinity, 163; bourgeois identity and, 51; citizenship and, 35, 152; of civilians, 156; English identity and, 50–51, 153, 219 n. 16; Indian identity and, 181, 184, 225 n. 13
Mayo, Katherine, 140–42, 223 n. 96
Medicine, 45; women's study of, 122–23, 126, 219 n. 25, 219 n. 31, 223 n. 94
Mehta, Pherozeshah, 188
Memoir, 132–33
Mercantilism, 42–43
Middle class, 158, 159, 160, 165, 209 n. 93, 227 n. 54; British women in, 10, 21, 124; as citizens, 14, 71, 172; competition-civilian as, 170, 172; Englishness and, 61; in India, 9, 51–53, 71, 153, 172, 173, 176; Indian

Middle class (cont.)
　women in, 139–40; middle-class "hero," 167
Mill, John Stuart, 13, 51, 154–55, 210 n. 51, 231 n. 27
Missionaries, 122; zenana and, 120, 135
Moderates: Indian nationalism and, 29, 151–52, 181, 187; politics of, 29, 64, 181–85, 187, 230 n. 108. *See also* Indian nationalism, nationalists
Modernity: bureaucratic, 34–35, 155–58, 167, 171–73, 177, 185–87; citizenship and, 4, 13, 142, 144; colonial, 115, 153; Indian negotiations with, 139, 144, 148, 153, 225 n. 13; metropolitan engagement with, 35, 152, 161, 162, 164, 167, 172; Sorabji and, 140, 147, 221 n. 57
Monstrosity, 71
Montagu-Chelmsford Report, 182
Morant Bay, 50
Mother India, 54
Mother India (Mayo), 140–46
Mourning: citizenship and, 35; rhetoric of, 188–90, 232 n. 140, 232 n. 145
Mutiny, 1, 22–23, 49–50, 166, 169

Nana Saheb, 50
Narrative: bureaucratic modernity and, 35; census and, 37; citizenship and, 4–6, 8–10, 12–13, 15–16, 30, 32, 97, 111, 148, 190, 200 n. 42; of credit, 32, 101–2; economy and, 38, 40; imperial citizenship and, 97, 115, 194; indentured laborers and, 105; of "Indian" identity, 94, 179; liminality and, 222 n. 77; nation as, 36, 197–98; of nationalism, 26, 186–87, 190; nationhood and, 17–18, 29, 31–32. *See also* Gothicity
Natal, 19, 22, 27, 34, 76–81, 83–87, 89–114
Natal Immigration Report, 79, 104
Natal Indian Congress, 101, 113

Nation: body politic as, 51, 52, 179, 181, 188; citizenship and, 6; national space, 28; national "we," 28; public sphere as, 177
Nationalism: modernity and, 34, 133, 138, 148, 219 n. 20; poetry and, 30. *See also* Anticolonialism; Indian nationalism, nationalists
Nation in Making, A, 32, 35, 151–52, 173–90
Nation-space, 29, 35, 36, 38, 189
Nation-state: anticolonialism and, 26; citizenship and, 16, 28, 192, 193, 198 n. 14; citizenship prior to, 4–6, 28; contingencies of, 29; women's property rights and, 222 n. 8
Nehru, Jawaharlal, 32
New Zealand, 19, 20, 50, 83
Noble, Margaret, 144, 210 n. 111
Northcote-Trevelyan Report, 155–56, 226 nn. 24–25

Oceana, 63
O'Connell, Daniel, 59, 72
O'Donnell, F. H., 209 n. 104

Parliament, 71, 73–76, 92, 122, 158, 165, 192. *See also* British Parliament
Parsee, 40, 65–66, 68, 69–70, 73–74, 93, 144, 146, 179
"Passenger Indians," 81–83, 111
Per capita income, 43–45, 110
Philanthropy, 132, 221 n. 66
Political economy, 8, 16, 47, 53–55, 206 n. 33, 206 n. 35, 207 n. 45; classical, 33, 36, 37, 40, 46; criticisms of, 42; free trade principles of, 38; moral improvement and, 43
Poll tax, 89, 108, 109, 113
Potato famine, 59, 201 n. 112
Poverty: Naoroji's analysis of, 52; petitions to British about, 206 n. 28
Poverty and Un-British Rule in India, 33, 36–57, 60, 205 n. 1, 208 n. 64
Proclamation of 1858, 22, 42, 50, 52, 91, 125, 165, 192

Professionalism, 8, 16, 22, 34, 115, 119, 120, 126, 129, 134, 146–48, 219 n. 16, 221 n. 57, 221 n. 66, 222 n. 68, 225 n. 13, 234 n. 119
Protector of Immigrants, 34; report of, 78–79
Provincial Service, 130, 221 n. 63
Purdahnashin, 34, 117, 128, 132, 134–42, 145, 218 n. 3, 219 n. 20

Queen's Proclamation, 22, 42, 50, 52, 91, 125, 165, 192

Race: citizenship and, 11, 38, 39, 75; colonial subjects and, 5, 22, 24, 27, 39, 56, 69; discrimination based on, 15, 24, 50, 63, 69, 82–83, 229 n. 31; empire and, 63; respectability and, 83; scientific notions of, 215 n. 13
Racialization: of colonial subjects, 38, 82–83, 161; of Zulus, 226 n. 116. See also "Black man" controversy
Rai, Lala Lajpat, 183–84
Ramakrishna, 153, 178, 226 n. 14
Ranade, M. G., 46, 53, 206 n. 33
Ranjitsinhji, 58
Rathbone, Elena, 143
Rendall, Jane, 202 n. 77, 202 nn. 79–80
Report on the Organization of the Permanent Civil Service, 155–56, 226 nn. 24–25
Revolt of 1857, 1, 22–23, 49–50, 166, 169
Rights: as British subjects, 1, 3, 23–24, 73, 77–78, 85; of citizenship, 1, 3, 4, 6, 12–13, 18–19, 25, 35; of imperial citizenship, 75–76; of indentured laborers, 79; of Indians, 2, 3, 13, 24–26, 50–52, 76, 80–89, 102–9, 118, 131, 191–92, 199; professional career and, 176, 183; women's, 140, 150
Rights of Citizenship, 232
Rukhmabai, 140, 213 n. 94
Ruskin, John, 42, 46, 105

Salisbury, Lord, 38, 48–49, 58, 61, 66
Sanyasi, 184
Sastri, Srinivas, 24

Sati, 52
Satyagraha, 88–89, 108–9
Satyagraha in South Africa, 88–89, 101, 103, 108–9, 112, 213 n. 54
Satyagrahi, 120, 122
Satyamurthy, S., 232
Sayani, R. M., 63
Second Reform Act, 19, 56, 83, 98, 170
Self-government, 20, 22, 42, 85–86, 182, 186
Self-Help (Smiles), 99
Sen Haimabati, 123, 221 n. 68
Settler colonies, 19–20, 21, 23, 27, 33, 83–84, 191
Sinha, Satyendra, 27
Slade, Madeleine, 144
Slavery, 44, 76–78, 84, 113
Smith, Adam, 40, 55, 205 n. 17, 208 n. 72
Social Service Institute, 144
Soldier-hero, 166, 169, 170, 171
Sorabji, Frascina, 120, 124, 125
South Africa, 19, 21–22, 33–34, 76, 81–92, 95–106, 108, 110, 113–14, 120, 191
South African Republic, 83
Southwood Smith, 45, 47
Spectralness, 16, 31, 34, 114
Subaltern, 120, 219 n. 20
Subjecthood, 1–3, 17, 18, 25–26, 80, 115, 117, 202 n. 71
Suffrage, 57, 98. See also Franchise
Suffragists, 19, 20, 21, 70, 117
Surat, 168, 182, 187
Swadeshi, 36
Swaraj, 182, 187
Sympathy, in economic analysis, 54–55

Tagore, Rabindranath, 210 n. 111, 230 n. 112, 232 n. 140
Tagore, S. N., 173
Telang, Kashinath, 188
Thakur, Sripad Babaji, 174
Third Reform Act, 56, 98
Three Clerks, 228
Tilak, Balgangadhar, 64, 181, 183, 187, 230 n. 107
Transnationalism, 6, 118

Trevelyan, Charles, 101, 155, 160, 162. *See also* Northcote-Trevelyan Report
Trevelyan, George Otto, 35, 154, 164, 166–67, 169, 172
Tyabji, Badruddin, 188

Universality: as basis of citizenship, 4, 9, 12–19, 23, 85, 93, 114, 118, 134, 191–93, 197 n. 5; ideal of, 42, 95, 97, 112, 149, 193–94 n. 38, 199 n. 42, 201 n. 56, 201 n. 58; liberalism and, 11, 14, 85; modernity and, 223 n. 91
Use value, 105, 111, 200 n. 44, 216 n. 111, 217 n. 135

Vanity Fair, 170
Victoria, Queen, 18, 27, 58, 67, 70, 165
Visram, Fajalbhai, 86, 105
Vivekananda, 181, 184
Voting. *See* Franchise

Weber, Max, 156, 185–86, 226 n. 33, 231 n. 127
Williams, Ivy, 126
Women's reform, 117, 139, 144; Indian feminist movement, 118, 130, 140, 223 n. 91, 223 n. 93; women's labor and, 119, 127, 131
Wood, Charles, 160, 226 n. 28
Wyllie, J. W. S., 162–64, 171

Zenana, 10, 22, 34, 117, 120, 127–49
Zenana Bible and Medical Mission, 135
Zoroastrians, 68, 120. *See also* Parsee
Zulu, 107, 116, 216 n. 116

An earlier version of the first section of chapter 1 appeared as "Political Economy, the Gothic, and the Question of Imperial Citizenship" in *Victorian Studies* 47, no. 2 (winter 2005): 260–71. A version of chapter 3 was published as "Empire, Nation, and the Professional Citizen: Reading Cornelia Sorabji's *India Calling*" in *Prose Studies* 28, no. 3 (winter 2006): 291–317 (http://www.informaworld.com). I am grateful to Indiana University Press and Francis and Taylor, respectively, for granting permission to reproduce revised versions of these articles.

SUKANYA BANERJEE IS AN ASSOCIATE PROFESSOR OF ENGLISH
AT THE UNIVERSITY OF WISCONSIN, MILWAUKEE.

Library of Congress Cataloging-in-Publication Data

Banerjee, Sukanya, 1973–
Becoming imperial citizens : Indians in the late-Victorian Empire / Sukanya Banerjee.
p. cm. — (Next wave : new directions in women's studies)
Includes bibliographical references and index.
ISBN 978-0-8223-4590-9 (cloth)
ISBN 978-0-8223-4608-1 (pbk)
1. Indian—History—19th century.
2. Citizenship—Indian—History—19th century.
3. Nationalism—Indian—History—19th century.
I. Title. II. Series: Next wave.
DS479.B37 2010
323.6089'9140171241—DC22   2010004453

www.ingramcontent.com/pod-product-compliance
Lightning Source LLC
Chambersburg PA
CBHW050211240426
43671CB00013B/2300